Social Work Pra
Populations

MW01286289

Social Work Practice with LGBTQIA Populations provides an overview of key issues for social workers working with LGBTQIA clients. Each chapter considers clients' experiences in different social and interpersonal contexts. This text encourages students to think critically about the barriers and discriminations clients might face in their lives and how social workers can be equipped to address these issues. Students are challenged to develop approaches that extend support to these clients and that remove structural barriers that clients face within the systems they encounter. Utilizing intersectionality theory, students will gain an understanding of the risks and protective factors unique to this population in social work contexts.

Claire L. Dente is a licensed clinical social worker in the Commonwealth of Pennsylvania. She received a BA from Chestnut Hill College in Philadelphia, PA, an MSW from The National Catholic School of Social Service at The Catholic University of America in Washington, DC, and a Ph.D. from Temple University in Philadelphia, PA. Her social work practice has included work in physical rehabilitation and ability services, college mental health and diversity issues. She is especially interested in the intersection of religion and spirituality with sexual orientation and gender identity. She has worked as a social worker on a stroke unit, as director of a university counseling center and disability services office, and as a social work faculty member.

As a Catholic nun involved in pastoral ministry to LGBTQIA persons since 1971, I have seen too much prejudice and outright hostility toward them. Claire Dente's book, *Social Work Practice with LGBTQIA Populations*, is just the right kind of tool social workers need to understand the experiences of LGBTQIA persons.

    —Sister Jeannine Gramick, *SL, Co-Founder of New Ways Ministry*

The authors thoughtfully challenge students and social work professionals to engage LGBTQIA clients in a culturally sensitive and competent manner. Dente masterfully weaves together the integration of social work knowledge, values, and skills in addition to providing valuable tools to support the individual. This text is a "must have" resource for any student or professional working within this community.

    —Troy L. Brindle, *LCSW, Past President NASW-PA and Co-Owner, Founder, and Director of Integrated Behavioral Health Services for Springfield Psychological, Springfield Pennsylvania*

Social Work Practice with LGBTQIA Populations

An Interactional Perspective

Edited by
Claire L. Dente

NEW YORK AND LONDON

First published 2019
by Routledge
711 Third Avenue, New York, NY 10017

and by Routledge
2 Park Square, Milton Park, Abingdon, Oxon OX14 4RN

Routledge is an imprint of the Taylor & Francis Group, an informa business

© 2019 Taylor & Francis

Library of Congress Cataloging in Publication Data
Names: Dente, Claire, editor.
Title: Social work practice with LGBTQIA populations : a relationship perspective / edited by Claire Dente.
Description: New York, NY : Routledge, 2018. |
Includes bibliographical references and index. |
Identifiers: LCCN 2018023910 (print) | LCCN 2018036058 (ebook) |
ISBN 9781315562506 (Master Ebook) | ISBN 9781317204558
(Web pdf) | ISBN 9781317204541 (ePub) | ISBN 9781317204534
(Mobipocket) | ISBN 9781138672420 (hardback) |
ISBN 9781138672437 (pbk.) | ISBN 9781315562506 (ebk.)
Subjects: LCSH: Social work with bisexuals. | Social work with gays. |
Social work with lesbians. | Social work with transgender people.
Classification: LCC HV1449 (ebook) | LCC HV1449 .S657 2018 (print)
| DDC 362.89/6--dc23
LC record available at https://lccn.loc.gov/2018023910

ISBN: 978-1-138-67242-0 (hbk)
ISBN: 978-1-138-67243-7 (pbk)
ISBN: 978-1-315-56250-6 (ebk)

Typeset in Bembo
by Taylor & Francis Books

Contents

Illustrations

Figure

Table

Boxes

About the Contributors

Austin J. Angiollilo, BA is an activist, community organizer, intersectional feminist, and an educator on social equity grounded in intersectionality theory. He has a BA in Psychology and a BA in Women's and Gender Studies from West Chester University. Austin is currently working toward his doctorate in Clinical Psychology at La Salle University and is pursuing a track in diversity studies. Austin plans to use this degree to provide psychological and mental health services for marginalized communities with a specific focus on LGBTQIA+ communities.

Michele Eggers Barison, Ph.D., MSW is an Assistant Professor in the Master of Social Work Program at Pacific University. Her work focuses on global inequities and the ways that social construction of laws and policies criminalize bodies and experiences. She also examines how environmental exploitation from the global north influences migration patterns to the United States. Dr. Barison focuses on the importance of integrating human rights into social work teaching and practice. She also addresses understanding and implementing ethical ways of using documentary filmmaking to communicate the human experience and larger global systemic issues of inequality.

Casey Bohrman, Ph.D., MSW, LSW is an Assistant Professor in the Graduate Social Work Department at West Chester University of Pennsylvania. She has a direct practice background in homeless and mental health services, with a focus on recovery-oriented approaches to care. Her research focuses on the criminal justice system, mental health services, and social media in the social work classroom.

Sandra S. Butler, Ph.D., MSW is Professor of Social Work and Graduate Coordinator at the University of Maine. She received a Ph.D. in Social Welfare from the University of Washington in Seattle. Her research has focused on poverty and economic security across the life span. Dr. Butler has collaborated with Maine Equal Justice Partners and testified before state legislative committees. She was a John A. Hartford Foundation Geriatric Social Work Faculty Scholar, and received a grant from the

National Institute on Aging to study home care workers. Dr. Butler is a member of the Maine Chapter of the Scholars Strategy Network. She regularly writes policy briefs and op-eds for the *Bangor Daily News* and co-authored a monthly column which profiled the impact of state welfare policies on Maine families. She has sat on a number of advisory boards during her career, including the Maine Women's Policy Center and the Maine Center for Economic Policy. She serves on the editorial board of the *Journal of Poverty* and the *Journal of Community Practice*. Dr. Butler also is the author or co-author of three books and over 100 articles, book chapters, and policy reports.

Christina M. Chiarelli-Helminiak, Ph.D., MSW is an Associate Professor and serves as the Department Chair and MSW Program Director in the Graduate Social Work Department at West Chester University of Pennsylvania. Her research focuses on the intersection of social justice and human rights especially within social work curriculum. Her practical experience includes working with survivors of domestic violence, sexual assault, and child abuse, which culminated with leading the development of a children's advocacy center providing community-based services in rural north Georgia. Dr. Chiarelli-Helminiak is also the Co-Chair of the Council on Social Work Education Council on the Role and Status of Women in Social Work Education. She received her BSW from Shippensburg University and her MSW from Marywood University, where she was the first social work student awarded the Sister M. Eva Connors Peace Medal. Dr. Chiarelli-Helminiak completed her doctorate at the University of Connecticut, where she was recognized as an Outstanding Woman Scholar.

Sara A. Chominski, MSW is a 2018 graduate of the Master of Social Work program at West Chester University of Pennsylvania. Sara plans to pursue the Licensed Social Worker (LSW) credential in Pennsylvania.

Lisa E. Cox, Ph.D., LCSW, MSW is Professor of Social Work and Gerontology in the School of Social and Behavioral Sciences at Stockton University, in Galloway, NJ. Dr. Cox holds a Ph.D. in Social Work and Social Policy from Virginia Commonwealth University (VCU); and a Masters in Social Work and Graduate Certificate in Aging Studies from VCU's schools of social work and allied health, respectively. Previously, Dr. Cox served as the administrative coordinator of Stockton University's social work program, and since 2007, she has been a Fellow and the Research Chair for Stockton University's Center on Successful Aging (SCOSA).

Joseph Nicholas DeFilippis, Ph.D., MSW is an Assistant Professor at Seattle University. Before entering the academy, he worked as an activist for almost two decades, including serving as the director of SAGE/Queens and as the founding executive director of Queers for Economic

Justice. He has authored numerous articles, and is the co-editor of *A New Queer Agenda* (2012, the Barnard Center for Research on Women), and three 2018 books for Routledge: *Queer Activism after Marriage Equality*, *The Unfinished Queer Agenda after Marriage Equality*, and *Queer Families and Relationships after Marriage Equality*.

Claire L. Dente, Ph.D., MSW, LCSW is a Professor of Social Work in the BSW program at West Chester University of Pennsylvania. She has worked in physical rehabilitation and ability services, mental health, and as an educator at both graduate and undergraduate levels. Dr. Dente's professional interests include LGBTQIA+ topics, including the intersection of identities with religion and spirituality. She also has interests in social work education and professional identity, autism spectrum disorders, sustainability, and creating trauma-informed environments in micro, mezzo, and macro contexts. Dr. Dente serves on the National Association of Social Workers-Pennsylvania Statewide Ethics Committee, and is a member of the Council on Social Work Education, the Association of Baccalaureate Social Work Program Directors, and the Association of Pennsylvania State College & University Faculties. She earned a BA from Chestnut Hill College in Philadelphia, PA; an MSW from The Catholic University of America, Washington, DC; and a Ph.D. in Counseling Psychology from Temple University, Philadelphia, PA.

Becky Duddy-Burke, MSW, LICSW earned her Master's in Social Work in 1995 from Boston College. She has worked in elder care, outpatient mental health, the Massachusetts prison system, and since 2002 as a psychotherapist in a private group practice in Boston. Becky is also a member of the Boston chapter of DignityUSA, a national organization of LGBTQI Catholics and allies working locally, nationally, and internationally for church reform and LGBTQI justice. It was at Dignity/Boston that Becky met her spouse, Marianne. They were married at a Dignity/Boston liturgy in 1998 and celebrated their civil union in Vermont in 2000. They legally married in 2004 when Massachusetts legalized same-sex marriage. Becky and Marianne are parents of two children, Emily and Finn. They adopted both children from foster care through the Massachusetts Department of Families and Children; Emily in 2003, and Finn in 2010. Becky resides with her family in Hyde Park, MA.

Anthony Estreet, Ph.D., MSW, LCSW-C, LCADC is an Associate Professor in the School of Social Work at Morgan State University. His research interest focuses on the prevention and intervention of mental health and substance use disorders among African Americans within the urban environment. He developed the addiction concentration for the MSW program, and has been researching program implementation and behavioral health treatment related outcomes for the past nine years. Dr. Estreet is the Co-PI of the HRSA Behavioral Health Workforce

Enhancement and Training Grant in the School of Social Work. He has worked with experts to develop a comprehensive Behavioral Health Training program for 90 MSW students over three years. He has been a practicing clinician for over ten years in the areas of mental health and addiction treatment and is licensed in the State of Maryland for both Social Work and Addictions Counseling. Dr. Estreet is also the CEO of Next Step Treatment Solutions, a behavioral health consulting firm, and serves as the lead consultant to health programs throughout Maryland. Dr. Estreet has significant experience in training and technical assistance on substance use disorders.

Kimberly A. Furphy, DHSc, OTR, ATP was granted a Doctor of Health Science Degree with concentrations in Assistive Technology and Gerontology at the University of St. Augustine for the Health Sciences, a Master of Science Degree in Occupational Therapy from Temple University, and a Bachelor of Arts in Psychology from the University of Virginia. Her clinical and research interests include assistive technology applications in the treatment and education of individuals with physical and cognitive disabilities as well as pedagogical innovations for professionals working in the field of assistive technology. She is an Associate Professor and current Program Director in the MSOT program at Stockton University, teaching assessment and treatment of adult and geriatric populations, upper extremity rehabilitation and splinting, and assistive technology interventions. She has numerous presentations at the American Occupational Therapy Association's Annual Conference and at the New Jersey Occupational Therapy Association's Annual Conference on assistive technology and home modification; she is invited frequently to speak on these topics. Dr. Furphy authored the chapter on assessment tools for Activities of Daily Living in the book *Occupational Therapy Assessment Tools: An Annotated Index, 4th Edition* and is co-author of 'Assistive Technology: Supports for Aging Adults' in *Occupational Therapy with Aging Adults: Enhancing Quality of Life through Collaborative Practice*.

Ona H. Grant is a student at West Chester University of Pennsylvania.

Erin Hipple, MSW, LSW, MA is an educator, activist, researcher, and therapist specializing in trauma-informed care and working with youth and LGBTQ+ client populations. Erin's educational background is in social work, psychology, and pre-medical studies. They are currently pursuing their Ph.D. in Social Work at Widener University. Erin's work focuses on disrupting dominant narratives to promote equity for people of marginalized race, gender, sexuality, socioeconomic status, level of ability, and body size statuses.

Tiffany Y. Lane, Ph.D., MSW is an Associate Professor at the Ethelyn R. Strong School of Social Work at Norfolk State University. Dr. Lane's work centers on providing awareness and support to youth who aged out of foster care and transition into post-secondary institutions. She founded 'Almatines Goodies,' an initiative that provides school supplies and toiletries to persons who were formerly in foster care and attend a post-secondary institution. She serves as the co-chair of the Council on the Role and Status of Women in Social Work Education for the Council on Social Work Education and is a member of the Association of Baccalaureate Social Work Program Directors.

Terrence O. Lewis, Ph.D., MSW, BASW, LICSW is an Associate Professor in the Graduate Social Work Department at West Chester University of Pennsylvania. Dr. Lewis has extensive clinical experience working with individuals and couples in community mental health settings and private practice. As a community-based researcher, he focuses on the relationships between churches and marginalized populations including LGBT and ethnic minority communities. His dissertation research was on the phenomenon of LGBT-affirming Black churches and their responses to the HIV/AIDS crisis. Building on the rich findings from the dissertation, Dr. Lewis's current research project is a narrative study with African-American pastors who develop and offer LGBT-affirming ministry within African-American communities.

Karen Myers, JD, MSW is an Assistant Professor at James Madison University (JMU), where she teaches practice classes in JMU's BSW program. She came to JMU in 2014 with over 15 years of experience as a school social worker and public interest lawyer. She enjoys qualitative research methods to examine diversity issues, specifically those related to the LGBTQIAP+ community. She is also a yoga and Bodyflow instructor, which is one of her favorite forms of self-care.

Tonya C. Phillips Ph.D., MSW, LCSW-C, LCADC is an adjunct professor at Coppin State University in Baltimore, Maryland. She has over 15 years of clinical practice experience with an expertise in substance use disorders. Over the past ten years, Dr. Phillips has provided specialty clinical services with military populations.

Noell L. Rowan, Ph.D., LCSW, LCAS, FNAP is Professor and Associate Director at University of North Carolina Wilmington in the School of Social Work. She also oversees the undergraduate social work program and is Founder and Coordinator of the graduate level Substance Use Disorders and Addictions Program. Her scholarship is in the areas of gerontology, mental health and addictions, and the LGBT populations. She has authored more than 20 peer-reviewed articles, book chapters, and reviews. She is also co-author of a book on LGBT aging. She is a recipient of several teaching and research awards. In 2018, she was inducted as a fellow in the National Academies of Practice. She has practiced in the fields of mental health and addictions for more than 20 years.

Michelle G. Thompson, Doctoral Candidate, MS, L.M.H.C. is a doctoral candidate of social welfare at the Robert Stempel College of Public Health & Social Work at Florida International University. Her research focuses on mental health disparities among sexual minorities with specific attention to the psychological well-being of sexual minorities of color. She holds both a MS and a BA in Psychology from Florida International University, and she is a licensed Mental Health Counselor in the State of Florida with more than a decade of clinical experience working with both youth and adults. Michelle has served as an adjunct lecturer for both the Department of Psychology and the School of Social Work at Florida International University for over five years.

Mohan Vinjamuri, Ph.D., LMSW is an Assistant Professor in the Department of Social Work at Lehman College/CUNY. His research interests include social work with LGBTQ populations, contemporary fatherhood, critical pedagogy, and evidence-based practice. Dr. Vinjamuri teaches courses in human behavior and the social environment, social work practice, research methods, and an elective on social work with LGBTQ populations. Most recently, he was co-author of *A Guide for Sustaining Conversations on Racism, Identity and Our Mutual Humanity* (Cognella) and a recipient of a Robert Wood Johnson Foundation grant for research on intergenerational social work with LGBTQ communities. Dr. Vinjamuri has practiced as a teacher and social worker for over 27 years in various educational and social service settings.

1 Introduction

Backgrounds and Assumptions

Claire L. Dente

PH.D., MSW, LCSW

Welcome! It is my desire and that of each chapter contributor that the content in these pages will challenge you to think more deeply about the next LGBTQIA client sitting in front of you, whether or not you are aware of their sexual orientation and gender identity. We bring to you our experience, our passion and our diligent efforts to present what we know and what continues to evolve in a process of lifelong learning. We hope these pages expand your commitment to engage in culturally sensitive social work with LGBTQIA individuals, families, groups, organizations and communities.

Learning Considerations

The purpose of this text is to provide an overview of key issues for LGBTQIA (lesbian, gay, bisexual, transgender, queer, questioning, intersex, asexual and ally) clients. Your reading will prepare you to consider the needs of LGBTQIA clients in many different service provision contexts. Overall, this text is not a collection of empirical studies or theoretical essays, although we do share relevant work in theory and research. Rather, the chapter authors invite you to consider the integration of social work knowledge, values and skills with LGBTQIA-specific cultural awareness and sensitivity. This text aims to help you to fill your professional social work "backpack" with more nuanced information about the needs and concerns of the LGBTQIA client in your specific service context. Our goal is to invite you to think critically about how LGBTQIA clients might face barriers and discrimination in the various contexts of their lives. We invite you to develop practice approaches that will extend support through your own encounters with LGBTQIA clients, to utilize a strengths-based approach, to advocate to remove structural barriers and to create policies that support LGBTQIA clients.

Students lead busy lives. Work, family, friends, social media and academic obligations pull us in many directions. We have worked hard to create readable and accessible content for you as a busy student, while maintaining scholarly integrity in the presentation of content. While geared primarily to BSW and MSW students, the content presented here is suitable for all levels of students and practitioners. It will supplement your social work readings that may provide limited content on LGBTQIA issues, yet we hope we will leave you wanting to know more. LGBTQIA cultural awareness is a life-long learning process. We approach social work practice with LGBTQIA clients broadly, providing an overview of key areas. The contributors present application considerations to engage you in LGBTQIA issues and to assist you in delving more deeply into culturally sensitive service delivery to this population.

A key theme throughout the book is to emphasize the social work knowledge, values and skills needed for the practice of social work with LGBTQIA clients in multiple practice contexts. The contributors approach social work practice with LGBTQIA clients from a **strengths perspective** and utilizing the construct of **intersectionality** at micro, mezzo and macro levels. Each chapter begins with a list identifying the recently revised social work competencies found in the Council on Social Work Education's 2015 Educational Policies (CSWE, 2015) that link with chapter content. These identify where the content will strengthen your social work competence.

Some chapters will include references to case examples to illustrate the application of concepts. Each chapter also provides resources such as relevant organizations and links to their websites, and contributors have **bolded** important terms defined in a glossary. We hope you will take away "don't leave home without it" information. Several contributors have also provided practice and discussion questions for you to consider and to test your knowledge.

In developing this text, we were aware that some of you are approaching LGBTQIA-specific practice in a more concentrated manner for the first time, while others may be highly informed. This text introduces some of you to new areas you may not have considered, while providing others a foundation from which to springboard into deeper reflection and more nuanced scholarship. We encourage you to challenge yourself to a new level of competence.

The LGBTQIA population faces unique challenges and concerns. As ecological systems theory postulates, many of these challenges are rooted in the systems where LGBTQIA clients interact. The experiences of oppression, discrimination and privilege for this population are not stagnant. Historical, political, religious and social currents affect the day-to-day experiences of LGBTQIA people. Policies and laws surrounding marriage, adoption and healthcare, as well as the growing acceptance or on-going rejection within many mainstream faith systems touch LGBTQIA people. Thus, addressing LGBTQIA issues is a fluid process in that it must be responsive to political, social, cultural and religious climates. The United States Supreme Court ruled in 2013 that the federal government could not deny marriage benefits to gay and lesbian people, but a ruling on the legality of gay marriage across the country only came from the Supreme Court two years later on June 26, 2015. These rulings instigated a backlash against

LGBTQIA people through religious freedom acts, transgender bathroom laws and other discriminatory actions. Federal law still does not list sexual orientation and transgender identity as protected classes, so LGBTQIA people are not afforded the protections that accompany protected class status. This demonstrates that social workers must be proactive about the rights of LGBTQIA people and the delivery of practice.

You will need to be vigilant to pressing needs within each generation. LGBTQIA issues will change and evolve over time within the service contexts presented in these chapters. We hope this content prepares you to address current and emerging issues here and in other contexts of practice not specifically discussed here, such as the military. Most of you who are reading this are interested in learning more, either for professional reasons or because you, a friend or a family member identify with this population. You are most likely highly motivated to learn more about issues relevant to people you know personally. Time and space realities prevent covering all that could be included here. Your reading offers breadth of exposure to the content, and you can choose to delve deeper into each area.

One very important resource for you as a social worker is to know your professional agencies and their positions on important issues. Are you familiar with the National Association of Social Workers, the Council on Social Work Education, the National Association of Black Social Workers, the Association of Baccalaureate Social Work Program Directors and the many other social work groups and organizations that exist? Are you aware that these and other agencies can offer resources, policies and position statements for LGBTQIA-affirmative social work practice? It is important to stay connected while a student and, even more importantly, long after your degrees are completed and you are engaging in social work practice.

Basic Concepts and Foundations

As noted previously, we are exploring LGBTQIA concerns through the frameworks of ecological systems theory, intersectionality and a strengths-based approach. Most social workers learn these concepts through courses on human behavior in the social environment. As a brief reminder, ecological systems theory considers the individual interacting within their environment, taking into consideration micro, mezzo and macro factors. Intersectionality considers the multiple identities of a client (age, gender and gender identity, race, ethnicity, sexual orientation, ability, etc.) and the dynamic and subtle ways these identities might privilege or marginalize an individual or group. A strengths-based approach avoids deficit thinking or blaming the victim and instead focuses on the resources and strengths available to the client.

These models guide our approach in the following chapters. We view LGBTQIA identities from a normative perspective of these identities along a continuum of variation of humanity. Thus, we do not pathologize sexual orientation or gender identity. The American Psychiatric Association removed homosexuality as a disorder from its *Diagnostic and Statistical Manual (DSM)* in 1973; in 2015, they reframed our understanding of gender in the *DSM-5* by replacing Gender Identity Disorder with Gender Dysphoria. You will not find scientific explanations, arguments or justifications for or against a person's sexual orientation or gender identity here; nor will you find theological debates about the sinfulness of LGBTQIA identities. I do encourage you to explore the nature vs. nurture debate, the studies on "a gay gene," and the arguments theologians and scholars make pro or con about what the holy readings, spiritual leaders and prophets have to say about sexual orientation and gender identity. While these may be important questions, they often originate from an attempt to seek moral and legal justification for the existence of LGBTQIA people. Justification is not the foundation of this text; rather, we start here from a position of strength, acceptance and normativity. We begin with the belief that for those of us who are believers, the Creator loves us all.

Background and History

There are many identity development models for you to consider as you think about social work practice with LGBTQIA clients. While we do not go into depth about them here, researchers consider Cass's Homosexual Identity Formation Model a milestone in understanding identity (Cass, 1979). Chapters 7 and 9 will include discussion of additional models for you to consider. Other researchers extend these theories and develop new applications relevant for current generations and contexts (Dickey, Burnes & Singh, 2012; Kenneady & Oswalt, 2014). What other models have you learned that help to frame our understanding of LGBTQIA identity and development?

As you consider social work practice with LGBTQIA clients, consider what you know about LGBTQIA history. In addition to the removal of homosexuality and gender identity disorder from the DSM, there are many markers in the history and experiences of LGBTQIA people. What happened to LGBTQIA people in the Holocaust? What do you know about Stonewall? Where did symbols like the rainbow flag and pink triangle originate? Can you identify the other LGBTQIA flags and symbols? What do you know about the HIV/AIDS crisis, breast cancer and healthcare for transgender people? How have religious traditions approached sexual orientation and gender identity? In what ways have LGBTQIA people challenged oppression and pursued civil rights? What is the history of gay marriage, how have LGBTQIA people been treated in schools or the military, and how has the media evolved in LGBTQIA representation? The following chapters will answer some of these questions with you; for others we challenge you to explore on your own.

Terminology and Language: Defining LGBTQIA

It is important to remember about whom we are speaking when we use the LGBTQIA acronym. Definitions and language are important to LGBTQIA people. The following explanations are extremely basic and will seem insufficient and incomplete to most LGBTQIA people. It is always important for us to get to know our clients and to ask them how they identify.

To define simply, **lesbians** (L) are women attracted to women, **gay** men (G) are men attracted to men and **bisexual** people (B) can be attracted to men or to women. **Transgender** (T) people are individuals who may identify internally as a gender other than that presented by their biology from birth (see Chapter 8 for more intricate definitions). **Queer** (Q) is an umbrella term, formerly a derogatory slur against LGBTQIA people, reclaimed by some to reframe its original meaning and to provide an inclusive space. It can include anyone who identifies as LGBTQIA, **gender non-binary** (those who do not identify gender as consisting solely of two traditional options of male or female), **pansexual** (those who may be attracted to members of all gender identities and expressions) and **gender non-conforming** (those who do not adhere to societal expectations and rules regarding gender expectations and presentation). **Questioning** (Q) refers to individuals who are exploring or unsure of their sexual orientation and/ or gender identity. Individuals with **intersex** (I) conditions, also referred to as Disorders/Differences of Sex Development (DSD), are individuals with "congenital conditions in which development of chromosomal, gonadal, or anatomic sex is atypical" (Accord Alliance, 2018; Chavhan et al., 2008, p. 1893; Houk, Hughes, Ahmed & Lee, 2006). It is important to know that some of these individuals prefer not to be included under the LGBTQIA umbrella, while others do. Individuals who identify as **asexual** (A) tend not to be sexually attracted to others, but there are many nuances and depths to this identity that could challenge that assertion. Historically, **allies** (A) are **heterosexual** (men attracted to women; women attracted to men) and **cisgender** (individuals whose internal gender identity matches their external biology) individuals who support LGBTQIA people. It is important to be aware that LGBTQIA people vary greatly in their use of terminology, and that terminology evolves. We aimed for greater inclusion by using the broad LGBTQIA umbrella, while humbly recognizing that even this may over- or under-represent, and that not all content in every chapter applies to all populations.

Terminology and Language: Clarifying Concepts

Now that we know 'who's who,' let us examine 'what's what.' I am grateful to Dr. Rodney Mader and Dr. Jackie Hodes at West Chester University of Pennsylvania (with thanks to Jason Stansberry, Dr. Rita Drapkin of Indiana University of Pennsylvania, and the West Chester University of Pennsylvania LGBTQ Advocacy Committee). Their tireless efforts developed ally training content that discussed biological sex, gender identity, gender role and expression, sexual orientation, sexual behavior and sexual identity (Mader & Hodes, 2009). Sometimes these concepts can be confusing, so let us take a closer look at their subtle distinctions.

Biological sex refers to the body with which I was born. It consists of my chromosomes, genitalia and hormones. The majority of individuals are born with a biological sex that we know as male or female, which is why society often considers gender to be binary (having only two options). Yet, others are born with atypical presentation or conditions (DSD and/or intersex) that do not fall neatly into these categories. **Gender identity** refers to my internal sense of my gender. This could be male, female, transgender, genderqueer, or perhaps I do not find any of these appropriate and thus might identify as label free. **Gender role or expression** captures how I choose to present myself outwardly. Do I wear extremely feminine or masculine clothing, or present with traditionally gender-specific hairstyles, mannerisms, gestures or make-up? If you research LGBTQIA history you can find discussions of butch/femme, drag and androgyny, but gender expression is also important today. How do members of our society treat individuals who do not fit traditional gender roles and expression? When does society find this acceptable or not? A man wearing a skirt might turn heads in one context, yet be viewed as normative in another context, especially if that dress is a kilt and it is March 17 in New York City. Thus, social norms influence our understanding.

Sometimes there is confusion between gender and sexuality, but these concepts differ. My **sexual orientation** indicates to whom I am attracted physically, emotionally and sexually. Heterosexual/straight people are attracted to the "opposite sex" while gay/lesbian people are attracted to the "same" sex. As noted earlier, there are also people who do not fit neatly into these categories, such as those who identify as asexual, bisexual, pansexual, queer or label free. My **sexual behavior** is the activity I choose to engage in and with whom. One might identify as a lesbian but engage in sexual behavior such as heterosexual intercourse with a close male friend, perhaps even a gay male friend. Social workers need to remember that identity and behavior may appear contradictory; thus, it is important to avoid presumptions. Finally, my **sexual identity** involves how I view myself. An individual might question if the lesbian or gay man mentioned earlier are bisexual, as each engaged in traditionally heterosexual behavior, yet each clearly self-identifies as lesbian and gay. It is important to listen to our clients about their identities.

Your Journey in the Pages Ahead

As you read the chapters ahead, you will find some common threads across chapters. This should highlight for you the importance of certain historical events and social and cultural issues. Consider those issues within the context of the chapter topic and through the lens of a social worker practicing there.

These reappear because of their significance to the LGBTQIA community and history. Note this through the lens of the content in each chapter.

It has been my honor and privilege to edit this textbook. I want you as readers to know how much the chapter contributors have poured their hearts and souls into these chapters. Some contributors identify as lesbian, gay, bisexual, transgender, queer, questioning, intersex/DSD or asexual, while others stand supportively and proudly as heterosexual and cisgender allies. I invited each contributor to write their chapter because of their professional expertise and/or personal experience in their chapter topic. I reached out to those I knew had a passion for knowledge. I invited contributors with a depth of spirit and integrity about their work who tirelessly support all people, including LGBTQIA people.

Karen Myers presents thought-provoking content and touching cases in her discussion of LGBTQIA relationships and gay marriage in Chapter 2. She also delves deeply into considerations for school social workers and others who work with LGBTQIA youth in Chapter 6 on education and schools. Mohan Vinjamuri explores LGBTQIA family and parenting issues in Chapter 3, which is a nice complement to my work with Becky Duddy-Burke and Sara Chominski's in Chapter 4 on issues and cases related to LGBTQIA adoption. Tiffany Lane highlights concerns for LGBTQIA clients interacting with social service agencies in Chapter 5, especially youth in the foster care system, and paying close attention to the needs of those who are aging out of the system. In Chapter 7, Terry Lewis provides a solid theoretical background to his discussion on race, ethnicity and practice approaches to engage in affirmative social work practice. In Chapter 8, Erin Hipple, Austin Angiollilo and Ona Grant have provided an exceedingly thoughtful and challenging discussion for affirmative practice with transgender and nonbinary people.

Anthony Estreet, Tonya Phillips and Michelle Thompson offer important considerations surrounding addiction issues and LGBTQIA people in Chapter 9, while Lisa Cox and Kimberly Furphy collaborated to provide a compelling overview of healthcare issues, access and disparities LGBTQIA people may face in Chapter 10. Noell Rowan and Sandy Butler will challenge your awareness of aging and the needs of older LGBTQIA adults in Chapter 14, while I address religious and spirituality issues in Chapter 13.

To help us to understand some of the mezzo and macro level areas for developing competency and advocacy skills, Casey Bohrman takes a closer look at ways our LGBTQIA clients may encounter the legal system in Chapter 11. In Chapter 12, Joseph Nicholas DeFilippis advocates for LGBTQIA concerns related to issues of poverty, economics and employment. Finally, Tina Chiarelli-Helminiak and Michele Eggers Barison broaden the perspective to consider social work concerns at global levels in Chapter 15. I am grateful to each of these devoted colleagues.

Many of us in social work education seek to mentor each other and to mentor our students; we want to see our students and colleagues succeed. Many contributors invited colleagues and students to co-author their chapters as a way to mentor others and/or to expand the knowledge base for the content provided here for you. When you meet them at a conference someday, I hope you will greet them with gratitude!

I am personally grateful to Samantha Barbaro, Erik Zimmerman, Emily Boyd and Francesca Hearn at Tayor & Francis Routledge, for their guidance to me in this first-time endeavor. I extend thanks to my university, West Chester University of Pennsylvania, to our president, Dr. Christopher Fiorentino, to the Association of Pennsylvania State College and University Faculties (APSCUF) and to my colleagues who have provided a climate of support for LGBTQIA people and scholarship on campus. Our department graduate assistants, Riley Hellings and Sarah Chominski, have provided numerous hours of assistance with details. I am extremely grateful to the chapter contributors (Karen, Mohan, Becky, Sara, Tiffany, Terrence, Erin, Austin, Ona, Anthony, Tonya, Michelle, Lisa, Kimberly, Casey, Joseph, Noell, Sandra, Christina, and Michele) for their commitment and patience through this first-time project. Your courage to stand up for the most marginalized among us and to speak out for social justice inspires me.

My dear family and friends have supported this endeavor with enthusiasm and encouragement. Our dog (Stickeen) and cat (Ellie) have kept me loved and humble. Most especially, my dear wife Leslie, you have stood by me faithfully with a hand on my shoulder through the challenges and joys of this project. I am blessed and grateful to journey through this life with you, and I love you very much.

Questions to Consider

1   What are the strengths perspective, intersectionality and ecological systems theory? How do these apply to LGBTQIA populations at micro, mezzo and macro levels?

2   What does Cass's *Homosexual Identity Formation Model* (Cass, 1979) say about sexual orientation? What other models and theories exist to help us to understand sexual orientation and gender identity development?

3   Examine a specific event, group or era in history, such as the Holocaust, the Civil Rights Movement or the Feminist Movement in the United States. Explore how LGBTQIA people were engaged in these events. How were they included or marginalized?

4   What has been the experience of LGBTQIA people in the military? What did the "Don't Ask, Don't Tell" policy mean for LGBTQIA service members and veterans? What policies have recently affected LGBTQIA transgender individuals in the military?

5   Look up something you have always wondered about, such as LGBTQIA symbols. Why were these important historically?

Resources

Council on Social Work Education https://cswe.org/
Human Rights Campaign (HRC) www.hrc.org
Lambda Legal www.lambdalegal.org/cgi-bin/iowa/index.html
National Association of Black Social Workers https://nabsw.site-ym.com/
National Association of Social Workers (NASW) www.naswdc.org/
Parents, Families and Friends of Lesbians and Gays (PFLAG) www.
  pflag.org/

References

Accord Alliance (2018). *Learn about DSD, FAQs. Terminology & frequency: What is useful about the terminology of DSD? What is unhelpful?* Retrieved from www. accordalliance.org/

Cass, V. C. (1979). Homosexual identity formation: A theoretical model. *Journal of Homosexuality*, 4(3), 219–235.

Chavhan, G. B., Parra, D. A., Oudjhane, K., Miller, S. F., Babyn, P. S., & Pippi Salle, J. L. (2008). Imaging of ambiguous genitalia: Classification and diagnostic approach. *RadioGraphics*, 28(7), 1891–1904. doi: doi:10.1148/rg.287085034

Council on Social Work Education (CSWE). (2015). *Educational policy and accreditation standards.* Alexandria, VA: Author.

Dickey, L. M., Burnes, T. R., & Singh, A. A. (2012). Sexual identity development of female-to-male transgender individuals: A grounded theory inquiry. *Journal of LGBT Issues in Counseling*, 6(2), 118–138. doi: doi:10.1080/15538605.2012.678184

Houk, C. P., Hughes, I. A., Ahmed, S. F., & Lee, P. A. (2006). Summary of consensus statement on interssex disorders and their management. International Intersex Consensus Conference. *Pediatrics*, 118, 753–757.

Kenneady, D. A. & Oswalt, S. B. (2014). Is Cass's model of homosexual identity formation relevant to today's society? *American Journal of Sexuality Education*, 9(2), 229–246. doi: doi:10.1080/15546128.2014.900465

Mader, R. & Hodes, J. (2009). LGBTQ 101: Learning what it means to be part of the LGBTQ community [PowerPoint slides]. Created by Drs. Rodney Mader & Jackie Hodes, with thanks to Jason Stansberry, Rita Drapkin (Indiana University of PA), and the West Chester University of PA LGBTQ Advocacy Committee.

2   Marriage Equality, Relationships, and Divorce

Karen Myers

JD, MSW

CSWE 2015 EPAS Competencies

Competency 1: Demonstrate ethical and professional behavior
Competency 2: Engage diversity and difference in practice
Competency 3: Advance human rights and social, economic and environmental justice
Competency 5: Engage in policy practice
Competency 7: Assess individuals, families, groups, organizations, and communities
Competency 8: Intervene with individuals, families, groups, organizations, and communities

Introduction

Imagine you have been with the love of your life for 35 years, sharing a home, vacations, chores, joys, and sorrows together. One day the love of your life is in a serious car accident. You rush to the hospital desperate to be there even if it is just to say goodbye but are barred admittance to your love's bedside because you are not considered family since you are not legally married.

Imagine you have fallen in love and have just accepted a wedding proposal. You are eager to begin planning your wedding at the church where you have attended your whole life and where your siblings have both gotten married. You eagerly call to set up an appointment to meet with your pastor but are told the church will not allow your marriage to take place there because you are a same-sex couple.

The first scenario was a common occurrence for members of the LGBTQIA community prior to **marriage equality** becoming the law of the land in June 2015. The United States Supreme Court's decision in Obergefell v. Hodges (2015) changes the legal landscape for gay and lesbian couples, allowing them to access more than 1,000 legal protections and benefits that come along with marriage; however, there may be other risks for these couples that continue to prevent them from taking advantage of the change in marriage laws. Furthermore, the right of same-sex couples to enter into civil marriages does not mean they can marry in many faith communities across the United States, where conservative beliefs make the second scenario all too common.

Social workers can celebrate marriage equality as a positive step towards recognizing the importance of human relationships while also acknowledging that there is more work to do in the fight for social justice. Legal protections are important but they cannot legislate inclusion nor guarantee safety. In some cases, the dismantling of such systems of oppression even creates backlash. For example, the right to marry legally ensures some legal protections for couples, but they may remain vulnerable socially, emotionally, economically, and in other ways.

Historical Background

Marriage is a social institution that invokes a wide variety of reactions from different people. Regardless of one's personal views, it is a civil right that was denied to an entire class of people until June 2015 when the United States Supreme Court ruled in favor of **same-sex marriage** in the *Obergefell* case. Some of the rights and protections related to marriage include tax benefits, employment benefits, disability benefits, estate planning benefits, government benefits, family benefits, consumer benefits, housing benefits, immigration benefits, medical benefits, and death benefits. In June 2013, United States v. Windsor (2013), a separate United States Supreme Court case, overturned the **Defense of Marriage Act (DOMA)** allowing married gay couples to benefit from the 1,138 related federal protections and rights; however, gay couples living in states where marriage was not an option for them still did not have access to any of these federal rights.

The first lawsuit related to legal recognition of same-sex marriage was filed in Minnesota in 1970. It was unsuccessful and few additional legal challenges occurred until 1993 when several gay couples, who had been denied marriage licenses, filed a discrimination suit, Baehr v. Lewin (1993), against the state of Hawaii. That case was effectively defeated by an amendment to the state constitution banning **gay marriage**s. Additional states passed their own marriage bans. In September 1996, President Bill Clinton signed DOMA, which prevented federal recognition of same-sex marriages and did not require states to recognize the marriage licenses of same-sex couples from other states.

DOMA inspired LGBTQIA people and their allies to increase advocacy for equal rights in different states. The first state to have a successful ruling was Vermont in 1999, which led to the establishment of **civil unions** for gay couples starting in July 2000. **Domestic partnerships** were another form of legal recognition offered in 1999, first in California. Civil unions and domestic partnerships did not offer equal benefits to marriage and neither status was recognized at the federal level. In 2003, Massachusetts became the first state to legalize gay marriage with Connecticut following in 2008. California also briefly allowed gay couples to marry in 2008 until Proposition 8 opened the way for the state constitution to ban same-sex marriage and brought significant media attention to gay marriage, igniting outrage on both sides of the debate. Proposition 8 remained in effect until 2013 when California became the 13th state to recognize same-sex marriage.

By the end of 2008, the entire country seemed polarized over the issue of marriage equality with a few states choosing to allow it and many other states banning it. At the time of the 2013 *Windsor* decision, only a dozen states and the District of Columbia allowed gay couples to marry. Two years later in June 2015, that number had more than doubled. The same-sex marriage timeline in Box 2.1 depicts some of the rapid changes that occurred in this country, particularly between 2008 and 2015. It also highlights the interplay between court rulings, legislation, and voter referendums.

Throughout this time, members of the LGBTQIA community continued to meet, date, fall in love, and make commitments to each other as they have since long before the issue of marriage equality became a national debate. Based on found documents and stories passed down, there is evidence that same-sex relationships are not a new or recent configuration. The couple at the heart of the *Windsor* case, Edith Windsor and Thea Spyer, had been together for more than 40 years before they were able to legally marry. Another couple, Charity Bryant and Sylvia Blake, spent 44 years together in the 1800s without ever being able to marry each other although original letters and journals suggest many in their community recognized their relationship (Cleves, 2014).

Box 2.1 Same-Sex Marriage Timeline

[Brackets [ ] indicate where same-sex marriage was legalized.]

1972 MN gay marriage case dismissed by **SCOTUS** (Supreme Court of the United States)

1973 MD is first state to pass a statute banning same-sex marriages

1993 HI Supreme Court rules that denying same-sex marriage violates state constitution

1996 President Clinton signs the Defense of Marriage Act (DOMA)

1998 HI voters approve a constitutional amendment banning same-sex marriage

1999 CA becomes first state to pass domestic partnership statute

2000 VT offers civil unions to same-sex couples

2003 MA Supreme Court legalizes same-sex marriage [MA]

2004 Eleven states pass constitutional amendments making same-sex marriage illegal

2005 CA legislators pass bill to legalize same-sex marriage but Governor vetoes

2006 Seven additional states ban same-sex marriage through constitutional amendments

2007 CA legislators pass bill to legalize same-sex marriage but Governor vetoes

2008 CA Supreme Court strikes down same-sex marriage ban but CA voters approve Prop 8 banning same-sex marriage

2008 CT Supreme Court legalizes same-sex marriage [MA, CT]

2009 IA, VT, ME, NH, DC legalize same-sex marriage but ME voters overturn same-sex marriage law [MA, CT, IA, VT, NH, DC]

2011 NY legalizes same-sex marriage [MA, CT, IA, VT, NH, DC, NY]

2012 MD, ME, WA, NJ legalize same-sex marriage but NJ Governor vetoes [MA, CT, IA, VT, NH, DC, NY, MD, ME, WA]

2013 SCOTUS invalidates a key portion of DOMA and state courts begin to overturn state bans [MA, CT, IA, VT, NH, DC, NY, MD, ME, WA, RI, DE, MN, CA, NJ, HI, IL, NM]

2014 More states legalize same-sex marriage [MA, CT, IA, VT, NH, DC, NY, MD, ME, WA, RI, DE, MN, CA, NJ, HI, IL, NM, OR, PA, IN, OK, UT, WI, VA, CO, KS, NV, WV, NC, SC, AK, ID, WY, AZ, MT]

2015 SCOTUS affirms same-sex couples' right to marry across the United States

Social Work Knowledge, Values, and Skills

In the following are some core elements and competencies covered in this chapter to take with you into practice.

What a Social Worker Needs to Know

- In many ways LGBTQIA couples are not all that different from heterosexual couples. They come together for similar reasons, including love and companionship. They also experience many of the same challenges related to finances, fighting, and figuring out household chores. However, there are also unique challenges based on societal structures that support **heteronormativity**.
- LGBTQIA couples often face oppression and marginalization as part of a minority group, which creates added stress on their relationships; however, stressors and challenges are situation specific and social workers should be careful not to make assumptions or generalize. Social workers should also be aware that the **intersectionality** of different identities can lead to added oppression and discrimination.
- There are still potential risks involved for gay couples choosing to marry. Each couple's experience is different and should be treated with openness and empathy.

Relevant Social Work Values and Ethical Considerations

- Dignity and worth of the person
- Importance of human relationships
- Social justice
- **Cultural humility**
- Confidentiality
- Empathy
- Non-judgmental approaches
- Self-determination
- Individualization

Social Work Skills to Strengthen Competency

- Engagement is a critical first step with all clients, but particularly members of the LGBTQIA community. There are ways to engage before even meeting a client by offering a welcoming environment. Display a rainbow flag or safe space sticker, hang photos that show diversity, and stock inclusive magazines in waiting areas. It is also important to make sure agency policies and paperwork do not presume heterosexuality. As you begin work with a client, listen to the language they use to describe themselves and those close to them and then use that language with them. A woman in a relationship with another woman might identify as lesbian, bisexual, queer, questioning, or male-to-female transgender. A gay couple may refer to each other as husband and husband, wife and wife, partner and partner, or spouse and spouse.
- During assessment, practice active listening skills. Many LGBTQIA clients have been judged harshly without ever being asked their stories. Having a safe space to talk is a powerful intervention all on its own. At the same time, be respectful and mindful of boundaries, avoiding needlessly intrusive questions so as not to make clients feel like they are an unnatural phenomenon.
- Make sure the client feels comfortable with suggested interventions because clients know their situations best. Be open to new and different ideas. Always respect client self-determination and acknowledge that what might be your choice may not be the right one for the client.
- Evaluation should be ongoing; incorporate suggestions for improvement whenever they are possible. Ask clients for their opinions and respectfully consider them even when they may not be opportunities for change.
- Throughout the time spent with a client, be mindful of client safety. Confidentiality is important with all clients but breaches about sexual orientation and gender identity can have devastating effects. If necessary, allow groups to meet in confidential locations. During advocacy efforts, ask clients what they are comfortable sharing and how.

- Critically analyze power imbalances and systemic oppression, identifying macro level work to be done for the benefit of all members of the LGBTQIA community.
- Practice self-awareness and self-reflection as part of cultural humility. Be aware of biases and assumptions that may hinder working effectively with LGBTQIA clients.

Implications for Social Work Practice

It is important for social workers to understand that while marriage equality is a recent development, LGBTQIA relationships are not. There is a rich and resilient history of LGBTQIA people coming together and staying together even in unsupportive and sometimes dangerous environments. The current backlash, occurring due to advances like marriage equality, requires awareness and navigation and underlines the need for additional legal protections for the LGBTQIA community. Equality for the LGBTQIA community remains a social justice issue, which also means it should be a priority for social workers who recognize it as one of their core values (NASW, 2008).

A gay couple may want to marry legally for many reasons, including simply publicly celebrating and acknowledging their relationship. There may be practical considerations, like putting a spouse on a company health insurance policy or seeking a change in immigration status. Often alongside these benefits, gay couples are considering potential costs and risks, like having a conservative church body expel the couple or unsupportive parents withdraw inheritance gifts. Sometimes couples are unaware of the limitations of marriage equality and the lack of protection in other legal arenas, like employment discrimination, which provides an opportunity for social workers to identify and educate others about those policies as well as advocate for necessary changes in those policies.

Views on morality grounded in religious beliefs remain the primary objection for same-sex marriage in the United States (Franck, 2011). Many faith communities welcome and affirm gay relationships, but the ones that do not often refuse to allow same-sex marriages to take place within their walls and may even expel members who are involved in a same-sex relationship. Judgment and rejection by one's faith community can result in deep pain as well as shame and embarrassment. A same-sex couple excitedly planning a wedding may have their joy marred by exclusion from their faith community (Blauch, 2004). An individual experiencing marginalization by their faith community can struggle with internalizing that experience, which can have reverberations into that person's desire and ability to form a positive, loving relationship (Frost & Meyer, 2009; Otis, Rostosky, Riggle & Hamrin, 2006).

Consider the following cases and your own social work practice. In what ways would you support these clients? Consider Alex and Cade, who experience challenges after legal marriage.

> ### Box 2.2 Case: Alex and Cade
>
> Alex and Cade have been dating for five years and engaged for two. They had thought about traveling to another state to marry legally but wanted to wait until they could legally marry in their home state of Virginia. They eagerly began planning their wedding when they knew their marriage would receive legal recognition. They were saddened when some of Cade's relatives refused to attend due to their religious convictions but they tried not to allow that to deter their excitement. They enjoyed a beautiful wedding day and a fabulous honeymoon to the Bahamas. Soon after they returned, Alex was fired from his job after his employer found out about his wedding to a man. Virginia law does not prohibit employment discrimination in the private sector so Alex is now unemployed, taking away income the couple counted on to pay their mortgage.

While Alex and Cade's situation is not an uncommon one for gay couples, it is important to remember that each situation is unique, which means the most important first step is to discover what these circumstances mean specifically for Alex and Cade. It would be important to use a strengths-based perspective looking for positive and protective factors to build upon while also acknowledging the systemic factors that created the problem for this newly married couple. The implications of Alex's job loss could be exacerbated by factors like where they live, the current job market, his particular skill level, the extent of their existing financial obligations, and/or the availability of familial support or alternative financial resources.

A social worker could become involved with Alex and Cade at the micro level, helping them to process the job loss and referring them to potential resources. They may need support individually and as a family to deal with this significant unexpected stressor so early in their marriage. This incident of discrimination may cause past experiences of oppression and marginalization to resurface. A support group could be a valuable mezzo-level intervention to provide another environment where they can receive support. Social workers should also be involved in macro practice, spreading awareness and advocating for protections so that others do not find themselves vulnerable to job loss due to exercising their legal right to marry. At all levels of practice, social workers should seek to understand the influence diversity has had on their clients' lives.

Situations like Alex and Cade's should also enhance a social worker's cultural humility and empathy towards similarly situated clients. It might be easy to assume that an unmarried couple is not serious about their relationship as opposed to them recognizing the potential costs of making the decision to marry if they are gay and privately employed in an unsupportive environment. Additionally, some couples may be discouraged from legal marriage by familial or religious resistance (Beagan & Hattie, 2015; Subhi & Geelan, 2012).

Members of the LGBTQIA community frequently experience rejection within their **family of origin**. The resulting isolation can be devastating to an individual and stressful for a couple. A healthy adaptation is to create a **family of choice**, which may include accepting members of the family of origin, but expanded to include others who are supportive. This network of people provides validation and support for the couple's relationship and may be the family with whom the couple celebrates holidays (Clunis & Green, 2005). Minimizing these relationships reaffirms the heteronormative nuclear family and marginalizes those closest to the couple (Peterson, 2013). Social workers should be mindful of the significance of these relationships and acknowledge them when using assessment tools like ecomaps or genograms. Let us now consider the case in Box 2.3.

Box 2.3 Case: Mark and Andrea

Mark and Andrea have been married for seven years. They have two young children. Andrea has always known Mark to be a gentler, quieter man than is considered typical. That is what drew her to him initially and what she continues to love in him. When they got together, he was estranged from his parents. She was close to her family who adore Mark, so in some ways it has felt easier not to have to divide time constantly between two families as her sister does. She comes home from grocery shopping one day to find Mark sobbing inconsolably with an open box in front of him. There is a large photo album on his lap and a small scrap of paper, which has fallen to the floor. Mark is crying so hard he cannot speak so she picks up the note and reads its simple line, "She never got over losing you until the day she died." Looking at the photo album, she realizes the "she" must be Mark's mother. She holds her husband close and allows him to weep. Later she looks more closely through the album and realizes that Mark often dressed as a girl and had long hair in the pictures. He tends to wear his hair longer now and has occasionally dressed up in her clothes for costume parties but she never thought much about it. Over the coming weeks, Mark pours out his story of growing up convinced he was a girl named Marly. His parents would hear nothing of it and his father punished him severely when he persisted. They finally kicked him out as a teenager and he went to live with a friend, but not before considering suicide. He reveals that he has tried to suppress his feelings for years, but admits he has never felt like a man. He loves Andrea and their children deeply. He cannot bear the thought of living the rest of his life as a man but he also does not want to lose the family he loves. Andrea is devastated but sees how heartbroken Mark is and wants to support him even though it will mean the loss of her husband and a major change in their family make-up.

The empathy social workers should extend here encompasses both Marly and Andrea. Marly felt pressured into a life as Mark. As a result, she and Andrea are now both in pain because of the consequences. Confidentiality would be incredibly important as Marly determines if and how she wants to transition. Social workers need to extend sensitivity around supporting her identity while also providing Marly with protection she may feel she needs. Andrea needs space to grieve without judgment. Individual and family-level interventions could include supportive counseling, family counseling, referrals to support groups and/or organizations, and assistance with finding appropriate medical and legal help. A social worker may collaborate with other professionals with the client's permission to help insure the provision of high quality and effective services.

Marly and Andrea could remain a couple, transitioning from a heterosexual marriage to a same-sex one, if both of them want to remain in the marriage. If the change in Marly's gender identity impacts their attraction to each other, they may continue to co-parent while uncoupling romantically. Gay men and lesbians can also find themselves in heterosexual marriages they entered at a time when they did not feel free to be who they are. Some choose to stay in those relationships, referred to as **mixed marriages**, while others find they can no longer continue living that life. Break-ups can be a time of intense pain as well as experiences of joy and freedom. Hannah and Brooke present another situation in the next scenario, Box 2.4.

Box 2.4 Case: Hannah and Brooke

Hannah and Brooke have been married for almost one year. They just bought a little house in their town and spend more of their monthly income than they would like on their mortgage. They both work weekdays and whoever wakes up first usually makes the coffee and lets the dog out. They mow their yard, do their laundry, and pay their taxes. They do not make their bed because they figure they will just be crawling right back into it at night. Neither of them likes to clean the bathroom so they toss a coin to decide who has the honor each week. They sometimes eat at home and sometimes go out. They argue at times but try to make up by the end of the day because they do not think it is good to go to bed angry. Their last vacation was their honeymoon. They would like to get away for their first anniversary but are not sure they can afford it. Hannah's parents did not attend their wedding and say they cannot approve of their "alternative lifestyle."

For many gay couples, the idea that they are living some kind of alternative lifestyle is alienating but also perplexing when their lives often do not seem that different from their neighbors. In fact, there are probably ways in which Hannah and Brooke wish their lifestyle was more alternative when it comes to chores and paying taxes. Depending on where they live, they may choose not to hold hands when they are walking down a street. They may not refer to each other as "honey" or "sweetheart" when they are out in public. They may not have their wedding picture displayed on their desks at work. They may be exhausted with being treated differently when they are out in public, when at home they feel perfectly normal.

It is quite possible a social worker could work with Hannah and Brooke around issues having nothing to do with their sexual orientation. Brooke's father could be hospitalized and a social worker could interact with her entire family as they are planning for his discharge to a rehab facility. One of their grandmothers could be in the late stages of Alzheimer's and entering hospice. There are times when the most culturally sensitive response a social worker can provide is one of normalcy. It may seem counterintuitive, but the very act of drawing attention to the diversity could be the experience that is marginalizing to the couple.

Strengths and Challenges in LGBTQIA Families

Resiliency is a common denominator among many gay couples. In spite of the significant external challenges gay couples face, many of them have been successful in establishing long-term, satisfying relationships. In *Together Forever*, Marcus (1998) interviewed 40 different gay couples who had been together for nine to 50 years. Marcus wrote that they had all successfully coped with challenges and were eager to share their stories "as an example to the next generation of gay and lesbian people, to offer themselves as the kinds of role models they themselves never had" (p. xiii). Building this type of community is important because lack of social supports can be a difficult challenge for some gay couples (Berzon, 1990; Stiers, 2000). There is more legal support now for couples who feel they can access that right without negative ramifications, but social support is still lacking in many communities.

Gay couples can feel isolated if they lack support in their community. They often have to work harder to establish positive relationships with family members, depending on the level of acceptance in their family (Berzon, 1997). Their faith community may ostracize them if their religion holds conservative beliefs around sexual orientation. Exclusions can lead to increased closeness as the couple comes to depend on each other, but the stress of being stigmatized based on their marginalized status can also place undue pressure on a couple's relationship (Mohr & Daly, 2008). How a couple responds to any given situation and its attendant stressors is not generalizable; therefore, social workers should build their cultural competence by learning about the oppression and marginalization gay couples can face without falling into the trap of making assumptions based on the knowledge they gain.

The intersection of different identities can compound already stressful situations. Some couples may experience oppression based on their sexual orientation as well as another identity or multiple identities, such as gender identity, race, religion, nationality, and/or ability (Addison & Coolhart, 2015). Women continue to advocate for equal pay in the United States, so a lesbian couple's income may be less than a similarly situated gay male couple's earnings. Immigration status can impact a gay couple by increasing their desire not to have attention drawn to them, which may limit the services they feel able to access. Transgender people and their partners live with even fewer protections under the law, which may increase the risks of visibility.

Intimate partner violence is a reality in the gay community, as it is in the heterosexual community (Jacobson, Daire & Abel, 2015). Partners can exert control through physical violence, emotional abuse, and/or financial restrictions. An added dimension in gay relationships, which social workers need to know, is that fear of disclosure can be used as an additional method for control and entrapment. A person in a gay relationship, who fears others knowing about their sexual orientation, may feel unable to leave the situation. There are also times when responders to incidents of physical violence may make assumptions about what is happening, not recognizing the situation as domestic violence since it is a same-sex relationship. This can leave the victim with fewer protections and the perpetrator with more power and access.

Intimate Relationships: Forming, Sustaining, and Endings

As with some heterosexual couples, there are gay couples who meet, date, marry, and stay together for the rest of their lives. Other relationships do not make it past the meeting or dating stage or dissolve after marriage. Some couples choose to stay together without making a public or legal commitment to each other. Some couples dream of and plan a lavish wedding. Each couple knows their own situation best and makes decisions based on their own considerations.

Forming Relationships

LGBTQIA couples meet in many of the same ways heterosexual couples meet: social gatherings, work, bars, through friends, and online. In some areas of the country, particularly large metropolitan areas, there are many places where gay people can gather. In other places, meeting people can be more challenging and risky. Some couples may conduct their entire relationship online because of the inability to find a way to be together in person.

For transgender people, there is often a question of when and how to disclose their identity to a romantic interest. They may be concerned for their safety if the person is angry or they may fear rejection. Mock (2014) writes about her feelings when she was deciding how to disclose her identity to a love interest, "I'm afraid you won't love me once you know me" (p. 7). She dedicated her book in a beautiful, loving tribute to that same love interest with the words, "For Aaron, who loved me because of myself, held me accountable to my truth, and became home" (Mock, 2014).

Once a couple starts dating, it is often a heady time of romance although there may be related emotions of shame and guilt depending on the individuals' upbringing and self-acceptance (Levy & Lo, 2013; Levy & Reeves, 2011). Both members of the couple are likely beginning to assess their compatibility and desire to pursue a longer relationship. Location again can play a big part in what a couple's dating relationship looks like. It may be that they are in an unsupportive area and so choose to spend time alone in places where their romantic relationship will not be detected. They may be in a location where there is more support but one or both of them has not come out and fears being found out.

Sustaining Relationships

The choice to commit to a relationship can be a formal one with legal documents, including a marriage certificate, the purchase of a home, and/or preparing powers of attorney and wills. It can also be an informal one. Some couples live together. Some couples do not. Some couples choose to share a last name. Some couples do not. Some couples commit to monogamy. Some do not. Some couples merge finances. Some do not. Each couple's situation is different and as such, social workers should treat each respectfully. Social workers should not judge the seriousness of a couple's relationship based on whether or not they have chosen to marry legally.

There are gay couples who choose to divide household responsibilities in traditional gender roles. There are gay couples who are more egalitarian in their approach. It is not uncommon for insensitive questions to be presented to gay couples based on heteronormative ideas about relationships. Social workers should be sensitive to this bias in their own questions and approaches to avoid further alienation and marginalization.

For some couples, choosing to sustain their relationship may mean the loss of social supports (Blumer & Murphy, 2011). Families may reject the couple. Faith communities may reject the couple. Neighbors may reject the couple. A lack of community support can isolate a couple and place added pressure on the relationship. Social workers "have an important role in addressing the 'minority stress' same gender couples experience" and "should explicitly attend to the social context of their gay and lesbian clients" (Fasbinder, Monson, Montero, Sanders, & Williams, 2013, p. 427).

Ending Relationships

Gay relationships end in similar ways to heterosexual ones. Couples break up. They divorce. Sometimes someone dies. There are amicable, mutually agreed upon separations and there are contentious, protracted ones. There can be a supportive network or that can be lacking. If the couple experienced ostracism and marginalization due to their relationship, the loss of that relationship can be even more isolating. In the documentary, *Bride-groom* (2013), Tom dies in a tragic accident. His partner, Shane, is excluded from his funeral, which further compounds his devastation. In similar situations with unsupportive family members, rights to a couple's assets have been challenged, leaving the surviving partner with financial difficulties during an emotionally devastating time. Legalized marriage does offer some protection now to limit this.

If one person wants to end the relationship and the other does not, the threat of outing can entrap the person who wants to leave. Threats of disclosure and the possible repercussions can force a person to stay in a relationship they no longer desire. Sometimes gay people are in heterosexual marriages because they feel that is their only option. They may maintain those relationships even if they are unhappy because they believe it is the only way to be accepted. **Heterosexism** can prohibit some relationships from ever starting and keep other relationships from ending.

Conclusion

Social workers use critical self-reflection to increase awareness about how their own experiences may impact their work with their clients, whether that is an individual, a couple, a family, a group, an organization, or a community. When working with diverse populations, social workers build cultural competence by remaining open and welcome to new understandings in order to provide culturally sensitive, effective services. Consider one last case in Box 2.5.

Box 2.5 Case: Karen and Sue

Karen and Sue have been together for 16 years. They have married three times but never divorced. This is not a riddle. This is their story. The first time they married was April 2001 when the two of them climbed to the site of their first date and exchanged vows and rings. They were worried Sue might lose her job if they did something publicly. Sue's employer ultimately discovered their relationship anyway and summarily fired her in September 2001, after 15 years of exemplary employment and promotions. Karen and Sue were devastated and significantly impacted by the loss of income and benefits, but also now felt free to have a public commitment ceremony, which they did in April 2002. All of Karen's immediate family attended; none of Sue's immediate family did. The church where they held the ceremony was kicked out of their church conference and one of the people who participated in their ceremony was stripped of her pastoral credentials as a result of providing the homily. For the first 11 years of their relationship, they always had to mark "single" on the forms they filled out because in the eyes of the law they were single in spite of the commitments they had made to each other. After Sue was fired, they had to figure out private health insurance for her because she could not be put on Karen's insurance since she was not her legal spouse. Throughout this time, Sue's family continued to ostracize them. In April 2011, after gay marriage became legal in the District of Columbia, they married for a third time in a small civil ceremony. While this third marriage was a legal marriage, they were still not considered legally married in their home state of Virginia, so they could take advantage of federal benefits but not state benefits. This meant filing their federal taxes jointly as spouses but their state taxes as single adults. Karen was still unable to add Sue on her health insurance. In many ways, Karen and Sue do not feel that different from their friends who are in heterosexual marriages; however, the discrimination they have faced simply due to their desire to create a life and home together is very different and very painful.

The case example in Box 2.5 is the story of the author of this chapter. I share it in the spirit of authenticity and honesty. It would be impossible for me to write about gay marriage without drawing on my own experience; however, there are many, many different experiences and stories within the LGBTQIA community. I would make an easy but regrettable mistake if I were to assume because I am a member of the LGBTQIA community that I know what someone else's experience has been like for them. I do not know what it is like to worry about deportation. I did not lose my home when Sue was fired. While I have experienced rejection by some family members, I have also been lovingly supported by others.

Whether the information in this chapter is new or known, it should serve as a reminder that there is diversity within diversity. Each individual is a compilation of identities and experiences, occurring within their environments. Social workers practice at these intersections of life, bringing knowledge, values, and skills, which should adapt as needed as part of life-long learning and cultural humility.

Questions to Consider

1 Why are marriage equality and legal recognition for LGBTQIA couples important? How do they provide greater security than civil unions or domestic partnerships?

2 What is the significance of the United States Supreme Court rulings in the cases, *United States v. Windsor* (2013) and *Obergefell v. Hodges* (2015)?

3 What effects and backlash at micro, mezzo, and macro levels are occurring and have occurred for LGBTQIA couples following the United States Supreme Court decisions on marriage equality?

4   What is the difference between a civil marriage and a religious marriage? Where do they intersect, and how are they different?

5   You work at an agency with an increasing number of LGBTQIA couples seeking services. Your supervisor approaches to start a support group for these couples. Identify what your role might be and describe some specific considerations you would keep in mind as you begin to plan.

6   What type of situation can you think of in working with an LGBTQIA couple that may challenge your own biases? How would you go about addressing these biases? If you were to provide training for your colleagues, what important information would they need to know about LGBTQIA couples to raise their awareness of their own biases?

Selected Resources

Websites

The following websites are excellent resources for social workers and their clients:

The Human Rights Campaign (HRC) www.hrc.org/ is the largest national lesbian, gay, bisexual, and transgender civil rights organization. Its website includes excellent federal and state information and resources.

Lambda Legal www.lambdalegal.org/ is "A national organization committed to achieving full recognition of the civil rights of lesbians, gay men, bisexuals, transgender people and those with HIV through impact litigation, education and public policy work." Its website includes personal stories, information, and resources.

The National Center for Lesbian Rights (NCLR) www.nclrights.org/ continues to work towards "LGBT Equality Through Litigation, Legislation, Policy, and Public Education." Its website has many personal stories from clients as well as numerous resources.

Parents, Families and Friends of Lesbians and Gays (PFLAG) http:// community.pflag.org/ is a grassroots organization founded in 1972 with the simple act of a mother publicly supporting her gay son. With over 400 chapters located throughout all 50 states, "PFLAG is committed to advancing equality and full societal affirmation of LGBTQIA people through its threefold mission of support, education, and advocacy."

Films

The following films provide poignant examples of LGBTQIA relationships:

The Danish Girl (2015) is a feature film loosely based on the lives of Danish artists Lili Elbe and Gerda Wegener. The story follows their marriage and deep abiding love for each other as they struggle through Lili's journey as a transgender pioneer.

Bridegroom (2013) http://bridegroommovie.com/ is a documentary about a beautiful love story between two young men who are tragically torn apart when one of them dies in an accident. The surviving young man is completely shut out and ostracized since he has no legal protections.

Edie & Thea: A Very Long Engagement (2010) www.ediewindsor.com/edietheal.html is a movie about the couple at the heart of the 2013 United States Supreme Court case which overturned DOMA.

Chris & Don: A Love Story (2007) is the true story of the 30 year love-filled relationship between British writer, Christopher Isherwood, and American portrait painter, Don Bachardy.

Inlaws & Outlaws (2007) www.inlawsandoutlawsfilm.com/ From the film's website, "with remarkable honesty, good humor, great music and real heart, Inlaws & Outlaws weaves together true stories of couples and singles, gay and straight, to embrace what we all have in common: we love."

Tying the Knot (2004) http://1049films.com/ provides a look at the importance of civil marriage for real life couples who have to face the harsh reality that their relationships mean nothing in the eyes of the law.

If These Walls Could Talk 2 (2000) is a movie with three different vignettes, which take place in the same house in different time periods. The first, set in 1961, provides a tragic look at what can happen to a couple without the legal rights and protection afforded by marriage.

References

Addison, S. M., & Coolhart, D. (2015). Expanding the therapy paradigm with queer couples: A relational intersectional lens. *Family Process*, 54(3), 435–453.

Baehr v. Lewin, 852 P.2d 44 (Haw. 1993).

Beagan, B. L., & Hattie, B. (2015). Religion, spirituality, and LGBTQ identity integration . *Journal of LGBT Issues in Counseling*, 9(2), 92–117.

Berzon, B. (1997). *The intimacy dance: A guide to long-term success in gay and lesbian relationships*. New York: Plume.

Berzon, B. (1990). *Permanent partners: Building gay and lesbian relationships that last*. New York: Plume.

Blauch, S. (2004). From the inside out. In R. S. Kreider (Ed.), *The cost of truth: Faith stories of Mennonite and Brethren leaders and those who might have been* (pp. 74–83). Kulpsville, PA: Strategic Press.

Blumer, M. L. C., & Murphy, M. J. (2011). Alaskan gay males' couple experiences of societal non-support: Coping through families of choice and therapeutic means. *Contemporary Family Therapy*, 33, 273–290.

Cleves, R. H. (2014). *Charity & Sylvia: A same-sex marriage in early America*. Oxford University Press.

Clunis, D. M., & Green, G. D. (2005). *Lesbian couples: A guide to creating healthy relationships*. Berkeley, CA: Seal Press.

Council on Social Work Education (CSWE). (2015). Educational policy and accreditation standards. Retrieved from www.cswe.org/File.aspx?id=81660.

Fasbinder, J., Monson, E., Montero, D., Sanders, J., & Williams, A. C. (2013). Same-gender marriage: Implications for social work practitioners. *Advances in Social Work*, 14(2), 416–432.

Franck, M. J. (2011). Religion, reason, and same-sex marriage. *Institute of Religion and Public Life*, 21, 47–52.

Frost, D. M., & Meyer, I. H. (2009). Internalized homophobia and relationship quality among lesbians, gay men, and bisexuals. *Journal of Counseling Psychology*, 56, 97–109.

Jacobson, L., Daire, A. P., & Abel, E. M. (2015). Intimate partner violence: Implications for counseling self-identified LGBTQ college students engaged in same-sex relationships. *Journal of LGBT Issues in Counseling*, 9(2), 118–135.

Levy, D. L., & Lo, J. R. (2013). Transgender, transsexual, and gender queer individuals with a Christian upbringing; The process of resolving conflict between gender identity and faith. *Journal of Religion & Spirituality in Social Work: Social Thought*, 32(1), 60–83.

Levy, D. L., & Reeves, P. (2011). Resolving identity conflict: Gay, lesbian, and queer individuals with a Christian upbringing. *Journal of Gay & Lesbian Social Services*, 23(1), 53–68.

Marcus, E. (1998). *Together forever: Gay and lesbian couples share their secrets for lasting happiness*. New York: Anchor Books.

Mock, J. (2014). *Redefining realness*. New York: Atria Books.

Mohr, J. J., & Daly, C. A. (2008). Sexual minority stress and changes in relationship quality in same-sex couples. *Journal of Social and Personal Relationships*, 25(6), 989–1007.

National Association of Social Workers (NASW). (2008). NASW Code of Ethics (Guide to the Everyday Professional Conduct of Social Workers). Washington, DC: NASW.

Obergefell v. Hodges, 576 U.S. (2015).

Otis, M., Rostosky, S., Riggle, E., & Hamrin, R. (2006). Stress and relationship quality in same-sex couples. *Journal of Social and Personal Relationships*, 23(1), 81–99.

Peterson, C. (2013). The lies that bind: Heteronormative constructions of "family" in social work discourse . *Journal of Gay & Lesbian Social Services*, 25(4), 486–508.

Stiers, G. A. (2000). *From this day forward: Commitment, marriage and family in lesbian and gay relationships*. New York: Macmillan.

Subhi, N., & Geelan, D. (2012). When Christianity and homosexuality collide: Understanding the potential intrapersonal conflict. *Journal of Homosexuality*, 59(10), 1382–1402.

United States v. Windsor, 570 U.S. 744 (2013).

3 Families and Parenting

Mohan Vinjamuri

PH.D., LMSW

> If you want to do this, you've got to really want it. This is something you have to really, really struggle for and fight for in your life... I waited for so long to be a parent, and I am so glad to be a parent right now, there's a real joy when I'm spending time with [Cody]. We have hard moments like every parent, but I think people really react to that, the strength of our relationship and the joy that each of us feels in our parent/son relationship
>
> (Theo, father of 3-year-old Cody)

CSWE 2015 EPAS Competencies

Competency 1: Demonstrate ethical and professional behavior

Competency 2: Engage diversity and difference in practice

Competency 3: Advance human rights and social, economic, and environmental justice

Competency 5: Engage in policy practice

Competency 6: Engage with individuals, families, groups, organizations, and communities

Competency 7: Assess individuals, families, groups, organizations, and communities

Competency 8: Intervene with individuals, families, groups, organizations, and communities

Introduction

Social workers, regardless of whether they work with individuals, groups, or communities, are invariably affected by families. They and their clients are part of families. The family is a fundamental social institution that helps to shape how we look at the world, our development, the ways we form relationships, and the ways we see our futures. This chapter discusses families with LGBTQIA parents and families in which a child comes out as LGBTQIA. In discussing the experiences of families with LGBTQIA members, this chapter encourages you the reader to become curious about your own definitions, beliefs, and assumptions about what it means to be a family. As family diversity in the United States and worldwide continues to expand (Brown & Perlesz, 2007), it is especially important for social workers to uphold their core professional values (National Association of Social Workers, 2008) as they work with LGBTQIA families. In this chapter, I use the term "LGBTQIA families" to signify a family with an LGBTQIA-identified family member.

The chapter begins by introducing queer theory as a theoretical framework to discuss LGBTQIA families. The chapter then goes on to discuss the experiences of families with LGBTQIA parents, including the pathways LGBTQIA people follow in becoming parents, and their experiences as parents in their communities. Following this, the experiences of LGBTQIA youth will be described, with a focus on their relationships with their parents, caregivers and other family members. This chapter highlights unique issues at various developmental stages in a family from early childhood to middle childhood, adolescence and young adulthood.

Social Work Knowledge: Queering the Family *(Competencies 2 and 3)*

Family is a social construct, that is, an idea or set of ideas about a set of relationships among a group of people. Human beings are a part of different kinds of groups. Families share characteristics that make them a particular kind of group. When something is socially constructed, ideas about it have been embedded into our thinking to the point that we take these ideas for granted as though they are unquestioned truths (Danto, 2008). What do you take for granted about families? What do you hold dear? Do you think of anything as essential to being a family and, if so, what? How do you react when you see a family that challenges your beliefs or vision of what it means to be a family? A key element of strengths-based social work practice (Saleebey, 2009) is being willing to identify, question, and challenge our assumption and pre-conceived ways of viewing individuals, relationships, and societal institutions.

Let's discuss some commonly held notions about parenting and family. One notion is that all children need a mother and a father. There are, of course, children raised by only a mother or a father, and they develop and grow in healthy ways. Often though, these children are labeled and judged as coming from "mother-absent" or "father-absent" households. Not being raised by two parents, one male and one female, is often considered a deficit. Another commonly held belief is that mothers and fathers are different by nature in what they offer as parents, and therefore for a child to be cared for fully, they need both a mother and a father. Implicit in this belief is the assumption that parental characteristics and functions are primarily gender specific. Even when a parent does something typically associated with the opposite gender, it may not be considered as legitimate. For example, if a father nurtures, it is not considered the same (i.e. less than) as the nurturing provided by a mother.

Often, we use the word "normal" to describe a family. What assumptions and beliefs do you have about what is a "normal" family? Assumptions about what makes a family "normal" are socially constructed, in that they are based on ideas about what it means to be "good parents" and what is needed for "healthy child development" (Istar Lev, 2010; Riggs, 2006; Stacey & Biblarz, 2001). The idealized notion of a family being comprised of a married opposite sex heterosexual couple and their biologically produced children still has considerable influence on the public psyche and in framing laws and policies affecting personal relationships, such as marriage and adoption laws (Hodson, 2012).

It is interesting that while these ideas, which have a deep history, continue to hold sway over people's psyches and societal institutions, the family itself has been undergoing social changes (Stacey, 2006). These include divorce, people choosing not to marry and to have children "out of wedlock", adoptive families, single parents, and people having children through reproductive technologies. Parents headed by LGBTQIA parents fit within this body of change. According to Hodson (2012), "'the family' is neither a static or unitary concept" (p. 502).

How can you as a social worker view families in a way that embraces and honors their diversity? Queer theory offers a useful lens to do so. Queering anything means exposing and interrogating what we assume to be normal. Peterson (2014) explains that there is an inextricable link between what it means to be a "family" and the formation of states and international relations. Families serve multiple purposes for individuals, communities, and societies as a whole. They provide emotional support, kinship, and interpersonal growth. In addition, they perform economic functions and are often the subject of political debate. To queer the family means to expose these relationships by disrupting, destabilizing, and then re-envisioning what is considered a "normal" family (Peterson, 2014). According to Browne (2006), "queer theory aims to 'make strange' – disrupt, destabilize, deconstruct, effectively to *queer* – what is considered normal, commonplace, taken-for-granted, or the 'natural order of things'" (Browne, 2006, p. 886 as cited in Peterson, 2014, p. 604). Queerness, thus, is about *owning* strangeness. Usually, when we describe something or someone as strange, it has a negative, pejorative connotation. In using the word queer from a strengths-based standpoint, we reframe strangeness as something powerful in that it challenges accepted ideas and gives space to new ideas about what we take for granted. Doing so can help you as a social worker advance social justice.

LGBTQIA-parented families are in many ways similar to families with heterosexual parents. At the same time, they face unique issues because of the ways a heteronormative society treats sexual orientation and gender identity. Queerness is about owning and celebrating difference. It is about questioning what we treat as the "gold standard." Thus, while it is important to determine how families with LGBTQIA parents are similar and different from families with heterosexual parents, we need to be careful not to convey the message that LGBTQIA-parented families need to somehow "measure up" to heterosexual-parented families (Hicks, 2005; Stacey & Biblarz, 2001). We need to be curious continually about understanding LGBTQIA families in their own right.

Families with LGBTQIA Parents (*Competencies 5, 6, and 7*)

How many families in the United States have an LGBTQIA parent? This question is complicated to answer for several reasons. First, there are many families with an LGBTQIA family member, but the family member has not come out. These families include LGBTQIA parents, sisters, sons, daughters, brothers, and grandparents who are living in silence in their families. Coming out to one's family members can be one of the most difficult experiences for an LGBTQIA person. We need to remember that when we ask how many families have LGBTQIA family members, we do not truly know.

A number of LGBTQIA people became parents while they were in heterosexual relationships and then later came out as LGBTQIA. These families have their own unique needs. Our discussion here primarily focuses on "planned" LGBTQIA families, that is, families in which LGBTQIA adults became parents as openly LGBTQIA people. Think about why this distinction matters. How might these two scenarios lead to different experiences of parenting? How might they lead to different experiences for the child? This chapter focuses on the unique challenges and opportunities of becoming parents within the context of an openly LGBTQIA committed relationship.

According to Gates (2015), as many as 2 to 3.7 million U.S. children under 18 may have an LGBTQIA parent; about 19% (one in five) of same sex couples and 19% of LGB individuals not in a couple are raising children under 18. Compared to a decade ago, same sex couples are increasingly having children within the context of an openly LGBTQIA committed relationship. The use of adoption, artificial insemination, and surrogacy is increasing among same sex couples. Increasing social acceptance has led to fewer LGBTQIA people having children while being in the closet in a heterosexual relationship (Gates, 2015). Also, LGB people of color are more likely to report raising or having children than White LGB people (Gates, 2015). A survey of more than 6,000 transgender individuals in the United States showed that 38% reported having been a parent at some time in their lives (Gates, 2015). The largest number of families with LGBTQIA parents, by proportion of the population, were found to reside in the South, Midwest, and Mountain West (Gates, 2013). This counters a common expectation that the largest percentage would be living in large cities in the Northeast and in California, regions that are associated with more liberal or progressive attitudes towards LGBTQIA people.

Notice any questions that come up for you at this point. Perhaps you are asking: What are the similarities and differences between heterosexual and LGBTQIA parenting? How do LGBTQIA people go about becoming parents? What is it like for them to be parents and to be an LGBTQIA person in the world? How do their children experience having LGBTQIA parents? How does having LGBTQIA parents affect their development, if at all? Does a parent's sexual orientation or gender identity matter, and if so, how does this make a difference?

Becoming Parents

One of the most important qualities many LGBTQIA parents bring to parenting is the fact that they made a deliberate choice to become parents, a choice that was fueled by a strong desire to raise children (Boyer, 2007; Matthews & Cramer, 2005). Some LGBTQIA individuals "view partnering and parenting as central to the legitimization or full expression of their humanity and citizenship" (Weber, 2008, p. 602). According to Hodson (2012), "no one template exists for how [LGBTQIA] families are formed" (p. 503). Multiple routes to parenthood exist for LGBTQIA people (Istar Lev, 2010). Gay men, for example, become parents through adoption, surrogacy, and co-parenting arrangements (Patterson & Tornello, 2010). One key factor in making this decision is the degree to which having a biogenetic tie with one's child is important. Cultural norms often presume that having a biogenetic connection with someone necessarily creates deeper emotional connections (Riggs, 2006; Murphy, 2013) and that the absence of such a connection creates negative consequences for children (Golombok, 2013). It is important to realize that many LGBTQIA people either cannot or choose not to have a child biologically. Gay men who choose to adopt rather than have a child through surrogacy, for example, have expressed that providing a home for a child who needed one was a priority over creating a child from their own genetics (Goldberg, 2012; Mallon, 2004).

Regardless of the path chosen, one of the distinguishing features of the parenting journey for LGBTQIA people is that they need the involvement of a "facilitating other," be they a sperm donor, surrogate, or (in the case of adopted or foster children) birth parents (Mitchell & Green, 2007, p. 81). In the absence of producing a child biologically through a heterosexual relationship, part of the effort in becoming a parent is finding a child through an external system or bureaucracy (Mallon, 2004), be it an adoption agency, surrogate mother, the foster care system, or a sperm bank. Mitchell and Green (2007) explain it well:

> Between the wish and the actuality of being at home with the baby, gay and lesbian parents travel a long and winding road of choices and chances taken. And, as their children grow, they cannot rely on a legacy of cultural givens, but rather must establish – in their own

minds, in their couples and families, within their extended families and friendship networks, and in the larger world – the meaning, significance and legitimacy of their parental roles and family structures.

(p. 82)

One issue that has historically affected all families with LGBTQIA parents is heterosexual bias and discrimination in social policies that can lead to a lack of legal protection (Hodson, 2012; Joslin, 2010). Thankfully, there has been social and legal progress in this area. With the legalization of same sex marriage by the United States Supreme Court in 2015, all 50 states now legally recognize both parents in a same sex relationship as the parent of a child born through donor insemination (Family Equality Council, 2017). Additionally, all states now permit same sex couples to adopt children jointly, which means they can petition to become the legal adoptive parents for a child at the same time (Family Equality Council, 2017).

LGBTQIA Families-in-Environment: Looking at Families through a Systems Lens

The challenges and opportunities LGBTQIA parents and their children face may depend on whether they are lesbian parents raising a child they had through assisted reproduction technologies; a gay male couple who adopted their child; a single gay man who had his child through surrogacy; or a transgender parent. Discussing each of these families in depth is beyond the scope of this chapter. Nevertheless, we can ask the following: What is it like for LGBTQIA parents and their children to be in the world? Building on the "person-in-environment" construct, which stems from ecological systems theory (Bronfenbrenner, 1989) and is at the heart of social work, we can examine this question using a "family-in-environment" perspective, particularly LGBTQIA families living in a heteronormative world.

What kinds of responses do LGBTQIA people receive from their families of origin to becoming and being parents? The responses vary and can range from celebration to outright rejection. Unlike heterosexual people for whom becoming a parent may be seen as a rite of passage and an expectation, LGBTQIA people may face messages and reactions that being LGBTQIA and being a parent is incongruent (Vinjamuri, 2015). Why might this be? Parenting by LGBTQIA people challenges several myths. It is important for you to become familiar with social science research to debunk the many myths about LGBTQIA parents and their children (Lebow, 2015). Some of these myths include:

- Children of LGBTQIA parents will be harmed by their parents.
- LGBTQIA people are not emotionally stable enough to be parents.
- A child will experience undo hardships from teasing, bullying, and discrimination related to having LGBTQIA parents.

- LGBTQIA parents have an agenda to make their children LGBTQIA.
- The absence of two parents of opposite genders will harm children. Children raised by two women will be developmentally harmed by not having a father; children raised by two men will be developmentally harmed by not having a mother.
- Children raised by same sex parents will become "confused" about their gender.

We can convert each of these myths into quantifiable questions, which is what social scientists have done over the past three decades. Does the gender composition of two-parent families affect children's health and well-being? How does having an LGBTQIA parent affect sexual orientation and gender identity development? Much of the political, social, and academic discourse on this topic has focused on the "impacts" LGBTQIA parents have on their children, such as their children's psychological and emotional development, the effects of the parent's sexual orientation on the sexual orientation of their children, and bullying and other forms of harassment children face in school and other community settings. Extensive reviews of research conducted over the past three decades have unequivocally shown that children of gay and lesbian parents are as emotionally, psychologically, and socially healthy as children raised by heterosexual parents (Gates, 2015; Goldberg, 2010). In fact, some studies have shown that children raised by same sex parents do better in certain areas of development than their counterparts in heterosexual-parented families (Patterson, 2005). The gender composition and sexual orientation of parents have been shown to have no effect on children's development (Biblarz & Stacey, 2010).

Families are by themselves complex systems that interact with many other complex systems in society. These interactions can be both formal and informal. Formal interactions involve being part of and participating in social and community institutions like schools, health care facilities, recreational facilities, religious institutions, and social service agencies. They also include activities like meeting with your child's teacher, taking your child to the doctor, and attending your church, synagogue, mosque, or temple. Informal interactions include everyday situations like playing with your child in the playground, traveling through an airport or subway station, shopping at the store, having a meal in a restaurant, or walking down the street. Given that attitudes, knowledge, and beliefs about LGBTQIA people and LGBTQIA parents in particular vary, LGBTQIA families have to deal with the uncertainty of how they may be treated within these formal and informal interactions (Vinjamuri, 2015). This uncertainty in how others may respond leads to complicated questions about disclosure and visibility. Just as LGBTQIA individuals need to make decisions about coming out, so do LGBTQIA parents and their children in various social settings.

How do LGBTQIA parents navigate their children's schools? What kinds of decisions do they have to make about being open about their families and advocating for themselves and their children? In what ways do they face heteronormative attitudes and practices in the schools? There has been an overall trend towards lesbian and gay parents being fully open with their children's teachers and schools about their sexual orientation (Goldberg, 2014). Goldberg (2014) studied lesbian, gay, and heterosexual adoptive parents in the preschool environment, and found that while most lesbian and gay parents did not encounter any challenges related to their sexual orientation in their children's schools, some experienced their children's teachers being uncomfortable or not understanding their family structure. Some of the barriers teachers face are myths they hold about LGBTQIA parents, lack of training, and lack of resources (Glass et al., 2016). Some queer parents want to be regarded as a "normal" family with children who have typical needs similar to children raised in other types of families; at the same time, parents want teachers and schools to celebrate the uniqueness of their family form (Glass et al., 2016). Interestingly, Glass et al. (2016) found that both preschool teachers and gay and lesbian parents of preschoolers strived to achieve "balancing normalcy" (p. 225) when working with queer families. So, the challenge for teachers and social workers is to find the balance between normalizing an LGBTQIA family experience while not diminishing the significance of LGBTQIA people becoming parents and forming the families they desire.

An Intimate Look within LGBTQIA Families: Parent–Child Relationships

Social workers need to work with the whole family. By this, I mean that social workers need to explore and build on the relationships within the family and support the family in nurturing and strengthening these relationships. Let's have an intimate look within an LGBTQIA family. How do the LGBTQIA parents and their children build their relationships and attachments? How do they communicate with one another? Research has shown that what matters most in building strong parent–child relationships between LGBTQIA parents and their children is what matters in parent–child relationships in other families, namely nurturing, support, empathy, and consistency (Ashbourne et al., 2011; Ryan et al., 2010). That is, the sexual orientation of the parent has been shown to have no influence on the ability for the parent and child to form a strong attachment with one another. That does not mean, however, that we should ignore the fact that a child has an LGBTQIA parent and say that "parenting is parenting, sexual orientation does not matter." It is important to pay attention to how the sexual orientation or gender identity of their parents may influence the types of reactions children encounter, namely stigma and discrimination, and how LGBTQIA parents support their children through these experiences (van Gelderen et al., 2012; Vinjamuri, 2016). Vinjamuri (2016), in a study with gay adoptive fathers from 20 families, found that open communication is the tool and bedrock that helps gay fathers support their children through the questions, challenges, and stressors they encounter as a result of not having a mother, having gay fathers, and being adopted. How will you as a social worker intervene with LGBTQIA families to help them to grow in their communication skills, to reduce the negative impact of external stressors, and to build a cohesive family identity with loving relationships?

LGBTQIA Youth, Adolescents, and Young Adults (*Competencies 2, 6, and 7*)

Having discussed families with LGBTQIA parents, consider families consisting of heterosexual parents and LGBTQIA children. How many families have an LGBTQIA child? This is a difficult question to answer, since not all children who are LGBTQIA have come out. One thing we do know is that young people are coming out as LGBTQIA at younger and younger ages (Schroeder, 2015). Some youths come out at 14 years of age or younger (Willoughby et al., 2010).

How do LGBTQIA youth experience their families? What do LGBTQIA youth need and want? How are their needs and desires similar to non-LGBTQIA youth and how are they unique? Discussions about LGBTQIA youth tend to become binary. By this I mean that experiences of LGBTQIA youth in their families are often described as either positive or negative, affirming or rejecting (Schroeder, 2015). Schroeder (2015) reminds us that LGBTQIA youth live between these extremes, which illustrates how the "relational and cultural worlds of queer youth remain complex" (Harvey & Stone Fish, 2015, p. 397). How will you challenge yourself as a social worker to see beyond this binary identity?

LGBTQ adolescents face multiple life stressors due to their minority status and experience of minority stress, including discrimination, risk of harassment, violence, and sexual abuse (Bebes et al., 2015). Consider the following statistics. Twenty-six percent of LGBTQ youth are kicked out of their homes and rejected solely because of their sexual orientation and/or gender identity (National Coalition for the Homeless, 2009). Eighty-two percent of LGBTQ youth experience some form of mistreatment in the classroom (Kosciw et al., 2012). Up to 40% of homeless youth identify as LGBTQ (Durso & Gates, 2012). Finally, LGBTQ young adults who reported high levels of family rejection during adolescence were 8.4 times more likely to report having attempted suicide and 5.9 times more likely to report high levels of depression compared with peers who experienced little to no family rejection (Ryan et al., 2009).

One of the most important and difficult experiences LGBTQIA youth have is coming out to their families about their sexual orientation and/or gender identity. Coming out to parents is one of the most difficult developmental milestones for queer youth (Woodward & Willoughby, 2014). The coming out process can be "a growth-enhancing event and is highly important to developing an integrated identity and for strengthening self-esteem" (Henry, 2013, as cited in Baiocco et al., 2015, p. 1490). Harvey and Stone Fish (2015) stated that "gender and sexuality are uniquely expressed in every person's specific developmental trajectory" (p. 398). While defining identity is a core developmental task for all youth (and adults, as well), this task can be more complex for queer youth who have to navigate living in a cultural and familial environment where their identities may not be validated. Many develop resiliencies in this process (Harvey & Stone Fish, 2015), but some face greater challenges. LGBTQIA youth are similar to heterosexual youth in needing to integrate gender and sexuality into their identities. The core needs behind coming out (self-acceptance, identity development, validation, support) are common to all of us; however, decisions around coming out create unique stressors and opportunities for LGBTQIA youth (Harvey & Stone Fish, 2015). What complications arise in coming out for youth with mental health challenges, unsupportive families, or other barriers to success? How might you as a social worker intervene with these youth to ensure a safe transition to adulthood?

Coming out is a complex process that is unique to each individual. At the same time, coming out reminds us of our fundamental need for safety and how being LGBTQIA and coming out can be unsafe. According to Schroeder (2015), the family, as well as the closet, can be both a sanctuary and a prison for LGBTQIA youth. Coming out to one's family is an ongoing process (Schroeder, 2015). Even after coming out to family in the home, one has to come out in spaces outside the home (Schroeder, 2015), such as schools, workplaces, etc. LGBTQIA youth adopt our culture's heteronormative standards and goals. They may contrast their own success against standards they cannot achieve because our culture excludes their identity from the definition of success in these standards. Perrin-Wallqvist and Lindblom (2015) state it well: "It is very difficult to bear the fear of not being accepted for who one is" (p. 477).

Disclosing one's sexual orientation to family members is an important psychological decision that is often fraught with uncertainty, fear, and both real and perceived threat (Perrin-Wallqvist & Lindblom, 2015). Think about what it may feel like to be in this position, to face a possible threat from your family members. This is not the sole experience of LGBTQIA youth; anyone who has defied social expectations in their family for whatever reasons likely faces such feelings. Disclosure involves exposure: "to 'expose' means to make oneself unprotected against inspection" (Perrin-Wallqvist & Lindblom, 2015, p. 476). When we are exposed, we feel unprotected and may feel overly scrutinized. We feel our vulnerability.

Even though societal and cultural attitudes are becoming more accepting, most parents tend to have negative responses to a child coming out as LGBTQIA (Woodward & Willoughby, 2014). LGBTQIA youth are at added risk for parental rejection due to their sexual orientation, gender identity, and/or gender atypical behavior, and are at greater risk for a wide range of psychological symptoms, due in part to negative parental reactions

(Bebes et al., 2015; Ryan et al., 2010). Bebes et al. (2015) found that higher levels of psychological control – which includes conditional love, withdrawal, guilt induction, and invalidation – was associated with higher levels of psychological symptoms. Riley et al. (2013) found that transgender adults, in reflecting back on their childhoods, remember facing ongoing negative and hostile reactions from their families and felt that lack of knowledge and awareness hindered their family's ability to move forward towards accepting their gender variance.

Conversely, LGBTQIA adolescents perceiving acceptance from their parents was associated with their psychological welfare (Samarova et al., 2013). Additionally, supportive parental relationships are especially protective and contribute to better educational outcomes for sexual minority youth (Watson et al., 2016). Samarova et al. (2013) found that, among a sample of Israeli adolescents aged 14 to 21, most adolescents perceived their parents to be moderately to fully accepting at the time they disclosed their sexual orientation. Many of these adolescents also perceived their parents to become accepting over time.

Following a strengths-based approach which sees struggle as planting the seeds of opportunity (Saleebey, 2009), it is important to examine "queer youth agency" (Schroeder, 2015, p. 786). Despite the potential hostile and negative reactions a young person may face by coming out, they still choose to do so. Sexual orientation and gender identity are not choices; however, how a young person chooses to present in the world and what they choose to share with others about themselves are choices they must make day to day.

We need to think beyond binary terms about acceptance versus rejection. Most families experience a mixture of both. We need to see parents and children as continually evolving and changing, and therefore we need to ask what can facilitate change (Ryan et al., 2009). Disclosure can happen in stages and occurs over time (Baiocco et al., 2015). It is important to recognize that most parents become more accepting or at least more tolerant over time with their LGBTQIA children (Diamond & Shpigel, 2014). At the same time, some "remain persistently intolerant or even rejecting" (Diamond & Shpigel, 2014, p. 258).

What helps parents become more accepting over time? Samarova et al. (2013) found a combination of factors assisted with acceptance, including adolescents being "catalysts of change" (p. 686), exposure to information about LGBTQIA people, and a parent's commitment to their relationship with their child. There is often, rightly so, so much focus on the challenges LGBTQIA parents experience when their children come out. Parents also speak about the positive aspects of parenting an LGBTQIA child. These include: personal growth (open mindedness, new perspectives, awareness of discrimination, compassion); positive emotions (pride and unconditional love); engaging in activism; social connection; and closer relationships to their child and within their family as a whole (Gonzalez et al., 2013).

Social Work Skills and Values: How Can Social Workers Support LGBTQIA Families? *(Competencies 1, 2, 3, and 8)*

Informed Practice

Becoming culturally sensitive in working with LGBTQIA populations requires identifying and challenging heteronormative attitudes and beliefs about LGBTQIA people (Mallon, 2008). Ideas about motherhood, fatherhood, and the "best interests of a child" become embedded in practice and social policy and then derive their power by becoming taken for granted and "natural" (Riggs, 2006). LGBTQIA parents challenge each of us personally to look beyond gender norms and gender roles in the family and reflect on what it means to be a caring and effective parent. On a policy practice level, social workers can lead the charge in challenging notions in child welfare and other practice settings about "who counts" as a family (Hicks, 2005) and about what constitutes the "best interests of the child" (Riggs, 2006). Social workers need to be knowledgeable of both local and national policy developments regarding gay parenthood (Robinson & Brewster, 2014). Asking for the names of the mother and father and providing only two choices for one's gender render non-heterosexual and non-gender conforming people invisible and not valid enough to be represented. Thus, practitioners in all settings can develop language on agency forms that does not presume that everyone is heterosexual and that a family has both a female and male parent. All of these actions further the core social work value of challenging social injustice and pursuing social change (NASW, 2008).

Choosing to parent may be greeted with a variety of reactions ranging from celebration and surprise to disapproval and rejection. Social workers need to attune to these social realities and to provide affirmation, support, and resources to those aspiring to become parents. Social workers have the opportunity to affirm families headed by LGBTQIA parents by exploring deeply how LGBTQIA parents cultivate their relationships with their children and how their experiences in their communities affect these relationships. Social workers in school settings need to be sensitive to the needs of children raised by LGBTQIA parents. They can be proactive in addressing and preventing bullying and other harassment of children raised by same sex parents. While doing so, it is important that they use a strengths-based perspective (Saleebey, 2009) to view these young people not as victims but as creative and resilient individuals in negotiating these challenges. These steps are in line with social work's core value of service and addressing social problems on individual and systemic levels (NASW, 2008).

Finally, as social workers, we may deliberately or inadvertently make being LGBTQIA central for LGBTQIA parents and their children. At the same time, we must realize that different aspects of their experiences as parents related to race, class, and other factors may intertwine with and can at times be more prominent than being LGBTQIA.

Ecological and System Considerations for Coming Out

As a social worker, you must develop skills to advocate and intervene at the micro, mezzo, and macro levels for LGBTQIA clients. Following ecological systems theory, it is important to view coming out from a person-in-environment perspective. When an LGBTQIA youth comes out, they are coming out within an environment created by many systems: their own psychological system, their family, their peer group, their community, and the larger society. We need to hold all of these systems accountable for the positive and negative consequences a youth faces when they come out. Over recent years, there has been more attention from practitioners and researchers on how to work with families in supporting and affirming their children and youth.

It is important to understand that coming out can create stress for a family. How a family handles this "stress" depends on a number of factors. Social workers can reframe it as an opportunity for a family to grow together, rather than solely as something harmful and negative. We need to look at a family's response to stress in terms of the family's relational capabilities and beliefs about the meaning of stress and other stressors in the family, in addition to looking at the meaning the family places on having an LGBTQIA family member (Baiocco et al., 2015; Ryan et al., 2010). We must consider coming out as a unique experience related to disclosure of sexual orientation, and at the same time we can examine this event as an example of a shake-up to the homeostasis of the family (Baiocco et al., 2015). Harvey and Stone Fish (2015), in discussing family therapy with queer youth and their families, emphasized that practitioners need to understand how queerness intersects with cultural, familial, and individual variables. It is important to understand parental reactions to a child coming out within the context of how important family cohesion is to the family and the degree to which the cultural scripts of the family emphasize family cohesion. Coming out "has the potential to disrupt boundaries, shift relationships, and increase conflict within the family system" (Woodward & Willoughby, 2014, p. 381). Working with families from these perspectives can help you keep social work's core value of recognizing the central importance of human relationships (NASW, 2008) at the heart of practice.

In helping families who may be unaccepting of their child but seem willing and able to change, it is important to focus on improving the quality of young adult-parent relationships and promote connection and mutual acceptance within the family (Diamond & Shpigel, 2014). It is essential to think of disclosure as a "whole family experience" (Baptist & Allen, 2008, as cited in Baiocco et al., 2015) and "interpersonal in nature" (Mohr & Fassinger, 2003, as cited in Baiocco et al., 2015). Neither parents nor LGBTQIA youths should elicit blame; rather, social workers must view them as resources in the coming out process (Woodward & Willoughby, 2014). Many parents struggle with how to make sense of their child being

LGBTQIA. When working with parents, explore the unique meanings parents ascribe to their child coming out and help parents become more aware of their beliefs and emotions that arise in relation to their child being an LGBTQIA individual (Woodward & Willoughby, 2014). In doing so, you will be honoring and practicing the core value of respecting the inherent dignity and worth of each person (NASW, 2008).

Conclusion

Greater LGBTQIA visibility in American society can affect cultural attitudes to LGBTQIA families. Social workers can promote more attitudes of acceptance towards LGBTQIA people. As these changes occur, our entrenched ideas about parenting, family, gender, and sexuality are exposed and challenged. It is imperative that social workers learn to work with LGBTQIA family systems in ways that are non-judgmental and strengths-focused. Doing so requires collaborating with all members of the family, seeing the potential for change in every interaction, finding ways to build on existing attachments and connections, and honoring what makes LGBTQIA families unique. It is important to assist our culture and LGBTQIA families to recognize the joys, aspirations, and struggles they share with all families.

Questions to Consider

1   How can the concept of "queering the family" be helpful to you as a social worker?
2   Discuss several ways you can promote social justice for LGBTQIA families.
3   In what ways might families with LGBTQIA families be similar to families with heterosexual parents? In what ways might they be different?
4   In what ways can you empathize with and support the coming out process for LGBTQIA young people?
5   What current policies at the local, state, and federal levels affect LGBTQIA families? What policies are harmful, helpful, or still needed?

Resources

PFLAG www.pflag.org provides support to LGBTQIA individuals and their families, friends, and allies.

Family Equality Council www.familyequality.org provides resources, education, and advocacy for families headed by LGBTQIA parents.

Family Acceptance Project https://familyproject.sfsu.edu/ is a research and intervention initiative providing information and resources to strengthen families with LGBTQIA youth.

The Trevor Project www.thetrevorproject.org provides crisis intervention
and suicide prevention for LGBTQIA youth.

The Williams Institute http://williamsinstitute.law.ucla.edu/ a think tank
providing cutting edge research and policy action related to LGBTQIA
individuals, families, and communities.

Hetrick Martin Institute www.hmi.org is a leading professional provider
of services and support for LGBTQIA youth.

Children of Lesbians and Gays Everywhere (COLAGE) www.colage.
org is a national organization uniting people with LGBTQIA parents into
a network of peers and supports.

References

Ashbourne, L. M., Daly, K. J., & Brown, J. L. (2011). Responsiveness in father-child relationships: The experience of fathers. *Fathering*, 9(1), 69–86. doi: doi:10.3149/fth.0901.69.

Baiocco, R., Fontanesi, L., Santamaria, F., Ioverno, S., Marasco, B., Baumgartner, E., Willoughby, B. L. B., & Laghi, F. (2015). Negative parental responses to coming out and family functioning in a sample of lesbian and gay young adults. *Journal of Child & Family Studies*, 24, 1490–1500.

Bebes, A., Samarova, V., Shilo, G., & Diamond, G. M. (2015). Parental acceptance, parental psychological control and psychological symptoms among sexual minority adolescents. *Journal of Child & Family Studies*, 24, 882–890.

Biblarz, T. J., & Stacey, J. (2010). How does the gender of parents matter? *Journal of Marriage and Family*, 72, 3–22.

Boyer, C. A. (2007). The impact of adoption issues on lesbian and gay adoptive parents. In R. A. Javier, A. L. Baden, F. A. Biafora, & A. Camacho-Gingerich (Eds.), *Handbook of adoption: Implications for researchers, practitioners, and families* (pp. 228–241). Thousand Oaks, CA: Sage Publications.

Bronfenbrenner, U. (1989). Ecoligical systems theory. In R. Vasta (Ed.), *Annals of child development: Six theories of child development: Revised formulations and current issues* (pp. 187–247). Greenwich, CT: JAI Press.

Brown, R., & Perlesz, A. (2007). Not the other mother: How language constructs lesbian co-parenting relationships. *Journal of GLBT Family Studies*, 3(2), 267–308.

Browne, K. (2006). Challenging queer geographies. *Antipode*, 38(5), 885–893. doi: doi:10.1111/j.1467-8330.2006.00483.x

Council on Social Work Education (CSWE) (2015). *Educational policy and accreditation standards for baccalaureate and master's social work programs*. Alexandria, VA: Council on Social Work Education.

Danto, E. (2008). Same words, different meanings: Notes toward a typology of postmodern social work education. *Social Work Education*, 27(7), 710–722.

Diamond, G. M., & Shpigel, M. S. (2014). Attachment-based family therapy for lesbian and gay young adults and their persistently nonaccepting parents. *Professional Psychology: Research and Practice*, 45(4), 258–268.

Durso, L. E., & Gates, G. J. (2012). *Serving our youth: Findings from a national survey of service providers working with lesbian, gay, bisexual, and transgender youth who are homeless or at risk of becoming homeless*. Los Angeles, CA: The Williams Institute with True Colors Fund and The Palette Fund.

Family Equality Council (2017). www.familyequality.org.

Gates, G. J. (2013). *LGBT parenting in the United States*. Los Angeles, CA: The Williams Institute.

Gates, G. J. (2015). Marriage and family: LGBTQIA individuals and same-sex couples. *Future of Children*, 25(2), 67–87.

Glass, V. Q., Willox, L., Barrow, K. M., & Jones, S. (2016). Struggling to move beyond acknowledgment: Celebrating gay and lesbian families in preschool environments. *Journal of GLBT Family Studies*, 12(3), 217–241.

Goldberg, A. E. (2010). *Lesbian and gay parents and their children: Research on the family life cycle*. Washington, DC: American Psychological Association.

Goldberg, A. E. (2012). *Gay dads: Transitions to adoptive fatherhood*. New York: New York University Press.

Goldberg, A. E. (2014). Lesbian, gay, and heterosexual adoptive parents' experiences in preschool environments. *Early Childhood Research Quarterly*, 29, 669–681.

Golombok, S. (2013). Families created by reproductive donation: Issues and research. *Child Development Perspectives*, 7(1), 61–65. doi: doi:10.1111/cdep.12015.

Gonzalez, K. A., Rostosky, S. S., Odom, R. D., & Riggle, E. D. B. (2013). The positive aspects of being the parent of an LGBTQIA child. *Family Process*, 52(2), 325–337.

Harvey, R. G., & Stone Fish, L. (2015). Queer youth in family therapy. *Family Process*, 54(3), 396–417.

Hicks, S. (2005). Is gay parenting bad for kids? Responding to the 'very idea of difference' in research on lesbian and gay parents. *Sexualities*, 8(2), 153–168.

Hodson, L. (2012). Ties that bind: Towards a child-centered approach to lesbian, gay, bisexual and transgender families under the ECHR. *International Journal of Children's Rights*, 20, 501–522.

Istar Lev, A. (2010). How queer! – The development of gender identity and sexual orientation in LGBTQIA-headed families. *Family Process*, 49(3), 268–290.

Joslin, C. G. (2010). Travel insurance: Protecting lesbian and gay parent families across state lines. *Harvard Law and Policy Review*, 4, 31–48.

Kosciw, J. G., Greytak, E. A., Bartkiewicz, M. J., Boesen, M. J., & Palmer, N. A. (2012). *The 2011 National School Climate Survey: The experiences of lesbian, gay, bisexual and transgender youth in our nation's schools*. New York: GLSEN.

Lebow, J. L. (2015). Editorial: LGBTQIA families in the 21st century. *Family Process*, 54(3), 391–395.

Mallon, G. P. (2004). *Gay men choosing parenthood*. New York: Columbia University Press.

Mallon, G.P. (Ed.) (2008). *Social work practice with lesbian, gay, bisexual, and transgender people* (2nd ed.). NY: Routledge.

Matthews, J. D., & Cramer, E. P. (2005). Parallel process issues for lesbian and gay adoptive parents and their adopted children. *Journal of Family Social Work*, 9(3), 35–56.

Mitchell, V., & Green, R. J. (2007). Different storks for different folks: Gay and lesbian parents' experiences with alternative insemination and surrogacy. *Journal of GLBT Family Studies*, 3(2/3), 81–104.

Murphy, D. A. (2013). The desire for parenthood: Gay men choosing to become parents through surrogacy. *Journal of Family Issues*, 34(8), 1104–1124.

National Association of Social Workers (NASW) (2008). *Code of ethics*. Washington, DC: NASW Press.

National Coalition for the Homeless (2009). *LGBTQ homelessness*. Washington, DC.

Patterson, C. J. (2005). *Lesbian and gay parenting* (pp. 5–22). Washington, DC: American Psychological Association. Retrieved from www.apa.org/pi/lgbt/resources/parenting.aspx

Patterson, C. J., & Tornello, S. L. (2010). Gay fathers' pathways to parenthood: International perspectives. *Journal of Family Research*, 103–116.

Perrin-Wallqvist, R., & Lindblom, J. (2015). Coming out as gay: A phenomenological study about adolescents disclosing their homosexuality to their parents. *Social Behavior and Personality*, 43(3), 467–480.

Peterson, V. S. (2014). Family matters: How queering the intimate queers the international. *International Studies Review*, 604–608.

Riggs, D. W. (2006). Developmentalism and the rhetoric of best interests of the child: Challenging heteronormative constructions of families and parenting in foster care. *Journal of GLBT Family Studies*, 2(2), 57–73.

Riley, E. A., Clemson, L., Sitharthan, G., & Diamond, M. (2013). Surviving a gender-variant childhood: The views of transgender adults on the needs of gender-variant children and their parents. *Journal of Sex & Marital Therapy*, 39, 241–263.

Robinson, M. A., & Brewster, M. E. (2014). Motivations for fatherhood: Examining internalized heterosexism and gender-role conflict with childless gay and bisexual men. *Psychology of Men & Masculinity*, 15(1), 49–59.

Ryan, C., Huebner, D., Diaz, R. M., & Sanchez, J. (2009). Family rejection as a predictor of negative health outcomes in white and Latino lesbian, gay and bisexual young adults. *Pediatrics*, 123(1), 346–352.

Ryan, C., Russell, S. T., Huebner, D., Diaz, R., & Sanchez, J. (2010). Family acceptance in adolescence and the health of LGBT young adults. *Journal of Child and Adolescent Psychiatric Nursing*, 23(4), 205–213.

Saleebey, D. (2009). *The strengths perspective in social work practice* (5th ed.) Boston, MA: Allyn & Bacon.

Samarova, V., Shilo, G., & Diamond, G. M. (2013). Changes in youths' perceived parental acceptance of their sexual minority status over time. *Journal of Research on Adolescence*, 24(4), 681–688

Schroeder, C. G. (2015). Sanctuary or prison: Queer youth and the family, household, and home. *Social & Cultural Geography*, 16(7), 783–797.

Stacey, J. (2006). Gay parenthood and the decline of paternity as we knew it. *Sexualities*, 9(1), 27–55.

Stacey, J., & Biblarz, T. J. (2001, April). (How) does the sexual orientation of parents matter? *American Sociological Review*, 66, 159–183.

van Gelderen, L., Gartrell, N. N., Bos, H. M. W., & Hermanns, J. M. A. (2012). Stigmatization and promotive factors in relation to psychological health and life satisfaction of adolescents in planned lesbian families. *Journal of Family Issues*, 34(6), 809–827. doi: doi:10.1177/0192513X12447269.

Vinjamuri, M. K. (2015). Reminders of heteronormativity: Gay adoptive fathers navigating uninvited social interactions. *Family Relations*, 64, 263–277. doi: doi:10.1111/fare.12118.

Vinjamuri, M. K. (2016). "It's so important to talk and talk": How gay adoptive fathers respond to their children's encounters with heteronormativity. *Fathering: A Journal of Research, Theory, and Practice about Men as Fathers*, 13(3), 245–270.

Watson, R. J., Barnett, M. A., & Russell, S. T. (2016). Parent support matters for the educational success of sexual minorities. *Journal of GLBT Family Studies*, 12(2), 188–202.

Weber, S. (2008). Parenting, family life, and well-being among sexual minorities: Nursing policy and practice implications. *Issues in Mental Health Nursing*, 29, 601–618.

Willoughby, B. L. B., Doty, N. D., Lindahl, K. M., & Malik, N. M. (2010). Parental rejection of adolescent same-sex attractions: Negative LGB identity as a mediator. Paper presented to the Society for Research in Adolescence, Philadelphia, PA.

Woodward, E. N., & Willoughby, B. (2014). Family therapy with sexual minority youths: A systematic review. *Journal of GLBT Family Studies*, 10, 380–403.

4 Adoption Considerations

Becky Duddy-Burke

MSW, LICSW

Sara A. Chominski

MSW

Claire L. Dente

PH.D., MSW, LCSW

CSWE 2015 EPAS Competencies

Competency 1: Demonstrate ethical and professional behavior
Competency 2: Engage in diversity and difference in practice
Competency 3: Advance human rights and social, economic and environmental justice
Competency 4: Engage in practice-informed research and research-informed practice
Competency 5: Engage in policy practice

We are on a tremendous journey of fighting for civil rights for LGBTQIA people in the United States. Numerous milestone experiences reflect this progress, including the Stonewall Rebellion in 1969 and removal of 'homosexuality' from the Diagnostic and Statistical Manual of Mental Disorders (DSM) by the American Psychiatric Association (APA) in 1973. More recently, we have experienced the establishment of marriage equality by the United States Supreme Court in 2015, ruling the Defense of Marriage Act (DOMA) as unconstitutional. In 2015, the APA also removed 'gender identity disorder' in the DSM-5 (the most recent edition of the DSM), and, in 2016, the last of the states recognized the right of LGBTQIA people to adopt.

In spite of changes regarding LGBTQIA rights, **adoption** still elicits biased opinions, prejudicial attitudes and discrimination at multiple levels in the lives of LGBTQIA people. The focus of this chapter is to explore working with the LGBTQIA population regarding adoption through the lens of the social work profession. We will discuss types of adoption, past and current legal and political trends that impact **LGBTQIA adoption**, challenges and obstacles in LGBTQIA adoption, and LGBTQIA youth in the United States foster care system.

Background

As social workers, we want to improve the lives of our clients, and work toward social justice in our communities, in society and in our world. CSWE 2015 EPAS remind us that,

> The purpose of the social work profession is to promote human and community well-being. Guided by a person-in-environment framework, a global perspective, and knowledge based on scientific inquiry, the purpose of social work is actualized through its quest for social and economic justice, the prevention of conditions that limit human rights, the elimination of poverty, and the enhancement of the quality of life for all persons.
>
> (CSWE, 2015, p. 5)

Additionally, CSWE identified social work competence as "the ability to integrate and apply social work knowledge, values, and skills, to practice situations in a purposeful, intentional, and professional manner to promote human and community well-being" (CSWE, 2015, p. 6). The National Association of Social Workers (NASW) *Code of Ethics* enhances this approach by providing us with guidelines that assist us further in carrying out these goals for competent practice through the core values of the heart of our profession.

LGBTQIA Adoption Statistics in the United States

The Williams Institute on Sexual Orientation and Gender Identity Law and Public Policy at UCLA School of Law studies LGBTQIA issues, including research on parenting and families. Through the Williams Institute, Gates (2013) studied LGBT parenting and reported the following statistics specific to LGBT parenting, adoption and foster care in the United States. We encourage you to download this report and to explore the Williams Institute's website for a wealth of data and resources on LGBTQIA issues (Gates, 2013). Some highlights of Gates's (2013) report included:

- More than 111,000 same-sex couples…are raising nearly 170,000 biological, step, or adopted children;
- Same-sex couples raising children are four times more likely than their different-sex counterparts to be raising an adopted child;
- More than 16,000 same-sex couples are raising an estimated 22,000 adopted children in the US;
- Same-sex couples are six times more likely than their different-sex counterparts to be raising foster children;
- Approximately 2,600 same-sex couples are raising an estimated 3,400 foster children in the United States. (Gates, 2013, p. 3)

This data highlights the importance of LGBTQIA parenting for children in foster care and adoption. Many LGBTQIA parents are supporting our communities by fostering and adopting children who might otherwise not have a family or home. Gates (2013) highlights the importance of providing culturally sensitive social work services to LGBTQIA parents in these roles.

NASW Policy Statements

Given the significant role that LGBTQIA parents play in adoption and foster care, it is important for social workers to understand our profession's stance on LGBTQIA issues. In addition to CSWE's LGBTQIA-positive focus in social work education standards, NASW's standards for professional practice require that social workers demonstrate cultural awareness, sensitivity and humility in practice with all LGBTQIA clients. Social workers should also apply this approach to work with LGBTQIA people within the area of adoption and foster care. NASW has emphasized support for the civil rights of all people, including the fight for full legal rights for the LGBTQIA community. Additionally, NASW policies encompass the expectation to practice nondiscriminatory attitudes toward people of every sexual orientation and gender identity, as well as to have awareness of the oppression the LGBTQIA population faces.

NASW issued a policy statement, *Lesbian, Gay, and Bisexual Issues*, approved by the NASW delegate assembly in August of 2014, superseding the earlier 2005 document (NASW, 2018a, pp. 211–219). This policy required that members of the LGBTQIA community receive the same opportunities as heterosexual couples, including child custody. "NASW supports the adoption of local, state, federal, and international policies and legislation that protect the rights and well-being of the children of LGB people" (NASW, 2018a, p. 215). With specific attention to parenting and diverse family systems, NASW further stated, "NASW recognizes the increasing number of LGB people opting to create families through biological reproductive technologies, adoption, foster caregiving, and the formation of alternative family systems and encourages the establishment of legal, medical, and social-psychological supports for these families" (NASW, 2018a, p. 216). Thus, our profession expects us to be vigilant in our work to attend to the unique circumstances and needs of LGB families and children.

NASW has also clearly addressed the rights and needs of transgender individuals through its policy statement on *Transgender and Gender Non-conforming People* (NASW, 2018b, pp. 323–331). This document stated that social workers must gain an understanding of human variation, communicate this understanding to the public in order to eliminate stigma, and support the rights of transgender individuals. It is through the expression of support and understanding that NASW hopes to promote a society that allows for equal rights for people of diverse gender, including those who identify as members of the transgender community. Similarly, NASW asserted that:

> discrimination and prejudice directed against any individuals on the basis of gender identity or gender expression, whether actual or perceived, are damaging to the social, emotional, psychological, physical, and economic well-being of the affected individuals, as well as society as a whole.
>
> (NASW, 2018b, p. 327)

This policy statement emphasized NASW's support of education and professional development for social workers, antidiscrimination efforts, expanding public awareness and advocacy. It calls for the provision of health and mental health services, and legal and political action to end discrimination against transgender individuals (NASW, 2018b, pp. 327–329). This policy emphasized the importance of social workers standing at the forefront of culturally sensitive service and advocacy for transgender and gender nonconforming people (NASW, 2018b).

Types of Adoptions

Social workers should be knowledgeable of the various types of adoption and issues frequently encountered when working with clients who are exploring adoption. The Child Welfare Information Gateway is a US government website offering a tremendous amount of adoption information and resources (see www.childwelfare.gov/). The Child Welfare Information Gateway defines **adoption** as, "the social, emotional, and legal process in which children who will not be raised by their birth parents become full and permanent legal members of another family while maintaining genetic and psychological connections to their birth family" (Child Welfare Information Gateway, 2015a). Many adoption agencies provide potential adoptive families links to this site to deepen their knowledge of foster care, adoption and the impact of these processes on children and families. It is important that social workers assisting potential LGBTQIA adoptive parents have an understanding of this important material, and recognize the ways it applies (or does not apply) to their unique family situation. There are many children at various stages in the foster care and adoption systems who present to us in other contexts: schools, healthcare settings, community centers, shelters, clinical work and other social work settings. All social workers should have a foundation of knowledge on adoption and be prepared for the families they may meet in their own service agencies.

Adoption has evolved and there are now many more iterations of adoption. In the past, adoption usually involved a heterosexual couple who were most likely adopting an infant child, but that has changed tremendously for both heterosexual and LGBTQIA people. Now that LGBTQIA people can adopt legally and openly in every state, adoption may be a **joint adoption** where a same-sex couple adopts a child together. It also could involve a **second-parent adoption**, where one partner of a same-sex couple adopts the other's biological child, or, adoption by a single LGBTQIA person. There are other adoption considerations. In **domestic adoption**, the child was born in the United States, and in **intercountry adoption**, the child was born in another country. Regardless of the type of adoption, contact between adoptive families and birth families varies. In an **open adoption**, the adoptive parents and birth parents/families have access to varying degrees of one another's personal information and have an option to maintain contact. Contact may range from the exchange of cards, letters and/or photos to face-to-face visits. A **closed adoption** maintains information about the birth parents as confidential (Child Welfare Information Gateway, 2015b). In the past, closed adoption policies prevailed; currently, there is support for open adoption as serving children better through having some connection to their biological family, medical histories, and other important information.

Domestic Adoption

There are four main types of agencies or service providers in domestic adoption. These include public agency adoption, licensed private agency adoption, independent adoption and facilitated/unlicensed adoption (Child Welfare Information Gateway, 2015b).

Public agency adoption seeks to find homes for children in the child welfare system, such as foster care. Public agencies generally include those facilitated by state, county and other governmental groups and are usually funded by taxes. Sometimes governmental child welfare agencies will contract with private agencies to provide services. The role of public agencies and private agencies contracted by public agencies is to find potential adoptive families for children in foster care. Once the court terminates parental rights, a social worker from the agency places the child with pre-adoptive foster parents. It is the role of the social worker to find and place the child with qualified and trained foster and pre-adoptive foster parents (Child Welfare Information Gateway, 2015b).

In **licensed private agency adoption**, parents that wish to adopt work with an agency, and the birth parents give up their parental rights to the agency. The agencies are required to abide by a set of procedures, licenses and standards. These adoptions frequently involve younger children or infant adoptions. It is common practice for agencies to allow birth parents to choose the potential adoptive family based on profiles created by the agency, and social workers will work with both families. Ultimately, the birth parents give consent after the birth of the child; many states include this condition to provide opportunity for the birth parents to change their minds after the birth (Child Welfare Information Gateway, 2015b).

- Attorneys conduct the **independent adoption** process, and parents do not utilize an agency in this process. The attorney will work with the prospective adoptive parents and the birth parents through the adoption process. Families typically use this process for the adoption of an infant. The infant usually is placed with the adoptive parents at birth, and the adoption becomes legalized when the birth parents relinquish their parental rights. The timing of the release of parental rights by the birth parents, and their rights to revoke that action, vary depending on the state law in these cases as well, providing birth parents an opportunity to change their minds (Child Welfare Information Gateway, 2015b).
- Finally, **facilitated/unlicensed adoption** involves a third party facilitator. Any individual who brings about the connection of a birth mother and prospective adoptive parents, which requires a fee, would constitute the facilitator. This method lacks security, supervision and standards. If the adoption falls through, there is no one to advocate for either party. For this reason, several states *prohibit* this method of adoption (Child Welfare Information Gateway, 2015b).

Intercountry Adoption

Intercountry adoption, also known as "international" or "transnational" adoption, involves the process where an individual or couple become the legal and permanent parent(s) of a child who is a national of a different country. Generally, the prospective adoptive parent(s) must meet the legal requirements of their country of residence and those of the home country of the child.

There are two types in intercountry adoption, those adhering to the Hague Convention on Protection of Children and Co-operation in Respect of Intercountry Adoption, and non-Hague Convention adoption (Child Welfare Information Gateway, 2015b). The Hague Convention constitutes "an international agreement to safeguard intercountry adoptions" (U.S. Department of State, n.d.). The United States ratified the Hague Convention in April 2008. The Hague Convention's goal is to protect children worldwide and to ensure their well-being. It has helped to protect children from kidnapping and human trafficking situations. The Hague Convention requires participating countries to have a Central Authority; the U.S. Department of State fulfills that role for the United States (U.S. Department of State, n.d.).

- **Hague Convention adoptions** require adoptive parents to use a provider specifically approved or accredited for Hague Convention adoption services. Parents must identify a desired country *prior to* a home study; children must be determined 'adoptable' by their country of origin and must meet the 'adoptee' definition of the Hague Convention. A child also needs an immigrant visa prior to entering the United States (Child Welfare Information Gateway, 2015b). In **non-Hague Convention adoption**, prospective adoptive parents may undergo a home study prior to choosing a country, which must meet state and federal requirements. The adoption agency must also satisfy licensure requirements in the home state. The child must meet the U.S. Citizenship and Immigration Services (USCIS) definition of 'orphan' and must obtain a visa prior to entering the United States (Child Welfare Information Gateway, 2015a).

LGBTQIA Considerations in Intercountry Adoptions

Many LGBTQIA people believe they cannot adopt internationally due to restrictive laws and policies, or that they will need to find ways to maneuver through the system of the country from which they want to adopt. Not only do prospective adoptive parents need to meet U.S. laws of adoption, but also the country from which they are adopting (Mertus, 2011). The number of countries recognizing same-sex marriage as legal has been increasing, and most of the same countries permit adoption of children by same-sex couples. Additionally, for those countries opposing LGBTQIA adoption, some follow a 'don't ask, don't tell' approach. The countries from which U.S. people adopt, considered the 'top sending countries,' include China, Ethiopia, South Korea, Russia and Ukraine (Mertus, 2011, pp. 283–288).

Mertus (2011) categorized potential LGBTQIA adoptive parents as follows: individual, coupled partner, couple and married spouses (pp. 276–277). 'Individual' refers to a member of the LGBTQIA community who is adopting as an individual who is not in a committed relationship and does not currently plan to have another person adopt or parent the child. 'Coupled partner' refers to LGBTQIA individuals who are in a committed relationship but who adopt as individuals. The individual who is the prospective adoptive parent has the intention to have the partner parent the child, but not necessarily adopt the child in the future. If so, the second individual may go through the process of a second-parent adoption in the United States. 'Couple' refers to a same-sex couple that are not legally married, but desire to adopt as a couple. 'Married spouses' refers to married couples who want to adopt in the foreign country as a married couple (Mertus, 2011, pp. 276–278). In addition, Mertus (2011) lists the countries with the highest rates of intercountry adoption. Mertus (2011) summarized the various laws and policies for each of these 'top sending' countries. The following list is a brief description of highlights from Mertus's (2011, pp. 283–288) findings by country:

- China: Laws were enacted in 2007 allowing only married heterosexual couples to adopt (pp. 283–284);
- Ethiopia: Expressly forbids adoption by gay or lesbian parents (p. 285);
- Russia: In 2014, Russia passed a law forbidding international same-sex couples to adopt children from Russia (Human Rights Campaign, 2014). Russian law does not recognize same-sex marriage (pp. 285–286);

- South Korea: Laws only permit married couples to adopt and South Korea does not recognize same-sex marriage (pp. 286–287);
- Ukraine: Laws permit only married couples to adopt and Ukraine does not recognize same-sex marriage (pp. 287–288).

In working with LGBTQIA clients seeking intercountry adoption, a social worker will need to be knowledgeable about the current laws and policies regarding adoption by LGBTQIA people in those countries. These may ebb and flow in level of support as countries abroad expand and contract their laws involving sexual orientation and gender identity. Brodzinsky and Goldberg (2017) found that families headed by sexual minority women had greater contact with intercountry birth families than did heterosexual families, particularly with birth families from some African countries that reject LGBTQIA identities. How would you as a social worker support these families? Social workers may experience countertransference reactions or may not want to see their clients go through the difficulties, bias and discrimination LGBTQIA people can face in intercountry adoption. It is important that social workers "engage with clients as experts in their own experiences" (CSWE 2015, Competency 2). Consider the experience of Meg, Dana and Lin described in the case in Box 4.1.

Box 4.1 Case: Meg, Dana and Lin

Meg and Dana are a lesbian couple who adopted their daughter, Lin, from China. At the time of Lin's adoption, Meg and Dana lived in a mid-Atlantic state on the U.S. East Coast. They adopted Lin in the early 2000s at the age of 14 months. Meg was 50 years old, and Dana was 53 at the time. Lin is currently 15 years old, Meg is 65 and Dana is 68. Meg is a scholar and professor of theology, and Dana is a therapist who is also actively involved in her faith community. Meg and Dana 'got together' in the late 1970s, and were together 23 years when they adopted Lin. They were not married at the time of Lin's adoption, but were married after same-sex marriage became legal in their state.

> We had been together for many years with plenty of love to share and saw other people forming families. We felt that we could share our lives with another person. There was a great need in China for girls to be cared for given the one-child policy. We spent several years discussing adoption, weighed the pros and cons and finally decided that it would be a good idea, something we could do that would give a child a home and us a family. We had no idea then – how can you – how enriching it would be to bring another person into our lives. We could not anticipate the challenges and struggles, but on balance would not trade Lin 'for all the tea in China!' Relatives in Meg's family had adopted over the years, both domestically

and internationally. Her sister adopted a baby in China so we knew how that worked. Given our age, and coupled status, we knew there would be limits on all fronts. We decided on China given the need there, and that our girls would be cousins with similar experiences. We also knew that China would allow one of us to adopt and we could simply 'hide' the other for legal purposes as necessary. It all worked out well despite our preference to do everything transparently.

We found an adoption agency in a state on the U.S. West Coast that was reportedly LGB-friendly and a local social worker who took a 'don't ask, don't tell' attitude. We had strong support across the board from anyone who mattered to us. Some people were quizzical at first, but eventually came to see this was something we planned to do. Chinese government policies prevented us from being out; however, the agency we used simply finessed everything. The man who ran the program was gay and Chinese, so we did not really worry. When we got back to the U.S., we utilized an excellent lawyer who does LGBTQIA legal work. Our attorney made sure our adoption (re-adoption for Meg, second parent adoption for Dana) was smooth. In fact, a judge in the state urged attorneys for LGBT families to waive venue and bring all such cases to his court where he would assure a fair hearing. We did that and had a wonderful experience.

Our Roman Catholic roots involved a tradition that was generally non-supportive of LGBTQIA identities. Conservative Catholic teaching insisted on male/female marriage and one mother/father for every child, so we did not expect that it would be progressive on gay adoption. We believe in the right to a safe, dignified life for all children and the importance of family. Our local women-church based community deeply supported our family process, and our home state was fine legally with our adoption. Federal law made our daughter a citizen on arrival. Chinese laws and regulations kept us from both adopting in China.

The example of Meg, Dana and Lin illustrates the importance of social workers respecting the choices clients make. This family wanted to adopt from China in part based on their experience of family members adopting from China. In this case, their value system included support for the rights of women globally and influenced their desire to parent a girl from China. Given the need for Chinese girls to have loving homes, these parents desired to affect macro-level issues by adopting a girl from China. They chose to provide their daughter with an opportunity to share a history and similar cultural experiences with cousins also adopted from China. This approach enhanced the quality of life for the children at a micro-level and provided support for the families at mezzo-level interventions.

The Home Study Process and LGBTQIA Considerations

The laws of all 50 states and the District of Columbia require prospective adoptive parents to undergo a home study, conducted by a licensed social worker or caseworker. The purpose of the home study process is to educate and prepare the prospective family for adoption, evaluate the capability and suitability of the prospective family to adopt, and for the social worker to gather information from the family that will help the social worker match the family with a child or youth whose needs they can best meet. Prospective adoptive parents are required in most states to receive numerous hours of training. Training assists with understanding the needs of children awaiting adoption, issues including attachment and trust, trauma-informed care, successful approaches to understanding and working through challenges, and addresses other agency requirements. Sometimes social workers provide aspects of training directly to prospective families, and other times families attend formal trainings. Some faith-based organizations involved in adoption and foster care will provide trainings or host settings for trainings. Social workers should be aware that some faith-based organizations have historically been unsupportive of LGBTQIA people, and thus, we should be sensitive to identifying training options in both faith- and non-faith-based settings for potential LGBTQIA adoptive parents when available. During home visits, the social worker wants to ensure that the home environment is safe and meets state licensing standards. Social workers are usually required to view all of the areas of the house, including the children's sleeping area and the property.

The home study process includes gathering information. Information includes a criminal background check and child abuse clearance; education and employment history; relationship history and relationship dynamics for a couple adopting, and social life and supports for a single person adopting; daily living; parenting experiences and other experiences with children; support systems; religious/spiritual belief system; and, feelings and motivation for adoption. The home study concludes with a written report of the information gathered and the social worker's recommendations. Confidentiality of the home study varies from agency to agency, therefore it is important for the prospective adoptive parents to ask the social worker and agency if and with whom the information is shared (Child Welfare Information Gateway, 2015c).

For LGBTQIA individuals and couples, the prospect of a home study may cause anxiety and fear. Members of the LGBTQIA community may ask questions in reference to whether or not they should disclose their sexual orientation (Child Welfare Information Gateway, 2016a). It is the responsibility of the social worker to assess with the clients their feelings and thoughts of possible risks and benefits of self-disclosure. It is also important for the social worker to provide the client with the perspective of the birth parents and agency. The agency may view non-disclosure as a 'red flag.' Disclosure would provide a fuller picture of the prospective adoptive parent(s) and family in order for the social worker to make the best possible placement decisions (Child Welfare Information Gateway, 2016a). In general, transparency works best for greater integrity.

The home study is an extremely personal process for any person or couple seeking to adopt, but can be even more so for LGBTQIA people. The prospective adoptive parent(s) may feel vulnerable and anxious about having a professional assess their lives, and fear being judged by the social worker conducting the home study. It is the role of the social worker conducting the home study to demonstrate competency and sensitivity throughout this process.

Social workers need to practice self-awareness regarding biases they may have regarding LGBTQIA couples and individuals seeking to adopt. What are *your* beliefs about LGBTQIA people as parents? In the past, many believed unsubstantiated ideas that all gay men are pedophiles, that children raised by gay or lesbian parents would themselves become gay or lesbian, or that not having two parents consisting of one man and one woman is pathological, unhealthy or immoral. Some faith-based agencies have included policies against placing children in LGBTQIA households. As social workers, we ought to reflect on our own background and belief system, and consciously address any biases we hold. We need to be able to manage and self-regulate these biases and values to be able to work with clients who may differ from us in sexual orientation and gender identity. Social workers should demonstrate that we respect human relationships as expressed by the couple or individual undergoing the home study. We need to empathize with the prospective parent(s) if they express anxiety about aspects of the home study, such as revealing sexual orientation or gender identity, or revealing experiences of bias or discrimination during the process.

Additional Case Examples

In addition to the case of Meg, Dana and Lin described in Box 4.1, the following examples illustrate various types of adoption and the decision-making process of each couple. The couples' experiences demonstrate diverse ways to form a family. It is important for social workers to respect this diversity. The cases are based on information from real and compiled experiences of actual LGBTQIA couples, who shared information about their experiences in adoption with one of the authors of this chapter. Couples provided demographic information and information about the adoption process: their decision to start a family, their decision to adopt, their decision process regarding type of adoption, and type of agency used. They also discussed areas of support and challenges. These included obstacles and/or discrimination from families, friends, social service agencies, adoption agencies, faith communities, the teachings of the religion(s) in which they are or were affiliated, and/or obstacles and discrimination through state, federal and/or international laws. We have changed specific identifying information and demographics to protect the identities and privacy of the families.

Box 4.2 Case: Lakeisha, Dameka and Adam

Lakeisha and Dameka are a lesbian couple who live in Massachusetts. Lakeisha gave birth to their son, Adam, in the late 1980s. Lakeisha was 37 years old, and Dameka was 35. Lakeisha is currently 64 years old; Dameka is 62; Adam is currently 27 years old. This is their story as told by Lakeisha:

> Dameka and I had been together for about 5 years when we started talking about whether to start a family. At that time, same-sex marriage was not legal in our home state (or any state in the U.S.), so we had various legal documents in place as domestic partners. After an initial period of ambivalence and 'is now the right time,' we decided that I would try to get pregnant using donor insemination. Dameka wanted to have a child, but was not at all interested in being pregnant. We used a local OB-GYN practice known to be receptive to lesbian couples, and switched to another practice after almost a year of not getting pregnant. The previous practice had so many lesbians inseminating that they kept running out of sperm! Eventually, it happened. Our son was born in the late 1980s, and we were thrilled. We had an attorney draw up a bunch of legal documents that we hoped would enable us to co-parent (take him to the doctor, etc.). At some point in those first few months, I spoke with my parents to express explicitly my wishes that if anything happened to me, Dameka was to continue as Adam's mother and guardian. They were supportive, as I had expected, but you never know. I remember that I developed laryngitis just before talking to them, and had to croak out my words. I wondered at the time if this symptom related to my plan to talk with my parents! In the meantime, we constantly had to explain to neighbors, relatives, health care professionals and work colleagues that yes, we were raising him together; he had two moms. No one was rude, but we got a lot of questions about 'male role models.' Ultimately, many people thought we were not being fair to this 'poor little boy' to raise him without a father.
>
> When Adam was 4, a ruling in our state made second-parent adoption legal for same-sex couples, and we immediately started pursuing this. A lesbian attorney friend referred us to another

attorney in our county to handle the request. We were extremely nervous about the outcome, as the judge had a lot of leeway in terms of whether or not to grant second-parent adoptions. When we met with the attorney, she said that she was going to handle it the way she had handled many other second-parent adoptions for heterosexual married couples, and not do anything extra. Of course, we were not married, as same-sex marriage was not legal at that time. There was a requirement that in cases where the biological father is unknown, a newspaper notice had to be placed to give the father a chance to come forward. The OB-GYN that handled the insemination provided us with a letter explaining that the donor was anonymous, and the court agreed to waive that requirement – phew! Other than that, the attorney prepared a statement based on information we provided that described the length of our domestic partner relationship, our living situation, education, and employment, and basically tried to make us sound as upstanding as possible.

We had not been going to church, but included in that letter our plans to attend the Universalist Church in our town in the fall when Adam started kindergarten. I had been raised Methodist, and wanted our child to have a loving faith community that supported our family without institutional ambivalence. We did not have a home study. Our attorney said it was not typically done for straight married couples, so why should we need to do it? One thing that was kind of weird about the process was that in order for Dameka to adopt Adam, I had to relinquish my parental rights immediately prior to both of us then adopting him as co-parents. That freaked me out a bit. What if there was an earthquake in that 10-second interval in between (ha-ha?), but all went according to plan.

We had friends in the area who were pursuing a same-sex second-parent adoption at around the same time, but their attorney advised them to wait a few weeks in order to avoid the judge that was going to be ruling on our adoption, as he had a reputation to be difficult at times. This did not make me feel very good, but as it turned out, the judge could not have been nicer, and we ended up being the first same-sex couple to complete a second-parent adoption in our county. Adam had just turned 5, and he was adorable (of course). He was cool as a cucumber in the judge's chambers. We had explained to him that the judge would make it so that people outside our family understood that he had two moms. The judge asked Adam a few questions about his daily life and his family. I do not remember the details of this, but Dameka remembers the judge asking Adam who taught him to throw a ball. He looked over our papers, and then congratulated the three of us. The whole process took 10 minutes, at most. We were deliriously happy, and went from the courthouse to my workplace to share the good news with my colleagues and to show off our little boy. A few weeks later, we completed the process of changing his birth certificate to name both of us as co-parents.

We did not experience any discrimination in the process of adoption; the discrimination was in the fact that until then, we had not been able legally to pursue a same-sex second-parent adoption. Dameka felt validated as a parent to be able to adopt Adam legally. As the biological parent, I experienced a feeling of relief that I did not expect. While I did not doubt Dameka's commitment to raise and support our son, on some level I was aware that legally, he was not totally my responsibility. For example, prior to the adoption, the only insurance option was to include him on my insurance, so I had to work full-time in order to insure the two of us, regardless of any other factors. I might have chosen to work full-time anyway, but it would have been nice to have the option of working part-time.

We also experienced greater ease in dealing with health care providers and with the public school system once the adoption was in place. It required a lot less explanation of Dameka's role to be able to state she was his adoptive parent. Dameka and I got married in the 2000s, immediately after our state (one of the first) legalized same-sex marriage. Adam was 14 years old, and he walked us down the aisle of the church we had started attending when he was in kindergarten. Last year, we had the joy of walking Adam down the aisle as he married his beautiful wife.

Lakeisha, Dameka and Adam's case demonstrates the potential bias that could enter into the adoption process. Whenever an LGBTQIA person seeks to adopt, the individual or couple are at the mercy of the biases of others. This couple was concerned about the feelings of their family of origin. In the past, there have been cases where even biological parents lost custody of their own children after entering a gay or lesbian relationship. In other cases, grandparents assumed custody if something happened to the birth mother, cutting off the other partner from the child. Thus, the passage of gay marriage and adoption laws protecting the rights of LGBTQIA parents has serious implications for LGBTQIA families. If the judge had been opposed to this family constellation for any reason, he may have ruled against the adoption. When the judge asked Adam who taught him to throw a ball, was this suggesting that only a male figure could do so and thus their family was inadequate? Social workers must remain vigilant for these subtleties that may still persist, even with laws in place.

Box 4.3 Case: Carson, Dante and James

Carson and Dante are a gay couple who live in the Northeast. Their son, James, is 15 years old; Carson is 49 years old, and Dante is 48 years old. Carson and Dante met 22 years ago and were legally married ten years later, about three years before meeting James. James met Carson and Dante when he was 7 years old, and moved in after 4 months. The agency intentionally proceeded through the foster process at a slow pace to help with adjustment. The adoption finalized after 20 months, when James was almost 9 years old. Carson and Dante adopted James through the Department of Children and Families (DCF), the social services agency for children and youth. All three are American-born and from the same state.

Carson and Dante are still married, and James still lives with them. Carson works as a marketing director and Dante is a real estate agent. This is their story of adoption through the child welfare process:

> Carson and Dante initially dismissed the idea of raising children when they started dating in their late 20s. After about eight years together, they began to contemplate raising a family. As friends started having children, they realized they, too, yearned for a way to bring a child into their lives.
>
> As a gay couple, Carson and Dante realized their options were more limited; for example, most foreign countries prohibited adoption of children by same-sex couples. They were attracted to the notion of helping a local child in need, so they considered state adoption. Friends of theirs, a lesbian couple, had successfully adopted a baby through DCF, so it seemed like a realistic option. They attended training classes through DCF, and began to attend local adoption 'parties,' where they met eligible children and their social workers. A social worker there told them about James. In the two years since his mother had lost custody of him, James had unsuccessful placements in at least two foster homes. He was living in a residential school at the time and was not yet legally free for adoption.
>
> After nearly 20 months of regularly scheduled supervised visits with James, the birth mother consented to an open adoption. DCF, Carson and Dante, and the birth mother's lawyer negotiated for two visits with the birth mother per year. In addition, James would be able to visit his biological great-grandparents on a regular basis.
>
> Carson and Dante reported experiencing very little discrimination as gay adoptive parents. Although there was no explicit discrimination, they did detect some discomfort during the foster and adoption process from a few DCF social workers about placing a child in the home of two men. Carson and Dante based this on subtle clues such as body language. At one adoption event, they inquired about

a certain boy they had met, and they attempted to give a printout of their home study to the boy's social worker. She initially stared at them, refusing to extend her hand to accept the home study from them. After an uncomfortable few moments, she reluctantly offered her hand and accepted the home study from them, but they never heard back from her. Their length of time to receive a placement was also much longer than it was for other families in their training class. Twenty-one months passed between the time Carson and Dante finished their training until they received a placement, whereas all of their classmates (which included two straight couples, a lesbian couple, and a single man) received placements within three months, in some cases even a few weeks. Carson and Dante knew other lesbian couples who received DCF placements much more quickly than they did as well. In the years since the adoption, they received only positive support from social services, law enforcement, schools, and churches; nonetheless, they did wonder about subtle bias from some in the process.

Carson and Dante were raised Catholic, but did not raise James in their faith. Instead, they attended a progressive Episcopal church. The church welcomed them, and James attended Sunday school for several years. Although the faith community was accepting (as was Carson and Dante's previous faith community), they no longer attend church as a family. Carson continues to attend church on a semiregular basis, and Dante now practices Buddhism. In his teens, James stopped attending religious services altogether.

Carson and Dante's families and friends have generally been accepting and supportive. A few of them initially voiced skepticism that two men, both of whom were employed full-time and neither of whom had prior experience raising children, would be able to raise a young child; however, the skepticism was short-lived. After they met James, they fully embraced him.

Carson and Dante 'reported experiencing very little discrimination,' yet social workers might regard some components of this case as indicating bias. Where do you think bias may have existed? Why was it easier for a lesbian couple to be matched with a child than a gay couple? Could anti-gay bias or concerns have entered into the extended time it took for the birth mother's decision to consent to an open adoption? What about the social worker's reaction at the adoption event? Why did she 'freeze' when she saw two men? Although many people believe these types of situations do not occur anymore, there are times and places when they do occur this obviously, and other times when bias may present in more subtle ways. Let us look at some of the research about LGBTQIA parenting and adoption.

Research of LGBTQIA Parenting and Adoption

Although tremendous gains have been made regarding LGBTQIA rights in marriage and adoption, there are still many derogatory beliefs, myths and misperceptions continue to exist when it comes to LGBTQIA adoption. Many people believe that children raised in a family with a father and mother are better adjusted than those raised in families headed by same-sex couples. There also is widespread belief that children raised by two mothers or two fathers will be ostracized by their peers, or will 'become' lesbian, gay, bisexual or transgender. Many people believe that gay men are pedophiles, and that children are at risk to experience sexual abuse if adopted by gay men. It is important for social workers to be critical thinkers and to know the distinction between scientific research and myths. Social workers need to apply this knowledge in working with our clients, to advocate for LGBTQIA parents, and to counter misinformation.

Recent literature on LGBTQIA adoption and parenting is expanding (Brodzinsky & Pertman, 2012). There have been significant findings supporting the notion that LGBTQIA parenting does not negatively harm children or their development into adulthood (Clarke & Demetriou, 2016; Farr, 2017; Manning, Fettro, & Lamidi, 2014; Moore & Stambolis-Ruhstorfer, 2013). While there is some debate about the impact of methodological issues on research outcomes in LGBTQIA parenting and adoption (Schumm, 2016), studies have found that children *do* prosper in LGBTQIA families which often have their own strengths (Ausbrooks & Russell, 2011; Lassiter, Gutierrez, Dew & Abrams, 2017; Tasker, 2013). Data has also begun to indicate that sexual orientation of parents alone may not be as strong of a reason for discrimination as it has in the past (Steffens, Jonas, & Scali, 2015). While this progress is welcome, many LGBTQIA adoptive families have faced a history of challenges in adopting children (Montero, 2014; Washington, 2013; Wiley, 2017). Institutions are making efforts to train healthcare workers and other professionals to expand cultural awareness in working with LGBTQIA families in service delivery (von Doussa et al., 2016).

The Child Welfare Information Gateway (2016b) provided a summary of research findings that supported the following conclusions:

- Children raised by LGBT parents do not differ in key areas of adjustment or function;
- Quality of parenting and level of family functioning are not related to sexual orientation of the parents;
- Adults who have been raised by LGBT parents report feeling more tolerant of all types of human diversity;
- The sexual orientation of youth does not have any correlation of the families in which they were raised.

(Child Welfare Information Gateway, 2016b)

Although the United States has made major strides toward inclusion and equality since the legalization of same-sex marriage in 2015, there are still vast amounts of prejudice and discrimination that exist in our country. This lack of acceptance affects many, if not all, aspects of the LGBTQIA community's life, including their experience with adoption agencies. Research has found that although many public adoption agencies have moved toward inclusion of same-sex couples, it is not without challenges. Stigma, anti-gay bias, negative attitudes and marginalization still impact LGBTQIA individuals and those who are choosing to parent (Carroll, 2018; George, 2016; Stern, Oehme, & Stern, 2016; Webb, Chonody, & Kavanaugh, 2017; Weber, 2010; Weiner & Zinner, 2015). Despite support for LGBTQIA people as parents and evidence of positive outcomes, some agencies still discriminate against prospective parents based on their sexual orientation or gender identity.

Laws in the United States Regarding LGBTQIA Adoption

It is imperative for social workers to know about adoption laws that have affected LGBTQIA people seeking to adopt. In the United States, there was a pattern of inconsistency regarding LGBTQIA adoption. Despite strides toward equality for the LGBTQIA population in recent years, older laws regarding LGBTQIA adoption in various states still prove to be significant in today's society in reference to the LGBTQIA community and their obstacles with adoption. Adoption laws varied from state to state, as states oversee adoption regulation and licensing. Decisions on allowing or not allowing LGBTQIA people to adopt involved complex processes. In some states, legislatures passed laws permitting same-sex couples to adopt. In other states, courts made decisions based upon lawsuits brought about by LGBTQIA people who faced discrimination in their attempts to adopt. Before gay adoption was ruled legal in all 50 states in 2016 (Reilly, 2016), many states made it difficult for the LGBTQIA community to adopt. Depending on the state, some judges refused to grant LGBTQIA parents the custody of their children, biological or adoptive, solely based on their sexual orientation (Pertman, 2000). States such as Florida banned same-sex couples outright from adopting children.

In 1999, Utah legally mandated that a couple must be heterosexual and married in order to adopt, and several other states at this time considered enforcing similar laws. These states included Arizona, Indiana, Michigan, Oklahoma, and Texas (Pertman, 2000). Arkansas also enforced that only heterosexual married couples had the right to serve as foster parents to children (Pertman, 2000). In 2010, the Florida Court of Appeals declared the Florida law banning LGBTQIA adoption unconstitutional (NCLR, 2014). Despite marriage equality in 2015, it was not until March 31, 2016, that LGBTQIA adoption became legal in all 50 states. Mississippi was the last state in which LGBTQIA adoption became legal; thus, the ruling prevented the state from enforcing its previously mandated law of banning LGBTQIA adoption (Reilly, 2016).

While same-sex marriage is now legal in the United States, it does not eliminate the oppression created by these past laws. Nor does marriage equality alter the reality of the significant struggles the LGBTQIA community still faces when going through the adoption process, depending on the state and agency. These oppressive laws and practices have created a validated feeling of fear and hesitation for LGBTQIA individuals or couples to participate in self-disclosure of their sexual orientation or gender identity when navigating the adoption and foster care processes. It historically has not been an uncommon theme for LGBTQIA people to pretend to be straight, single or gender-conforming in order to adopt (Pertman, 2000).

Obstacles to LGBTQIA Adoption

LGBTQIA people continue to face discrimination by social, religious and political systems. It is important for social workers to understand historical and public policy affecting the human rights of LGBTQIA people. Two current policy issues affecting the rights of LGBTQIA persons to adopt are the Religious Freedom Restoration Act of 1993 (RFRA) and state laws permitting faith-based adoption agencies to deny LGBTQIA people from adopting. Before exploring state RFRA's, let us look at the historical development of the federal RFRA, passed in 1993. The First Amendment to the United States Constitution includes the Free Exercise Clause, proclaiming that Congress shall not pass laws prohibiting the free exercise of religion. In the 1960s court case, *Sherbert v. Verner*, a woman was fired from her employment. Her employer denied her benefits due to her refusal to work on a Saturday in accord with her religious practices as a Seventh Day Adventist (Berkley Center, n.d.). The Supreme Court found the denial of unemployment compensation unconstitutional, as it was a violation of the First Amendment (Berkley Center, n.d.).

In 1978, the government enacted the American Indian Religious Freedom Act (AIRFA, n.d.) to protect the religious rights of American Eskimos, Aleuts and Native Hawaiians (U.S. National Library of Medicine, n.d.). It included protection of the freedom to worship through ceremonial and traditional rites, the use and possession of objects considered sacred, and access to sacred sites (U.S. National Library of Medicine, n.d.). The AIRFA prohibited all government agencies from interfering in the free exercise of Native religion. Criticism of the AIRFA focused on the successful enforceability of the Act.

Throughout the 1980s, the United States Supreme Court began to allow legislation that incidentally prohibited religiously mandatory activities as long as the ban was 'generally applicable' to all citizens (Kearney, 2015). In 1993, opposition to these U.S. Supreme Court's rulings led to the creation of the Religious Freedom Restoration Act (RFRA).

On March 11, 1993, Congressperson Chuck Shumer (D-NY) and Senator Ted Kennedy (D-MA) introduced bills to their respective chambers of Congress. Both the House of Representatives and the Senate passed the Act, and then President Bill Clinton signed it. As a result of the RFRA, laws would be overturned if those laws burdened the practice of a religion. The RFRA reinstated the United States Supreme Court ruling in *Sherbert v. Verner* (Berkley Center, n.d.). The RFRA mandated that the federal government be responsible for protecting the exercise of religious practices (Civil Impulse, 2017).

In 1997, the United States Supreme Court ruled that the application of the federal RFRA to states was unconstitutional. This ruling came about in the court case *City of Boerne v. Flores* (Berkley Center, n.d.). In this case, the Roman Catholic Archdiocese of San Antonio wanted to enlarge a church in the city of Boerne, Texas. A Boerne ordinance protected the church as an historical landmark, and prohibited the Archdiocese from making significant structural changes. The Archdiocese sued, citing the federal RFRA as a way to protect its decision to tear down the church. The United States Supreme Court ruled against the Archdiocese, stating that the application of the federal RFRA to states violated the Fourteenth Amendment of the United States, and the RFRA is not a proper exercise of Congress' enforcement of power. As a result, many states created their own RFRA's (Berkley Center, n.d.).

Governor Mike Pence of Indiana, the 48th Vice President of the United States, signed what is perhaps the most familiar RFRA, also known as the 2015 RFRA. Business owners had claimed they had the right to deny services to LGBTQIA customers based on their religious beliefs. The Indiana RFRA stated that the government of Indiana may not burden a person's right to exercise religious freedom. The Indiana RFRA defined a person as "an individual, partnership, organization, company, corporation, or firm," whether the entities are for-profit or non-profit. The Indiana RFRA has been controversial for a few reasons. Conservative perspectives view it as a legitimate way to fight legalization of same-sex marriage. On the other hand, progressive and liberal lenses view it as anti-LGBTQIA and allowing discrimination toward LGBTQIA people and groups. Reacting to protest by several groups, Governor Pence signed a bill in April of 2015 amending the RFRA, with the intent to protect LGBTQIA people (Lowery, 2015). The bill stated, "No provider…may deny service to anyone on basis of sexual orientation, race, religion or disability" (Lowery, 2015). It appears that the goal of this bill would be to ensure that a business could not deny service to a group or individual based on their sexual orientation or gender identity; however, a criticism of the act is that it is still unclear who the Indiana RFRA protects. Engel (2016) noted that,

> according to proponents, the [Indiana RFRA] is aimed to protect individuals from being compelled to act contrary to their religious

beliefs. But the scope was unclear: would it protect from being forced to provide services for same-sex weddings or would it enable discrimination against gay, lesbian, bisexual, or transgender persons, and is there a substantial difference between the two questions?

(Engel, 2016, p. 6)

Engel also questioned the impact of the amendment: "Whether or not the revision ameliorated the prospect of discrimination is open to question, particularly as Indiana has no statute barring discrimination based upon sexual orientation or gender identity" (Engel, 2016, p. 6). It is important for social workers to understand the impact of RFRA's and legal considerations surrounding LGBTQIA identities and religious institutions and agencies (Issa, 2017).

Another obstacle to LGBTQIA adoption is the reality that faith-based adoption agencies that do not support LGBTQIA identities can find ways to deny adoption services to LGBTQIA people. In 2015, the state of Michigan passed a law permitting religious adoption agencies to reject prospective parents who do not conform to their religious beliefs, including LGBT couples (Green, 2015). Additionally, in some areas, religious organizations have chosen to stop adoption services rather than follow non-discrimination laws. For example, Catholic Charities in Boston, Massachusetts, Washington, D.C., and Illinois have stopped doing adoption work because of the legal mandate to provide services to same-sex couples. Other faith-based organizations opposed to LGBTQIA marriage and adoption may slow the process for couples, avoid returning contacts to potential adoptive parents in a timely manner, or not return them at all. Carson and Dante's case in Box 4.3 exemplifies some examples of these types of interactions. While this may be contrary to the NASW Code of Ethics, these more subtle and at times unconscious interactions do still occur and may interfere with an LGBTQIA family's attempt to foster or adopt a child. Although Carson and Dante may have sought to adopt through the public child welfare agency, social workers should know that many faith-based organizations still have contracts with states and child welfare departments. These alliances can help to expand placement services for children and present many strengths when they include all potential parents in the process.

On May 24, 2017, U.S. Representative John Lewis (D-GA) introduced a bill to the U.S. House of Representatives Ways and Means Committee entitled *Every Child Deserves a Family Act* (ECDFA, HR 2640). Senator Kirsten Gillibrand (D-NY) introduced the ECDFA to the U.S. Senate on June 7, 2017 (Human Rights Campaign, 2018). This Act would "prohibit discrimination in adoption or foster care placements based on the sexual orientation, gender identity, or marital status of any prospective adoptive or foster parent, or the sexual orientation or gender identity of the child involved" (Every Child, 2017a; Every Child, 2017b). As of this writing, this bill awaits passage before enacting it as law.

LGBTQIA Youth in Foster Care in the United States

LGBTQIA youth in general face discrimination and prejudice related to their sexual orientation or gender identity. Specifically, LGBTQIA youth in the foster care system face added stressors and obstacles. Youth who identify as LGBTQIA are more likely to be placed in foster care than their heterosexual and cisgender peers (Ryan, 2015; Wilson & Kastanis, 2015; Wilson, Cooper, Kastanis & Nezhad, 2014). These youth may have higher rates of runaway and throw away experiences (Pearson, Thrane, & Wilkinson, 2017), thus increasing their chances for entering the child welfare system. Many have already experienced rejection from their biological family.

LGBTQIA youth in the foster care system are over-represented and under stress, and the percentage of LGBTQIA youth in foster care is greater proportionally than that of the general population (CASA, 2009; Wilson, Cooper, Kastanis & Nezhad, 2014). A 2014 report in Los Angeles, California, found that LGBTQIA youth of color were particularly at risk for stressors, obstacles, abuse and violence (Wilson, Cooper, Kastanis & Nezhad, 2014). Social workers must consider the intersectionality of sexual orientation, gender identity, race and ethnicity for many LGBTQIA children in foster care. The primary goal of foster care is to provide a temporary safe space for children and adolescents who are unable to be cared for by their parents; however, due to the prevalence of **homophobia** and **transphobia**, LGBTQIA youth have not always experienced the safety that foster care is intended to provide (Gilliam, 2004). For example, LGBTQIA youth in the foster care system have experienced physical, emotional and sexual abuse by adults who were supposed to be providing a safe living environment (Gilliam, 2004). Additionally, many LGBTQIA youth in foster care have faced conversion therapy as an attempt to convince them that their sexual or gender identity is wrong (Gilliam, 2004). As a result of the lack of support, advocacy and understanding for LGBTQIA youth in the foster care system, many of these individuals experienced negative outcomes including suicidal ideation, substance use and/or homelessness (Gilliam, 2004).

The challenges that LGBTQIA youth in the foster care system face often result from the lack of acceptance toward the LGBTQIA community at macro levels within society, religious traditions, belief systems and laws and policies at all levels of government. Social workers must consider the complexity of experience for an LGBTQIA child who is struggling to understand their gay, lesbian, bisexual or transgender identity. Under ideal circumstances, the coming out process can be fraught with fear and uncertainty (Klein, Holtby, Cook & Travers, 2015). An LGBTQIA child 'in the system' may feel overwhelmed, especially if there are other intersectional factors such as race, ethnicity and ability status that make their negotiation of coming out and their place in the child welfare system even more complex.

How does the LGBTQIA child find support and/or come out if placed in a faith-based family that rejects these identities? Can they seek support by contacting their social worker at the faith-based agency that placed them there if this agency espouses similar beliefs? What is their confidence level that their social worker will be supportive? Social workers must consider these many intersecting dimensions of diversity and identity. Many faith-based organizations contract with child welfare agencies to provide foster and/or adoption services. Social workers both within and outside of public, private and faith-based foster and adoption agencies must be vigilant to protect LGBTQIA children in the system and advocate for their needs, regardless of the social worker's own beliefs.

LGBTQIA youth in foster care are facing lower levels of permanency. It is less common for LGBTQIA youth to find permanent homes by way of reunification or adoption than for their heterosexual, cisgender counterparts (CASA, 2009; McCormick, Schmidt, & Terrazas, 2017; Wilson & Kastanis, 2015). Despite efforts to increase the rates of permanency for youth in the foster care system, the literature reveals little formal study of interventions to address the lack of permanency outcomes for LGBTQIA youth (Jacobs & Freundlich, 2006; Wilson & Kastanis, 2015). It is not uncommon in the field of child welfare for some to believe that these children and adolescents will never achieve permanency (CASA, 2009). Data is lacking on intervention attempts to increase permanency for LGBTQIA youth in foster care (McCormick, Schmidt, & Terrazas, 2017).

Although challenges still remain, positive actions can and are occurring for LGBTQIA youth in the foster care system. A CASA (Court Appointed Special Advocates) program in Prince Georges County, Hyatsville, MD, offers training to social workers in the Department of Social Services who work with LGBTQIA youth. The staff of another CASA program in Miami, Florida, the 11th Judicial Circuit Guardian ad Litem Program, has participated in a training jointly offered by NASW and Lambda Legal (CASA, 2009). States should be more proactive about placing LGBTQIA youth with parents who identify as LGBTQIA, in order to promote a more positive experience and environment of acceptance and understanding for the youth (Gilliam, 2004). Schools of social work must also heed the call to address biases against LGBTQIA people (Dentato et al., 2016).

Social workers can host and facilitate trainings and community collaborations through their agencies to support LGBTQIA families. For example, the *Chicago Tribune* highlighted a story on community groups using this approach (Davis, 2016). The Illinois Department of Children and Family Services joined with *Let It Be Us*, a Chicago non-profit adoption and foster care advocacy group, and other adoption and foster care agencies to conduct workshops providing encouragement and advice to potential gay and lesbian parents. This was particularly helpful for the family highlighted in this story: the future parents (a lesbian couple) and the child (a 13 year old who self-described as gender non-conforming). In this case, it was particularly relevant for the child, as the youth reported feeling safer in gender expression and sexuality in growing up with these particular individuals as parents (Davis, 2016). In working with LGBTQIA youth in foster care and advocating for their well-being, it is important to demonstrate social work knowledge, practice and skills.

Conclusion

Although society continues to make great strides regarding LGBTQIA adoption, LGBTQIA people seeking to adopt continue to face challenges. Social workers need to explore evidence-based interventions to facilitate successful foster care and adoption processes. We must strive to listen and to understand the experiences of the LGBTQIA community surrounding adoption from the perspectives of the children as well as the parents. It is imperative as social workers to provide services at the micro, mezzo and macro levels that are rooted in our profession's Code of Ethics. It is also necessary that we continuously demonstrate cultural humility and lifelong learning toward competency. It is our role as social workers to assist clients and to work toward social justice in our local and global contexts.

Questions to Consider

1   What are the differences between open and closed adoptions? What are factors affecting an LGBTQIA family in each type of adoption?
2   How does intersectionality provide a framework for understanding the experiences of LGBTQIA children in foster care and adoption, and LGBTQIA people who desire to adopt?
3   What unique challenges arise for LGBTQIA people considering domestic and intercountry adoption? What is the Hague Convention and why is it important?
4   Discuss legislation affecting the lives of LGBTQIA children and families. How do RFRAs affect the adoption process for LGBTQIA people?
5   What supports would you provide to LGBTQIA adoptive families? How would you support these families through the adoption process?
6   What social work values and ethics are important to consider when working with LGBTQIA children and families in foster care and adoption?

Resources

Books

Making it legal: A guide to same-sex marriage, domestic partnerships, and civil unions (4th edition) by Attorney Frederick Hertz and Attorney Emily Doskow (2016).
Journey to same-sex parenthood: Firsthand advice, tips and stories from lesbian and gay couples by Eric Rosswood (2016).

Websites

Adoption Exchange Association www.adopt.org
Adoptions Together www.adoptionstogether.org
Adopt US Kids www.adoptuskids.org
Child Welfare Information Gateway www.childwelfare.gov/
Family Equality Council www.familyequality.org
Gay Parenting/LGBT Magazine www.gayparenting.org
Human Rights Campaign www.hrc.org
Lambda Legal www.lamdalegal.org
National Center for Lesbian Rights www.nclrights.org
National Court Appointed Special Advocate Association (CASA for Children) www.casaforchildren.org/site/c.mtJSJ7MPIsE/b.5301295/k.5573/National_CASA_Association.htm supports court-appointed volunteer advocacy to promote permanency for children who have experienced abuse or neglect.

References

American Indian Religious Freedom Act (AIRFA). (n.d.). Retrieved from https://coast.noaa.gov/

Ausbrooks, A. R., & Russell, A. (2011). Gay and lesbian family building: A strengths perspective of transracial adoption. *Journal of GLBT Family Studies*, 7(3), 201–216. DOI:doi:10.1080/1550428X.2011.564936

Berkley Center for Religion, Peace & World Affairs, Georgetown University (Berkley Center). (n.d.). *Sherbert v. Verner*. Retrieved from https://berkleycenter.georgetown.edu/cases/sherbert-v-verner

Brodzinsky, D. M., & Pertman, A. (Eds.). (2012). *Adoption by lesbians and gay men: A new dimension in family diversity*. New York: Oxford University Press.

Brodzinsky, D., & Goldberg, A. E. (2017). Contact with birth family in intercountry adoptions: Comparing families headed by sexual minority and heterosexual parents. *Children & Youth Services Review*, 74, 117–124. DOI:doi:10.1016/j.childyouth.2017.02.003

Carroll, M. (2018). Gay fathers on the margins: Race, class, marital status, and pathway to parenthood. *Family Relations*, 67(1), 104–117. DOI:doi:10.1111/fare.12300

Court-Appointed Special Advocates for Children (CASA). (2009, Fall). Addressing the needs of LGBTQ youth in foster care. *The Connection*. Retrieved from www.f2f.ca.gov/res/pdf/AddressingTheNeeds.pdf

Child Welfare Information Gateway. (2015a). Introduction to adoption. *U.S. Department of Health and Human Services, Administration for Children & Families, Children's Bureau*. Retrieved from www.childwelfare.gov/topics/adoption/intro/

Child Welfare Information Gateway. (2015b). Adoption options: Where do I start? *U.S. Department of Health and Human Services, Administration for Children & Families, Children's Bureau*. Retrieved from www.childwelfare.gov/pubPDFs/f_adoptoption.pdf#page=2&view=Step%201:%20Explore%20adoption%20options

Child Welfare Information Gateway. (2015c). *The adoption home study process*. Washington, D.C: U.S. Department of Health and Human Services. Children's Bureau.

Child Welfare Information Gateway. (2016a) *Frequently asked questions from lesbian, gay, bisexual, transgender, and questioning (LGBTQ) prospective foster and adoptive parents*. Washington, D.C: Department of Health and Human Services.

Child Welfare Information Gateway. (2016b). *Working with lesbian, gay, bisexual, transgender,and questioning (LGBTQ) families in foster care and adoption*. Washington, D.C: U.S. Department of Health and Human Services, Children's Bureau.

Civil Impulse. (2017). H.R.1308–1103rd Congress: Religious Freedom Restoration Act of 1993. Retrieved from www.govtrack.us/congress bills/103/hr 1308

City of Boerne v. Flores. (1997, February 19). Retrieved from www.law.cornell.edu/supct/html/95-2074.ZS.html

Clarke, V., & Demetriou, E. (2016). 'Not a big deal'? Exploring the accounts of adult children of lesbian, gay and trans parents. *Psychology & Sexuality*, 7(2), 131–148. DOI: doi:10.1080/19419899.2015.1110195

Council on Social Work Education (CSWE). (2015). *Educational policy and accreditation standards*. Alexandria, VA: Author.

Davis, T. (2016, August 22). Groups encourage more gay couples to adopt children, be foster parents. *The Chicago Tribune*. Retrieved from www.chicagotribune.com/news/ct-gay-adoption-met-20160814-story.html

Dentato, M. P., Craig, S. L., Lloyd, M. R., Kelly, B. L., Wright, C., & Austin, A. (2016). Homophobia within schools of social work: The critical need for affirming classroom settings and effective preparation for service with the LGBTQ community. *Social Work Education*, 35(6), 672–692. DOI: doi:10.1080/02615479.2016.1150452

Engel, S. M. (2016). Introduction: Fragmented citizens. In *Fragmented citizens: The changing landscape of gay and lesbian lives* (pp. 1–20). New York, NY: New York University Press.

Every Child (2017a). Every Child Deserves a Family Act of 2017, HR 2640, 115th Congress. (2018).

Every Child (2017b). Every Child Deserves a Family Act of 2017, Senate 1303, 115th Congress. (2018).

Farr, R. H. (2017). Does parental sexual orientation matter? A longitudinal follow-up of adoptive families with school-age children. *Developmental Psychology*, 53(2), 252–264. DOI: doi:10.1037/dev0000228

Gates, G. J. (2013). LGBT parenting in the United States. *The Williams Institute on Sexual Orientation and Gender Identity Law and Public Policy at UCLA School of Law*. Retrieved from https://williamsinstitute.law.ucla.edu/wp-content/uploads/LGBT-Parenting.pdf

George, M. (2016). Agency nullification: Defying bans on gay and lesbian foster and adoptive parents. *Harvard Civil Rights-Civil Liberties Law Review*, 51(2), 363–422.

Gilliam, J. W., (2004). Toward providing a welcoming home for all: Enacting a new approach to address the longstanding problems lesbian, gay, bisexual, and transgender youth face in the foster care system. *Loyola Los Angeles Law Review, Digital Commons at LMU and LLS*, 37(4), 1037–1064. Retrieved from http://digita lcommons.lmu.edu/llr/vol37/iss4/4

Green, E. (2015, July 27). Gay rights may come at the cost of religious freedom. *The Atlantic*. Retrieved from www.theatlantic.com/politics/archive/2015/07/legal-rights-lgbt-discrimination-religious-freedom-claims/399278/

Human Rights Campaign. (2014, February 14). *Russia officially bans LGBT international adoption*. Retrieved from www.hrc.org/blog/russia-officially-implements-anti-lgbt-international-adoption-ban

Human Rights Campaign. (2018, March 29). *Every child deserves a family act: H.R. 2640; S.1303*. Retrieved from www.hrc.org/resources/every-child-deserves-a-family-act

Issa, M. A. (2017). Guaranteeing marriage rights: Examining the clash between same-sex adoption and religious freedom. *Georgetown Journal of Gender & The Law*, 18(1), 207–228.

Jacobs, J., & Freundlich, M. (2006). Achieving permanency for LGBTQ youth. *Child Welfare League of America*, LXXXV(2), 299–314.

Kearney, J. D. (2015). The Supreme Court and religious liberty. *Marquette Law Review*, 99(2), 427–445.

Klein, K., Holtby, A., Cook, K., & Travers, R. (2015). Complicating the coming out narrative: Becoming oneself in a heterosexist and cissexist world. *Journal of Homosexuality*, 62(3), 297–326. DOI: doi:10.1080/00918369.2014.970829

Lassiter, P. S., Gutierrez, D., Dew, B. J., & Abrams, L. P. (2017). Gay and lesbian parents. *Family Journal*, 25(4), 327–335. DOI:doi:10.1177/1066480717731204

Lowery, W. (2015, April 2). Gov. Pence signs revised Indiana religious freedom bill into law. *The Washington Post*. Retrieved from www.washingtonpost.com/news/post-nation/wp/2015/04/02/gov-pence-signs-revised-indiana-religious-freedom-bill-into-law/?utm_term=.270887f18433

Manning, W. D., Fettro, M. N., & Lamidi, E. (2014). Child well-being in same-sex parent families: Review of research prepared for American Sociological Association amicus brief. *Population Research and Policy Review*, 33(4), 485–502. DOI: doi:10.1007/s11113–11014–9329–9326

McCormick, A., Schmidt, K., & Terrazas, S. (2017). LGBTQ youth in the child welfare system: An overview of research, practice, and policy. *Journal of Public Child Welfare*, 11(1), 27–39. DOI: doi:10.1080/15548732.2016.1221368

Mertus, J. B. (2011). Barriers, hurdles, and discrimination: The current status of LGBT intercountry adoption and why changes must be made to effectuate the best interests of the child. *Capital University Law Review*, 39, 271–311.

Montero, D. M. (2014). America's progress in achieving the legalization of same gender adoption: Analysis of public opinion, 1994 to 2012. *Social Work*, 59(4), 321–328. DOI: doi:10.1093/sw/swu038

Moore, M. R., & Stambolis-Ruhstorfer, M. (2013). LGBT sexuality and families at the start of the twenty-first century. *Annual Review of Sociology*, 39, 491–507. DOI:doi:10.1146/annurev-soc-071312–145643

National Association of Social Workers (NASW). (2018a). Lesbian, gay, and bisexual issues. In National Association of Social Workers, *Social work speaks: National Association of Social Workers policy statements, 2018–2020*, (11th ed.), (pp. 211–220). Silver Spring, MD: Author.

National Association of Social Workers (NASW). (2018b). Transgender and gender nonconforming people. In National Association of Social Workers, *Social work speaks: National Association of Social Workers policy statements, 2018–2020*, (11th ed.), (pp. 323–331). Silver Spring, MD: Author.

National Center for Lesbian Rights (NCLR). (2014). *Adoption by lesbian, gay, and bisexual parents: An overview of current law*. Retrieved from www.nclrights.org/wp-content/uploads/2013/07/adptn0204.pdf

Pearson, J., Thrane, L., & Wilkinson, L. (2017). Consequences of runaway and thrownaway experiences for sexual minority health during the transition to adulthood. *Journal of LGBT Youth*, 14(2), 145–171. DOI: doi:10.1080/ 19361653.2016.1264909

Pertman, A. (2000). Special needs, diverse families. *Adoption nation: How the adoption revolution is transforming America.* (pp. 209–235). New York, NY: Basic Books.

Reilly, M. (2016, March 31). Same-sex couples can now adopt children in all 50 states. *The Huffington Post*. Retrieved from www.huffingtonpost.com/entry/m ississippi-same-sex-adoption_us_56fdb1a3e4b083f5c607567f

Ryan, H. (2015, June 5). Crisis of America's LGBT youths in foster care. Retrieved from www.takepart.com/article/2015/06/05/crisis-americas-lgbt-youth-foster-care

Schumm, W. R. (2016). A review and critique of research on same-sex parenting and adoption. *Psychological Reports*, 119(3), 641–760. DOI: doi:10.1177/ 0033294116665594

Steffens, M. C., Jonas, K. J., & Scali, T. (2015). Putting prejudice into perspective: Does perceived suitability for adoption depend on sexual orientation more than on other applicant features? *Sensoria: A Journal of Mind, Brain & Culture*, 11(1), 41–57.

Stern, M. J., Oehme, K., & Stern, N. (2016). A test to identify and remedy anti-gay bias in child custody decisions after Obergefell. *UCLA Women's Law Journal*, 23(2), 79–100.

Tasker, F. (2013). A Review of "Lesbian, gay and queer parenting: Families, intimacies, genealogies." *Journal of GLBT Family Studies*, 9(3), 302–304. doi: doi:10.1080/1550428X.2013.781910

U.S. Department of State. (n.d.). Understanding the Hague convention. *U.S. Department of State, Bureau of Consular Affairs.* Retrieved from https://travel.state. gov/content/travel/en/Intercountry-Adoption/Adoption-Process/understa nding-the-hague-convention.html

U.S. National Library of Medicine. (n.d.). Native voices: Native peoples' concepts of health and illness. *U.S. National Library of Medicine, National Institutes of Health, Health & Human Services.* Retrieved from www.nlm.nih.gov/nativevoices/tim eline/545.html

von Doussa, H., Power, J., McNair, R., Brown, R., Schofield, M., Perlesz, A., & … Bickerdike, A. (2016). Building healthcare workers' confidence to work with same-sex parented families. *Health Promotion International*, 31(2), 459–469. DOI: doi:10.1093/heapro/dav010

Washington, T. M. (2013). Once born, twice orphaned: Children's constitutional case against same-sex adoption bans. *Journal of Law & Family Studies*, 15(1), 19–42.

Webb, S. N., Chonody, J. M., & Kavanagh, P. S. (2017). Attitudes toward same-sex parenting: An effect of gender. *Journal of Homosexuality*, 64(11), 1583–1595. DOI: doi:10.1080/00918369.2016.1247540

Weber, S. (2010). A stigma identification framework for family nurses working with parents who are lesbian, gay, bisexual, or transgendered and their families. *Journal of Family Nursing*, 16(4), 378–393. DOI:doi:10.1177/1074840710384999

Weiner, B. A., & Zinner, L. (2015). Attitudes toward straight, gay male, and transsexual parenting. *Journal of Homosexuality*, 62(3), 327–339. DOI: doi:10.1080/ 00918369.2014.972800

Wiley, M. O. (2017). Adoption research, practice, and societal trends: Ten years of progress. *American Psychologist*, 72(9), 985–995. DOI: doi:10.1037/amp0000218

Wilson, B. D. M., & Kastanis, A. A. (2015). Sexual and gender minority disproportionality and disparities in child welfare: A population-based study. *Children and Youth Services Review*, 58, 11–17. DOI: doi:10.1016/j.childyouth.2015.08.016

Wilson, B. D. M., Cooper, K., Kastanis, A., & Nezhad, S. (2014). Sexual and gender minority youth in foster care: Assessing disproportionality and disparities in Los Angeles. *The Williams Institute on Sexual Orientation and Gender Identity Law and Public Policy at UCLA School of Law*. Los Angeles, CA: The Williams Institute, UCLA School of Law.

5 LGBTQIA Youth and Social Service Systems

Tiffany Y. Lane

PH.D., MSW

CSWE 2015 EPAS Competencies

Competency 1: Demonstrate ethical and professional behavior
Competency 2: Engage diversity and difference in practice
Competency 3: Advance human rights and social, economic and environmental justice
Competency 4: Engage in practice-informed research and research-informed practice
Competency 5: Engage in policy-practice
Competency 6: Engage with individuals, families, groups, organizations and communities
Competency 7: Assess individuals, families, groups, organizations and communities
Competency 8: Intervene with individuals, families, groups, organizations and communities

Individuals who are interested in the profession of social work are influenced to join the profession because of their personal experiences with social workers, their desire to help others in need and their passion to be a change agent to improve the conditions of marginalized groups. Social work students often enter into the major with a predetermined field of interest and the population they would like to serve. As they advance in the social work program, they discover the diverse populations and fields of practice and how best to serve clients based on their unique circumstances. Consideration of client and community distinctiveness is key in the social work profession, particularly when it comes to effective social service delivery. Members of the LGBTQIA community have unique lived experiences, and often experience discrimination because of their sexual orientation and gender identity. The challenges that LGBTQIA youth faced position them at risk of **homelessness**, suicide and physical and emotional abuse (Quintana, Rosenthal & Krehely, 2010). Social workers must be at the forefront of providing **culturally sensitive** services to this vulnerable population in social service settings. This chapter will address how social workers may encounter LGBTQIA youth in providing services that address homelessness and child welfare concerns, with a specific focus on the needs of LGBTQIA youth.

Social Services (Competencies 1 and 6)

Social services are services provided by public, private or non-profit agencies to individuals, families and communities. The U.S. Department of Health & Human Services (HHS) is the federal organization that oversees the multiple social service programs on the state and local level in the US. The mission of the U.S. Department of Health & Human Services is to improve and shield the health and welfare of all Americans through effective human service delivery (U.S. Department of Health & Human Services, 2016). The social service programs and services that HHS oversees include: Temporary Assistance for Needy Families and Children (TANF), Special Supplemental Nutrition Program for Women, Infants, and Children (WIC), Supplemental Nutrition Assistance Program (SNAP), Head Start, child support enforcement, foster care, adoption, homelessness, home energy assistance, programs for persons with disabilities, and programs for seniors and military families (U.S. Department of Health & Human Services, 2016; United States Department of Agriculture, 2016). Both private and non-profit social service agencies provide similar programs.

Social service agencies provide diverse services at the state and local levels. Social workers employed with a social service agency may work in diverse roles based on the area of practice. NASW Center for Workforce Studies & Social Work Practice (2011) highlighted key tasks that social workers may carry out within a social service agency. They include:

- Identifying and intervening with at-risk families;
- Analyzing an individual's or family's social support networks;
- Assessing clients for substance abuse, support systems, physical and emotional functioning, financial stability, safety and other concerns;
- Assisting individuals and families in the development and management of coping skills;
- Assisting individuals and families with processing information and resolving personal issues;
- Building effective client relationships;
- Collaborating with treatment teams;
- Conducting intake interviews and assessments;
- Conducting home visits;
- Conducting psychosocial assessments and social histories;
- Determining client eligibility for services;
- Assessing abuse or neglect;
- Coordinating out-of-home placements and adoptions;
- Developing and implementing intervention, treatment and discharge plans;

- Educating and linking clients to local community resources;
- Providing case management services

(NASW Center for Workforce Studies & Social Work
Practice (2011), pp. 1–2)

Social service agencies play a vital role in the lives of people who are in need of assistance. Agencies charge social workers to provide quality care through their role and function, and to be sensitive to the unique needs and challenges faced by individuals, families and communities. Social workers will encounter LGBTQIA youth who are in need of services, and should be well-informed of their challenges and needs. Social workers should work to address issues that affect the LGBTQIA community at micro, mezzo and macro levels of practice.

Getting Started: What a Social Worker Needs to Know

Homelessness (Competency 4)

Box 5.1 Case: Nassir and Homelessness

Nassir is a 19-year-old African American male who recently graduated from high school. While in his senior year of high school, he informed his family that he was gay. His younger siblings and his father seemed fine about his sexual orientation; however, his mother was extremely upset and told Nassir that she was "hurt by his decision to be gay." The following day after Nassir told his family, his mother confronted him and told him that he had to be "straight" or he could not stay in her home. Nassir immediately went to speak with his father, but his father was very passive. Frustrated and hurt, Nassir left his home of 18 years. His siblings were very upset with their mother's decision, but felt helpless. Nassir was able to stay with a close friend for a couple of weeks but eventually ran out of places to stay. His boss at his part time job fired him due to lateness. He was frequently late because of the multiple moves from friends' homes in different geographical locations. Nassir refused to call his mother and was upset with his father because he felt that he had let him down.

Imagine if your parents kicked you out of your home as a teenager because your caregiver(s) did not approve of your sexual orientation or gender identity. What would you do? How would you survive? Would you have somewhere to stay? Would you have a support system? These questions are dilemmas that LGBTQIA youth face far too often in their daily lives. Nassir's case illustrates the experience of a gay male forced to leave his home because of his sexual orientation. He became homeless and separated from his primary social supports. This abrupt transition can be frightening for youth who do not have other means of stable supports in their lives. It is not uncommon for LGBTQIA youth to find themselves homeless once they come out to their families. LGBTQIA youth represent a disproportionate amount of the homeless population. They make up 7% of the US population but comprise 40% of the homeless youth population (True Colors Fund, 2016). LGBTQIA youth of color are overrepresented in the homeless population (Choi, Wilson, Shelton & Gates, 2015).

In 2014, *Rolling Stone* published an article, "*The Forsaken: A Rising Number of Homeless Gay Teens Are Being Cast Out by Religious Families*" (Morris, 2014), which highlighted a resilient woman named Jackie, who was disowned by her religious family because she was a lesbian. She came out to her parents during her sophomore year in college and they instantly refused to support her financially and emotionally. As a result, she became homeless. She discussed her internal struggles of being a lesbian due to her religious upbringing, and her battles with homelessness at that time in her life. Some may ask how her parents could reject her. Why is this such a big deal to her family? The reality is that many LGBTQIA youth confront dismissal from their families and/or loved ones for multiple reasons, not just religious beliefs. Research suggests that one of the main reasons that LGBTQIA youth are homeless is because of their families' negative response to their gender identity, gender appearance and/or sexual orientation (Whitbeck, Chen, Hoyt, Tyler, & Johnson, 2004). A survey of social service providers that work with LGBTQIA youth reported that more than half indicated they were homeless because their parents forced them out or they ran away because of their sexual orientation, gender identity and/or gender expression. Choi, Wilson, Shelton and Gates (2015) found that the primary reason for LGBTQIA homelessness was being "forced out by parents/ran away because of sexual orientation, gender identity and gender expression" (p. 5). Other reasons for LGBTQIA homelessness included:

- Family issues
- Family poverty and/or lack of affordable housing
- Forced out by parents and/or ran away because of other issues
- Aged out of the foster care system
- Physical, emotional or sexual abuse at home
- Lack of culturally competent services
- Youth untreated mental illness
- Substance use by youth(Choi, Wilson, Shelton & Gates (2015), p. 5)

Homelessness affects LGBTQIA youths' social, emotional and overall well-being. These youth are more at risk of sexual and physical harm being on the streets without a secure residence. Additional risk factors associated with LGBTQIA homelessness are health and mental health concerns, contracting sexually transmitted diseases and HIV, unemployment, non-completion of high school and/or legal issues (Ferguson & Maccio, 2015; Ryan, 2009).

Box 5.2 Policy Highlight: The Runaway and Homeless Youth Act (RHYA)

Runaway and Homeless Youth Act (RHYA) is a federal law that funds essential services for homeless youth. The act ensures funding for three key programs that provide critical services and support homeless youth in the US. The programs include:

- Support agency outreach work: The funding provides agencies with funds to do outreach work in the community to get youth off the street.
- Provide shelters: The funding provides shelters, family preservations services, counseling services and basic needs.
- Transitional housing: The funding support housing and supportive services to homeless youth for a longer duration.

This policy has an explicit effect on the LGBTQIA population, considering the overwhelming number of LGBTQIA youth who are homeless. This policy contains a nondiscrimination clause to safeguard that all youth are treated fairly. This protects LGBTQIA youth from unjust treatment and ensures equitable programs and services provided.

(True Colors Fund, 2016; Wilber, 2015)

In addition to risk factors, LGBTQIA youth also face societal discrimination. Despite federal policy (see Box 4.2) and basic human rights, LGBTQIA youth have difficulties finding shelters that will admit them or acknowledge their sexual orientation and/or gender identity (National Coalition on Homelessness, 2014). Although there are shelters that welcome LGBTQIA youth and shelters that exclusively serve LGBTQIA youth, some choose not to stay in shelters and related social services because they want to avoid being harassed, abused, marginalized or feeling unsafe in these settings (Ferguson & Maccio, 2015). Discriminatory practices by agencies towards LGBTQIA youth who are seeking housing assistance also contribute to the number of homeless LGBTQIA youth. Due to these prejudices, LGBTQIA homeless youth are less likely to access social services than heterosexual homeless youth and more likely to live on the streets (Gattis, 2013; Youth.gov, 2016). Transgender homeless youth are at higher risk of physical harm due to social stigmas and are more likely to be turned away from shelters (National Coalition on Homelessness, 2014). Often times, social service agencies who serve transgender youth are not culturally sensitive to their distinct needs. Some discriminatory practices towards transgender youth include denying them shelter due to their gender identity, inconsiderately housing them in a gendered space with which they do not identify, and neglecting to address associated concerns that they may have (National Center for Transgender Equality, 2015). As a social worker in these settings, what might you do to make your agency more welcoming to homeless LGBTQIA youth?

While there are clear challenges, many LGBTQIA youth do seek out support from agencies. The report titled, *Serving Our Youth: The Needs and Experiences of Lesbian, Gay, Bisexual, Transgender, and Questioning Youth Experiencing Homelessness,* surveyed 138 youth homelessness social service agencies to explore homelessness among LGBTQIA youth (Choi, Wilson, Shelton & Gates, 2015). Agencies provided services to LGBTQIA and heterosexual youth. The services most frequently utilized by LGBTQIA youth were drop-in services, homeless prevention, permanent housing, host home, rental assistance, family service, emergency shelter, and transitional living, after care and street outreach (Choi, Wilson, Shelton & Gates, 2015, p. 15).

According to results of needs assessments conducted by the agencies studied, the primary needs of LGBTQIA homeless youth were: 1) respect and emotional support of identity; 2) health care; 3) education; 4) employment; and 5) housing (Choi, Wilson, Shelton & Gates, 2015, p. 15). Understanding the needs of vulnerable groups, such as LGBTQIA homeless youth, informs social work interventions on the micro, mezzo and macro levels. As a social worker in this context, how would you provide the respect and emotional support needed? In what ways would you assist LGBTQIA youth with accessing health care, education, employment and housing within the current parameters and regulations of social service systems and policies?

LGBTQIA Youth in Foster Care (Competency 4)

Foster care is defined as a temporary arrangement provided by a public or private social agency that removes children from their homes because of a serious or dangerous situation and moves them to a setting that provides them full-time care (Downs et al., 2008). The primary reason that children are placed in foster care is the family breakdown or incapacity, intensified by severe environmental pressures (Downs et al., 2008). Many LGBTQIA children and youth are in foster care for the same reasons as non-LGBTQIA children and youth. The reasons for placement in care are generally due to some form of abuse and/or neglect, and related to poverty, mental illness, substance abuse and parental imprisonment (Human Rights Campaign, 2016). Nonetheless, LGBTQIA youth are more at risk of placement in foster care due to the rejection from their families when they come out, which at times can lead to physical abuse and/or neglect. Although characteristics such as race/ethnicity, gender and age are thoroughly examined through the Adoption and Foster Care Analysis and Reporting System (a system that collects case-level information on all children in foster care and those who have been adopted through title IV-E agency involvement), there is a lack of comprehensive data on LGBTQIA children and youth in foster care. In spite of the general disparity of data on LGBTQIA children and youth in foster care, there are studies on LGBTQIA youth in foster care.

LGBTQIA youth are overrepresented in the child welfare system (Child Welfare Information Gateway, 2013). Research suggests that LGB children and youth are more at risk of experiencing child maltreatment than children who do not identify as LGB (Office of Planning, Research and Evaluation, 2015). LGB foster care youth are less likely to be reunited with their families and/or adopted comparted to non-LGB youth; however, *transgender* youth are at the greatest risk of not attaining a permanent and stable home (Wilson, Cooper, Kastanis & Nezhad, 2014). Transgender youth often are belittled for their gender identity and tormented for expressing that identity (National Center for Transgender Equality, 2015). Studies have also shown that children who do not conform to gender identities are at a higher risk of child maltreatment (Roberts et al., 2012; Corliss et al., 2009).

In 2015, the FOX network debuted a hit show, "Empire." The show was about a successful African American family who owns an entertainment company (Daniels, Strong & Hamri, 2015). The family system included a mother, father and three sons. One of the sons, Jamal, identified as gay and in his early 20s. Throughout the episodes, the show depicted Jamal's experiences growing up with his family and their reactions to his gender expression. One of the most shocking episodes was a flashback scene showing Jamal as a toddler being thrown in the trash can by his father because he dressed up in his mother's scarf and high heels and walked around their home. Multiple episodes showed the verbal and emotional abuse Jamal suffered as a child and adult by his father. The abuse that Jamal endured was due to non-conformity of gender roles, and later because he came out as a gay male. Although he was not placed in foster care, there was plausible evidence for an investigation. This scenario is an example of the likely risk of maltreatment that exists in the society among LGBTQIA youth from childhood to adulthood, often resulting in placement.

LGBTQIA youth placed in foster care because of abuse and/or neglect are similarly subject to risk while in foster care. The study on sexual and gender minority in Los Angeles foster care by Wilson, Cooper, Kastanis and Nezhad, 2014 found that almost 13% of LGBTQIA youth experienced inadequate treatment by the foster care system, compared to 6% of non-LGBTQIA foster care youth. They are at risk of abuse and/or neglect when they come out to their foster care parents and/or residential placements (Child Welfare Information Gateway, 2013). This can result in the youth experiencing multiple placements in foster care or running away and becoming homeless. Some LGBTQIA youth ran away from their foster placements due to the host parents' resentment towards their sexual orientation or gender identity/expression (Feinstein et al., 2001). Social workers in child welfare need to tune in and be sensitive to signs to ensure a child's wellbeing. They can screen potential foster and adoptive resource parents for their capacity to support LGBTQIA children.

Box 5.3 Policy Highlight: California Senate Bill 731: Foster Children: Housing: Gender Identity

California is the first state to pass legislation for the welfare of transgender children and youth in foster care. Senate Bill 731 provided transgender youth the right to live in homes and institutions that consider and acknowledge their gender identity—irrespective of the sex listed in their records. This policy also specified that youth have the right to have foster care parents and child welfare professionals who have completed a cultural competency and sensitivity training on best practices for delivering suitable care to lesbian, gay, bisexual, and transgender youth in out-of-home care.

(California Legislative Information, 2016)

The Human Rights Campaign (2016) reported that "experiences of bias and discrimination come from interactions with social workers and group home staff as well as policy and structural barriers preventing LGBTQIA youth from receiving the services they need" (p. 2–3). To address the barriers that exist for LGBT youth, The LGBTQIA center located in Los Angeles launched the RISE (Recognize, Intervene, Support and Empower) program for LGBTQIA youth in foster care. The federally funded program "aims to reduce the number of lesbian, gay, bisexual, transgender, or questioning (LGBTQIA) youth in long-term foster care, and improve permanency by decreasing heterosexism and transphobia in caregiving settings" (Permanency Innovations Initiative Evaluation Team, 2016, p. 1). The components of the program are care coordination team and outreach and relationship building. In cooperation, these interventions included case management, family support and engagement, education and training about LGBTQIA youth. Box 5.3 provides a summary of this recent legislative progress.

Youth Who Age Out of Foster Care

A population within the foster care system that are often forgotten are youth who age out. Youth who age out of foster care are individuals who have reached their states' defined legal age of independent status, and the foster care system is no longer required to provide assistance and support. The transition for aged out foster care youth can be a difficult adjustment, as the services and support end abruptly, ignoring their developmental and social needs. A wealth of empirical evidence identifies the challenges that foster care youth **aging out** may encounter. The major issues include homelessness, substance abuse, mental health illness, early parenting, reliance on public assistance, involvement in the criminal justice system, dropping out of high school, and incarceration (Casey Family Programs, 2008; Courtney et al., 2007; Leathers & Testa, 2006; Munson, Narendorf & McMillen, 2011; White et al., 2011).

Research on youth who age out of foster care is minimal (Dworsky, 2013). Some suggest that it is difficult to pinpoint how many youth age out because they often do not share their identities regarding sexual orientation or gender identity. Despite the lack of data to determine the percentage of youth who age out, Dworsky (2013) suggested that LGB youth have more challenges to becoming financially and socially independent than non-LGB youth. Detrimental experiences in foster care may have an effect on their ability to be self-reliant. These factors also are the reason why some youth voluntarily leave foster care before aging out and become homeless. LGB youth who have no ties to social supports can struggle to be self-sufficient once they exit foster care. There are policies that attempt to address the social barriers of older foster care youth. The Chafee Foster Care Independence Program and the Fostering Connections to Success and Increasing Adoptions Act of 2008 addressed the needs of older foster care youth beyond the age of 18. Both policies provide diverse supports to older foster care youth employed and/or enrolled in school. Box 5.4 provides a summary of the Foster Care Independence Act (FCIA) of 1999. Social workers must be advocate for policies that address the needs of youth in foster care and support those policies that can assist these youth.

Box 5.4 Policy Highlight: Support for Youth Aging Out of Care: The Foster Care Independence Act (FCIA) of 1999

The Foster Care Independence Act (FCIA) of 1999 provided states with a dedicated funding stream for foster youth and increased federal spending on independent living programs. The act established the John H. Chafee Foster Care Independent Living Program which provides supports to help foster youth successfully transition to independence. The services are available to youth up to the age of 21. These services include financial assistance for post-secondary education, training, and employment support. In addition, some states use some of the funds to help youth with room and board for former foster care youth. The Chafee funding permits states to develop their programs and services based on the needs of the foster care youth.

(Oldmixon, 2007)

Relevant Social Work Values and Ethical Consideration (Competency 1)

Social work values guide the mission of the social work profession. All are relevant to the issues facing LGBTQIA youth who are in need of social services. The NASW Code of Ethics identifies our core social work values of service, social justice, dignity and worth of the person, importance of human relationships, integrity and competence (NASW, 2017, para 3). To better understand how the social work core values apply to social work practice with diverse populations in need of social services, consider the social work ethical principles relative to working with LGBTQIA youth on the micro, mezzo and macro levels of practice.

Social workers' primary goal is to help people in need and to address social problems (NASW, 2017). There are many unique needs of LGBTQIA youth who are homeless and in foster care. Social workers in the social service field must support LGBTQIA youth to improve their wellbeing and safety in society. Social workers must be at the forefront to promote social change related to the societal issues plagued by this population. Some major social problems related to LGBTQIA youth are societal and family rejection, discrimination, heterosexism and risk of violent attacks.

Social workers challenge social injustice (NASW, 2017). Injustices related to providing services to LGBTQIA youth are apparent and should be addressed. Social services should be accessible to all people despite their race, gender, sexual orientation and/or sexual expression and identity. Our Code of Ethics charges us as social workers to address inequalities through advocacy, practice, research and education. Social workers should empower LGBTQIA youth to understand their rights to social services and encourage them to seek services when needed.

Social workers respect the inherent dignity and worth of the person (NASW, 2017). Social service agencies must respect and acknowledge LGBTQIA youth and their intersections of social identities. Social workers should support LGBTQIA youths' potential to address their needs and respect their self-determination. Social workers should engage in social actions and other forms of demonstrations on behalf of and with LGBTQIA youth to eradicate power and discrimination on the bases of sexual orientation, gender identity or expression.

Social workers recognize the central importance of human relationships. Social workers should develop a rapport with their LGBTQIA clients to build healthy helping relationships. Social service agencies should strengthen relationships with the LGBTQIA community to support, preserve and improve the welfare of the community. Expanding networks with the LGBTQIA community can raise awareness of need and areas for service delivery.

Social workers behave in a trustworthy manner. It is important that social workers are honest and consistent with the social work profession's mission, values and ethical standards. Social workers should encourage ethical practices at their agencies to ensure that the agencies provide services to vulnerable populations, including members of the LGBTQIA community, with respect and cultural sensitivity.

Social workers practice within their areas of competence and develop and enhance their professional expertise. Social workers and social service agencies who work with LGBTQIA youth should actively engage professional development activities that will enhance their knowledge base and skill set to work effectively in practice. Knowledge grows over time and research provides new insights for practice, sometimes even discrediting other practices. Social workers should strive to be lifelong learners to remain aware of relevant study for greater competence in providing services to LGBTQIA people.

Social Work Skills to Strengthen Competency in Micro, Mezzo and Macro Levels of Practice (Competencies 2, 3, 5, 6, 7 and 8)

The skills that social workers apply vary based on the needs of their client(s). One key approach to working in practice with individuals, groups, families and/or organizations is to consider the person-in-environment. This perspective views the clients and their various environments as an active system, in which each factor concurrently influences and is influenced by the other. This is vital to the application of social work skills. Cournoyer (2014) defines social work skills as:

> a circumscribed set of discrete cognitive and behavioral actions that are consistent and congruent with (1) social work values, ethics and obligations; (2) research-based knowledge; (3) the dimensions of professionalism; and (4) a legitimate social work purpose with the context of a phase or process of practice.
>
> (p. 13)

Some vital social work skills relevant to practice in the social service field, particularly while serving LGBTQIA youth include:

- Engagement
- Assessment
- Planning
- Advocacy

Engagement sets the tone in the helping relationship. In social service settings, clients are usually referred to agencies or walk in to seek help. Depending on the social service setting you are working in you may be working one-on-one with clients or working with groups. It is important for the worker to be aware of the challenges faced by LGBTQIA youth.

For example, a transgender youth may come into your agency and seem guarded; perhaps they won't open up right away. This may be due to societal discrimination and marginalization of people who are transgender. Social workers must be patient, exert empathy and warmth, and be sensitive to their needs and experiences. It is important that the client knows that you are a social support. It is crucial to actively listen and build a rapport, even if you are only meeting with them one time, for example, if you are working in a drop in center or a food pantry. What types of questions might you ask to establish trust and to engage an LGBTQIA client in a social service setting? How can they know that you are trustworthy and will treat them respectfully?

If a client shares that they identify as LGBTQIA, the worker should validate that client by demonstrating understanding and respect for their sexual orientation and gender identity. Clients who are LGBTQIA often experience invisibility, meaning that their sexual orientation is not always a known part of their identity. It is important to "see" your client(s) and respect them in all of their identity constellations. Be familiar with your clients' culture, which may include, but not be limited to, language, dress, ethnicity and their preferred use of gender neutral or gender inclusive pronouns. Valuing and understanding a client's viewpoint is important to the development of a helping relationship for the assessment process.

Assessment of social service needs for LGBTQIA youth requires awareness of the unique challenges faced by this vulnerable group. It is important that the social worker has an idea of the structural barriers that exist and risk factors faced so that the social worker can focus on areas of greater need and risk for the client during the assessment. For example, questions about the client's family and support system, social relationships, living situation, pronouns the person prefers to use and other situations that might be strengths for the client or put the client at risk. While assessing for social service needs, the social worker should ask clear questions, probe, seek clarification when needed and reflect on the information that the client offers. It is important to inquire about the clients' biological, psychological, social, cultural and spiritual factors so that you have a holistic view of your client's resources and needs.

Planning to support a client's need will require the client and social worker to work together. Based on needs identified by the social worker and client working together, that worker can help the client to create a plan specific to their situation. The plan may be one they address together, identifying goals, objectives and action steps that must be met to reach the desired outcomes within specific timeframes. Social workers may also *refer* a client to appropriate social service providers based on their needs. It is important for the social worker to follow-up with the client to determine if they are achieving their goals, and if the referred social service agency is helpful. Social workers must advocate for culturally sensitive services for LGBTQIA youth in their own and other social service agencies. Research suggests that LGBTQIA youth experience marginalization in multiple systems; thus, it is important to address these biases to ensure equitable services. Advocacy should occur on all levels of practice. Social workers should work to empower their clients to advocate for fair and respectful treatment from social service providers. On the mezzo level, social workers should work to address the discriminatory practices within social service agencies and in communities. Some ways to work towards inclusive practices are: 1) to provide educational trainings; 2) to develop culturally sensitive policies and practices in agencies on topics such as using preferred pronouns, inclusive forms and paperwork, and ensuring the availability of safe, gender-neutral bathrooms; 3) to hold community forums; and 4) to increase LGBTQIA specific services within the community.

Social workers should also contest inequitable policies and programs that do not support LGBTQIA youths' general wellbeing, and promote equitable policy and program initiatives that provide quality social services to LGBTQIA youth. The case in Box 5.5 illustrates how a social worker, Alma, uses social work skills to address the unique needs of a client.

Box 5.5 Case: Josh

Alma is a social worker working in a community support program that provides educational and employment resources to youth in an urban area. Josh is a 17-year-old male who came to her agency to inquire about GED prep services. Alma could tell that he was very nervous, so during the *engagement* phase she asked him general questions to make him feel comfortable and warm up. During Alma's *assessment* of Josh, he informed her that his parents kicked him out of their home because he told them he was gay, and they did not approve. He reported that he was staying with a friend and the situation was stable. Josh dropped out of school but wanted to get his GED and find a suitable job to pay for rent when he is ready to live on his own. Alma inquired about his housing plans until he earned an income, and he reported that he could stay with his friend until he was able to afford an apartment. He also informed Alma that he did not have any formal social supports. Based on the information collected, Alma was able to *refer* Josh to a local GED program, *link* him to a career counselor at her agency and *coordinate* a mentor for Josh with a local agency that provides supports to LGBTQIA youth. Alma felt that Josh could benefit from a social support who serves with LGBTQIA youth.

Conclusion

This chapter addressed how social workers might encounter LGBTQIA youth and adults in providing social work services through public social services agencies. LGBTQIA youth are at risk of homelessness and placement in foster care; they are more likely to need social services for housing and other related needs. Understanding LGBTQIA youths' experiences, challenges and needs will better prepare you as a social worker to work in the social service field. Services that are sensitive to the unique needs of LGBTQIA youth will support better outcomes and overall wellbeing of LGBTQIA youth. The NASW Code of Ethics reminds us of the "importance of human relationships" and this is essential in working with LGBTQIA clients who may have experienced rejection. Social workers need to be aware of the systematic barriers that marginalize LGBTQIA youth and discourage them from seeking social services. The social work profession aims to change systems that oppress groups; thus, advocating for culturally sensitive policies and programs must be at the forefront of our work on the mezzo and macro levels of practice. Community outreach is also vital to increase the awareness of the social services available to LGBTQIA youth, and to gain local partnerships.

Questions to Consider

1   A social worker at a city homeless agency notices that there seem to be many LGBTQIA youth as clients seeking services. What might you do to ensure that your agency is providing culturally sensitive services to these clients?

2   Transgender youth are overrepresented in the foster care system. How can social workers address their needs at micro, mezzo and macro levels?

3   What are the Runaway and Homeless Youth Act (RHYA) and the Foster Care Independence Act (FCIA) of 1999? As a social worker, how might these Acts support your efforts to provide services to LGBTQIA youth?

4   Why might sexual orientation and gender identity increase the level of homeless youth? How can social workers intervene and advocate for youth to prevent homelessness? Identify and discuss some *unique* experiences of LGBTQIA youth in foster care. How might their experiences differ from heterosexual and/or cisgender youth?

5   Describe two *societal issues* faced by LGBTQIA youth who age out of foster care. How might social workers assist clients facing these issues?

6   Social service agencies include a wide range of areas of need, including food (SNAP) and cash assistance (TANF), health care (CHIP and Medicaid), housing assistance (Section 8), employment, aging (Medicare) and child welfare services. How can social workers in these diverse departments raise awareness of LGBTQIA clients, prepare for their unique needs and advocate within social service systems?

Resources

The following websites are great resources for social workers and their clients.

National Resource Center for Permanency for Family Connection
www.nrcpfc.org/is/lgbt-parents-in-childwelfare.html provides professional
assistance and information to help strengthen the capacity of state, local, tribal
and other publicly supported child welfare agencies.

True Colors Fund https://truecolorsfund.org/about/ works to end
homelessness among lesbian, gay, bisexual and transgender youth, creating a world in which young people can be their true selves.

RISE (Recognize Intervene Support Empower) https://lalgbtcenter.
org/RISE is a federally funded initiative that has developed and tested a
new service model that will reduce the number of LGBTQ youth in
long-term foster care and help them find loving, permanent homes.

Substance Abuse and Mental Health Services Administration (SAMHA)
www.samhsa.gov/behavioral-health-equity/lgbt provides resources on the
LGBT population including national survey reports, agency and federal
initiatives, and related behavioral health resources.

National Center for Transgender Equality www.transequality.org/ is
the nation's leading social justice advocacy organization winning life-
saving change for transgender people.

Chapin Hall at the University of Chicago https://voicesofyouthcount.
org/brief/lgbtq-youth-homelessness/ is an independent policy research
center at the University of Chicago conducting and exploring research on
vulnerable youth. It oversees the policy research initiative on youth homelessness, Voices of Youth Count. This initiative has studied LGBTQIA
youth homelessness and published the report, *Missed opportunities: LGBTQ
youth homelessness in America* (Morton, Samuels, Dworsky, & Patel, 2018).

References

California Legislative Information (2016). *SB-731 Foster children: Housing: gender
identity*. Retrieved from https://leginfo.legislature.ca.gov/faces/billNavClient.
xhtml?bill_id=201520160SB731

Casey Family Programs (2008). *The Casey young adult survey: Findings over three years*.
Seattle, WA: Author. Retrieved from www.casey.org/Resources/Publications/Ca
seyYoungAdultSurveyThreeYears.htm

Child Welfare Information Gateway (2013). *Supporting your LGBTQ youth: A guide for
foster parents*. Retrieved from www.childwelfare.gov/pubPDFs/LGBTQyouth.pdf

Choi, S., Wilson, B., Shelton, J., & Gates, G. (2015). *Serving our youth 2015: The
needs and experiences of lesbians, gays, bisexuals, transgender, and questing youth experiencing homelessness*. (William Institute and True Funds Report). Retrieved from
https://williamsinstitute.law.ucla.edu/wp-content/uploads/Serving-Our-Youth-
June-2015.pdf

Corliss, H. L., Cochran, S. D., Mays, V. M., Greenland, S., & Seeman, T. E. (2009). Age of minority sexual orientation development and risk of childhood maltreatment and suicide attempts in women. *American Journal of Orthopsychiatry*, 79(4), 511–521. doi:doi:10.1037/a0017163

Cournoyer, B. (2014). *The social work skills workbook*. (8th ed.). Belmont, CA: Thomson Brooks/Cole.

Courtney, M. E., Dworsky, A., Cusick, G. R., Havlicek, J., Perez, A., & Keller, T. (2007). *Executive summary: Midwest evaluation of the adult functioning of former foster youth: Outcomes at age 21*. Chicago: Chapin Hall Center for Children at the University of Chicago.

Daniels, L., Strong, D. (Writers), & Hamri, S. (Director) (2015) The pilot [*Episode 1 Season 1*]. In Strong, D., Grazer, B., Munic, R., Calfo, F., Chaiken, I. & Hamri, S. (Executive Producers). *EMPIRE*. Chicago, Illinois: FOX

Downs, S. W., Moore, E., McFadden, E. J., Michaud, S. M., & Costin, L. B. (2008). *Child welfare and family services: Polices and practice* (8th ed.). Boston, MA: Pearson Education.

Dworsky, A. (2013). The economic well-being of lesbian, gay, and bisexual youth transitioning out of foster care. (Issue Brief). Retrieved from www.acf.hhs.gov/sites/default/files/opre/opre_lgbt_brief_01_04_2013.pdf

Feinstein, R., Greenblatt, A., Hass, L., Kohn, S., & Rana, J. (2001) *Justice for all?* Retrieved from www.prisonlegalnews.org/media/publications/urban_justice_center_lesbian_and_gay_youth_project_report_on_lgbt_youth_in_the_juvenile_justice_system_2001.pdf

Ferguson, K. M., & Maccio, E. M. (2015). Promising programs for lesbian, gay, bisexual, transgender, and queer/questioning runaway and homeless youth. *Journal of Social Service Research*, 41(5), 659–683. doi:doi:10.1080/01488376.2015.1058879

Gattis, M. N. (2013). An ecological systems comparison between homeless sexual minority youth and homeless heterosexual youth. *Journal of Social Science Research*, 39, 38–49.

Human Rights Campaign (2016). *LGBTQ youth in the foster care system*. Retrieved from www.hrc.org/resources/lgbt-youth-in-the-foster-care-system

Leathers, S. & Testa, M. (2006). Foster youths emancipating from care: Caseworkers' reports on needs and services. *Child Welfare*, 85(3), 463–498.

Morris, A. (2014). The forsaken: A rising number of homeless gay teens are being cast out by religious families. *Rolling Stone*. Retrieved from www.rollingstone.com/culture/features/the-forsaken-a-rising-number-of-homeless-gay-teens-are-being-cast-out-by-religious-families-20140903

Morton, M. H., Samuels, G. M., Dworsky, A., & Patel, S. (2018). *Missed opportunities: LGBTQ youth homelessness in America*. Chicago, IL: Chapin Hall at the University of Chicago. Retrieved from https://voicesofyouthcount.org/brief/lgbtq-youth-homelessness/

Munson, M., Narendorf, S. & McMillen, J. (2011). Knowledge of and attitudes towards behavioral health services among older youth in the foster care system. *Child & Adolescent Social Work Journal*, 28(2), 97–112. doi:doi:10.1007/s10560-010-0223

National Association of Social Workers (NASW) Center for Workforce Studies & Social WorkPractice (2011). *Social workers in social services agencies: Occupational profile. Overview of Functions* (pp. 1–2). Retrieved from www.socialworkers.org/LinkClick.aspx?fileticket=cPGKXbFAxsw%3D&portalid=0

National Association of Social Workers (NASW). (2017). *Code of ethics of the National Association of Social Workers (NASW)*. Retrieved from www.socialworkers.org/About/Ethics/Code-of-Ethics/Code-of-Ethics-English

National Center for Transgender Equality (2015). *Issues: Housing and homelessness*. Retrieved from www.transequality.org/issues/housing-homelessness

National Coalition on Homelessness (2014). *LGBT homelessness*. Retrieved from http://nationalhomeless.org/issues/lgbt/

Office of Planning, Research and Evaluation (OPRE) (2015). An Office of the Administration for Children & Families, U.S. Dept. of Health and Human Services. *LGBT populations and the child welfare system: A snapshot of the knowledge base and research*. (OPRE Report #2015–2024). Retrieved from www.acf.hhs.gov/sites/default/files/opre/chapter_brief_child_welfare_508_nologo.pdf

Oldmixon, S. (2007). *State policies to help youth transition out of foster care (issue brief)*. Retrieved from www.nga.org/files/live/sites/NGA/files/pdf/2007/0701YOUTH.PDF

Permanency Innovations Initiative Evaluation Team. (2016). *Findings from the RISE youth qualitative interviews*. (OPRE Report 2016–2005). Retrieved from http://files.lalgbtcenter.org/pdf/rise/Los-Angeles-LGBT-Center-RISE-Youth-Quantitative-Interview-Brief.pdf

Quintana, N., Rosenthal, R., & Krehely, J. (2010). *On the streets: The federal response to gay and transgender homeless youth* (Center for American Progress Report). Retrieved from www.americanprogress.org/wpcontent/uploads/issues/2010/06/pdf/lgbtyouthhomelessness.pdf.

Roberts, A. L., Rosario, M., Corliss, H. L., Koenen, K. C., & Austin, S. B. (2012). Childhood gender nonconformity: A risk indicator for childhood abuse and posttraumatic stress in youth. *Pediatrics*, 129(3), 410–417. doi:doi:10.1542/peds.2011-1804

Ryan, C. (2009). Helping families support their lesbian, gay, bisexual, and transgender (LGBT) children. *National Center for Cultural Competence, Georgetown University Center for Child and Human Development Report*. Retrieved from https://nccc.georgetown.edu/documents/LGBT_Brief.pdf

True Colors Fund (2016). *Our issues*. Retrieved from https://truecolorsfund.org/our-issue/

United States Department of Agriculture (2016). *Women, infants, and children (WIC)*. Retrieved from www.fns.usda.gov/wic/women-infants-and-children-wic

U.S. Department of Health & Human Services (2016). *About HHS*. Retrieved from www.hhs.gov/about/index.html

Whitbeck, L., Chen, X., Hoyt, D., Tyler, K., & Johnson, K. (2004). Mental disorder, subsistence strategies, and victimization among gay, lesbian, and bisexual homeless and runaway adolescents. *Journal of Sex Research*, 41(4), 329–342.

White, C. R., Gallegos, A. H., O'Brien, K., Weisberg, S., Pecora, P. J., & Medina, R. (2011). The relationship between homelessness and mental health among alumni of foster care: Results from the Casey young adult survey. *Journal of Public Child Welfare*, 5(4), 369–389. doi:doi:10.1080/15548732.2011.599754

Wilber, S. (2015). New guide promotes the safety and well-being of LGBT youth in the justice system. [National Center for Lesbian Rights Blog Post]. Retrieved from www.nclrights.org/new-guide-promotes-the-safety-and-well-being-of-lgbt-youth-in-the-justice-system/

Wilson, B., Cooper, K., Kastanis, A., & Nezhad, S. (2014). *Sexual and gender minority in Los Angeles foster care [Executive Summary]*. Retrieved from http://williamsinstitute.law.ucla.edu/wp-content/uploads/LAFYS_report_final-aug-2014.pdf

Youth.gov (2016). *LGBTQ*. Retrieved from http://youth.gov/youth-topics/lgbtq-youth

6 Education and Schools

Karen Myers

JD, MSW

CSWE 2015 EPAS Competencies

Competency 2: Engage diversity and difference in practice
Competency 3: Advance human rights and social, economic, and environmental justice
Competency 5: Engage in policy practice
Competency 6: Engage with individuals, families, groups, organizations, and communities
Competency 7: Assess individuals, families, groups, organizations, and communities
Competency 8: Intervene with individuals, families, groups, organizations, and communities

Introduction

Imagine that you are required to be in a building you are not allowed to leave for the next eight hours. There are no bathrooms in the entire building for you to use. Many people in the building push you, call you names, and torment you in various ways at every opportunity. Every time you learn a new way to protect yourself, the rules seem to change and you have to figure out all over again what it is you must do differently to be safe. You feel like there is no one in the whole building who understands you and is on your side. Given this situation, how likely would you be to feel good about yourself and be able to focus on learning new academic concepts?

Imagine you are 12 years old. Your peers are all starting to talk about having crushes on each other. You have a crush too but your crush is on someone of the same sex as you. Every day on the bus, in the cafeteria, in the locker room, or hanging out in the halls, you hear your friends pick on other classmates, saying things like, "What are you, a disgusting homo?" or, "Stop acting like such a queer!" Thus, you conclude that what you are is not something that is acceptable within your group of friends. You also hear your parents talking at home about how much they oppose gay people being able to marry and how they are glad your family's church would kick a gay person out; hence, you know that what you are is not something that is acceptable to your parents or your church, either. You try to change that part of you but you cannot. You try to bury that part of you as deeply as you can but the more you try not to think about it the harder it is to think about anything else. You are tormented by your thoughts and terrified someone will find out about them. Given this situation, how likely are you to develop a positive self-esteem and be able to learn new academic concepts?

Most young people in the United States spend a minimum of 13 years in school beginning in kindergarten and finishing when they graduate from high school after their 12th grade year. Acquiring academic knowledge is an important component of the years spent in school, but that is only one part of the tremendous amount of development and education that happens during that time. Building character, discovering personality traits, learning social skills, developing relationships, and identifying interests all occur alongside lessons in subjects like reading, writing, math, history, and science. Some young people seem to excel in all areas while others experience areas of struggle. For LGBTQIA youth, educational settings can be difficult environments to navigate as they identify differently from the norm. Their experiences run the gamut from desperately trying to hide in outright hostile, dangerous environments to feeling openly accepted, even celebrated, in supportive ones.

Social workers are involved with young people in school settings in a wide variety of ways. School social workers, therapeutic day treatment counselors, home-school liaisons, parental outreach coordinators, and residential facility staff are often employed directly by school systems and educational programs. Other social workers interface with school settings through social services, community-based services, healthcare, homeless shelters, counseling programs, and family treatment programs. LGBTQIA youth have as much likelihood, if not more, than their peers to show up in any of these settings so it is imperative for social workers to be sensitive to the specific issues they may face due to their minority status. Their status as youth makes them even more vulnerable to the marginalization and oppression faced by the LGBTQIA community. This is particularly true for LGBTQIA youth **coming out** in families, schools, and faith communities where intolerance and violence remain structurally supported.

It is equally important that LGBTQIA parents are welcomed into school settings where their children attend. Supportive parental involvement in a child's education is valuable, but discrimination in the school setting may hinder parents. Social workers should attune to policies and practices that marginalize these families, making it difficult for LGBTQIA parents and their children to feel fully engaged at their school. Furthermore, the visibility and support of LGBTQIA families in schools sets an important example for LGBTQIA youth who are in the process of coming out and their peers who see acceptance for diversity modeled for them.

Getting Started

What a Social Worker Needs to Know

- Young people need the space and freedom to figure out who they are. Social workers should be mindful of the developmental process and careful not to rush to conclusions or make assumptions based on how a young person presents.
- LGBTQIA youth are particularly vulnerable as targets for ostracizing and bullying by their peers. These incidents can happen in all settings but are particularly commonplace in less supervised areas. Students must be protected so school is a safe place and a conducive learning environment. This means addressing incidents as they happen but also putting proactive programs and policies in place.
- LGBTQIA parents should be welcomed in schools where their children attend. Social workers should analyze and critique policies and practices which may marginalize LGBTQIA families due to the effect on those families as well as the impact on the school environment for LGBTQIA youth.
- The behavior of LGBTQIA youth can be mislabeled and misdiagnosed when the effects of living in a hostile, unsupportive environment are ignored. Social workers bring valuable training in looking at systemic issues which may be causal by focusing on youth in their environments.
- ALL young people benefit from supportive, affirming environments. Ideas and strategies targeted for LGBTQIA youth have a much wider impact than that specific population.

Relevant Social Work Values and Ethical Considerations

These social work values and ethics are important to consider in working with LGBTQIA youth:

- Dignity and worth of the person
- Importance of human relationships
- Social justice
- Empathy
- Confidentiality
- Non-judgmentalism
- Self-determination
- Individualization
- Access to services

Social Work Skills to Strengthen Competency

When you consider core social work skills, practicing nuances can help you to become more culturally sensitive to the specific needs of LGBTQIA youth in educational environments. The following recommendations can help you to provide inclusive services:

- Engagement is a critical first step with all clients, but particularly youth within the LGBTQIA community. Make support widely known and highly visible by displaying a rainbow flag and/or safe space sticker, hanging photos that show diversity, and being vocal about acceptance. As you begin work with young people, listen to the language they use to describe themselves and use that language with them. Honor their name and pronoun choices. Allow them the freedom to change these names and pronouns. Recognize that a young person might identify as **asexual, questioning, queer, gender fluid, gender non-conforming, genderqueer, bisexual, lesbian, gay, transgender, pangender, pansexual, intersex**, or something else. Know the difference between biological **sex, gender identity**, and **sexual orientation** and do not conflate them.

- During assessment, be an active listener. Many LGBTQIA youth have been quieted or judged harshly without ever being asked their stories, so having a safe space to talk is a powerful intervention all on its own. As much as possible, allow the young person to guide the conversation without leading them with a set agenda or questions; however, there are times when it is paramount to determine that they are safe. When asking questions, be careful not to reinforce heteronormativity or the gender binary. Think about the difference between asking "Do you have a girlfriend/boyfriend?" and "Is there someone special you like?"

- Young people are deserving of self-determination so work with them to identify interventions they feel comfortable about implementing. Be a vocal **ally** but also support self-efficacy by creating safe environments for them to advocate for themselves. DO NOT disclose a student's identity/identities without their permission, even to people you believe are supportive.

- LGBTQIA youth are often highly resourceful out of necessity. Be open and willing to learn from them. Evaluate interventions and programs frequently within the rapidly changing environment of educational settings.

- Be aware of the significant risks LGBTQIA youth face. Honor confidentiality. Develop readily available resource lists you can access quickly. Recognize the value of hotlines and online resources which offer support but allow a student to remain **closeted** if they choose.

- Embody social work values and ethics. Work towards social justice for LGBTQIA people by treating them with dignity and respect; challenge oppressive factors which undermine and discriminate against them.

- Practice self-awareness and self-reflection as part of cultural humility. Be aware of biases and assumptions that may hinder working effectively with LGBTQIA youth.

Implications for Social Work Practice

While positive changes are occurring, there is significant work which remains to be done in respecting the dignity and worth of all people and seeking inclusivity and social justice for the LGBTQIA community, including its young people. Social workers are bound professionally and ethically to be a part of these efforts (CSWE, 2015; NASW, 2008). Despite increased visibility in media portrayals of the LGBTQIA community, societal structures continue to be designed around **heteronormativity**, leaving some young people feeling isolated and vulnerable at a particularly critical time of exploration and development. The social exclusion faced by LGBTQIA-identified or questioning youth has led to verbal harassment, physical assault, inaccessibility to LGBTQIA-sensitive healthcare and information, and a decline in physical and emotional health and well-being (Ahuja et al., 2015; Aragon, Poteat, Espelage, & Koenig, 2014; Espelage, Rao, & De La Rue, 2013). According to recent statistics, they experience higher incidences of self-harm and/or suicide, increased use of alcohol and drugs, homelessness, and a greater likelihood of incarceration (Padilla, Crisp, & Rew, 2010; Robinson & Espelage, 2011; Russell, Sinclair, Poteat, & Koenig, 2012).

Social workers value an ecological perspective, recognizing that sexual orientation and **gender expression** are but two aspects of youth identity; the complexities of coming out for an adolescent are layered with other factors such as race, immigration status, religion, class, and ability. For example, youth of color who identify as LGBTQIA may face mistreatment on a variety of levels; this **intersectionality** may lead to compounded oppression and marginalization (Jamil & Harper, 2010). The experiences of LGBTQIA youth with disabilities have been virtually "ignored by the academic, special education, and social services establishments" (Duke, 2010, p. 151). At the same time that positive changes are occurring, the systematic silencing of those on the margins is no less intense.

Too many youth feel the agony of rejection from family, peers, and faith communities when they come out in non-accepting environments. While young people who share a marginalized status with their family may experience significant support and guidance from family members, the majority of LGBTQIA youth have heterosexual and cisgender parents. Coming out to family may mean further ostracization or homelessness (Shpigel, Belsky, & Diamond, 2015). Awareness of this risk can keep a young person closeted, causing further isolation and distress.

Young people who identify outside of the normative structures of sexuality and **gender** face many challenges and struggles, but social workers are trained to identify the strengths and protective factors of LGBTQIA youth. Within school settings, gay–straight alliances (GSAs) and other student organizations have provided support for some, but there remains an alarming lack of such resources. More disturbingly, there are often school policies that penalize non-normative expressions of gender and sexuality or that serve to punish students who decide to stand up for themselves against harassment and bullying (Snapp, Hoenig, Fields, & Russell, 2015). Social workers can provide positive support, educate others, and create changes so that school becomes a positive learning environment and safe space for LGBTQIA young people and their families.

It is imperative that social workers identify and implement immediate interventions at the micro and mezzo levels to keep LGBTQIA youth safe and supported in school settings while simultaneously working towards systemic change at the macro level to dismantle the institutional practices that marginalize and discriminate against these youth. Legal protections vary state by state and even school district by school district so it is important for social workers to be informed in order to advocate that existing protective policies are followed and absent ones are put into place.

School Environments for LGBTQIA Young People and Their Families

Bullying

Bullying creates a hostile environment and is a persistent problem for marginalized students, which includes a high incidence of LGBTQIA bullying (GLSEN, 2014). Some students who are bullied openly identify as LGBTQIA; others do not. Bullying can take many forms. A student may experience teasing, taunting, physical violence, the spread of rumors, and/or exclusion. One mean person can be a bully but bullying also happens when groups gang up on a vulnerable person. Cyberbullying occurs when the internet becomes the tool for the bullying process. It can include sending unkind messages to an individual, posting those messages and/or pictures online, and spreading hurtful things about another person. Sometimes cyberbullies hide behind a fake identity.

Box 6.1 Case: Brian

Brian spends all day every day trying to go unnoticed at school. He surreptitiously watches the popular guys and tries to walk the way they walk. He also buys similar clothes in an effort to blend in with them. He tries to talk about the things they talk about even though he could care less who won the most recent NBA game. He avoids locker rooms and bathrooms whenever possible. He gets up extra early each morning so his mom can drop him off at school and stays in the library until she can pick him up in the evenings because nothing good has ever happened on the bus. He goes as quickly as he can from one class to the next; nonetheless, others have often cornered him in the hall and shoved him up against the lockers with a menacing "faggot" whispered in his ear. He has lost track of how many painful wedgies he has had. The time he tried to avoid one, he received in-school suspension for "roughhousing" in the hallway. He attempted to explain but the assistant principal told him he was not interested in the details. He loves theater, but would not dream of drawing attention to himself by trying out for the school play. He always makes sure he misses at least a couple of questions on his homework assignments and tests so he never has the top score lest a teacher highlight that. He spends the majority of his school day figuring out how to disappear in a crowd.

Students who experience bullying often try to find ways to avoid it, but when their evasions fail, they come to dread school. If they react, defend, or stick up for themselves, they are often the ones who get into trouble rather than receive the protection they need. The stress and trauma they experience can make learning difficult if not impossible. Too often school administrators and teachers are unaware or unhelpful. LGBTQIA students' poor school performance can be misinterpreted as academic deficits when the capability is there but hindered by what is happening in the school environment. The following statistics come from The 2013 National School Climate Survey (GLSEN, 2014):

- 55.5% of LGBT students felt unsafe at school because of their sexual orientation
- 74.1% of LGBT students were verbally harassed in the past year because of their sexual orientation and 55.2% because of their gender expression
- 49.0% of LGBT students experienced cyberbullying in the past year
- 61.6% of the students who reported an incident said that school staff did nothing in response
- 30.3% of LGBT students missed at least one entire day of school in the past month because they felt unsafe or uncomfortable
- 71.4% of LGBT students heard "gay" used in a negative way frequently or often at school, and 90.8% reported they felt distressed because of this language
- 64.5% heard other **homophobic** remarks frequently or often.

These statistics are troubling but what is even more disturbing is the number of LGBTQIA students who are not included in those numbers because they are no longer alive. This is not close to an all-inclusive list. The following teenagers died by suicide after having experienced significant bullying and discrimination:

- **Taylor Alesana, 16 –** In April 2015, this California transgender teen died by suicide after speaking in a heart-breaking video posted on YouTube www.youtube.com/watch?v=aU2YywE3JJI about being bullied in school and online.

- **Blake Brockington, 18** – In March 2015, this North Carolina teenager died by suicide. He had become an advocate for LGBTQIA youth; however, he continued to struggle in his own life.
- **Aubrey Shine, 19** – In February 2015, this Maryland teenager died by suicide after reportedly struggling to have her identity recognized by others, including her family members.
- **Zander Mahaffey, 15** – In February 2015, this Georgia teen died by suicide, claiming his identity in a final message – "I'm a boy in my heart."
- **Ash Haffner, 16** – In February 2015, this North Carolina teenager died by suicide after enduring years of bullying, which reportedly worsened after his transition to identifying as male.
- **Leelah Alcorn, 17** – In December 2014, this Ohio teenager posted a suicide note expressing hope that her death would bring attention to the discrimination, abuse, and lack of support transgender people face.
- **Carlos Vigil, 17** – In July 2013, this New Mexico teenager posted a heart-breaking letter online before he killed himself after being bullied. In the brief message he said: "The kids in school are right, I am a loser, a freak and a fag and in no way is that acceptable for people to deal with."
- **Alexander "AJ" Betts Jr., 16** – In July 2013, this Iowa teen reportedly died by suicide after being subjected to intense bullying at his high school due to his sexuality (he identified as gay) and his mixed race background.
- **Jadin Bell, 15** – In January 2013, this Oregon teen hung himself on an elementary school playground structure after being bullied for being gay.
- **Josh Pacheco, 17** – In November 2012, this Michigan teen reportedly died by suicide after being bullied in and out of school for being gay.
- **Kenneth "Rodney" Weishuhn Jr., 14** – In April 2012, this Iowa teen hung himself. He was reportedly targeted for being gay, having come out shortly before his suicide.
- **EricJames Borges, 19** – In January 2012, just one month after filming an "It Gets Better" video www.youtube.com/watch?v=InWhEIaCFkg in support of LGBTQIA youth, this California teen took his own life. He wrote in his suicide note, "My pain is not caused because I am gay. My pain was caused by how I was treated because I am gay."
- **Phillip Parker, 14** – In January 2012, this Tennessee teen reportedly died by suicide after experiencing constant bullying for being gay.
- **Jamey Rodemeyer, 14** – In September 2011, this New York teenager, who identified as bisexual and tried to be a support to other LGBTQIA youth www.youtube.com/watch?v=-Pb1CaGMdWk, hung himself after facing severe bullying himself.
- **Zach Harrington, 19** – In October 2010, this Oklahoma teen took his own life after experiencing anti-gay bullying throughout his

schooling. He had recently sat through an intense anti-gay exchange at a local city council meeting.

- **Terrell Williams, 17** – In October 2010, this Washington State teen died by suicide soon after being attacked at his high school.
- **Seth Walsh, 13** – In September 2010, this California teen died after spending nine days on life support. He reportedly attempted suicide over relentless bullying because he was gay.
- **Billy Lucas, 15** – In September 2010, this Indiana teenager, who never self-identified as gay, hung himself. He was reportedly tormented by anti-gay bullying at school.
- **Tyler Clementi, 18** – In September 2010, this Rutgers University student reportedly died by suicide after his roommate secretly filmed him kissing another man and posted it online.
- **Asher Brown, 13** – In September 2010, this Texas teen reportedly died by suicide after repeated bullying. His mother and stepfather reported that kids accused him of being gay, some of them performing mock gay acts on him in his physical education class.
- **Justin Aaberg, 15** – In July 2010, this Minnesota teen reportedly died by suicide after experiencing merciless harassment due to his sexual orientation.
- **Carl Joseph Walker-Hoover, 11** – In April 2009, this Massachusetts boy reportedly hung himself after school bullies repeatedly called him "gay."
- **Eric Mohat, 17** – In March 2007, this Ohio teenager shot himself after being taunted relentlessly for being gay. He was allegedly called "gay," "fag," "queer," and "homo" often in front of his teachers.

These lives were cut short by events that should have been prevented. Many of these teenagers reached out for support but were denied what they needed. All of them had strengths – resiliency, creativity, intelligence, motivation, musical talent, humor, and kindness to name a few. Their potential contributions to their communities, their country, and their world will never be realized.

School environments can be terrifying for LGBTQIA employees as well as students. Fear of being outed and losing one's job can hinder school staff from feeling free to speak up and advocate on behalf of students (Endo, Reece-Miller, & Santavicca, 2010; Hardie, 2012; Russell, 2010). **Heterosexual** and cisgender teachers can also fear professional repercussions for simply including LGBTQIA perspectives and curricula in their classrooms (Flores, 2014; Fredman, Schultz, & Hoffman, 2015; Smith, 2015). LGBTQIA parents can feel unwelcome and even face outright discrimination when they try to participate in their children's education. They often have to spend time counteracting the heteronormative messages their children receive at school, which detract from their own family's reality.

Lack of Representation

LGBTQIA students often do not see themselves represented in what they are learning in school, which leaves them feeling more marginalized. LGBTQIA-inclusive curriculum is an important component of a welcoming school environment (Horn et al., 2010; Snapp, Burdge, Licona, Moody, & Russell, 2015). This includes school-based sexuality education, which should provide safe sex practices for all young people not just heterosexual youth (Abbott, Ellis, & Abbott, 2015; Elia & Tokunaga, 2015; Gowen & Winges-Yanez, 2014). In the words of lesbian poet, Adrienne Rich:

> when someone with the authority of a teacher, say, describes the world and you are not in it, there is a moment of psychic disequilibrium, as if you looked in to a mirror and saw nothing. Yet you know you exist and others like you, that this is a game with mirrors. It takes some strength of soul—and not just individual strength, but collective understanding—to resist this void, this nonbeing, into which you are thrust, and to stand up, demanding to be seen and heard.
>
> (Rich, 1984, p. 199)

Social workers in schools should stand alongside LGBTQIA students and LGBTQIA parents who feel invisible to make sure their experiences are seen and heard. This does not mean outing people but rather making sure to provide visible and vocal support for LGBTQIA inclusivity.

School assignments and events should acknowledge and allow for diversity among individuals and families as a way to support inclusivity and set an example of embracing difference. School personnel, school forms, and school events should not assume heterosexual parents for all students. LGBTQIA students who want to display who they are should not be excluded or marginalized or forced into gender normative behavior. Openly self-identifying as LGBTQIA can be very risky so these students should be supported and protected as they figure out who they are. Dismissal of identity disengages students but also creates an environment where ostracism is encouraged, which increases the likelihood of bullying (Snapp, McGuire, Sinclair, Gabrion, & Russell, 2015). Teachers who model acceptance and inclusivity are crucial in creating safe school environments for all students (Wernick, Kulick, & Inglehart, 2013). Social workers in school settings also play a critical part and can fill a variety of generalist practice roles – advocates, educators, facilitators, mobilizers, and trainers, as they work towards the inclusion and safety of all LGBTQIA people.

Box 6.2 Case: Charlie

Charlotte wants to be called Charlie. He hates the color pink. He hates long hair and cuts his as soon as it starts to grow out. He refuses to use the girls' bathroom at school because he is not a girl. He does not understand why his outsides do not match his insides. He is frustrated and angry that what seems so simple to him is such a big deal to everyone else. He does not understand why he cannot be on the boys' team when they divide boys and girls in his class at school. His teacher makes him sit out or go talk to the guidance counselor instead. She does not hang up his "About Me" poster as she does for all the other students for parents' night. She does not let him read the boy parts when they practice for the class play. She has his name and birthday on a pink cake on the calendar rather than a blue balloon like the other boys. When he took it down, she sent him to the principal's office. He heard her call him "confused" when she is the one who cannot seem to understand. He is starting to hate school because he cannot be himself. He is 7 years old.

The earlier inclusive practices are started in school settings, the greater the likelihood that young people will be accepting of themselves and others. LGBTQIA issues should not be viewed as reserved for middle and high school. The seeds of acceptance are sown early. Furthermore, there may be young people who have LGBTQIA parents or other family members. Transgender youth tend to have very early experiences of **gender dysphoria** and need openness and acceptance in their journey of self-discovery. As their gender identity emerges, it is often very confusing why others cannot see what is so clear to them and the way they feel about themselves. The lack of acceptance by others can quickly turn into shame and lack of acceptance of oneself, which can lead further into anxiety, depression, and suicidal thoughts/actions.

Lack of Support

All young people in school environments are on a journey of self-exploration. They need a safe, supportive, affirming environment to be themselves freely. Ambiguity can be a part of the process but depends on the individual. LGBTQIA young people are in a precarious place trying to figure out who they are while often facing pressure to be someone else, someone who fits the norm. While their gender identity and sexual orientation are parts of the person they are becoming, those aspects can feel all-consuming when they are the source of marginalization and discrimination.

Box 6.3 Case: Karen (a)

Karen has straight "A" grades. She plays viola in the school orchestra. She was inducted into the National Honor Society. She gets along with her classmates and tries to be a friend to everyone. She attends church regularly with her family and has participated in youth group activities to collect and donate clothing, provide gifts at holidays, feed the homeless, and build low-income housing. She wants to help people in her future career so has thought about being a social worker or a public interest lawyer. Her mother caught her kissing a girl when she was younger and made it very clear that the problem was not so much the kissing as "who" she was kissing. She has tried dating guys. She even likes some of them but she has never felt kissing them the way she felt kissing that girl. She likes them as friends, but she is not attracted to them beyond that. She wants a girlfriend. She wants to fall in love and get married someday. She hears at least once a week what a terrible sin – an "abomination" – it is to feel that way. She has prayed with all her heart to have those feelings taken away. She feels like a terrible person for continuing to have them. She does not know how to be free of them. They feel as natural to her as breathing. She has come to believe nothing else she does will make any difference in how her family and her church perceive her if she cannot change this about herself. She is tortured by her thoughts and feelings. She is exhausted by the struggle and has started to loathe herself. She contemplates suicide as a means of escape.

The case in Box 6.3 is written about the author of this chapter who felt so unable to be her true self while she was a teenager that dying felt more conceivable than continuing to struggle. I write this chapter and share my own story in the hopes of helping other LGBTQIA young people to avoid this level of despair. Youth who feel isolated and alone need people around them who reflect back their strengths and offer hope. A lesbian student identifying what she would have liked her teachers to know while she was in school wrote, "All I really wanted was to be looked in the eye and told: 'You're okay.'" (Imber, 2005, p. 11).

Letting a student know they are okay means honoring their journey of self-discovery, respecting their right to self-determination, and using their preferred name and pronouns. It means carefully and consciously protecting them from bullying, allowing them to use a bathroom and locker room that reflects their identity, encouraging them to attend prom with the person they choose, inviting them to read books by authors with similar backgrounds and experiences, offering inclusive curricula and supporting diverse alliances, programs, and events. Social workers can be instrumental in school systems on many different levels in many different roles engaging, assessing, intervening, and evaluating to insure LGBTQIA young people have these rights and the social justice they deserve.

Establishing Supportive School Environments for LGBTQIA Young People

Safety

Safety and education are basic human rights. School environments need to be safe and welcoming for all students. Too often, that is not the case for

LGBTQIA young people. Social workers must recognize these human rights and advocate for them at the individual and system levels (CSWE, 2015). Social workers also engage diversity and difference in practice and seek understanding about how oppression and marginalization impact and shape people's life experiences (CSWE, 2015). Social workers have opportunities in various roles within school systems to provide individual support to LGBTQIA youth, facilitate small groups, initiate awareness programs, intervene in bullying incidents, educate others, collaborate in team meetings, and advocate for school policy changes. Supportive school personnel are extremely valuable in helping to make school a safer place for LGBTQIA youth (Marshall, Yarber, Sherwood-Laughlin, Gray, & Estell, 2015).

Social workers can recommend intentional planning to insure that all school spaces are safe, including bathrooms, locker rooms, hallways, cafeterias, gyms, stadiums, outside areas, and buses. They can evaluate school facilities and events to promote welcoming and safe environments. Social workers can advocate for inclusion at homecoming dances and proms when LGBTQIA youth want to bring a date of the same sex. Field trips, especially overnight ones, can be terrifying times for young people who do not feel safe. Social workers can include LGBTQIA youth as integral voices in discussions and planning, as these youth know their situations best.

Social workers should also be mindful of students' larger environments and look at safety issues from a broader perspective, including a student's home life and community. Drawing an ecomap with a LGBTQIA student is a way to visualize how their supports and stressors constellate and social workers can use this tool to identify absent systems and needs. Available resources should be identified, compiled, and made readily available to students, who may face expulsion from their homes as a result of coming out. Hotlines and online resources are valuable for students who want to seek support but maintain anonymity.

Support

While it is critical to address incidents as they happen in schools, it is equally important to be proactive in fostering an environment that embraces diversity and welcomes difference, which benefits LGBTQIA students as well as other vulnerable student groups. If systemic change does not occur, the roots of oppression are not dug up, and structurally supported inequality continues (Payne & Smith, 2013). Social workers can play a vital role in assessing school climates by engaging LGBTQIA students and learning about their experiences and needs. Interventions can be implemented based on those meetings and should include support groups and alliances, which build community and are especially important for young people who do not have family support (Craig, Austin, & McInroy, 2014).

LGBTQIA youth identify having LGBTQIA school personnel to serve as role models and mentors as important to their well-being (Sadowski, Chow,

& Scanlon, 2009); therefore, social workers should serve as allies to those adults who are willing to be out at school and advocate for employment protections based on sexual orientation and gender identity. Affirming and supportive school personnel also make it more likely that youth will report homophobic or **transphobic** incidents rather than suffer them in silence (Moe, Bacon, & Leggett, 2015).

Social workers should intentionally build their own cultural awareness so they can take the lead on providing training for school staff around risk factors for LGBTQIA youth and the importance of protective factors, like diverse representation and inclusive curricula (Graff & Stufft, 2011). Information can also be made readily available by creating a handbook that openly addresses LGBTQIA issues and implements supportive school-related policies, like using respectful terminology, eliminating stereotypes, honoring preferred name and pronoun of students, and intervening immediately when discriminatory incidents occur. Supportive adults who are willing to provide safe spaces should be identified and available to engage LGBTQIA youth, which has shown to have a positive effect on students' school engagement (Seelman, Forge, Walls, & Bridges, 2015).

Social workers should also seek out effective models of inclusion, like restorative justice practices, which "engender respect for others" and "lead to greater social responsibility among students, ultimately reducing the amount of hurt and harm inside and outside the school community" (Miller & Endo, 2012, p. 37). Peer relationships are a significant part of young people's school experiences, particularly during adolescence. Supportive friends, even a single friend, have been identified as a vital source of social support and an important protective factor for LGBTQIA youth in school settings (Roe, 2015). These relationships become even more critical when young people have difficulty accessing support from their parents (Needham & Austin, 2010).

Respect for Privacy

LGBTQIA young people need to be protected and connected but they also deserve to be respected. Their identities should not be diminished due to their age or disclosed without their permission. When they have the courage to speak up about their preferred name and pronouns, those should be used at school. Many LGBTQIA adults struggle to be out so when youth self-identify as part of a vulnerable group, it should be recognized and treated as an act of courage. They may not be ready to come out to everyone, but if they choose to trust someone with their identity and story, a respectful response can significantly affect how they choose to proceed. Supporting them in that process should be an honor to a social worker but navigated carefully so the young person is not outed to anyone else, including their parents, before they are ready. They are the ones who will deal with any repercussions, so they must be prepared to take that step rather than prematurely forced into it. If they have not experienced respect in the past, they may feel understandably reluctant to trust someone again.

Conclusion

It is easy to make assumptions based on appearances and prior experiences. The pervasiveness of heteronormativity leaves us all prey to unconscious bias. Critical self-reflection and self-awareness are important practice tools for all social workers in working with diverse populations (CSWE, 2015).

Box 6.4 Case: Karen (b)

Karen is terrified of worms and snakes and anything that slithers. Her sister seeks them out. Karen loves skirts and dresses and bows. Her sister is most comfortable in jeans, shorts, and t-shirts. Karen enjoys reading books and playing with dolls. Her sister is very active and makes all sports look easy. Karen's Christmas wish list includes a dollhouse. Her sister's wish list includes a John Deere tractor. Karen is in the house canning with her aunts while her sister is in the barn gutting a pig with her uncles. Karen's favorite chore is doing the laundry. Her sister's favorite chore is mowing the lawn. Karen cries when a mouse gets caught in a trap. Her sister likes to shoot at squirrels. Karen grew up and married a woman; her sister grew up and married a man.

I turn to my own story again to illustrate another important takeaway. Were you surprised by the last sentence in Box 6.4? Why? What in the case example made you think there might be a different ending? I surprised quite a few people when I came out, and had my sexual orientation openly questioned because I was too girly to be a lesbian. Think for a moment about all the ways in which that is problematic and reinforcing of misinformed assumptions and stereotypes. In my life, those expectations created walls to a closet I was unsure I could escape.

Young people need the freedom and support to embrace their emerging identities without the crippling effects of stereotypes and discrimination. LGBTQIA young people are not the only youth who will benefit from increased openness and inclusion in school settings. Oppression and marginalization as the result of one's identity can be deadly. Social workers committed to the dignity and worth of all people work towards social justice by creating safe spaces for those at the margins while simultaneously working to expand those margins so all can be included within. There is no place that is more imperative than in our educational settings.

Questions to Consider

1   A seventh grade student in a public middle school tells you as the social worker that she is a lesbian. How might you respond to this student?

2   What is the role and function of the school social worker in an academic environment to support LGBTQIA students?

3   What bullying prevention strategies does your local school district utilize? Are these strategies effective? Are there evidence-based strategies for bullying prevention that might work better? As a social worker, how might you raise awareness of ways to decrease bullying and its effects on LGBTQIA children with teachers, students, parents, principals, administrators, and school board members?

4   Consider one of the teens listed in this chapter who died by suicide. Read what you can about their story through an online search, and imagine how things might have turned out differently. In identifying their challenges, including their experiences at school, what would you do now to support a student in a similar situation? How can you implement strategies to identify risks and protective factors for LGBTQIA students?

5   Michaela is in second grade and refuses to answer to the name Michaela, preferring the name Michael. He also refers to himself using male pronouns and corrects his teacher when she continues to use female ones. The teacher scheduled him on the agenda of the next student study meeting to address his "disruptive" behaviors. What should you do as a social worker before, during, and after this meeting?

6   Reflect on your own personal experience growing up. What messages did you receive about sexual orientation and gender? What were your own experiences of bullying? How can your experience help and/or hinder your work with LGBTQIA young people?

Selected Resources

Websites

The following websites provide excellent resources for social workers and their clients:

The Gay Lesbian & Straight Education Network (GLSEN) www.glsen.org/ is a leading national education organization that began in 1990 when a concerned group of teachers in Massachusetts came together to improve an education system for its LGBTQIA students. GLSEN's current goal is:

> every student, in every school, to be valued and treated with respect, regardless of their sexual orientation, gender identity or gender expression. We believe that all students deserve a safe and affirming school environment where they can learn and grow.

The Gay-Straight Alliance Network (GSA Network) http://gsanetwork.org/ is a next-generation LGBTQIA racial and gender justice

organization that empowers and trains queer, trans and allied youth leaders to advocate, organize, and mobilize an intersectional movement for
safer schools and healthier communities.

Human Rights Campaign https://hrc.org/resources/topic/children-youth

Welcoming Schools www.welcomingschools.org/, a Project of the Human
Rights Campaign Foundation, offers concrete steps that schools can take to
demonstrate their commitment to LGBT inclusiveness so that all students
and families are fully welcome.

The California Safe Schools Coalition www.casafeschools.org/ is a CA
state-based organization but their website offers many valuable resources
including their Safe Schools Resource Guide.

Parents, Families and Friends of Lesbians and Gays (PFLAG)
http://community.pflag.org/ is a grassroots organization founded in
1972 with the simple act of a mother publicly supporting her gay son.
With over 400 chapters located throughout all 50 states, "PFLAG is
committed to advancing equality and full societal affirmation of
LGBTQIA people through its threefold mission of support, education,
and advocacy."

The Trevor Project www.thetrevorproject.org/ "provides crisis intervention and suicide prevention for LGBT youth," including a 24/7 hotline
at 866-488-7386.

Trans Student Educational Resources (TSER) www.transstudent.org/ is:

> a youth-led organization dedicated to transforming the educational
> environment for trans and gender nonconforming students through
> advocacy and empowerment. In addition to our focus on creating a
> more trans-friendly education system, our mission is to educate the
> public and teach trans activists how to be effective organizers. We
> believe that justice for trans and gender nonconforming youth is con-
> tingent on an intersectional framework of activism.

The It Gets Better Project www.itgetsbetter.org/ communicates to lesbian,
gay, bisexual, and transgender youth around the world that "it gets better"
by providing gay adults and mentors who share words of encouragement
with them.

Films

The following films provide poignant portrayals of the experiences of
LGBTQIA youth:

Growing Up Trans (2015) www.pbs.org/wgbh/frontline/film/growing-up
-trans/ takes an intimate and eye-opening journey inside the struggles
and choices facing transgender kids and their families. This clip of Ariel's
story, www.youtube.com/watch?v=io6SfkqUGBo, can be used in

practice classes to portray the profound impact of showing a person dignity and respect by honoring their choice of a name.

Matt Shepard is a Friend of Mine (2014) http://mattshepardisafriendofmine.com/ provides a compassionate and compelling look into the life of the gay freshman who was murdered in October 1998. It is a great catalyst for conversation in the classroom about social justice, sexual violence, hate crimes, and the importance of equality. Be sure to click on the tab for educators on the website. While progress has been made since 1998, LGBTQIA inequality and hate crimes are still a reality today and parts of Matt's story remain true for other young people. This film reminds us of the importance of their safety.

Tomboy (2011) is a French film about a 10-year-old transgender child (identified and named as a female at birth), who, after moving with his family to a new neighbourhood, introduces himself to his new friends as the boy he sees himself to be.

Bullied (2010) www.tolerance.org/kit/bullied-student-school-and-case-made-history is "a documentary film that chronicles one student's ordeal at the hands of anti-gay bullies and offers an inspiring message of hope to those fighting harassment today. It can become a cornerstone of anti-bullying efforts in middle and high schools." The website offers excellent resources to be used alongside the film.

Creating Gender Inclusive Schools (2010) http://youthandgendermediaproject.org/films/ chronicles what happens when a public elementary school in Oakland, CA, goes through gender training. It demonstrates the power of an open and honest conversation about gender and provides many excellent resources for other schools to follow suit.

I'm Just Anneke (2010) http://youthandgendermediaproject.org/films/ is a film about 12-year-old Anneke, who is determined to be her true self whether that is a girl, a boy, or something in-between. Even though she's been rejected by her friends and struggles with depression and suicidal thoughts, she's decided to maintain a fluid gender identity – she wants to make sure her insides matches her outsides but isn't sure she fits into a binary conception of gender. Additional resources are offered through the website.

The Family Journey: Raising Gender Nonconforming Children (2010) http://youthandgendermediaproject.org/films/ captures through frank, vulnerable interviews with families how critical loving and accepting a gender nonconforming child is in the face of ignorance and outright hostility. Additional resources are offered through the website.

It's Elementary (1996) http://groundspark.org/our-films-and-campaigns/elementary and *It's Still Elementary* (2007) www.newdaydigital.com/It-s-Still-Elementary.html are companion films about gay issues in schools. *It's Still Elementary* tells the fascinating history of why and how *It's Elementary* was made, the response it provoked from the conservative right, and the questions it raises about the national safe schools movement today.

The Truth About Jane (2000) www.mylifetime.com/movies/the-truth-about-jane is a coming out story of a high school girl's first sexual experience with another girl and the ensuing ostracism at school as well as family difficulties at home.

Out of the Past (1998). In 1995, Kelli Peterson started a gay and straight club at her Salt Lake City high school. The story of her ensuing battle with school authorities is interspersed with looks back at historic events, including the 30-year love affair of Sarah Orne Jewett and Annie Adams Fields, Henry Gerber's attempt after World War I to establish a gay-rights organization, Bayard Rustin's role in the civil rights movement, and Barbara Gittings' taking on of the American Psychiatric Association's position that homosexuality is illness.

Books

The following books are wonderful resources as they provide diverse experiences of LGBTQIA youth:

Redefining Realness by Janet Mock (2014) – In her memoir, Janet shares her truth and personal history as a trans woman, including her transition during high school. She discusses intersectionality and how it plays out in her story. She also has a website for further information – http://janetmock.com/.

Some Assembly Required by Arin Andrews (2015) – In his memoir, Arin shares his story of transitioning during high school.

Rethinking Normal: A Memoir in Transition by Katie Rain Hill (2015) – In her memoir, Katie shares her personal story of transition.

Prairie Silence by Melanie Hoffert (2014) – Melanie Hoffert's memoir offers a glimpse into her internal struggle for self-acceptance and the courage it took to return home.

Being Jazz by Jazz Jennings (2016) – Jazz is a young advocate for transgender equality as she chronicles her own journey.

Beyond Magenta: Transgender Teens Speak Out by Susan Kuklin (2015) – Susan Kuklin's book is a compilation of her interviews with six transgender or gender-neutral young adults, including photographs and images portraying the emotional and physical journey each young person has taken.

Torn by Justin Lee (2012) – Justin Lee shares his personal journey of coming out and struggling to align his sexual orientation with his Christian upbringing. He is the founder and executive director of The Gay Christian Network (GCN), www.gaychristian.net/, a nonprofit interdenominational support organization.

Becoming Nicole: The Transformation of an American Family by Amy Ellis Nutt (2016) – Drawing from personal diaries, home videos, clinical journals, legal documents, medical records, and interviews with family members, Amy Ellis Nutt provides an extensive account of an American family raising and loving a child, who felt at odds with society's conventions and norms. There is significant information about the family's experience navigating the school environment for Nicole.

Oddly Normal: One Family's Struggle to Help Their Teenage Son Come to Terms with His Sexuality by John Schwartz (2013) – John Schwartz writes of his son's struggle with identity, which included a suicide attempt one day after school. The book offers critical lessons in helping gay kids in their coming out process.

Raising Ryland by Hillary Whittington (2015) – Ryland's mother, Hillary Whittington, writes about her experiences as the parent of a transgender child. A related YouTube video is at www.youtube.com/watch?v=yAHCqnux2fk

Beyond Progress and Marginalization: LGBTQ Youth in Educational Contexts edited by Corrine C. Bertram, M. Sue Crowley, & Sean G. Massey (2010) – This book highlights the stories of LGBTQ youth in their own words as they explore how oppression and opportunity interact to influence their identities.

LGBTQ Youth Issues: A Practical Guide for Youth Workers, Serving Lesbian, Gay, Bisexual, Transgender, and Questioning Youth by Gerald P. Mallon (2010) – This practical book provides a combination of personal stories, proven research, and practical tips to guide those who work with LGBTQIA youth.

Gay, Lesbian, and Transgender Issues in Education: Programs, Policies, and Practices edited by James T. Sears (2005) – The essays in this book offer many firsthand accounts of the struggles LGBTQIA youth face as they seek their education. Strategies for improving educational systems are also offered.

References

Abbott, K., Ellis, S., & Abbott, R. (2015). "We don't get into all that": An analysis of how teachers uphold heteronormative sex and relationship education. *Journal of Homosexuality*, 62(12), 1638–1659.

Ahuja, A., Webster, C., Gibson, N., Brewer, A., Toledo, S., & Russell, S. (2015). Bullying and suicide: The mental health crisis of LGBTQ youth and how you can help . *Journal of Gay & Lesbian Mental Health*, 19(2), 125–144, DOI: doi:10.1080/19359705.2015.100741

Aragon, S. R., Poteat, V. P., Espelage, D. L., & Koenig, B. W. (2014). The influence of peer victimization on educational outcomes for LGBTQ and non-LGBTQ high school students. *Journal of LGBT Youth*, 11(1), 1–19, DOI: doi:10.1080/19361653.2014.840761

Council on Social Work Education (CSWE). (2015). Educational policy and accreditation standards. Retrieved from www.cswe.org/File.Aspx?id=81660.

Craig, S. L., Austin, A., & McInroy, L. B. (2014). School-based groups to support multiethnic sexual minority youth resiliency: Preliminary effectiveness. *Child and Adolescent Social Work Journal*, 31(1), 87–106.

Duke, T. S. (2010). Working with LGBTQ youth with disabilities: How special educators can reconceptualize CEC standards. In C. C. Bertram, M. S. Crowley, & S. G. Massey (Eds.), *Beyond progress and marginalization: LGBTQ youth in educational contexts* (pp. 149–173). New York: Peter Lang Publishing.

Elia, J. P., & Tokunaga, J. (2015). Sexuality education: implications for health, equity, and social justice in the United States. *Health Education*, 115(1), 105–120.

Endo, H., Reece-Miller, P. C., & Santavicca, N. (2010). Surviving in the trenches: A narrative inquiry into queer teachers' experiences and identity. *Teaching and Teacher Education*, 26, 1023–1030.

Espelage, D. L., Rao, M. A., & De La Rue, L. (2013). Current research on school-based bullying: A social-ecological perspective. *Journal of Social Distress and the Homeless*, 22(1), 7–21. doi:doi:10.1179/1053078913Z.0000000002

Flores, G. (2014). Teachers working cooperatively with parents and caregivers when implementing LGBT themes in the elementary classroom. *American Journal of Sexuality Education*, 9, 114–120.

Fredman, A. J., Schultz, N. J., & Hoffman, M. F. (2015). "You're moving a frickin' big ship": The challenges of addressing LGBTQ topics in public schools. *Education and Urban Society*, 47(1), 56–85.

Gay, Lesbian & Straight Education Network (GLSEN). (2014). The 2013 National School Climate Survey. Retrieved from www.glsen.org/article/2013-national-school-climate-survey.

Gowen, L. K., & Winges-Yanez, N. (2014). Lesbian, gay, bisexual, transgender, queer, and questioning youths' perspectives of inclusive school-based sexuality education. *Journal of Sex Research*, 51(7), 788–800.

Graff, C., & Stufft, D. (2011). Increasing visibility for LGBTQ students: What schools can do to create inclusive classroom communities. *Current Issues in Education*, 14(1).

Hardie, A. (2012). Lesbian teachers and students: Issues and dilemmas of being "out" in primary school. *Sex Education*, 12, 273–282.

Horn, S. S., Konkol, P., McInerney, K., Meiners, E. R., North, C., Nunez, I., Quinn, T., & Sullivan, S. (2010). Visibility matters: Policy work as activism in teacher education. *Issues in Teacher Education*, 19(2), 65–80.

Imber, M. (2005). What I would have liked my teachers to know. In J. T. Sears (Ed.), *Gay, lesbian, and transgender issues in education: Programs, policies, and practices* (pp. 9–12). New York: Harrington Park Press.

Jamil, O. B., & Harper, G. W. (2010). School for the self: Examining the role of educational settings in identity development among gay, bisexual, and questioning male youth of color. In C. C. Bertram, M. S. Crowley, & S. G. Massey (Eds.), *Beyond progress and marginalization: LGBTQ youth in educational contexts* (pp. 175–201). New York: Peter Lang Publishing.

Marshall, A., Yarber, W. L., Sherwood-Laughlin, C. M., Gray, M. L., & Estell, D. B. (2015). Coping and survival skills: The role school personnel play regarding support for bullied sexual minority-oriented youth. *Journal of School Health*, 85(5), 334–340.

Miller, P. C., & Endo, H. (2012). Restorative justice: A model for meeting the needs of LGBTQ youth. In A. Honigsfeld & A. Cohan (Eds.), *Breaking the mold of education for culturally and linguistically diverse students* (pp. 31–38). Lanham, MD: Rowman & Littlefield Education.

Moe, J., Bacon, K., & Leggett, E. (2015). School counselors as allies: The relationship between sexual orientation competence and open and affirming service for LGBTQ youth. *Journal of LGBT Issues in Counseling*, 9(2), 74–91.

National Association of Social Workers (NASW). (2008). Code of Ethics (Guide to the Everyday Professional Conduct of Social Workers). Washington, DC: NASW.

Needham, B. L., & Austin, E. L. (2010). Sexual orientation, parental support, and health during the transition to young adulthood. *Journal of Youth and Adolescence*, 39, 1189–1198.

Padilla, Y. C., Crisp, C., & Rew, D. L. (2010). Parental acceptance and illegal drug use among gay, lesbian, and bisexual adolescents. *Social Work*, 55(3), 265–275.

Payne, E., & Smith, M. (2013). LGBTQ kids, school safety, and missing the big picture: How the dominant bullying discourse prevents school professionals from thinking about systemic marginalization or... Why we need to rethink LGBTQ bullying. *QED: A Journal in GLBTQ Worldmaking*, 1, 1–36.

Rich, A. (1984). Invisibility in academe. In *Blood, bread, and poetry: Selected prose 1979–1985*. (pp. 198–201). New York: W.W. Norton & Company.

Robinson, J. P., & Espelage, D. L. (2011). Inequities in educational and psychological outcomes between LGBTQ and straight students in middle and high school. *Educational Researcher*, 40(7), 315–330. doi:doi:10.3102/0013189X11422112

Roe, S. L. (2015). Examining the role of peer relationships in the lives of gay and bisexual adolescents. *Children & Schools*, 37(2), 117–124.

Russell, S. T., Sinclair, K. O., Poteat, V. P., & Koenig, B. W. (2012). Adolescent health and harassment based on discriminatory bias. *American Journal of Public Health*, 102, 493–495. doi:doi:10.2105/AJPH.2011.30043

Russell, V. T. (2010). Queer teachers' ethical dilemmas regarding queer youth. *Teaching Education*, 21, 143–156.

Sadowski, M., Chow, S., & Scanlon, C. P. (2009). Meeting the needs of LGBTQ youth: A "relational assets" approach. *Journal of LGBT Youth*, 6(2–3), 174–198.

Seelman, K. L., Forge, N., Walls, N. E., & Bridges, N. (2015). School engagement among LGBTQ high school students: The roles of safe adults and gay–straight alliance characteristics. *Children and Youth Services Review*, 57, 19–29.

Shpigel, M. S., Belsky, Y., & Diamond, G. M. (2015). Clinical work with non-accepting parents of sexual minority children: Addressing causal and controllability attributions. *Professional Psychology: Research and Practice*, 46(1), 46–54.

Smith, M. J. (2015). It's a balancing act: The good teacher and ally identity. *Educational Studies*, 51(3), 223–243.

Snapp, S. D., Burdge, H., Licona, A. C., Moody, R. L., & Russell, S. T. (2015). Students' perspectives on LGBTQ-inclusive curriculum. *Equity & Excellence in Education*, 48(2), 249–265.

Snapp, S. D., Hoenig, J. M., Fields, A., & Russell, S. T. (2015). Messy, butch, and queer: LGBTQ youth and the school-to-prison pipeline. *Journal of Adolescent Research*, 30(1), 57–82, DOI: doi:10.1177/0743558414557625

Snapp, S. D., McGuire, J. K., Sinclair, K. O., Gabrion, K.,& Russell, S. T. (2015). LGBTQ-inclusive curricula: why supportive curricula matter. *Sex Education*, 15(6), 580–596.

Wernick, L. J., Kulick, A., & Inglehart, M. H. (2013). Factors predicting student intervention when witnessing anti-LGBTQ harassment: The influence of peers, teachers, and climate. *Children and Youth Services Review*, 35, 296–301.

7 Race, Ethnicity, Sexual Orientation, and Gender Identity[1]

Intersectionality in the Lives of LGBTQIA People of Color

Terrence O. Lewis

PH.D., MSW, BASW, LICSW

CSWE 2015 EPAS Competencies

Competence 1: Demonstrate ethical and professional behavior

Competency 2: Engage diversity and difference in practice

Competency 3: Advance human rights and social, economic, and environmental justice

Competency 6: Engage with individuals, families, groups, organizations, and communities

Competency 7: Assess individuals, families, groups, organizations, and communities

Competency 8: Intervene with individuals, families, groups, organizations, and communities

Introduction

Despite significant socio-political signs of progress on LGBTQIA rights in the United States, heterosexism, homophobia, and transphobia remain strong social forces that produce significant discriminatory experiences for LGBTQIA individuals and their families. For LGBTQIA individuals of color, **racism** and ethnocentrism compound the challenges of having a non-heteronormative identity. For example, to be African American and gay in the U.S. is to live at the intersections of two stigmatized identities (Lewis, 2015; Griffin, 2006). When considering **sexism** and misogyny, the challenges triple in their potential oppressive power. A Mexican-American lesbian may navigate three marginalized identities of race, gender, and sexual orientation. LGBTQIA individuals of color live within this complex reality of multiple marginalized identities. This type of life can have devastating effects on biological, psychological, social, and spiritual well-being (Lewis, 2015; Fullilove, 2006). This chapter will explore the intersectional realities of race/ethnicity, sexual orientation, and gender identity for LGBTQIA individuals of color.

The chapter will cover the current research-based knowledge about LGBTQIA individuals of color; the social work values, ethics, and skills for culturally sensitive practice with this population; and community resources for client support and empowerment. By the end of this chapter, students will be able to:

- Describe the basic tenets of **Stigmatization Theory, Minority Stress Theory**, and **Intersectionality**
- Describe the basic types of LGBTQIA stigmatization: **homophobia, heterosexism, bi-phobia**, and **transphobia**
- Identify potential effects of multiple types of stigmatizations on the biological, psychological, and social well-being of LGBTQIA individuals of color
- Identify the social work values and ethics that promote affirmative and competent practice with LGBTQIA populations
- Identify and apply the basic knowledge and skills that are necessary for culturally sensitive practice with LGBTQIA individuals and families within communities of color.

Theoretical Foundations

Competent social work practice must be rooted in a sound theoretical framework. When working with marginalized populations, such as LGBTQIA persons of color, the theoretical framework should include theories about stigmatization, the impact of social minority status on bio-psychosocial health, and the multidimensional challenges of life at the intersections of multiple marginalized identities. In this section, we will review the basic tenets of Stigmatization Theory, Minority Stress Theory, and Intersectionality. These three theories provide a framework for understanding the impact of living with multiple marginalized identities.

Stigmatization Theory

According to Goffman (1963), stigma is a trait that engenders social disregard, discredit, and shame. The stigma is not innate to the stigmatized person; rather, it is bestowed upon them by others who view themselves as "normal" or those in society who meet or effectively pass as meeting the standards of normalcy. They are the architects and/or overseers of these standards (Goffman, 1963). The process of stigmatization is an essential framework for identity formation in relation to peer groups, societal norms, identification of social deviance, and the consequences of deviations to personal and social identity. A central aspect of stigmatization is the intersectionality of power, knowledge, and culturally bound values and norms (Goffman, 1963; Foucault, 1990). According to Goffman (1963), there are three primary types of stigma:

Abominations of the body: Related to socially identified physical deformities;
Blemishes of individual character: Character traits perceived as signs of
moral weakness, unnatural desires, dangerous beliefs, dishonesty, and
treachery. This type of stigma can be a response to a history of mental
health problems, legal problems, addictions, non-heterosexual orientations, non-binary gender identities and expressions, and revolutionary
political ideologies;
Tribal stigma: Based on racial, ethnic, national, and/or religious identities,
these stigma can be transmitted through lineages and equally contaminate all
members of a family.

From this theoretical perspective, dominant or "normal" society attributes
multiple stigmatizing characteristics to LGBTQIA persons of color. The
history of racism in the U.S. (Miller & Garran, 2008) depicts the combination of tribal, abomination, and blemish stigma in the social narratives about
the inferiority of non-White individuals. Sexism and misogyny are born
from a similar combination to justify arguments that women are inferior and
should be governed by men. Individuals who identify as non-heterosexual
are often labeled as abominations with poor moral character. People who
identify as transgender often endure similar dehumanizing and marginalizing
labels (Hill, 2005). Garfinkel (1956) cautioned against the destructive power
of stigmatization. He argued that a *paradigm of moral indignation* fueled stigmatization and systematic degradation of person deemed to be deviant.
Once a stigmatized person is viewed as less than human, they become a
potential threat to humanity and normal society. When faced with such a
threat, the oppressor may justify any means necessary to eliminate the stigmatized person, from restricting their basic human rights to genocidal levels
of violence (Garfinkel, 1956; Miller & Garran, 2008).

Minority Stress Theory

Minority Stress Theory (MST) is rooted in years of sociological and psychological research regarding identity development, social stigma, and the
impact of stress on the bio-psychosocial functioning of individuals living
with a stigmatized identity. According to MST core assumptions, minority
stress is:

1   Unique…[and] in that stigmatized individuals experience higher levels
    of psychosocial stress than non-stigmatized individual because of the
    stigmatized identity;
2   Chronic…related to 'relatively stable and underlying societal and cul-
    tural structures'
3   Socially based…not inherently rooted in characteristics, traits, or heritage
    of the stigmatized individual; based on public beliefs, social processes and
    institutionalized structures. (Meyer, 2003, p. 676)

Minority stress is born out of interpersonal dynamics, environmental forces, and institutionalized structures that promote the marginalization of some groups and the privileging of others. Meyer (2003) proposes a *distal stressors–proximal processes* continuum of minority stress processes that LGBTQIA individuals experience. Distal stressors are objectively offensive actions or situations. They may include direct acts of stigmatization such as verbal insults, physical assaults, or denial of legal rights due to LGBTQIA identity.

Unlike distal stressors, proximal processes develop from the subjective interpretation of stressful social actions and situations by a stigmatized individual (Meyer, 2003). Instead of assuming that minority stressors affect every stigmatized person equally, MST recognizes the mediating factors of self-identity, self-acceptance, relational supports, group solidarity, and a supportive environment. Consistent with the strengths perspectives, MST acknowledges the ameliorating impact of health copings, resiliency, and social resources (Meyer, 2003; Alessi, 2014).

When applying MST to social work practice with LGBTQIA populations, it is important to consider the four factors that may influence an LGBTQIA individual's mental, emotional, behavioral and social functioning. These factors include: a) stigmatizing events (both chronic and acute); b) the vigilant anticipation and preparation for minority stress events and situation; c) the internalization of the oppressors' attitudes by the oppressed; and d) the hiding or social denial of non-heterosexual sexual orientation (Alessi, 2014; Meyer, 2003). It is a natural human instinct to protect oneself from potentially threatening situations. Homophobia, heterosexism, and transphobia can pose subtle and overt threats to the well-being of LGBTQIA individuals and their families. For an LGBTQIA person of color, these threats are exponentially amplified by the pain of racism and ethnocentrism. LGBTQIA persons of color live within the intersections of dual and triple marginalized identities. Competent social work practice with this population must include cultural awareness and responsiveness to the intersectionality of oppressions.

Intersectionality

Power (social, political, and economic) is inextricably linked to the process of knowledge production. The creation, legitimation, and dissemination of knowledge are essential components of social reality (Berger & Luckman, 1966; Freire, 2014). By controlling the process of knowledge production, oppressors promote the unequal distribution of resources and the privileging of dominant groups' identities, values, belief systems, and cultural perspectives (Freire, 2014). The privileging of one group requires the subjugation of another (Adams, Blumenfeld, Castañeda, Hackman, Peters, & Zúñiga, 2010; Miller & Garran, 2008). Intersectionality emerged as a revolutionary counterpoint to the traditional sources of power and knowledge. As one of the most marginalized groups in the U.S., women of color pushed back on the socio-political structures and social narratives that systematically silenced the voices of historically marginalized groups including women, persons of color, immigrants, and sexual minorities. Intersectionality is both an "analytic strategy" and a source of knowledge production (Dill & Zambrana, 2013, p. 142). As an analytic strategy, intersectionality seeks to deconstruct critically the micro, mezzo, and macro social structures that justify privileged identities, the unequal distribution of resources, and the subjugation of non-white, non-male, and non-heterosexual individuals. As a source of knowledge production, intersectionality helps society to construct multidimensional understandings of the lived experiences of all human beings, the complex systems of power and oppression, the consequences of those systems, and the guidelines for their deconstruction. Intersectionality unapologetically promotes a paradigm shift towards the reconstruction of society as more inclusive and human rights oriented.

As a theoretical framework for social work practice, intersectionality requires that social workers challenge each dimension of oppressive power and foster the creation of a society rooted in multi-cultural knowledge, wisdom, and values. According to intersectionality scholars, there are four domains of power: structural, disciplinary, hegemonic, and interpersonal. The structural domain includes the institutions and systems for "reproducing subordination over time" (Dill & Zambrana, 2013, p. 145). Disciplinary domain consists of the bureaucratic processes that maintain and protect the institutions and systems of power. The hegemonic domain shapes social consciousness through "images, symbols, ideas, and ideologies" that support the status quo systems of power as justifiable (p. 145). This domain creates the social narratives that normalize oppression. The interpersonal domain operates within the everyday relational interactions that promote oppressive narratives as an unchanging reality. The oppressive narratives manifest in verbal and behavioral micro-aggressions (Nadal, Issa, Leon, Meterko, Wideman, & Wong, 2011) that reinforce the dehumanizing and discriminatory forms of power. By using these four domains in intersectional analysis, social workers can construct a dynamic and substantive picture of the oppressive social realities that perpetuate stigmatization and discrimination of LGBTQIA persons of color.

Stigmatization Theory, Minority Stress Theory, and Intersectionality provide a strong foundation for assessing the lived experiences of LGBTQIA persons of color. With this theoretical foundation, social workers can develop multi-culturally based forms of knowledge, professional values, and practice skills. In addition to these three theories, scholars from these marginalized communities have developed other theories and perspectives to voice the unique narratives of specific communities. Readers are encouraged to learn the following theories and perspectives: Critical Race Theory, Latino/a Critical Theory, and Queer Theory (Kiehne, 2016; Miller & Garran, 2008).

Racial and Ethnic Identity Development

When discussing the lived experiences of LGBTQIA persons of color, it is important to consider the impact of stigmatization on their identity development process. Identity development is a complex series of events across the lifespan that shape a person's sense of self, their social identities in their family and local community, and their relationships with the larger world (Goffman, 1963; Miller & Garran, 2008). Several scholars have developed models of identity development about LGBTQIA individuals and people of color. Most racial and ethnic identity development theories (henceforth referred to as REIDT) propose that individuals experience transformative stages of identity development. The common themes across the REIDT models depict an intensive intra and interpersonal journey of self-discovery within the larger socio-political contexts of racism and ethnocentrism:

- Pre-awareness of difference
- Exposure to difference and initiation of self-exploration
- In-depth exploration, immersion, and challenging of relationships in pursuit of new or modified identity and sense of belonging
- Introspection and reflection in pursuit of a mature, integrated, and adaptive identity
- Internalization of a mature and adaptive identity with positive coping skills for navigating dominant cultures; and fighting racism, ethnocentrism, and other forms of oppression.

(Miller & Garran, 2008; Phinney & Kohatsu, 1999)

While REIDT models provide some helpful knowledge about the identity process for persons of color, most of the models have significant limitations. They often minimize or negate the realities of multi-ethnic and multi-racial identities, the intersectionality with diverse sexual orientations and gender identities, the intergenerational impact of oppression, and the multi-dimensional factors of socialization (Sisneros, Stakeman, Joyner & Schmidt, 2008; Miller & Garran, 2008). Based on these critiques, we recommend that social workers use REIDT models with caution and as one tool in a multi-dimensional assessment process.

LGBTQIA Identity Development

When discussing the identity development of LGBTQIA individuals, it is important to have a foundational understanding of the theories that attempt to explain the lived experiences of members in this heterogeneous community. There are several theories regarding LGBTQIA identity development. The Cass Model (Cass, 1984) is one of the most researched models for lesbian and gay identity development. In this model, there are six phases:

- Identity confusion
- Identity comparison
- Identity tolerance
- Identity acceptance
- Identity pride
- Identity synthesis (Cass, 1984)

In addition to this model, there are other models including the Coleman Model, the Minton and McDonald Model, and the Troiden model. While these models provide a framework of understanding the developmental processes of individuals that identify as gay and lesbian, some LGBTQIA scholars argue that the lived experiences of persons who identify as bisexual and/or transgender are distinctly different and not represented in these models (Hill, 2005). In response to these critiques, some scholars have constructed models that attempt to depict the developmental processes of these two under-represented groups within the LGBTQIA community. After a critical review of the existing research, Brown (2002) published a modified version of Weinberg, Williams and Pryor's Bisexual Identity Development model which includes the following stages:

- Initial confusion
- Finding and applying the label
- Settling into the identity
- Identity maintenance

Regarding transgender identity development, the Lev (2006) Model of Transgender Emergence is one of the most researched models. The six stages of this model include:

- Awareness
- Seeking information
- Disclosure to significant others
- Exploration – identity and self-labeling
- Exploration – transition
- Integration – acceptance and post transitioning. (Lev, 2006, p. 268)

To strengthen the evidence-based knowledge about LGBTQIA identity development, more research is needed, especially regarding bisexual, transgender, and intersex individuals. Social workers can play a critical role in developing this body of knowledge through rigorous community-based research with LGBTQIA clients and their families.

While this chapter provides a brief overview of REIDT and LGBTQIA developmental models, multi-culturally sensitive social work practice with LGBTQIA people of color requires a more in-depth exploration of the theories and evidence-based approaches developed by scholars and practitioners who have been committed to serving LGBTQIA individuals and their families. In the next section, the author will discuss Affirmative Social Work Practice (ASWP), a model for culturally competent practice with LGBTQIA populations.

From Theory to Practice: Affirmative Social Work

ASWP is consistent with professional standards for ethical and culturally sensitive practice (Dessel, Jacobsen, Levy, McCarty-Caplan, Lewis & Kaplan, 2017; NASW, 2015). ASWP resonates with the core tenets of Empowerment Theory, Stigmatization Theory, Minority Stress Theory, and Intersectionality. A social worker must be committed to providing the best services to clients regardless of race, ethnicity, nationality, immigration status, gender identity, sexual orientation, class status, or religious affiliation (NASW, 2015). ASWP requires a willingness to challenge beliefs and behaviors that marginalize the identities and lived realities of LGBTQIA individuals of color and their families (Alessi, 2014; Morrow & Messinger, 2006; Sue, 2006). The common tenets include:

- Developing a client–social worker relationship that is based on genuine positive regard and validation of the client's wisdom about their own life
- Consciousness-raising education and discourse with clients about their rights, sources of oppression, sources of strength, and their self-efficacy as change agents
- Increasing clients' access to knowledge, skills, and other resources for effective problem-solving on the individual, community, and societal levels
- Micro, mezzo, and macro interventions that foster social justice, human rights, and the dismantling of institutionalized forms of oppression. (Freire, 2014; Miller & Garran, 2008; Sue, 2006)

These tenets resonate with the National Association of Social Workers (NASW, 2015) ten standards for culturally sensitive practice. The standards emphasize the following aspects of social work: *ethics and values, self-awareness, cross-cultural knowledge and skills, service delivery, empowerment and advocacy, diversity of workforce, professional education, communication, and leadership* (NASW, 2015). In accordance with the NASW standards, the Council on Social Work Education (CSWE) integrated multi-cultural education standards into the core competencies that guide accredited social work degree programs in the U.S. (CSWE, 2015). While NASW and CSWE provide clear guidelines, the process of becoming a culturally sensitive social worker requires patience, persistence, and open-mindedness. Cultural sensitivity is built on the foundations of self-awareness, education, experience, and supervision. To facilitate student learning, this writer has developed a table (see Table 7.1) of cultural sensitivity standards and practice behavior

Table 7.1 Cultural Sensitivity Standards and Practice Behavior Guidelines

Cultural Competence Standard	Practice Behaviors
Ethics and Values	Intentionally learn and apply culturally relevant sources of information in ethical decision-making processes. Recognize, value, and promote diversity.
Self-awareness	Develop self-awareness about cultural identity, values, beliefs, strengths, and biases. Through supervision and reflective practice, explore and manage the influence of your identity, beliefs, and values on your practice.
Cross-cultural Knowledge	Continual development of evidence-based, culturally grounded knowledge that is relevant to the client populations that you serve.
Cross-cultural Skills	Continual development of evidenced-based culturally grounded practice skills that is relevant to the client populations that you serve.
Service Delivery	Development of culturally relevant resources and professional partnerships ensure competent community-based service for the client populations that you serve.
Empowerment and Advocacy	Collaboratively help clients to develop the knowledge, skills, and self-efficacy to act effectively as a change agent in their family and community.
Diverse Workforce	Utilize evidenced-based knowledge about Multi-cultural Organization Development to evaluate and promote the cultural diversity and cultural competency of social service agencies.
Professional Education	Promote and facilitate the hiring, training, and on-going supervisory support of a culturally sensitive social service workforce.
Language Diversity	Promote and facilitate the hiring, training, and on-going supervisory support of a multi-lingual and multi-culturally diverse social service workforce.
Cross-cultural Leadership	Promote and facilitate the hiring, training, and on-going supportive supervision of culturally sensitive leadership in the social service workforce.

(CSWE, 2015; NASW, 2015; Miller & Garran, 2008; Sue, 2006)

guidelines, based on the standards of NASW, CSWE, and scholars in multi-culturally competent social work practice.

In addition to these guidelines, LGBTQIA affirmative social work researchers and practitioners have constructed affirmative practice recommendations. They are consistent with strengths-based, collaborative social work models. While the practice literature includes some variations on the basic structure of the social work relationship, the common core phases include pre-engagement, engagement, assessment, goal setting and contracting, intervention, evaluation and termination (Kirst-Ashman & Hull, 2012; Murphy & Dillon, 2011; Poulin, 2010). Using this basic structure, social workers can integrate the LGBTQIA affirmative recommendations into their practice.

In the *pre-engagement* phase, the social worker has the primary goal of culturally sensitive preparation for initiating the client–worker relationship. When working with marginalized and stigmatized populations, this phase should include an on-going process of building self-awareness and culturally sensitive education. Regarding self-awareness, social workers can explore their beliefs, values, and knowledge about sexuality, sexual orientation, and socially conforming and non-conforming gender identities and gender expressions. Social workers should also examine their thoughts, feelings, and beliefs about family and relationships. What do you think, feel, and believe about non-heteronormative relationships and family systems, including LGBTQIA marriage and parenting and LGBTQIA youth? Social workers should also examine their self-awareness about stigma, oppression, and liberation for LGBTQIA populations.

These are just a few of the intersecting realities that shape the lives of LGBTQIA individuals and their families. Heterosexual privilege can foster overt and covert forms of bias, micro-aggressions, and discrimination. Self-awareness, on the other hand, can increase a social worker's open-mindedness, humble curiosity, non-judgmental perspectives, and genuine respect for diversity of gender identities and sexual orientations.

Culturally sensitive education is essential for ASWP. As social workers, we have many resources for formal and informal cultural education about LGBTQIA individuals, families, and communities. These resources include courses and conferences about the lived experiences, strengths, and needs of LGBTQIA populations; LGBTQIA affirmative local agencies, political organizations, and social groups; evidenced-based research journals and books about LGBTQIA affirmative social work practice; and regular supervision that fosters reflective practice, cultural sensitivity, and continuing education.

In the *engagement* phase, the social worker focuses on building rapport, establishing trust, nurturing emotional security, and initiating a working alliance. In addition to culturally sensitive self-awareness, the principles of mutual respect, genuine positive regard, cultural humility, and collaboration can inform the social worker's relationship stance. With this affirmative and culturally sensitive engagement process, the social worker and client can create a strong foundation for the assessment process.

During the *assessment* phase, the social worker conducts a multi-dimensional assessment that involves the gathering of multiple sources of data about the client's target problems for services, the bio-psychosocial and spiritual context of their life, strengths and resources. Applying the Minority

Stress Model and an ASWP model, the assessment process may include an exploration of the following dimensions of an LGBTQIA client of color's target problems, strengths, and the bio-psychosocial–spiritual context of their life:

- Minority stressors in their life as related to their multiple marginalized identities
- The impacts of the stressors on their identity, self-worth, and self-efficacy
- Their coping skills, strengths, and signs of resilience
- The client's level knowledge about sexual orientations, gender identities, and expressions
- The client's stages of development in their LGBTQIA identity, racial and ethnic identity, and their life cycle
- Levels of comfort/acceptance or discomfort/rejection of their own LGBTQIA identity
- Their familial and community beliefs, values, and behavioural responses to LGBTQIA individuals
- The client's level of openness and disclosure of their LGBTQIA identity at home, in their community (including religious affiliations and institutions), and at work.

By adding these areas of exploration, the social worker and client can develop an in-depth culturally sensitive assessment.

In the *goal setting and contracting* phases, ASWP emphasizes client-centeredness, collaboration, and empowerment. While the assessment process includes a thoughtful assessment of LGBTQIA related themes, it is important to remember that LGBTQIA clients participate in social work services for many reasons. There are LGBTQIA clients who do not want or need to focus on LGBTQIA identity and minority stress related issues (Alessi, 2014; Morrow, 2006). Social workers should foster a goal setting and contracting process that empowers the client to identify their target problems, the strengths, and the primary goals.

In ASWP, a social worker may implement *interventions* that focus on an LGBTQIA client's life narratives, identity development, self-acceptance, and empowerment to combat stigmatization and other minority stressors (Alessi, 2014; Messinger, 2006; Poulin, 2010). ASWP may be used in conjunction with other strengths-based and post-modernist treatment models. Consistent with narrative therapy, an affirmative social worker may encourage LGBTQIA clients to tell their life story, to reflect critically on major themes, to externalize and map the influence of target problems and to re-story their life narratives with increased hope and self-efficacy (Buckman & Buckman, 2016). Regarding LGBTQIA identity, an affirmative social worker may focus on the client's stages of identity development, self-acceptance, coming out processes, familial and community affirmation or stigmatization, and increasing the client's copings skills and self-acceptance (Alessi, 2014; Messinger, 2006). Consistent with empowerment theory, an affirmative social worker empowers LGBTQIA clients to re-claim their voice in their own life story, to acknowledge their equal worth and dignity, and to stand against the oppressive forces of LGBTQIA stigmatization and marginalization.

As a culturally sensitive and strengths-based approach, ASWP encourages collaborative *evaluation* and a supportive *termination* process. An affirmative social worker encourages the client's honest feedback about their working alliance, progress on goals, barriers, and next steps. The termination process may include a review of the client's journey, the strengths, new coping skills, and their plan for continued growth after termination.

A Portrait of Life as LGBTQIA Persons of Color

Black and LGBTQIA in America

There is ample documentation of the historical and current stigmatization of African Americans (Du Bois [1903] 2003, Lewis, 2015; Sherr, 2006). Using Goffman's (1963) terms, the *tribal stigma* of African ethnic heritage and the racial identification as Black have shaped the biological, psychological, social, political, economic, and spiritual functioning of the African American community in the U.S. since the beginning of the slave trade (Douglas, 2005; Miller & Garran, 2008; Raboteau, 2001). African Americans have survived slavery, the Civil War, the Reconstruction Era, Jim Crow, and the Civil Rights Movement. While there have been significant signs of progress towards equality, the painful legacy of racism permeates the U.S. in implicit and overt ways. Despite the historic eight years of President Barack Obama's administration, signs of institutionalized racism and volatile community racial tensions have increased significantly. The signs include the drastically disproportionate incarceration of African Americans, increased police brutality against unarmed African Americans, and the increased racialized rhetoric and violent acts of White supremacist (Alexander, 2011; Miller & Garran, 2008). When discussing the lived experiences of African American LGBTQIA individuals and their families, it is critical to explore the racialized reality of their lives in this nation (Miller & Garran, 2008; Sherr, 2006).

Despite the historical and current experiences of race-based trauma (Miller & Garran, 2008; Paris, 1995), the African American community has a profound history of resiliency, recovery, and capacity building. This community's resiliency is rooted in their collectivist worldview, the primacy of relational harmony, and a strong reliance on spirituality and religious institutions (Lewis, 2015; Sherr, 2006; Schieman, Pudrovska, Pearlin & Ellison, 2006; Lincoln & Mamiya, 1990). African Americans remain one of the most religious communities in the U.S. The complex cultural institution of the Historically Black Church (HBC) remains an essential touchstone and cornerstone for most African Americans. This is true for LGBTQIA and non-LGBTQIA African Americans (Bates, 2005, Lewis, 2015; Schieman et al., 2006; Sherr, 2006). The HBC has historically been both a source of strength and a stumbling block for many LGBTQIA African Americans (Griffin, 2006; Bates, 2005). While the HBC has promoted the protection and empowerment of the African American family, its message of empowerment has been based on a heterosexist and patriarchal paradigm about Black identity in America (Bates, 2005; Douglas, 2005; Griffin, 2006; Lewis, 2015). For example, to be Black and gay often requires balancing the weight of at least two stigmatized identities (Griffin, 2006; Lewis, 2015). Womanist scholars argue that a lesbian woman of color endures a triad of stigmatized identities: race, gender, and non-heterosexual orientation (Bates, 2005; Douglas, 2005). Black gay men endure a similar triadic stigmatization due to the demonization of blackness, black maleness, and gayness. In addition to marginalization by the dominant White society, LGBTQIA African Americans face rejection within the African American community by most HBC's and conservative community leaders who support the homophobic theological perspectives (Griffin, 2006; McBride, 1998; Orey, 2006).

In addition to the central role of religion, African Americans primarily approach life with a collectivist worldview and an emphasis on relational harmony. In contrast to the Euro-centric individualistic worldview, African American identity links to communal identity. Thoughts, feelings, and behaviors are viewed in terms of their implications for the individual, family, and community (Miller & Garran, 2008; Sherr, 2006). The values of rugged individualism and complete autonomy may be interpreted as selfish and detrimental to the growth of the family and the community. The African American history of survival, resilience, and achievement was built upon the foundations of a unified vision, collective collaboration, family preservation, and communal well-being (Sherr, 2006; Raboteau, 2001). While these cultural traits of African American communities have been sources of strength and empowerment, they have had a significantly deleterious effect on the lives of LGBTQIA African Americans. When working with LGBTQIA African American clients, it will be helpful for the social worker to explore the potential impact of these cultural factors in the clients' lives and the lives of their loved ones. To help you apply these cultural factors in ASWP, please review Shawn's story and the social worker's response.

Shawn's Story

Shawn is a self-identified 23-year-old single African American Christian male who lives in a metropolitan southern city. He is a full-time student in a Master of Divinity program at a prestigious private university. As a hometown son, he has earned accolades from his family, teachers, and pastor for his work as a student leader, peer minister, and community volunteer. Shawn has scheduled a counseling appointment with an off-campus clinical social worker to address his "recent bouts of confusion, anxiety, and depression."

During the initial visit, Shawn asked several questions about the confidentiality of the sessions. He shared that he did not want his family or friends to know that he was seeing a social worker. He explained that, "they would get overly concerned and I don't want to worry them, especially my parents." He shared that he has had problems with intense dreams, anxiety, poor concentration, and increasing sadness. He stated that the symptoms started about six months ago. When the therapist inquired about precipitating factors (major life changes, losses, traumas), Shawn paused, looked away and seemed to scan the room. Upon noticing the social worker's diploma from his school, he changed the focus of the conversation to their shared alma mater.

After a few minutes, the social worker redirected the conversation and noted that Shawn seemed uncomfortable with exploring the precipitants for his symptoms. Shawn paused again and stated that his junior year started with an exciting move into an off-campus apartment with his best friend, David. They met in their first year and became dear friends. Shawn looked down and stated, "Things have changed since he came out."

Using empathic responses, minimal prompts, and a non-judgmental stance, the social worker encouraged Shawn to continue telling his story. Shawn stated that David kissed him one night during an intense conversation right after they moved into their apartment. Shawn stated that he responded with a kiss, too, before pushing David away. David apologized and explained that he had feelings for Shawn and needed to be honest about the fact that he was gay. Shawn stated, "I don't know what to do with my feelings for David. I was raised to believe that homosexuality is a sin, but David is a good guy and a dear friend. I love him."

After stating his feelings for David, Shawn seemed stunned by his own words. He avoided eye contact with the social worker for the rest of that session. He cancelled the next two sessions due to "unforeseen school and church responsibilities." When he returned to counseling, he was tearful and started the session with a question. "What am I going to do?"

Discussion Questions

Stop for a moment to review these four questions. Reflect on how you feel about Shawn and how you think he and his social worker should proceed. Thoughtfully consider your own reactions and potential responses. Write down your responses and share them with classmates in a small group discussion. Then, read further to see the author's conceptualization of this case and recommendations for culturally sensitive practice:

1   What are your first impressions of Shawn: his strengths, resources, challenges, and target problems?
2   What are your thoughts and feelings about Shawn and David's relationship?
3   Considering the theories of oppression and culturally relevant concepts discussed in this chapter, what hypotheses do you have about the reasons for Shawn's level of distress? Why is he so upset? What are some of the stigmatizing factors and minority stressors that Shawn may be facing?
4   If you were Shawn's social worker, what would you do? What LGBTQIA affirmative social work practices may help Shawn through this distressing time in his life?

Now that you have your own thoughts and responses, read the responses provide here.

What are your first impressions of Shawn: his strengths, resources, challenges, and target problems?

Shawn appears to have significant strengths and resources including strong familial and community relationships, intelligence and academic achievements, a strong religious and spiritual identity, a strong African American identity, and financial resources. His challenges include significant anxiety symptoms related to emerging same-sex attraction to a dear friend, cognitive dissonance related to his religious beliefs about the "sin" of homosexuality, a lack of LGBTQIA affirmative relationships, and no LGBTQIA affirmative education to challenge his anti-LGBTQIA religious beliefs.

What are your thoughts and feelings about Shawn and David's relationship?

Shawn and David are consenting adults who have the right to explore their feelings for each other. Gay, lesbian, and bisexual relationships are normal, healthy, and non-pathological. All of the major health sciences support the affirmation of same-sex attraction as healthy, and repudiate attempts to pathologize or treat same-sex attraction as deviance or disease (CSWE, 2016; Dessel et al., 2017, Lewis, 2015).

Considering the theories of oppression and culturally relevant concepts discussed in this chapter, what hypotheses do you have about the reasons for Shawn's level of distress? Why is he so upset? What are some of the stigmatizing factors and minority stressors that Shawn may be facing?

Shawn appears to be experiencing emotional, psychological, and religious distress related to his emerging same-sex attraction to a dear friend. Shawn's distress may be exacerbated by his experiences of minority stressors as an

African American man, as well as his fears of additional stigmatization for a potentially emerging identity as a gay or bisexual man. Considering the existence and influence of homophobic theologies and LGBTQIA stigmatization within HBC, Shawn may be facing a major conflict between his intersecting identities and the religious beliefs of his family and community (Lewis, 2015). For Shawn, a non-heterosexual orientation may be perceived as a serious threat to his sense of self, his strong familial and community ties, and his religious identity.

If you were Shawn's social worker, what would you do? What LGBTQIA affirmative social work practices may help Shawn through this distressing time in his life?

It is important to create an emotionally supportive and affirming relationship with Shawn. An affirmative social worker would emphasize empathic responsiveness, a non-judgmental stance, validation of Shawn's feelings, genuine positive regard, and collaboration. With this foundation, Shawn and the social worker may develop a working alliance aimed at the following goals:

- Completing a multi-dimensional bio-psychosocial–spiritual assessment
- Decreasing Shawn's emotional distress symptoms by increasing his effective mindfulness stress-reduction coping skills
- Exploring Shawn's feelings and thoughts about his relationship with David
- Exploring Shawn's feelings and thoughts about homosexuality and LGBTQIA identities
- Exploring Shawn's intersecting cultural identities as an African American man and a Christian
- Exploring alternative life narrative that may help Shawn to develop an integrated sense of self that affirms all of his intersecting identities
- Increasing Shawn's knowledge about LGBTQIA affirming resources, including affirmative churches and affirmative LGBTQIA community groups.

With ASWP, the social worker can help Shawn to explore honestly and courageously his life story, his sexual orientation and possibly emerging LGBTQIA identity, his fears and challenges, and paths to empowered wholeness.

Shawn's story is just one of many stories in the multi-cultural realities experienced by LGBTQIA individuals of color. In addition to African American communities, LGBTQIA individuals of color have intersecting racial and ethnic identities within Latino/a, Asian, Pacific Islander, American Indian, Jewish, and Middle-Eastern communities. The theories and practice approaches in this chapter should be critically examined for their culturally valid applications in social work practice with LGBTQIA individuals from these racial and ethnic minority communities.

Conclusion

LGBTQIA individuals of color live at the intersections of multiple stigmatized and marginalized identities (race/ethnicity, sexual orientation, gender identity and expression). In this chapter, the author has provided a theoretical and research-based framework for culturally sensitive and affirmative social work practice with this marginalized population. Using Stigmatization Theory, Minority Stress Theory, and Intersectionality, social workers can create culturally sensitive knowledge, values, and skills for working with LGBTQIA individuals of color and their families.

ASWP models are consistent with the best practices for strengths-based and client-centered social work practice. With ASWP, culturally sensitive social workers can engage in LGBTQIA affirmative practices that support, honor, and empower this marginalized population to claim their equal worth, dignity, and human rights within their families, communities, and nation. Students are encouraged to build on knowledge in this foundational chapter with continued critical study, supervision, and reflective practice. LGBTQIA affirmative social workers must be committed to life-long learning, critical self-reflection, and culturally sensitive practice. To facilitate that process, please review the resources, glossary terms, and reference list at the end of this chapter.

Questions to Consider

1   Consider the primary elements of Stigmatization Theory, Minority Stress Theory, and Intersectionality. How can these theories inform your practice with LGBTQIA clients of color? In what ways does a strengths-based approach remain important in working with LGBTQIA clients?

2   Consider Jackie, a client who identifies as a transgender female. Jackie is a person of color who grew up in a religiously conservative family. In what ways might Jackie experience stigmatization and minority stress based on her identities? How can intersectionality frame strategies to understand and support this client?

3   How do clients experience stigma by race, ethnicity, sexual orientation, and/or gender identity? What might be some potential effects of multiple types of stigmatization on the biological, psychological, social, spiritual, and cultural well-being of LGBTQIA individuals, families, groups, organizations, and communities of color?

4   What social work values and ethics promote affirmative and competent practice with LGBTQIA populations of color? How can you and other social workers apply these values and ethics in practice?

5   Identify culturally relevant resources and professional partnerships at micro, mezzo, and macro levels to ensure culturally sensitive service for the LGBTQIA client populations that you serve within communities of color. What steps do you need to take to identify these resources? How can you build strong relationships?

6 Racial and ethnic identity development theories propose that individuals experience transformative stages of identity development. How might these identity development models inform your practice with LGBTQIA clients of color?

Resources

CSWE Council on Sexual Orientation and Gender Identity and Expression (CSOGIE) www.cswe.org/CentersInitiatives/Diversity/About Diversity/15550/15548.aspx

Family Equality Council www.familyequality.org/ is a national organization committed to promoting legal equality for LGBTQ families.

GLSEN www.glsen.org/ is a national network of educators and students who are committed to creating safer and more inclusive learning environments for students in K-12 schools.

Human Rights Campaign – Communities of Color www.hrc.org/explore/topic/communities-of-color is a research-based resource for learning about LGBTQIA communities of color.

National Black Justice Coalition http://nbjc.org/ is committed to the empowerment of Black LGBTQ individuals and their families.

National Queer Asian Pacific Islander Alliance www.nqapia.org is a federation of national organization committed the empowerment of LGBTQIA individuals within these communities.

Unid@s, The National Latina/o Lesbian, Gay, Bisexual &Transgender Human Rights Organization www.facebook.com/UNIDOSLGBT/ is an organization committed to creating a more inclusive and just world for LGBTQIA individuals and their families through education, advocacy, and collective social justice action.

YouthPrideAlliance http://youthpridealliance.org/ is an organization that promotes the healthy and affirmative development, visibility, equal rights, and support of LGBTQIA youth.

Note

1 Note that SOGI (which appears in the running head for this chapter) stands for Sexual Orientation and Gender Identity.

References

Adams, M., Blumenfeld, W. J., Castañeda, C., Hackman, H. W., Peters, M. L., & Zúñiga, X. (2010). *Readings for diversity and social justice* (2nd Ed). New York: Routledge.

Alessi, E. J. (2014). A framework for incorporating minority stress theory into treatment with sexual minority clients. *Journal of Gay and Lesbian Mental Health*, 18, 47–66.

Alexander, M. (2011). Go to trial: Crash the justice system. *The new Jim Crowe: Mass incarceration in the age of colorblindness* (revised edition). New York: The New Press.

Bates, A. (2005). Liberation in truth: African American lesbians reflect on religion, spirituality, and their church. In S. Thumma & E. R. Gray (Eds.), *Gay religion.* Walnut Creek, CA: AltaMira.

Berger, P. & Luckman, T. (1966). *The social construction of reality: A treatise on the sociology of knowledge.* New York: Anchor Books.

Brown, T. (2002). A proposed model of bisexual identity development that elaborates on experiential differences of women and men. *Journal of Bisexuality,* 2(4), 67–91 doi: doi:10.1300/J159v02n04_05

Buckman, R. & Buckman, J. (2016). Narrative therapies. In N. Coady & P. Lehmann (Eds.). *Theoretical perspectives for direct social work practice: A generalist-eclectic approach.* New York: Springer.

Cass, V. C. (1984). Homosexual identity formation: Testing a theoretical model. *The Journal of Sex Research,* 1(2), 143–167.

Council for Social Work Education (CSWE). (2015). *Educational policies and accreditation standards.* CSWE Press.

Council for Social Work Education (CSWE) (2016). *Position statement on conversion/reparative therapy.* Retrieved from www.cswe.org/File.aspx?id=85010

Dessel, A. B., Jacobsen, J., Levy, D. L., McCarty-Caplan, D., Lewis, T. O. & Kaplan, L. E. (2017). LGBTQ topics and Christianity in social work: Tackling the tough questions. *Social Work & Christianity,* 44(1/2), 11–30.

Dill, B. T. & Zambrana, R. E. (2013). Critical thinking about inequality: An emerging lens. In S. J. Ferguson (Ed). *Race, gender, sexuality, social class: Dimensions of inequality.* Los Angeles: Sage.

Douglas, K. B. (2005). *What's faith got to do with it? Black bodies/Christian souls.* Maryknoll, NY: Orbis Books.

Du Bois, W. E. B. ([1903] 2003). *The Negro Church,* introduction by Phil Zuckerman, Sandra Barnes and Daniel Cady. Walnut Creek, CA: AltaMira Press.

Foucault, M. (1990/1976). *The history of sexuality: An introduction, Volume I.* New York, NY: Vintage Books.

Freire, P. (2014/1970). *Pedagogy of the oppressed.* New York: Continuum.

Fullilove, R. E. (2006). *African Americans, health disparities, and HIV/AIDS: Recommendations for confronting the epidemic in Black America.* Washington, D.C.: National Minority AIDS Council.

Garfinkel, H. (1956, March). Conditions of successful degradation ceremonies. *American Journal of Sociology,* 61(5), 420–424.

Goffman, E. (1963). *Stigma: Notes on the management of spoiled identity.* New York, NY: Simon & Schuster.

Griffin, H. (2006). *Their own receive them not African American lesbians & gays in Black churches.* Cleveland, OH: Pilgrim Press.

Hill, D. B. (2005). Trans/gender/sexuality: A research agenda. *Journal of Gay and Lesbian Social Services,* 18(2), 101–109.

Kiehne, E. (2016). Latino critical perspective in social work. *Social Work,* 61(2), 119–126.

Lincoln, C. E. & Mamiya, L. H. (1990). *The Black church in the African American experience.* Durham, NC & London: Duke University Press.

Kirst-Ashman, K. K. & Hull, G. H. (2012). *Understanding generalist practice.* Belmont, CA: Brooks/Cole.

Lev, A. L. (2006). Transgender emergence within families. In D. F. Morrow & L. Messinger (Eds.), *Sexual orientation and gender expression in social work practice: Working with gay, lesbian, bisexual, and transgender people* (pp. 263–283). New York: Columbia University Press.

Lewis, T. O. (2015). LGBT-affirming Black churches' responses to the HIV/AIDS crisis. *Journal of Religion and Spirituality in Social Work: Social Thought,* 34(2), 140–157.

McBride, D. A. (1998, Spring). Can the queen speak? Racial essentialism, sexuality and the problem of authority . *Callaloo,* 21(2), 363–379.

Meyer, I. H. (2003). Prejudice, social stress, and mental health in lesbian, gay, and bisexual populations: Conceptual issues and research evidence. *Psychological Bulletin,* 129(5), 674–697.

Miller, J. & Garran, A. M. (2008). *Racism in the Unites States: Implications for the helping professions.* Belmont, CA: Brooks/Cole.

Morrow, D. F. (2006). Gay, lesbian, and bisexual identity development. In D. F. Morrow & L. Messinger (Ed.), *Sexual orientation and gender expression in social work practice: Working with gay, lesbian, bisexual, and transgender people,* (pp. 263–283), New York: Columbia University Press.

Morrow, D. F. & Messinger, L. (Eds). (2006). *Sexual orientation and gender expression in social work practice: Working with gay, lesbian, bisexual, and transgender people.* New York: Columbia University Press.

Murphy, B. C. & Dillon, C. (2011). *Interviewing in action in a multicultural world.* Belmont, CA: Brooks/Cole.

Nadal, K. L., Issa, M. A., Leon, J., Meterko, V., Wideman, M., & Wong, Y. (2011). Sexual orientation microaggressions: "Death by a thousand cuts" for lesbian, gay, and bisexual youth. *Journal of LGBT Youth,* 8(3), 234–259.

National Association of Social Workers (NASW) (2015). *Standards and indicators for cultural competence in social work practice.* NASW Press.

Orey, B. D. A. (2006). The politics of AIDS in the Black community. *Forum on Public Policy,* (3), 1–13.

Paris, P. (1995). *The spirituality of African peoples: The search for a common moral discourse.* MN: Augsburg Fortress.

Phinney, J. & Kohatsu, E. L. (1999). Ethnic and racial identity development and mental health. In J. Schulenberg, J. L. Maggs & K. Hurelmann (Eds.), *Health risks and developmental transitions during adeolescence* (pp. 420–443). New York, NY: Cambridge University Press.

Poulin, J. (2010). *Strengths-based generalist practice: A collaborative approach* (3rd Ed). Belmont, CA: Wadsworth Cengage Learning.

Raboteau, A. J. (2001). *Canaan land: A religious history of African Americans.* New York: Oxford University Press.

Schieman, S., Pudrovska, T., Pearlin, L. I., & Ellison, C. G. (2006). The sense of divine control and psychological distress: Variations across race and socioeconomic status. *Journal for the Scientific Study of Religion,* 45(4), 529–549.

Sherr, M. E. (2006). The Afrocentric paradigm: A pragmatic discourse about social work practice with African Americans. *Journal of Human Behavior in the Social Environment,* 13(3), 1–17.

Sisneros, J., Stakeman, C., Joyner, M., & Schmidt, C. (2008). *Critical multicultural social work.* Chicago: Lyceum Books.

Sue, D. W. (2006). *Multicultural social work practice.* Hoboken, NJ: John Wiley & Sons.

8 Working with Transgender and Nonbinary Client Populations

Erin Hipple

MSW, LSW, MA

Austin J. Angiollilo

BA

Ona H. Grant

CSWE 2015 EPAS Competencies

Competency 1: Demonstrate ethical and professional behavior
Competency 2: Engage diversity and difference in practice
Competency 3: Advance human rights and social, economic, and environmental justice
Competency 5: Engage in policy practice
Competency 6: Engage with individuals, families, groups, organizations, and communities

Introduction

As of June 2016, 0.6% of the US population (1.4 million) identified as transgender (Flores, Herman, Gates, & Brown, 2016, p. 3). Transgender and nonbinary individuals face unique challenges in a variety of social work settings. In this chapter, you will be provided with information and background related to transgender and **gender nonbinary** client populations that will assist you in supporting these individuals in both your professional and personal life.

US mainstream understanding of transgender and nonbinary experience is growing rapidly. As transgender and nonbinary individuals gain increased mainstream visibility, the language that we use to conceptualize their experiences will evolve in kind. This means that as social workers, we must remain willing to educate ourselves on updated terminology and methods of support. While this chapter introduces some concepts that may assist in preparing you to have cultural humility when working with transgender and nonbinary individuals, this information is in no way exhaustive, and the resources at the end of the chapter are a great place to go to further your understanding.

Transgender or **'trans'** is a term used to refer to individuals whose current **gender identity** does not align with the sex they were assigned at birth. The prefix *trans-* is Latin for 'other side.' **Cisgender** is a term used to refer to individuals whose current gender identity aligns with the sex they were assigned at birth. The prefix *cis-* (pronounced 'sis') comes from the Latin word, meaning 'same side.' While transgender people may also identify with the labels of 'man' and 'woman,' the trouble with excluding the prefixes *trans-* and *cis-* from conversations about gender is that often the cultural assumption in the United States is that the terms 'man' and 'woman' only refer to cisgender people. As this chapter will identify, transgender individuals face challenges unique to their gender identity.

Nonbinary is a term that encompasses gender identities that do not fall exclusively in man/male or woman/female categories of gender (Webb, Matsuno, Budge, Krishnan, & Balsam, 2015, p. 1). A nonbinary person may identify as being both a man and a woman at the same time, somewhere between those two genders, or off of the gender spectrum entirely. 'Within non-Western cultures, individuals from groups such as Two Spirit people [Native American], Fa'afafine [Polynesian], or Hijra [South Asian] are sometimes considered to comprise a 'third' gender, but may or may not identify as nonbinary or transgender' (Webb, Matsuno, Budge, Krishnan, & Balsam, 2015, p. 1). Two Spirit, more broadly, describes the presence of both a feminine and a masculine spirit in one person (Balestrery, 2012). For the purposes of this chapter, the term nonbinary will describe a myriad of individuals who fall in this identified subset of gender identity; however, there are several other terms that nonbinary people might use to describe their identities. It is important to respect the way that an individual conceptualizes and labels their gender identity.

Coming Out as Transgender or Nonbinary

For transgender or nonbinary people, coming out has its own set of unique challenges. For some, the coming out process might start with an individual questioning their gender. For others, it might begin with a feeling of identification with the 'other' sex, or not feeling like they belong in the body into which they were born. A transgender person might come out as a *trans woman*, a *trans man*, or they may refer to themselves as *transmasculine* or *transfeminine*. Nonbinary people may come out under a variety of labels, including **genderfluid, genderqueer, agender, bigender** and/or **pangender**, among other terms. Coming out is a fluid process, meaning it does not have a specific beginning or end. Some transgender individuals may know from a very young age that they are transgender, and some individuals may not know until later in their life. *The age at which a transgender person comes out does not have a correlation with the validity of their identity, and it is important to respect each transgender individual's personal process.* Lack of education about gender identity, restrictive gender norms, and lack of support and acceptance from peers might also impact the coming out process. While coming out can be an empowering time for transgender and nonbinary people, it can also be difficult and painful.

Intimate/Romantic Relationships

Transgender and nonbinary people, like any other population, have the capacity to cultivate and maintain satisfying intimate and romantic relationships. Intimate relationships for trans and nonbinary individuals may come with unique challenges. For example, disclosure of trans identity during the dating process has been identified as one of the most difficult aspects of being trans (Platt & Bolland, 2017). If a transgender person immediately discloses their transgender identity to a potential partner, they risk the potential of rejection in addition to the potential of verbal or physical violence. If they do not disclose their identity immediately and wait until they have formed a bond with a potential partner, the disclosure comes with similar risks, in addition to the risk of accusations of deception. Statistics indicate that one in two transgender people will be raped or assaulted by a romantic partner (TSER, 2013). These risks create the possibility of an incredibly stressful situation for transgender people with regard to identity disclosure in dating situations.

When a transgender or nonbinary person discloses their identity to an affirming partner(s), it can result in many positive relational outcomes for all parties (Joslin-Roher & Wheeler, 2009). With acceptance and understanding within the relationship, trans people may find that their partners become their biggest supporters.

Transitioning

Transitioning refers to the process a person may take to make their current gender identity more known to the world/people around them. Transition is often used as a means to alleviate gender dysphoria. **Gender dysphoria** categorizes the feelings of discomfort or disconnect a transgender person may have with his/her/their body. Transitioning happens differently for different people. Some transgender people may take measures to *socially transition* by coming out, asking to be referred to by the pronouns that match their identity, and/or altering their choice of clothing to better align with the gender that matches them. *Legal transition* refers to the process a transgender person may take to change their name and/or gender marker on legal documents such as IDs, drivers' licenses, passports, and birth certificates. For some transgender people, transition involves hormone replacement therapy and/or surgery. This is often referred to as *medical transitioning*, as it involves treatment by one or more medical professionals. Legally and medically transitioning is often seen as a privilege in trans communities because many transgender people do not have access to services that would allow them to medically transition. This may be due to their age, geographic location, or socioeconomic status. Medically transitioning can also be very expensive. While transgender individuals transition in different ways, it is important to be respectful and not inquire about a person's transition process or body unless that information is offered freely by the person as a topic of discussion.

Passing

Passing refers to the ability of a transgender person to move through public spaces confident that they will be correctly perceived by others as their gender, and it may also refer to the idea that other people wouldn't be able to readily identify them as transgender based on their appearance (Stryker & Whittle, 2006). Social and medical transitioning may be part of the process of passing for some transgender individuals, but not necessarily for all. Passing can be an affirming experience that allows a transgender person to feel physically and socially aligned with their identity; however, passing is not just a point of affirmation. Passing is often also a point of safety for transgender individuals, as they face the possibility of violence in public spaces if they are identified as transgender.

Violence and Discrimination against Transgender People

Hate Crime Violence

Nineteen percent of hate crime survivors identify as transgender. In 2017, 235 transgender people were murdered (this is not including those who may have been misgendered in police reports), an increase from the 75 transgender people killed in 2016 (Abernathey, 2017). Nearly all of the victims of these murders were transgender women of color. Statistics show that trans women have a one in twelve chance of being murdered, and that jumps to a one in eight chance for trans women of color (TSER, 2013). Of the 24 reported LGBTQA+ people killed by hate violence in 2016, 67% (16) were transgender and nonbinary people. Of the homicides, 54% (13) were transgender women of color (Schmider, 2016). Each year, November 20 is a Transgender Day of Remembrance, when people remember the lives of transgender people that were lost due to anti-transgender violence (Lang, 2017).

According to the American Medical Student Association (AMSA, 2015), 19% of transgender women have been incarcerated at some point in their lives. For trans women of color, that number is threefold (Reisner et al., 2014, p. 2). One in four transgender women in prison report being denied healthcare while incarcerated (AMSA, 2015). Not only are transgender women targeted by the police, they are often placed in prison settings that do not align with their identity, putting them at risk for further violence.

Healthcare Disparities

While transgender and nonbinary people are disproportionately targeted in hate crime related violence, they also face discrimination of other kinds. In 2015, 65% of transgender people reported discrimination in one or more public accommodation settings. According to Reisner, Bailey, and Sevelius (2014) 'one in five transgender people postponed or did not seek healthcare due to a fear of discrimination'. Additionally, 29% of transgender patients report having to teach their healthcare provider about transgender health issues. Trans man, activist, and orator, Leslie Feinberg, (2001) recounted an experience he had in a Jersey City, NJ emergency department:

> Five years ago, while battling an undiagnosed case of bacterial endo-carditis, I was refused care at a Jersey City emergency room. After a physician examined me and discovered that I am [assigned female at birth], he ordered me out of the emergency room despite the fact that my temperature was above 104°F. He said I had a fever 'because you are a very troubled person'.
>
> (pp. 897–898)

Due to these disparities in care, many transgender and nonbinary people distrust medical and mental health facilities.

Workplace and Housing Discrimination

Transgender and nonbinary individuals face discrimination on a regular basis, and depending on what state they live in, they may not receive legal protections for that discrimination. Only 20 states in the United States have legislation that prohibit employment and housing discrimination against transgender and nonbinary individuals (Human Rights Campaign, 2017). Currently, only 14 of 50 states in the United States facilitate gender marker changes on both birth certificates and drivers' licenses (Human Rights Campaign, 2017). Lack of legislation supporting transgender individuals in changing their legal forms of identification with their correct gender has profound implications with regard to discrimination, as these documents are often required to apply for employment and housing accommodations. This means that a transgender person has to out themselves in order to apply for work or housing, thus opening them up to discriminatory practices by employers and landlords.

Bathroom Access

Many transgender and gender nonbinary individuals have to spend inten-tional time thinking about whether they have safe bathroom access in public spaces. In a study from UCLA's Williams Institute (Flores, Herman,

Gates, & Brown, 2016), 18% of transgender people have been denied access to a gender-segregated public restroom, while 68% have experienced some sort of verbal harassment and 9% have experienced some form of physical assault when accessing or using gender-segregated public restrooms (Herman, 2013). Regarding bathroom access, crime statistics suggest that the population highest at risk for experiencing violence of all kinds is transgender people (Durso & Gates, 2012). Additionally, to date, there have been no instances of a transgender person perpetrating sexual assault in a public bathroom (National Center for Transgender Equality, 2018).

Language and Pronouns

Language and terminology used to describe transgender individuals and their experiences is rapidly evolving (Green & Maurer, 2015). The terminology in this chapter attempts to compile the most up-to-date language used by transgender and nonbinary individuals. As social workers, it is a matter of ethics and social justice to continuously educate ourselves on the most updated, affirming language and terminology in order to best advocate for transgender lives and experiences. We must also understand that language to describe transgender and nonbinary experience might be different depending on the culture of the transgender or nonbinary individual. What is important is that we respect the terminology used by any given transgender or nonbinary person and do our best to adjust our language accordingly. Along with respecting pronouns, choosing gender neutral language when addressing groups of people can create a more inclusive environment. An example of this would be to say 'Hello everyone/folks' instead of 'Hello ladies and gentlemen.'

More Up-to-date Language

Language is constantly shifting as time progresses and because of this, certain terms that were once acceptable to use are now outdated. Language such as 'sex change,' 'the surgery,' or 'sex reassignment surgery' are no longer used and instead, the most up-to-date terminology to refer to medical transition is 'medically transitioning' or 'gender affirmation surgery.' Additionally it is important to use the term 'trans man' instead of saying 'used to be a woman,' or 'FTM (female to male),' and 'trans woman' instead of 'used to be a man,' or 'MTF (male to female)'. Language has also shifted to avoid using the term 'transsexual' because it is a term that was used to imply that a particular person had already undergone gender affirmation surgery and many transgender people find this disclosure to be invasive. Instead, we opt to say 'transgender' or 'trans.' It is important to note that words such as 'transgender,' 'trans,' and 'nonbinary' are to be used as adjectives. Because of this, one should avoid saying 'a transgender,' 'transgenders,' or 'transgendered.' If you ever worry that you are using any of these words incorrectly, substitute in a different adjective and see how it sounds (i.e. 'a *transgender* person' is used as an adjective in the same way as 'a *tall* person'). Words to avoid all entirely when describing transgender people include: tranny/ trannie, transvestite, it, she-male, he-she, and shim. These words are highly derogatory.

Social Work Applications

As with the language available to describe transgender and nonbinary identities and experiences, the types of resources and supports for transgender and nonbinary individuals is rapidly growing and changing. At the end of this chapter, there is a list of resources for you and your clients. These resources may assist you in further education and support around language, concerns, and outcomes for transgender and nonbinary populations.

The information in this chapter can assist social workers in generalist and clinical contexts to support transgender and nonbinary client populations. While this may be a starting point for best practice in working with trans and nonbinary clients, it is important to remember that education about this population is ongoing. Additionally, just like any population, social workers must navigate transgender and nonbinary client concerns on a case-by-case basis. It is imperative that we as social workers continually educate ourselves regarding the needs of transgender and nonbinary clients. We must learn skills to integrate that understanding into our social work practice, but we must also remember that transgender identity is only one facet of an individual's experience and should not be the only factor we consider when we work with trans and nonbinary client populations.

Generalist Social Work Applications

Generalist social workers have the potential to offer a great deal of support to transgender and nonbinary clients, but this requires education and cultural humility. Just as transgender individuals report experiencing hostility in medical environments (Transgender Health, 2017), there are similar apprehensions when entering mental health facilities or social service agencies.

Case Management

For caseworkers, it can be helpful to have an understanding of the local resources available to transgender and nonbinary individuals in your area. In the resources section of this chapter, you will find websites that identify a number of legal, medical, housing, and social support organizations for transgender and nonbinary clients. Many of these websites provide state-by-state breakdowns of transgender resources and contact information should you need to reach out to identify applicable resource availability in your area.

Educating yourself about the laws in your area as they pertain to transgender issues can also be beneficial when supporting transgender and nonbinary clients in a generalist capacity, as legislation can vary widely from state to state, and even from county to county. There are legal resources at the end of this chapter that provide helpful legal information pertinent to transgender and nonbinary people that are easily accessible and updated often. Using your voice to encourage legislators to vote against transphobic legislation is a powerful way to support transgender clients on a macro level.

On Administrative Advocacy

If a transgender or nonbinary client is out and would like their pronouns and name to be used in all contexts at your agency, collaborate with the office manager and staff to note that in the client's chart, and/or in the agency's electronic client system. Talk to front desk staff about being aware of the client's name and pronouns. In many states, transgender and nonbinary people have to keep their assigned name on their state IDs and insurance cards, so front desk staff might not be privy to the client's name and pronouns. Having a conversation about this with office staff can be helpful in creating an inclusive environment for your client.

More Micro Practice Applications

Mental Health Outcomes and Clinical Considerations

There are many mental health diagnoses that may have a unique impact on trans and nonbinary clients. Transgender and nonbinary people are about nine times more likely to attempt suicide in their lifetime than cisgender people. These rates display that 40% of transgender people will attempt suicide at some point in their life (James et al., 2016). These rates may be elevated due to the transgender person's greater likelihood of experiencing discrimination, and/or the lack of a support system. It is important to note that while discrimination and lack of support do play a large role in a transgender person's level of life satisfaction, internal factors such as co-occurring experiences with depression and anxiety are prevalent, and these experiences may or may not be linked to experiences related to gender identity and issues of discrimination. Bockting, Miner, Romine, Hamilton, and Coleman (2013) surveyed 1,093 transgender men and women. Of that number, 44% had/have depression, 33% had/have anxiety, and 40% experienced overall psychological distress.

In 2015, the American Psychiatric Association updated the *Diagnostic Statistical Manual of Mental Disorders* (DSM) from the DSM-IV-TR to the DSM-5. One of the changes that occurred was the movement from the diagnosis of *Gender Identity Disorder* to the diagnosis of *Gender Dysphoria*. While shifting the language was a step in reducing the incorrect assertion that being transgender is a disorder, it is important to note that the gender dysphoria experienced by trans and nonbinary clients may be a response to rigid, socially constructed gender norms. Pathologizing that response has troubling implications; however, it is also important to understand that having the diagnosis in the DSM-5 works as a way for transgender people to receive insurance coverage for their medical transition. This can be an important benefit for individuals who need financial assistance in their medical transition.

On Misgendering a Client

Misgendering refers to the act of using the wrong name or pronoun for an individual, thus identifying them by a gender that is not theirs. It is unfortunately common that people misgender transgender and nonbinary people (both intentionally and unintentionally). While the impact of misgendering is different for each individual, it can be an invalidating and/or painful experience. It can be difficult to shift our language when someone identifies themselves as transgender or requests that we use a different name or pronouns to address them, but it is important that we respect their identity and follow their request to the best of our ability. Remember, no one is perfect. If you use the wrong name or pronouns, correct yourself and move on. Resist the urge to be performatively apologetic. We never want to elevate our feelings of guilt for making a mistake over the experience that the individual has had of being misgendered.

On Pronouns

You cannot assume that you know anyone's pronouns, and therefore, it makes sense to ask every new client what their pronouns are. You may want to start by introducing yourself with your pronouns the first time you meet any new client (i.e., 'Hello, my name is Kate, my pronouns are "she" and "hers"'), giving space for your client to then respond with their pronouns. By introducing yourself and identifying your pronouns, you are not only clarifying the client's pronouns for your own use, but also modeling the use of inclusive language, which benefits all clients. When inquiring about a person's pronouns, avoid asking a client what their 'preferred' pronouns are. Asking a client for 'preferred' pronouns implies preference over truth. A person's pronouns are their pronouns, it isn't about preference at all.

The most commonly used pronouns are she/her and he/him. Gender-neutral pronouns such as they/them/theirs (i.e. *They* are wearing a hat, *their* hat is nice, it looks good on *them*) are being used by trans and nonbinary individuals as well. Some people take issue with they/them/theirs pronouns because traditional grammatical use of those pronouns was in a plural context; however, the dictionary has recognized the singular form of 'they' since 2015 (Kozicka, 2016). Singular forms of gender-neutral pronouns such as ze/zir/zirs are also used. For more information on pronouns and pronoun usage, refer to the resources section at the end of this chapter.

Supporting a Transgender Client in Coming Out

Make a Plan. If a transgender client begins to talk about coming out to family and friends, support from a therapist can be very helpful. One way to help a transgender or nonbinary client in this process is providing them with affirming space to create a plan to come out. When a social worker or clinician offers a space that allows the client to introspect on the potential outcomes of coming out, as well as assessing and preparing for any potential safety issues or risk factors, this can help a transgender or nonbinary client gain perspective and confidence. Remember, it is never our role as a social worker or therapist to push a transgender or nonbinary client to come out if they are not ready. We must proceed with humility and allow the client to take the lead.

Supporting a Transgender Client in Medical Transition

There are several ways that clinicians can support trans clients who decide to undergo a medical transition. There are a few important considerations when working with a client who has medically transitioned or decides to do so while under your clinical care.

If you know that your client has already had surgery, it is not your place to inquire about it unless the client begins the conversation, and even then, proceed respectfully and remember that while you might be curious about elements of their experience, stick to only what is necessary for your clinical treatment of the client. It is highly inappropriate, for example, to ask a trans person to show you their body post-operatively.

For clients who decide to medically transition while in your care, you may be able to advocate for them by writing a letter of referral/recommendation for their procedure. According to the World Professional Association of Trans Health (WPATH) guidelines, letters of recommendation can be written by any mental or behavioral health provider with a Master's level of training or higher (Transgender Health, 2017). Encourage your client to speak with their surgeon and insurance provider regarding these requirements in order to be sure you are including all of the information needed. There are resources for the basic requirements of a transition letter of recommendation available at the end of this chapter.

Addressing the Needs of Transgender and Nonbinary Youth in a Clinical Context

Identity development is a necessary developmental task for all children and adolescents. For transgender and nonbinary youth, this task comes with the additional challenge of integrating their gender identity into their family, community, and cultural dynamics (Grossman & D'Augelli, 2006). This can be even further complicated by a lack of exposure to information about gender identity. Due to this lack of education, young people might experience distress or demonstrate behaviors that they might not know relate to their gender identity.

Some transgender and nonbinary youth may disclose their status to you without having done so with their primary caregivers. This may be a matter of physical or psychological safety. It is important to allow the client to guide the process of coming out to family, and *only* if they choose to do so. It is also imperative that therapists are intentional about not disclosing an individual's gender identity status to caregivers or parents unless the client has explicitly consented to this. Here is a helpful case example:

> You are assigned to work with an adolescent client named Jane. Jane was assigned female at birth, and is diagnosed with Major Depressive Disorder with a history of self-harm. Jane appears reserved in session, making limited eye contact and speaking very little. After a few sessions, Jane discloses to you that she believes herself to be a transgender boy. She tells you that she has her friends at school call her 'John' and 'he,' but that she has to be very careful that her mom doesn't find out because her mom says that transgender people are 'unnatural.'

How can you advocate for this client?

1   Ask Jane if she would like you to call her John and use he/him/his pronouns while in session. If Jane says 'yes,' follow through with this request consistently. If you misgender John by using the wrong name or pronouns, apologize and correct yourself; or, when discussing his identity, offer him the opportunity to correct you if it happens. If John is in a place of questioning his identity, make sure he is aware that you are always willing to change your language to keep him comfortable.

2   Ask John how he would like you to address him outside of meetings, (i.e. to his mom, other caregivers, in his chart). This might mean using she/her pronouns and John's assigned name (Jane) in notes, in case the notes become available to his caregivers. Social workers must be mindful in interactions with caregivers because outing clients may pose a risk to their safety.

3   Remember, your personal beliefs aside, you are there to be a support for John, and if that is the name and identity he feels comfortable with, aligning with him will help you build a relationship. It is not your job to convince John how to identify his gender, but to provide him with space to explore that for himself.

Trust that individuals (even young people) are able to assess their own level of identification and comfortability with an identity. See the resources at the end of this chapter for information about how to help in guiding this process.

Caregivers of Transgender and Nonbinary Youth

Working with parents and caregivers of transgender youth can come with its own set of unique considerations. Caregivers may span the gamut with regard to their willingness to accept the transgender identity of their child. Some caregivers are willing to accept their child's new identity and will actively and independently seek knowledge and education to help them better understand how to support their child. Parental closeness and support is often identified as a protective factor that may minimize psychological stress for transgender youth (Wilson, Chen, Arayasirikul, Raymond, & McFarland, 2016). For these caregivers, it is helpful to be prepared with some additional suggestions of where they can access resources for further education. The resource section of this chapter offers some potential places to direct caregivers for further education.

For many parents and caregivers, a transgender child 'coming out' can involve a process of grieving, where the caregivers experience a multitude of emotions related to the realization that their child does not identify with the gender that he/she/they were assigned at birth. Some caregivers are unwilling to accept their child's identity at all and may be introducing the child to a social worker, therapist, or clinical setting with the intention of 'fixing' the issue.

If your client is a transgender or gender nonbinary youth, it is important that you recognize that the caregiver may need to do their own processing, but that you do not allow their emotions to take precedence over the child's identity and lived experience in the context of your work with the child. You must remember that while there may be pressure to align with caregivers, you must advocate to the best of your ability for your client. This can be a dance, as caregivers may have the power and authority to halt or continue services for your client. It takes skill to walk that line between advocacy for your client and affirmation of caregiver feelings and expectations. Suggesting individual therapy for the caregiver might be an option, but should be navigated with care.

Family Sessions with Transgender or Nonbinary Youth

Offering to have a family session (when appropriate) is a powerful way to give the child an opportunity to be heard in a space where they have an advocate present to mediate the contact and help clarify communication. However, family sessions can easily devolve into a power struggle with the caregivers dominating the session, so prepare to mediate accordingly.

While it can be helpful for caregivers to express their feelings about their child's gender identity within a family session, we must not prioritize the emotions of the caregiver over the lived experience of the child. If we do so, we risk invalidating the child's identity and experience. It is not the role of a social worker or therapist to force the client to talk, but only to offer equal time if the client is willing to use it. It may take several sessions before a client is ready or willing to do so, and depending on the dynamics, they may choose not to do so at all.

Providing caregivers with trans-supportive education and resources can be a helpful way to support a transgender or nonbinary child. Not all caregivers are willing to seek education and understanding, and therapists must use their discretion. Some parents will want to come into sessions intermittently with little warning. There are many factors that may influence a social worker or therapist in whether this makes clinical or practice sense for the client. Additionally, as a social worker and/or therapist, you have the right to request that family sessions be planned in advance, although it might mean navigating some caregiver pushback.

If caregivers are unwilling to accept their child's identity, sessions may involve discussion of safety planning with your client. If the caregiver(s) are aware that their child identifies as transgender or nonbinary (and particularly if the caregivers are un-affirming and expect social workers or therapy to 'fix' their child by getting them to align with the sex and accompanying gender identity they were assigned at birth), they may intensely question their child about the topics discussed in therapy. Suggestions for clients who might have to engage in conversations with caregivers post-session are to speak generally to the topics of session (i.e. 'we discussed coping skills,' or 'we talked about what has been going on at school'). If a caregiver wants further details, the client might choose to provide details only related to other issues they are experiencing (i.e., anxiety or depression) without mentioning discussion of their gender identity. It can be helpful to educate clients that interactions with a social worker, and therapy in particular, are places for them to speak confidentially about the things that concern them; it can also help to educate them that they can relay to their caregiver(s) that they prefer to not share the details of their sessions for that reason. Of course, it is also the social worker or therapist's responsibility to assess for safety concerns (i.e., suicidal ideation, self-harm behavior, and/or abuse). We must be careful to remember that while we want to provide a confidential space for transgender and nonbinary youth clients with non-affirming parents, we may be required to break confidentiality if the client is at risk of serious harm or death. We do not want to encourage secret keeping of self-harm and suicidality and it is important that we are clear with our clients about that distinction.

If your client is the caregiver of a child who has come out as transgender or nonbinary, your role as a social worker or therapist is different. The caregiver is your primary client, at which time it makes sense to let their feelings and experiences take the forefront of your individual sessions. In this context, it is equally important for the therapist to be educated in issues of transgender and nonbinary populations, as it will allow you to direct sessions to help the caregiver potentially come to terms with their child's gender identity. That may not always be possible for some caregivers, but a therapist or social worker can help the caregiver to identify ways to support their child even if they cannot understand or agree with their child's gender identification. Being able to provide education and resources in this context can be helpful.

Conclusion

In the United States, transgender and nonbinary individuals are experiencing increased mainstream visibility. However, transgender and nonbinary individuals also continue to be subjected to a high threat of systemic and interpersonal violence. By practicing cultural humility, educating ourselves on trans issues, and disrupting attitudes and policies that promote transphobic ideals, social workers can play an important role in advocating for transgender and nonbinary clients in micro and macro contexts.

Questions to Consider

1   You run a group for individuals who struggle with depression symptoms in a mental health outpatient setting. What are some ways that you can make the group inclusive of transgender and nonbinary individuals?
2   You have a client and you feel unsure about their pronouns. What do you do?
3   You have a client who comes to you with questions about transition surgery: the procedure, insurance coverage requirements, and the possible drawbacks. How might you get the information your client seeks?
4   How may your work differ with a transgender person of color as compared to a white trans person?
5   When would you inquire about a person's gender identity?
6   What is the sexual orientation of a trans man who dates women?
7   You have a client that identifies as transgender and has spoken to you about the gender dysphoria they experience in relation to their identity. You notice that they exhibit disordered eating behaviors. How may you relate the disordered eating to their gender dysphoria? In what ways might the motives for disordered eating behavior be different for a transgender person as compared to a cisgender person? In what ways might they be similar?

Resources

General Educational and Informational Resources

'Transforming Gender' Documentary https://vimeo.com/124200023 gives an in-depth look at people's personal experiences living as transgender individuals.

Transgender Training Institute www.transgendertraininginstitute.com provides education for professionals, facilitators, and practitioners regarding transgender issues.

Human Rights Campaign (HRC) www.hrc.org/resources/topic/tra nsgender is the largest national lesbian, gay, bisexual, transgender, and queer civil rights organization. This section of the website offers general information on transgender people and terminology.

GLAAD www.glaad.org/reportdefamation is a place to report defamation of transgender people in media depictions.

Lambda Legal: Resources for LGBTQA+ Youth by State www.lambda legal.org/sites/default/files/publications/downloads/fs_resources-for-lgbtq-youth-by-state_1.pdf has state specific resources for transgender individuals.

Trevor Space www.trevorspace.org is a safe space for LGBTQA+ 13–24 year olds. It offers social interaction with other LGBTQA+ youth, as well as resources, support, and a 24-hour hotline for LGBTQA+ youth in crisis.

Lets Get Real: A Q&A Guide for Dating Trans Folks www.rainbow resourcecentre.org/files/GetReal-RRC.pdf is a Q&A guide for dating transgender individuals.

Legal Resources

Transgender Law Center https://transgenderlawcenter.org; grounded in legal expertise and committed to racial justice, TLC employs a variety of community-driven strategies to keep trans and nonbinary people alive and fighting for liberation.

ACLU www.aclu.org/other/know-your-rights-guide-trans-and-gender-nonconforming-students is a guide to inform transgender and nonbinary students of their rights in schools.

National Center For Transgender Equality www.transequality.org/issues/resources/responding-hate-crimes-community-resource-manual is a manual designed to help people develop a comprehensive and integrated response to hate crimes.

National Center for Lesbian Rights www.nclrights.org/legal-help-resources/resource/hidden-injustice-lgbt-youth-in-juvenile-courts/ discusses the hidden injustices that LGBTQA+ youth face in juvenile courts.

Ally Resources

National Center For Transgender Equality www.transequality.org/issues/resources/supporting-the-transgender-people-in-your-life-a-guide-to-being-a-good-ally is a comprehensive guide on how to be a good ally to transgender people.

Straight for Equality www.straightforequality.org/transresources provides a list of resources you may need access to in order to support a transgender person in your life.

Transgender Training Institute (TTI) www.transgendertraininginstitute. com provides training and consulting services that are informed/provided by transgender people, for the benefit of transgender people and communities.

Serano, J. (2013). *Excluded: Making feminist and queer movements more inclusive.* Berkeley, CA: Seal Press. A book that highlights how to be inclusive of transgender people in activism.

Transgender Women of Color

Trans Woman of Color Collective www.twocc.us; the celebration and uplifting of trans women of color's experiences and lives. They aim to help fight all oppressions trans women of color are experiencing.

National Black Justice Coalition (NBJC) http://nbjc.org/ is a civil rights organization dedicated to the empowerment of black lesbian, gay, bisexual, transgender, and queer (LGBTQA) people.

'Two Spirits' Documentary http://twospirits.org/; this documentary follows the life of a Native American person who identifies as two-spirit and what that means.

Health Resources

Center of Excellence for Transgender Health http://transhealth.ucsf. edu aims to provide health related or medical care, as well as being an inclusive, gender affirming resource for healthcare information for transgender individuals.

Gender Benders https://lgbtrightstoolkit.org/wp-content/uploads/2015/ 10/GB-Transition-Funding-Resource.pdf is a guide to funding a medical transition from grants and fundraising to utilizing insurance.

Social Service and Therapy Resources

National Center for Lesbian Rights www.nclrights.org/legal-help-resour ces/resource/a-place-of-respect-a-guide-for-group-care-facilities-serving-transgender-and-gender-non-conforming-youth/ is a guide for group facilities for the care of transgender and gender nonconforming youth.

American Psychological Association. (2015). Guidelines for psychological practice with transgender and non-binary people. www.apa.org/pra ctice/guidelines/transgender.pdf assists psychologists in the provision of culturally competent, developmentally appropriate, and trans-affirmative psychological practice with trans and nonbinary people.

Resources for LGBTQA+ People with Housing Insecurity and Homelessness:

National Coalition for the Homeless http://nationalhomeless.org/ issues/lgbt/ contains information on rates of homelessness for transgender people and what can be done to combat it.

Transgender Law Center https://transgenderlawcenter.org/resources/ housing contains information on housing rights for transgender people.

Teich, N. (2012). Transgender 101: A simple guide to a complex issue. Columbia University Press. https://cup.columbia.edu/book/transgen der-101/9780231157131. An in-depth exploration of transgender experience.

References

Abernathey, M. (2017). Transgender day of remembrance. *Remembering our dead project*. Retrieved from www.tdor.info/

American Medical Student Association (AMSA). (2015, November). *Transgender health*. Retrieved from www.amsa.org/advocacy/action-committees/gender-sexuality/transgender-health/

Balestrery, J. E. (2012). Intersecting discourses on race and sexuality: Compounded colonization among lgbttq American Indians/Alaska Natives. *Journal of Homosexuality*, 59(5), 633–655.

Bockting, W. O., Miner, M. H., Romine, R. S., Hamilton, A., & Coleman, E. (2013). Stigma, mental health, and resilience in an online sample of the US transgender population. *American Journal of Public Health*, 103(5), 943–951.

Durso, L. E., & Gates, G. J. (2012). *Serving our youth: Findings from a national survey of service providers working with lesbian, gay, bisexual, and transgender youth who are homeless or at risk of becoming homeless*. Los Angeles: The Williams Institute with True Colors Fund and the Palette Fund.

Feinberg, L. (2001). Trans health crisis: For us it's life or death. *American Journal of Public Health*, 91(6), 897–900.

Flores, A. R., Herman, J. L., Gates, G. L., & Brown, T. N. T. (2016). *How many adults identify as transgender in the United States? Introduction and summary* (p. 3). The Williams Institute. Retrieved from https://williamsinstitute.law.ucla.edu/research/how-many-adults-identify-as-transgender-in-the-united-states/

Green, E. R., & Maurer, L. (2015). *The teaching transgender toolkit*. Ithaca, NY: Planned Parenthood.

Grossman, A. H., & D'Augelli, A. R. (2006). Transgender youth: Invisible and vulnerable. *Journal of Homosexuality*, 51(1), 111–128.

Herman, J. L. (2013). Gendered restrooms and minority stress: The public regulation of gender and its impact on transgender people's lives. *Journal of Public Management & Social Policy*, 19(1), 65–80.

Human Rights Campaign. (2017). [Graph illustration the state policies that affect the LBGTQ community]. *State Maps of Laws & Policies*. Retrieved from www.hrc.org/state-maps/housing

James, S. E., Herman, J. L., Rankin, S., Keisling, M., Mottet, L., & Anafi, M. (2016). *The report of the 2015 U.S. transgender survey*. Washington, DC: National Center for Transgender Equality.

Joslin-Roher, E., & Wheeler, D. P. (2009). Partners in transition: The transition experience of lesbian, bisexual, and queer identified partners of transgender men. *Journal of Gay & Lesbian Social Services*, 21(1), 30–48. doi:doi:10.1080/10538720802494743

Kozicka, P. (2016, January 11). Singular 'they' named 2015's Word of the Year. *Global News*. Retrieved from https://globalnews.ca/news/2446364/singular-they-named-2015s-word-of-the-year/

Lang, A. (2017, November 20). *Why I don't believe in Transgender Day of Remembrance*. Retrieved from: www.them.us/story/why-i-dont-believe-in-trans-day-of-Remembrance?utm_source=social&utm_medium=facebook

National Center for Transgender Equality. (2018). *What experts say. Police departments across the country agree: There's been no increase in public safety incidents in cities and states with nondiscrimination laws*. Retrieved from https://transequality.org/what-experts-say

Platt, L. F., & Bolland, K. S. (2017). Trans★ partner relationships: A qualitative exploration. *Journal of GLBT Family Studies*, 13(2), 163–185.

Reisner, S., Bailey, Z., & Sevelius, J. (2014). Racial/ethnic disparities in history of incarceration, experiences of victimization, and associated health indicators among transgender women in the U.S. *Women & Health*, 54(8), 750–767. doi: doi:10.1080/03630242.2014.932891

Reisner, S. L., White, J. M., Dunham, E. E., Heflin, K., Begenyi, J., Cahill, S., & Project Voice Team. (2014, July). *Discrimination and health in Massachusetts: A statewide survey of transgender and gender non-conforming adults* (Executive Summary, p. 2). Fenway Health Institute. Retrieved from http://fenwayfocus.org/wp-content/uploads/2014/07/The-Fenway-Institute-MTPC-Project-VOICE-Report-July-2014.pdf

Schmider, A. (2016, November 9). 2016 was the deadliest year on record for transgender people. GLAAD. Retrieved from www.glaad.org/blog/2016-was-deadliest-year-record-transgender-people

Stryker, S., & Whittle, S. (Eds.). (2006). *The transgender studies reader*. Taylor & Francis.

Trans Student Educational Resources (TSER). (2013). November 19, 2017. Retrieved from www.transstudent.org/

Webb, A., Matsuno, E., Budge, S., Krishnan, M., & Balsam, K. (2015). *Non-binary gender identities fact sheet*. APA Division 44: The Society for the Psychological Study of Lesbian, Gay, Bisexual, and Transgender Issues. Washington, DC: APA. Retrieved from www.apadivisions.org/division-44/resources/advocacy/non-binary-facts.pdf

Wilson, E. C., Chen, Y. H., Arayasirikul, S., Raymond, H. F., & McFarland, W. (2016). The impact of discrimination on the mental health of trans★ female youth and the protective effect of parental support. *AIDS and Behavior*, 20(10), 2203–2211.

9 Addressing Behavioral Health Treatment among LGBTQIA Clients

Anthony Estreet

PH.D., MSW, LCSW-C, LCADC

Tonya C. Phillips

PH.D, MSW, LCSW-C, LCADC

Michelle G. Thompson

DOCTORAL CANDIDATE, M.S., L.M.H.C.

CSWE 2015 EPAS Competencies

Competency 1: Demonstrate ethical and professional behavior
Competency 2: Engage diversity and difference in practice
Competency 6: Engage with individuals, families, groups, organizations, and communities
Competency 7: Assess individuals, families, groups, organizations, and communities

As depicted in the following cases, addressing mental health and substance use disorders can be complex. Consider the following cases as you read through the content provided. We will revisit these cases after reviewing important clinical background material and LGBTQIA affirmative approaches for social work practice.

> **Box 9.1 Case: Adrian**
>
> A 40-year-old African American client named Adrian walks into your clinic seeking behavioral health services. During the assessment, Adrian reports that she has been experiencing depressed mood and anxiety since moving into her new neighborhood. Adrian also reveals that she is transgender and living with HIV. Adrian reports that she was born with male anatomy but always felt that she was living as someone else. She reports that her family does not accept her identity and has discontinued contact with her. Additionally Adrian reports that she is in a new

relationship with her boyfriend and identifies as being heterosexual. Adrian discloses that only a few close friends know that she is transgender

Box 9.2 Case: 16 Year Old Client

A 16-year-old adolescent client comes into the clinic due to increased depressed mood, suicidal ideations, isolation, lack of appetite, and decreased sleep. He reports having ongoing nightmares and flashbacks (during the day) which have caused panic attacks and fear of leaving the house. He reported being bullied online and in his neighborhood since he was "outed" as being gay following an online argument with a classmate over money for buying 20 Percocet's. The client reports that the neighborhood boys attacked him one day on his way home from school. He indicates that his family and parents have not said much to him since finding out that he had a boyfriend.

Background

Despite the increase in awareness and improvement regarding access to treatment following the passage of the Patient Protection and Affordable Care Act, mental health and substance use disorders continue to be reported at problematic levels (Briggs, Miller, & Briggs, 2016). The Substance Abuse and Mental Health Services Administration (SAMHSA) is a federal agency with a mission to reduce the impact of substance abuse and mental illness on America's communities. According to 2014 National Survey on Drug Use and Health (NSDUH; SAMHSA, 2014), an estimated 43.6 million adults ages 18 and up reported having a mental illness, while 20.2 million adults reported having a substance use disorder. Moreover, 7.9 million people reported both a mental health and substance use disorder, also known as co-occurring disorders. The ongoing need to address co-occurring behavioral health problems is a high priority for the social work profession (Briggs, Miller, & Briggs, 2016). This is also an area of much needed attention within the LGBTQIA community which have continuously experienced disparities in addressing their health and behavioral health needs (Erdley, Anklam, & Reardon, 2014).

According to Feldman and Wright (2013), LGBTQIA clients are at an increased risk for having mental health and/or substance use disorders when compared to their heterosexual counterparts. Moreover, individuals identifying as LGBTQIA are also less likely to seek treatment for mental health and/or substance use disorders when needed (McCabe et al., 2013). Research has demonstrated that individuals identifying as LGBTQIA experience stigma and discrimination which may affect their overall willingness and access to behavioral health treatment. According to Senreich (2010), substance use may be a method to cope with the stresses of societal discrimination, **internalized homophobia**, and/or feelings of shame which may result from consistent negativity expressed towards the LGBTQIA community. Furthermore, research has indicated that psychological stress associated with stigma and perceived or actual discrimination causes increases in mental health symptoms (Mereish & Poteat, 2015). Given this information, it is important to know that LGBTQIA clients could be at increased risk of mental health disorders such as depression, anxiety, or PTSD (SAMHSA, 2014).

Considerations Unique to LGBTQIA Clients in Treatment

Clients that identify as LGBTQIA present with multiple treatment needs that must be understood if treatment is to be successful (Wallace & Santacruz, 2017). Although the cases noted in Boxes 9.1 and 9.2 are fictional, these circumstances are very much a reality for many individuals in the community. Previous research has estimated that 9 million (about 3.8%) of Americans identify as gay, lesbian, bisexual, or transgender. Within that estimate, approximately 20 to 30% use drugs and alcohol, compared to approximately 9% of people in the general population (Wallace & Santacruz, 2017). As depicted in the case vignettes in Boxes 9.1 and 9.2, LGBTQIA clients often experience issues such as alienation from family members and fear of disclosing information about sexual orientation and gender identity (Schrimshaw, Siegel, Downing, & Parsons, 2013). Emotional distress and substance use may be increased for LGBTQIA clients with familial circumstances similar to those presented in the case vignettes. When working with LGBTQIA clients, social workers should be mindful that the family unit may not be a source of support (LaSala, 2013). It is important for social workers to utilize a culturally sensitive lens to apply their knowledge of engagement, assessment, and clinical intervention in order to provide appropriate clinical services (Craig, Austin, & Alessi, 2013).

Homophobia, stigma, and discrimination have a long history of affecting LGBTQIA clients and have been identified as a major barrier to help seeking and engaging in treatment (Calton, Cattaneo, & Gebhard, 2016; Wallace & Santacruz, 2017). This can be attributed to an ongoing history of overt stigma and discrimination. Prior to its removal in 1973, "homosexuality" was classified as a mental health disorder in the American Psychiatric Association's (APA) Diagnostic and Statistical Manual (DSM) (Kite & Bryant-Lees, 2016). Moreover, LGBTQIA clients were subjected to unethical treatment such as conversion therapy which was designed to change an individual's sexual orientation to the more acceptable heterosexual orientation (Drescher, D'Ercole, & Schoenberg, 2014). Given the ethical concerns and poor treatment outcomes from this clinical approach, the practice of conversion therapy has since been discontinued as an acceptable treatment approach (Drescher, D'Ercole, & Schoenberg, 2014). In fact, many major mental health organizations and associations have policy and position statements that directly oppose the use of conversion therapy. The National Association of Social Workers (NASW) and the APA both refute conversion therapy with position statements that highlight ethical concerns with reparative therapies (APA, 2009; NASW, 2015).

After much debate and policy changes, the attitudes of the general public have started to shift regarding the rights and freedoms of the LGBTQIA community; however, negative and discriminatory reactions remain a reality that continue to stigmatize this population (Feldman & Wright, 2013). In their survey of the LGBTQIA community, Pew researchers found that more than 90% of those surveyed believed that society had become more accepting in general of the LGBTQIA community (Taylor, 2013). Despite this increase in perceived acceptance, a significant portion of participants that were surveyed also reported experiencing societal stigmatization. Of those surveyed, 40% acknowledged experiencing rejection from friends and family and 30% had experienced physical attacks and/or threats. Sixty percent reported being the target of slurs or jokes with 21% of the sample reporting unfair treatment by employer and feeling unwelcomed at places of worship (30%) (Taylor, 2013).

The National Association of Social Workers Code of Ethics (NASW, 2017) has clear expectations for social workers working with LGBTQIA clients. Social workers cannot discriminate against clients or refuse to provide services for them solely because of their sexual orientation and/or gender identity. In keeping with the guiding principles of our profession and our Code of Ethics, social workers should create alliances with LGBTQIA clients (Eckstrand & Potter, 2017). Additionally, increasing their understanding within the community and enhancing access to care for clients that need support can strengthen a social worker's ability to assist their clients with working through issues related to stigma and discrimination based on sexual orientation and gender identity (Fredriksen-Goldsen et al., 2014).

Knowledge, Skill, and Ability (KSA) for Social Workers Working with LGBTQIA Clients

Social workers must be attentive to feelings of shame, doubt, and confusion in clients affected by anti-LGBTQIA discrimination, stigma, and prejudice (Senreich, 2010). Shame can be a significant trigger for increased mental health symptoms as well as avoidance of treatment (Mereish & Poteat 2015). Shame is classified as a painful belief in one's defectiveness as a human being which typically occurs as a result of negative self-images or beliefs about self-worth (Feldman & Wright, 2013). These issues are interwoven with existing mental health and/or substance use disorder treatment needs

(McCabe et al., 2013). Additionally, family discord is another factor which could increase the severity of symptoms and affect the happiness and quality of life among those affected by behavioral health conditions (Wallace & Santacruz, 2017). Additional areas of consideration include effective treatment interventions for substance use disorders which can become a mechanism for coping with social stigma and internalized homophobia (Wallace & Santacruz, 2017). Some of the most common reasons that people use drugs and alcohol are to cope with stress and peer socialization through avenues such as parties, nightclubs, and raves (Kelly, Davis, & Schlesinger, 2015).

Social networks can greatly influence quality of life for LGBTQIA clients. It can be beneficial to form positive associations that are able to provide support with addressing both substance use disorders and the stress associated with discrimination (Feldman & Wright, 2013). One form of social networks that social workers should be aware of are formed through Narcotics Anonymous or Alcoholics Anonymous. Many people with substance use disorders find hope and strength through 12-step programs. While many people benefit from engaging with 12-step programs, there are many who may choose not to attend 12-step meetings because of the religious/spiritual overtones within the approach. Spirituality and/or religious beliefs should be considered before recommending 12-step programs to LGBTQIA clients.

The following list highlights some additional key issues for social workers to consider when working with LGBTQIA clients:

- Complex dynamics of interpersonal relationships which can be a positive or negative influence on a client's behavioral health
- Understanding of the relationship between social life, social community, friends as family, and overall roles of bars and social life and drug use
- Recognizing the need for flexibility and be willing to adjust strategies in accordance with the client's characteristics
- Non-judgmental and respectfully accepting to the clients cultural, behavioral, and value differences.

Importance of Assessment Process

The assessment process is usually the first encounter with the client. It is during this phase that information is gathered to determine treatment needs and barriers to care; therefore, it is a critical component in the initial engagement phase of treatment. LGBTQIA clients with mental illness or substance use disorders often present to treatment with acute symptoms in advanced stages. In addition, the accompanying psychosocial stressors (homelessness, family rejection, coming out) exacerbate the potential for increase in substance use or mental health symptoms to include suicide risk. For this reason, comprehensive assessment tools that ask questions about many of the unique treatment needs of this population are recommended (Steele et al., 2017).

It is essential that the comprehensive assessment process is tailored to assess the psychosocial stressors as well as behavioral health and substance use needs. A suicide risk assessment should be completed at initial encounter and subsequent encounters to ensure ongoing safety (Steele et al., 2017). The suicide assessment should inquire about current as well as historical suicidal behaviors as well as family history of suicide. Much of the assessment tools used in treatment settings are designed to collect data that would pertain to traditional gender roles with limited query about other pertinent factors that may impact treatment outcomes. For example, most assessment forms assume marital status as married, single, separated, or widowed which does not capture all relationship types. Despite the legalization of same-sex marriage, there are still couples who may not live together or those who live together in closeted same-sex relationships (Feldman & Wright, 2013). The omission of this data is just an example of information that is not captured in an assessment, and could increase barriers for clinical practice, further isolating LGBTQIA clients. It is important to understand and assess the family system and the client's readiness or experience with disclosing sexual identity and coming out to others (LaSala, 2013). This could include the process of asking clients about sexual orientation, behaviour, and gender identity which is significantly important as they are different components of identity (Feldman & Wright, 2013).

Another component of the assessment process is understanding a client's family of origin. While these questions are pertinent to the overall clinical picture, there are some LGBTQIA clients that may have redefined what family means to them due to lack of support or acceptance from their family of origin (LaSala, 2013). Therefore, a thorough assessment of family (as defined by the client) and social networks is significant to understand the possible sources of support in the treatment process. Appropriately assessing and gathering this information can be helpful and increase willingness to engage and successfully complete treatment (Eckstrand & Potter, 2017). As illustrated in the cases of Adrian (Box 9.1) and the 16 year old client (Box 9.2), acceptance or rejection from the family has significant impact on mental health and/or substance use disorder symptoms as well as treatment related outcomes and should be included in a comprehensive assessment.

In the case of Adrian (Box 9.1), she reported that her relationship with her family of origin was impacted as a result of her gender identity; however, Adrian also identified that she does have friends that she felt comfortable disclosing her sexual identity to and that are also a possible source of support. Within this context, an assessment of how Adrian identifies her support would be critical to the overall engagement and support during the treatment process.

In the case of the 16-year-old client (Box 9.2), a clinical assessment of family supports would indicate that there is family discord with minimal communication. This particular case is exacerbated because of ongoing stigma, substance use, and depressed mood. This particular client would be further assessed for suicide risk as well as possible need for higher level of care if warranted. Additionally, identifying social supports would be critical in the treatment process given the clear indication of isolation, stigma, shame, and doubt. While working with the identified clients, social workers should ensure that treatment intervention strategies are developed based on assessment of these dynamics.

Clinical recommendations suggest programs should provide a safe space for LGBTQIA clients with substance abuse and emotional problems to talk freely about their lives (Briggs, Miller, & Briggs, 2016). The goal of comprehensive assessment is to identify needs and create safe spaces for treatment. As with every client, the social worker cannot assume a "one size fits all approach" and that all clients have the same clinical needs. The assessment phase can be used as a clinical approach to ensure that the complex needs of each client are addressed through a tailored and individualized treatment approach. For example, in Adrian's case (Box 9.1), there may be a need for additional questions around health and HIV management. Since Adrian indicated that she is in a relationship, gathering more information about health navigation and sexual behaviors may be informative. Additionally, information about why Adrian moved could be critical to the case. What about her new neighborhood is causing an increase in mental health symptoms?

Conversely, in the case of the 16 year old (Box 9.2), the earlier mentioned questions may not be as informative. Pertinent questions for this case could explore the onset and frequency of experiencing flashbacks and nightmares. Moreover, a deeper exploration of how long and often he has been bullied would be informative to his present symptomology. Understanding these symptoms in the context of isolation and lack of family support would also be imperative in both cases. An important aspect to consider during the assessment phase is how have previous treatment attempts impacted the client's view of treatment? Previous research has identified that negative treatment experiences such as experiencing stigma and discrimination from providers and other treatment participants, non-supportive environments, and hostility have impacted overall treatment outcomes among LGBTQIA clients (Mereish & Poteat, 2015; Pachankis et al., 2015). Understanding the importance of the clinical assessment is critical to good culturally sensitive social work practice with LGBTQIA clients. Engaging in a thorough yet sensitive clinical assessment can lead to increased engagement and the development of a more comprehensive individualized treatment approach.

Evidence Based Practice (EBP) Interventions and LGBTQIA clients

Throughout this chapter, there will be constant references to the overall importance of ongoing clinical assessment while working with your clients.

This ongoing process continues even during the clinical intervention phase. One of the more critical components to consider during the intervention phase is the issue of cultural sensitivity. Addressing mental health and substance use issues can be complex, however incorporating issues that often have effects among LGBTQIA clients such as lack of specialized treatment approaches, the "coming out" process, family isolation, socialization patterns, transference, countertransference, and self-disclosure could increase the complexity of the treatment experience. It is imperative that social workers are knowledgeable about these possible issues as well as competent and skilled to address them. Sue, Rasheed, and Rasheed (2015) offer several suggestions for increasing cultural sensitivity among social workers. They suggest that social workers consistently engage in a process of self-reflection and gain awareness of their own biases which could impact their clinical work. While this process may be difficult, it is a process that could inform the social worker of the overall ability to work with specific populations. Additionally, social workers can increase their cultural sensitivity by attending continuing education seminars which can greatly enhance their knowledge of working with LGBTQIA clients. Another suggestion is to engage with the community by attending community meetings or events to better understand the issues that could be affecting their clients (Drescher, D'Ercole, & Schoenberg, 2014; Erdley, Anklam, & Reardon, 2014; Fredriksen-Goldsen et al., 2014). In considering the overall complexities of addressing mental health and substance use issues among LGBTQIA clients, it is necessary to engage in culturally sensitive practice and consistently strive to provide individualized treatment options based on assessed clinical need (Sue, Rasheed, & Rasheed, 2015).

Screening, Brief Intervention, and Referral to Treatment (SBIRT)

As an important approach to working with LGBTQIA clients in behavioral health, it is critical to effectively address all aspects of the clinical needs. Several decades of research have shown that there are high rates of substance use and substance use disorders among the LGBTQIA adult population (Silvestre, Beatty, & Friedman, 2013). One way to ensure that clinicians are aware of possible issues is to integrate Screening, Brief Intervention, and Referral to Treatment (SBIRT) into the standard intake process. SBIRT is an evidence based practice (EBP) that employs a community-based approach to identify, reduce, and prevent substance use disorders and other health risk behaviors. The flexibility of this approach allows for implementation in diverse settings, including healthcare sites (e.g., community-based health clinics) and community events (e.g., Gay Pride) (Wallace & Santacruz, 2017). SBIRT programs have empirical support for reducing alcohol consumption or alcohol-related problems (Wallace & Santacruz, 2017) (for more information visit www.integration. samhsa.gov/clinical-practice/SBIRT). This approach consists of three steps which can be incorporated into ongoing social work practice with LGBTQIA clients:

1   **Screening**: A process that involves the use of standardized screening instruments to provide information for clinicians to understand risky health behaviors. Screening can occur in many social work settings.
2   **Brief Intervention**: The clinician reviews results of the screening with the client and engages the client in a short discussion reviewing substance using behaviors which allows for feedback and advice.
3   **Referral to Treatment**: The clinician makes a referral for further clinical assessment or intervention for clients whose screen indicates a need for additional services.

Utilizing the SBIRT approach in social work practice with LGBTQIA clients provides an opportunity to assess for substance use disorders on a continuum. This allows for the identification and intervention of substance using behaviors at various stages which include primary prevention, early intervention, and referral to treatment. In the primary prevention stage (abstinence/low risk use) which consists of approximately 75% of the general population, the social worker would complete the appropriate screenings and provide feedback to the client. As we progress to the early intervention stage (20% of general population), the social worker would engage in brief intervention or brief treatment as an opportunity to engage in dialogue about harmful/excessive substance use and the client's overall motivations and awareness of a possible concern. The final stage of the SBIRT process is the identification of a possible substance use disorder (5% of the general population). During this stage, the social worker would engage in a brief intervention to increase motivation and awareness followed by a referral to treatment. The integration of the SBIRT approach into social work practice increases the opportunities to identify those clients that are at risk or have risky substance using patterns and to provide an opportunity to address the identified substance use through a brief intervention (Russett, 2016).

Cognitive Behavioral Therapy

Cognitive behavioral therapy (CBT) approaches are encouraged to address stress associated with the coming out process, acceptance or emotional distress common among LGBTQIA clients, and for addressing many other mental health concerns such as self-esteem and self-worth. CBT can also be used as a treatment intervention to address beliefs related to stigma, discrimination, and internalized homophobia as well as to improve cognitive, affective, and behavioral stress among LGBTQIA clients (Pachankis et al., 2015; Pachankis, Cochran, & Mays, 2015; Wallace & Santacruz, 2017). The process of CBT challenges internalized negative beliefs while encouraging and supporting emotional regulation among many clients. Ongoing research supports the use of LGBTQIA affirmative CBT which emphasizes change, acceptance, tolerance, and understanding at an individual and societal level as a necessary component of behavioral health treatment (Craig, Austin, & Alessi, 2013; Pachankis et al., 2015).

Researchers have been increasingly adapting behavioral health interventions to address the ongoing complex needs of diverse populations. Craig, Austin, and Alessi (2013) adapted the foundation of CBT to create a CBT model specifically tailored to working with LGBTQIA populations. They proposed the following ten key considerations: 1) affirm identities, 2) foster collaboration with clients, 3) identify client strengths and supports, 4) clarify problem areas, 5) help client identify behavioral change, 6) validate client feelings, 7) collaborate over confrontation, 8) utilize cognitive restructuring, 9) help client identify positive thoughts, and 10) utilize homework as a supportive process. A detailed explanation of their ten considerations can be found in their manuscript (Craig, Austin, & Alessi, 2013, pp. 261–263). The use of EBP approaches provide the social worker and client with reliable and consistent therapeutic interventions which have been tested and accepted as beneficial within the social work profession (for more information visit www.samhsa.gov/nrepp).

Specialized Treatment Considerations

When engaging LGBTQIA individuals in behavioral health services, it is important that social workers utilize an LGBTQIA affirming practice approach. This approach to therapy embraces a positive view of LGBTQIA identities and relationships as well as recognizes and understands the importance of addressing macro, mezzo, and micro related issues (Rock, Carlson, & McGeorge, 2010). Some of the issues addressed using this approach which may impact clinical services and outcomes with your client include heterosexism, homophobia, marginalization, stigma, limited services, self-esteem, coming-out, and acceptance (Pachankis et al., 2015). One of the many benefits of this approach is that it is rooted in the person-in-environment (PIE) perspective and is strengths-based which means that it can be applied in a variety of practice settings. With its focus on 1) affirming LGBTQIA identities, 2) empowering clients, 3) supporting self-determination, 4) evaluating the effects of macro and micro forces, and 5) encouraging advocacy, this approach is particularly suitable for social work practice and could be beneficial to the overall clinical experience (Craig, Austin, & Alessi, 2013; Pachankis et al., 2015).

Treatment Considerations for Addressing Coming Out

As part of creating an LGBTQIA affirming therapeutic environment, clinicians should understand the importance of choosing to disclose one's sexual orientation and/or gender identity. This could be a significant issue during the clinical process especially if the client has not decided to disclose to their family and friends or they chose to disclose and received negative reactions. For LGBTQIA individuals, making the choice to disclose their sexual orientation and/or gender identity is an empowering decision in that the client does not feel the need to hide or remain "in the closet" regarding their identity (Feldman & Wright, 2013). The process of coming out can be therapeutic in addressing issues of self-esteem, secrecy, isolation, shame, anxiety, and depression for LGBTQIA clients (Drescher, D'Ercole, & Schoenberg, 2014). Consequently, the process can also contribute to increasing levels of depression, anxiety, and stress due to fear of negative responses and possible alienation by family and friends (Corrigan, Kosyluk, & Rüsch, 2013). These latter negative responses raise serious clinical concerns about the risk for suicide, substance abuse, and relapse. Coming out happens across one's lifetime in many contexts, and there are many factors that impact the process including social supports, environment, and overall perception of support (Feldman & Wright, 2013). For example, an LGBTQIA client can be out with close friends but not all friends, with their family but not within their community or work, or they can be out in all aspect of their lives. It is important for social workers to understand that for many LGBTQIA individuals, the burden of remembering where they are out or who they came out to can cause additional stress and related mental health concerns which impact overall wellness (Higa et al., 2014). Social workers should be supportive of the coming out process for their clients and provide a safe space for clients to work through the "balancing act" of this complex process (Craig, Austin, & Alessi, 2013; Pachankis, Cochran, & Mays, 2015). Additionally, it is important for social workers to consider the coming out process and differences based on race, culture, gender, age, and other forms of intersectionality (Feldman & Wright, 2013; Orel, 2014). The degree to which LGBTQIA clients come out is then dependent on a variety of aspects such as self-acceptance, safety, and overall support. This means that coming out may be a healthy decision which positively affects mental health for some but can also be an unhealthy decision which negatively impacts mental health for others (Mereish & Poteat, 2015; Schrimshaw et al., 2013).

As an integral part of addressing this process with clients, it is important for clinicians to understand the coming out process. Currently there are several models of identity development social workers can utilize during this process. One such model of identify formation is Fassinger's Model of Gay and Lesbian Identity Development (McCarn & Fassinger, 1996). Within this model, individual sexual identity and/or group membership identity occurs in four distinct phases: awareness, exploration, deepening/commitment, and internalization. One of the important aspects of this model is that identity formation occurs within the individual and the community. Another model used for identify development is the Transgender Identity Development

Model (Mathy & Kerr, 2014; Sloan, Berke, & Shipherd, 2017). Similar to Fassinger's model and the Cass model referenced earlier in this book, there are several steps within the transgender identity development model. These six steps consist of: understanding the role of gender identity, developing a personal transgender identity, developing a transgender social identity, becoming a transgender offspring, developing transgender intimacy status, and entering a transgender community (Evans, Forney, Guido, Patton, & Renn, 2010). While proponents of these models assert that these approaches occur in linear step-wise development stages, it is important to understand that each client is unique and that their identity development may not follow a linear approach (Feldman & Wright, 2013). Ultimately, clinicians working within this population should be aware of the importance and significance of this process and how it can affect the therapeutic process and client outcomes (Pachankis, Cochran, & Mays, 2015).

Gender and Treatment

When working with LGBTQIA clients in behavioral health treatment, research has consistently supported the need for treatment considerations that also take into account gender identity and/or expression (Steele et al., 2017). Addressing gender identity and expression in behavioral health treatment acknowledges the differences that may play a role in the overall clinical picture for those that identify as gay, bisexual, lesbian, transgender, and queer. Previous research has demonstrated ongoing disparities in the overall rates of mental health and substance use issues among and within LGBTQIA populations (Sloan, Berke, & Shipherd, 2017). As such, behavioral health clinical approaches should be informed by research and be culturally sensitive to address the wide variety of needs expressed by clients (Sue, Rasheed, & Rasheed, 2015). Previous research related to gender differences indicated that men and women experience different types of behavioral health issues as well as responses to treatment (Wallace & Santacruz, 2017). One criticism of behavioral health outcomes research is that participants have been historically classified using gender binary approaches. As a result, previous findings have indicated higher rates of mental distress among women when compared to their male counterparts (Steele et al., 2017). In addition, previous findings also indicated that women tend to experience "internalizing" disorders such as anxiety and depression whereas men typically experience "externalizing" disorder such as impulse control and substance use disorders (Needham & Hill, 2010). More recently, research has increased to examine health related issues among LGBTQIA individuals. Consequently, a large majority of the National Institutes of Health (NIH) funded research (79%) has focused on HIV/AIDS with substantially less focused on mental health (23.2%) and substance use disorders (30.9). Despite the low proportion of research funding, there has been a slight increase in studies that focus on identifying treatment related needs and specific interventions tailored to LGBTQIA clients (Coulter, Kenst, & Bowen, 2014).

Understanding the complexities of gender identity and expression within behavioral health treatment could lead to more culturally sensitive clinical interventions that specifically address the diverse needs within the LGBTQIA community instead of a treatment as usual approach. As previously mentioned, culturally sensitive behavioral health clinical interventions which address substance use disorders (Wallace & Santacruz, 2017) as well as mental health (Drescher, D'Ercole, & Schoenberg, 2014) among specific groups within the LGBTQIA community have increasingly emerged within the literature. More specifically, these clinical interventions are diverse in addressing older adults (Rogers et al., 2013), youth (Craig, Austin, & Alessi, 2013; Higa et al., 2014), gay and bisexual men (Pachankis et al., 2015), lesbian and bisexual women (Mathy & Kerr, 2014), and transgender individuals (Sloan, Berke, & Shipherd, 2017). Despite the modest progress towards identifying and evaluating clinical approaches, some research has identified the following as areas of concern in need of more investigation: parenting (LaSala, 2013), intimate partner violence (Calton, Cattaneo, & Gebhard, 2016), eating disorders (Duffy, Henkel, & Earnshaw, 2016), access to treatment (Steele et al., 2017), and trauma (Eckstrand & Potter, 2017).

Within the LGBTQIA population, there is also a need to highlight and address these differences in behavioral health treatment as well as acknowledge that within-group differences also exist when taking into account sexual orientation (Mathy & Kerr, 2014). For example, research has shown that women and men who engage in same-sex behavior or identify as LGBTQIA were found to be at higher risk for behavioral health disorders and treatment seeking behaviors when compared to their heterosexual counterparts (Steele et al., 2017). Moreover, LGBTQIA clients have been shown to demonstrate increased behaviors related to smoking, alcohol, and drug use when compared to their heterosexual counterparts (Eckstrand & Potter, 2017). These disparities have been related to a variety of factors such as acceptance, self-esteem, neighborhood violence, and other factors that affect the mental health of LGBTQIA clients and should be considered as a part of behavioral health treatment (Calton, Cattaneo, & Gebhard, 2016; Kelly, Davis, & Schlesinger, 2015; Silvestre, Beatty, & Friedman, 2013).

Another important treatment consideration is understanding that gender identity and sexual orientation exists on a continuum. As such, social workers should consistently check in with their clients to ensure that client treatment needs and expectations are being met. This is particularly important when working with clients that identify their sexual orientation as bisexual. Previous research has supported that some bisexual male clients may not identify as being bisexual or gay but may engage in sexual encounters with men (also known as men who have sex with men—MSM) (Schrimshaw et al., 2013). Moreover, given that many behavioral health treatment approaches for substance use disorders involve group treatment, some bisexual clients may be reluctant to identify themselves in treatment due to fear of being ostracized by both openly gay and lesbian clients as well as heterosexual clients (Schrimshaw et al., 2013). Previous findings have revealed that clients who identified as bisexual were less likely to disclose their sexual orientation and were more likely to discontinue treatment for negative reasons when compared to gay and lesbian clients (Senreich, 2010). In creating and considering an LGBTQIA affirmative therapeutic environment, it is important to understand these issues and be accepting of how they present in treatment.

Addressing HIV in Treatment

Addressing all aspects of behavioral health treatment needs for LGBTQIA clients include ongoing discussion and education around HIV transmission and safer sex practices, particularly among gay and bisexual males (Fonner et al., 2016). Addressing HIV education and monitoring risky behaviors such as substance use and unprotected sex is an important component of treatment (Miller et al., 2015). Clinicians should understand and incorporate knowledge regarding the HIV disease process and effective treatment and management. The integration of HIV education is especially important if the client also engages in risky substance use such as intravenous drug injections and sharing of needles (McCabe et al., 2013). Clinicians should become knowledgeable of medications used to treat and manage HIV such as antiretroviral therapy (ART) as well as the possible physical and mental health related side effects commonly associated with being HIV positive (Shelby, Aronstein, & Thompson, 2014). Some of these side effects include depression, anxiety, self-esteem, hypervigilance, and isolation. These side effects can compound existing behavioral health treatment concerns and need to be addressed as part of ongoing treatment (Fonner et al., 2016; Miller et al., 2015). Moreover, clinicians should be utilizing an integrated treatment approach and discussing medication adherence and reducing the stigma that may be experienced as a result of having HIV (Shelby, Aronstein, & Thompson, 2014). Addressing clients with HIV can bring up additional treatment issues such as safer sex vs abstinence (Miller et al., 2015). Clinicians should be knowledgeable about the use of pre-exposure prophylactic (PREP) medications as well as the affects that abstinence can have on existing relationships (Fonner et al., 2016; Shelby, Aronstein, & Thompson, 2014). There may also be a need to address grief and loss issues especially if the client has experienced the death of family and friends to AIDS (older LGBTQIA clients) (Rogers et al., 2013).

Family Therapy Considerations

Addressing family concerns during therapy with LGBTQIA clients is an important area to explore as this can reveal family dynamics which should be considered as part of ongoing treatment (LaSala, 2013). These issues could concern sexual orientation, assisting with disclosure or the "coming out" process, addressing shame and guilt from both client and family perspectives, as well as stigma. It is important to understand the role of the family in the client's life as well as how existent relationships could decrease or increase areas of clinical focus (LaSala, 2013). More to the point, the clinician should not disclose the sexual orientation of the client if this information is not known to the family. As part of family therapy, there may be a need for education regarding ongoing behavioral health issues and how such issues can be exacerbated by ongoing issues related to sexual orientation. This is particularly important when addressing issues such as substance use disorders and discussing the inclusion of family support. In helping the family to understand this, creating a safe LGBTQIA affirmative environment and alliance with the family and client is essential.

Behavioral Health among Older LGBTQIA Adults

Behavioral health treatment has been slow to address the needs of older adults in general and among LGBTQIA older adults specifically despite ongoing projections that the "baby boomer" population will contribute significantly to an increase in older adults by 2030 (Rogers et al., 2013). Research has estimated approximately 2.5% of adults age 50 and older identify as LGBTQIA (Erdley, Anklam, & Reardon, 2014; Fredriksen-Goldsen et al., 2014). This estimate accounts for more than 2.4 million older adults with projected estimates for 2030 greater than 5 million (Rogers et al., 2013). Despite this increase, behavioral health treatment among this population remains underdeveloped and poorly characterized as a large majority of treatment approaches are not culturally sensitive or adapted for older adults (Erdley, Anklam, & Reardon, 2014; Fredriksen-Goldsen et al., 2014).

It is important for social workers to understand the many complex issues facing older LGBTQIA adults. Previous research has described the complex nature of addressing mental health among older LGBTQIA clients as a "hidden epidemic" given the probability of older LGBTQIA clients having to hide their sexuality, substance abuse, and mental health (Erdley, Anklam, & Reardon, 2014). Moreover, older LGBTQIA adults have reported barriers to treatment such as living with stigma, long term discrimination, undiagnosed or under treated substance use and mental health disorders, grief and loss issues, isolation, and confronting the challenges of late life without traditional supports such as multigenerational families or legally sanctioned marriage between same-sex partners (Orel, 2014). It is important to engage this population and develop a thorough understanding of the psychosocial stressors that occur in their lives and that existing behavioral health concerns could be both a cause and consequence of being an LGBTQIA older adult (Erdley, Anklam, & Reardon, 2014; Fredriksen-Goldsen et al., 2014).

Conclusion

Social workers who practice within mental health and/or substance use disorder treatment settings must be aware of the ongoing and significant issues which may affect LGBTQIA clients. While addressing the client's immediate treatment need is a primary focus, it is equally important for social workers to engage clients through the use of LGBTQIA affirmative practice approaches. As this chapter has demonstrated, there are many complex client needs and barriers which impact treatment engagement, retention, and overall outcomes among LGBTQIA clients. As previously mentioned, LGBTQIA clients are at higher risk for mental health concerns including suicide and substance use disorder (Craig, Austin, & Alessi, 2013). As such, it is critical for social workers to utilize a culturally sensitive treatment approach to engage LGBTQIA clients and ensure that treatment needs and expectations are congruent. Moreover, it is imperative that social workers understand the complex needs of individual clients and understand the importance of starting where the client is and working through the process at a pace that is comfortable to the client. Given that research which has indicated poor treatment seeking behaviors among LGBTQIA clients has been associated with perceived stigma and discrimination from behavioral health professionals, the use of effective engagement strategies such as motivational interviewing will provide a space that is non-judgmental and empowering which has been shown to increase retention and utilization of clinical services (Shelby, Aronstein, & Thompson, 2014). Social workers should continuously demonstrate cultural sensitivity when working within LGBTQIA clients and use an appropriated clinical lens to validate the experiences of their clients. Each client that enters treatment is unique and different in their own way; it is up to the social worker to perform a thorough assessment to ensure that all treatment needs are met. Moreover, social workers should advocate within their treatment setting to ensure openness and acceptance of all clients by staff and other clients (Shelby, Aronstein, & Thompson, 2014).

Questions to Consider

1   Research in this chapter indicated that LGBTQIA people are at greater risk for substance use and for mental health challenges. What do you think contributes to these higher rates?
2   Strong skills in assessment are key to working with LGBTQIA clients, especially surrounding substance use and mental health. In what areas of assessment do social workers need to be particularly vigilant? Why is it as important to tune in to what a client is *not* saying as well as what they are actually saying?
3   What unique facets for LGBTQIA people must social workers consider in the intersection of coming out and substance abuse and/or mental health concerns?

4   Why is it important to engage in evidence based practices such as SBIRT and cognitive behavioral therapies? How would you utilize these approaches in your work with LGBTQIA individuals and communities?

5   Why is it important to consider the unique needs of older LGBTQIA? How might age impose different risks for older adults than for younger adults? What strengths and challenges unique to age cohort must social workers include in assessment, treatment, advocacy, and practice?

References

American Psychological Association (APA). (2009). Report of the APA task force on appropriate therapeutic responses to sexual orientation. Retrieved from www.apa. org/pi/lgbt/resources/sexual-orientation.aspx

Briggs, H. E., Miller, S. E., & Briggs, A. C. (2016). Enhancing behavioral health workforce in youth mental health through grand challenges in social work. *Journal of Child and Adolescent Behavior*, 4, 270. doi:doi:10.4172/2375-4494.1000270

Calton, J. M., Cattaneo, L. B., & Gebhard, K. T. (2016). Barriers to help seeking for lesbian, gay, bisexual, transgender, and queer survivors of intimate partner violence. *Trauma, Violence, & Abuse*, 17(5), 585–600.

Coulter, R. W., Kenst, K. S., & Bowen, D. J. (2014). Research funded by the National Institutes of Health on the health of lesbian, gay, bisexual, and transgender populations. *American Journal of Public Health*, 104(2), e105–e112.

Corrigan, P. W., Kosyluk, K. A., & Rüsch, N. (2013). Reducing self-stigma by coming out proud. *American Journal of Public Health*, 103(5), 794–800. doi: doi:10.2105/AJPH.2012.301037

Craig, S. L., Austin, A., & Alessi, E. (2013). Gay affirmative cognitive behavioral therapy for sexual minority youth: A clinical adaptation. *Clinical Social Work Journal*, 41(3), 258–266.

Drescher, J., D'Ercole, A., & Schoenberg, E. (2014). *Psychotherapy with gay men and lesbians: Contemporary dynamic approaches*. Routledge: New York, NY.

Duffy, M. E., Henkel, K. E., & Earnshaw, V. A. (2016). Transgender clients' experiences of eating disorder treatment. *Journal of LGBT Issues in Counseling*, 10(3), 136–149.

Eckstrand, K. L., & Potter, J. (Eds.). (2017). *Trauma, resilience, and health promotion in LGBT clients: What every healthcare provider should know*. Springer International Publishing AG: Gewerbestrasse, Switzerland.

Erdley, S. D., Anklam, D. D., & Reardon, C. C. (2014). Breaking barriers and building bridges: Understanding the pervasive needs of older LGBT adults and the value of social work in health care. *Journal of Gerontological Social Work*, 57(2–4), 362–385.

Evans, N., Forney, D., Guido, F., Patton, L., & Renn, K. (2010). *Student development in college: Theory, research, and practice*. Jossey-Bass: San Francisco, CA.

Feldman, S. E., & Wright, A. J. (2013). Dual impact: Outness and LGB identity formation on mental health. *Journal of Gay & Lesbian Social Services*, 25(4), 443–464.

Fredriksen-Goldsen, K. I., Hoy-Ellis, C. P., Goldsen, J., Emlet, C. A., & Hooyman, N. R. (2014). Creating a vision for the future: Key competencies and strategies for culturally competent practice with lesbian, gay, bisexual, and transgender (LGBT) older adults in the health and human services. *Journal of Gerontological Social Work*, 57(2–4), 80–107.

Fonner, V. A., Dalglish, S. L., Kennedy, C. E., Baggaley, R., O'reilly, K. R., Koechlin, F. M., ... & Grant, R. M. (2016). Effectiveness and safety of oral HIV preexposure prophylaxis for all populations. *AIDS (London, England)*, 30(12), 1973.

Higa, D., Hoppe, M. J., Lindhorst, T., Mincer, S., Beadnell, B., Morrison, D. M., ... Mountz, S. (2014). Negative and positive factors associated with the well-being of lesbian, gay, bisexual, transgender, queer, and questioning (LGBTQ) youth. *Youth & Society*, 46(5), 663–687. doi:10.1177/0044118X12449630

Kelly, J., Davis, C., & Schlesinger, C. (2015). Substance use by same sex attracted young people: Prevalence, perceptions and homophobia. *Drug and Alcohol Review*, 34(4), 358–365.

Kite, M. E., & Bryant-Lees, K. B. (2016). Historical and contemporary attitudes toward homosexuality. *Teaching of Psychology*, 43(2), 164–170.

LaSala, M. C. (2013). Out of the darkness: Three waves of family research and the emergence of family therapy for lesbian and gay people. *Clinical Social Work Journal*, 41(3), 267–276.

Mathy, R. M., & Kerr, S. K. (2014). *Lesbian and bisexual women's mental health*. Routledge: New York, NY.

McCabe, S. E., West, B. T., Hughes, T. L., & Boyd, C. J. (2013). Sexual orientation and substance abuse treatment utilization in the United States: Results from a national survey. *Journal of Substance Abuse Treatment*, 44(1), 4–12.

McCarn, S. R., & Fassinger, R. E. (1996). Revisioning sexual minority identity formation: A new model of lesbian identity and its implications for counseling and research. *The Counseling Psychologist*, 24(3), 508–534. Doi: doi:10.1177/0011000096243011

Mereish, E. H., & Poteat, V. P. (2015). A relational model of sexual minority mental and physical health: The negative effects of shame on relationships, loneliness, and health. *Journal of Counseling Psychology*, 62(3), 425–437.

Miller, C. T., Solomon, S. E., Bunn, J. Y., Varni, S. E., & Hodge, J. J. (2015). Psychological symptoms are associated with both abstinence and risky sex among men with HIV. *Archives of Sexual Behavior*, 44(2), 453–465.

National Association of Social Workers (NASW). (2015). *Sexual orientation change efforts (SOCE) and conversion therapy with lesbians, gay men, bisexuals and transgender persons: NASW position statement*. Washington, DC: Author.

National Association of Social Workers (NASW). (2017). *Code of ethics of the National Association of Social Workers*. NASW Press: Washington, DC.

Needham, B., & Hill, T. D. (2010). Do gender differences in mental health contribute to gender differences in physical health? *Social Science & Medicine*, 71(8), 1472–1479. doi:doi:10.1016/j.socscimed.2010.07.016

Orel, N. A. (2014). Investigating the needs and concerns of lesbian, gay, bisexual, and transgender older adults: The use of qualitative and quantitative methodology. *Journal of Homosexuality*, 61(1), 53–78.

Pachankis, J. E., Cochran, S. D., & Mays, V. M. (2015). The mental health of sexual minority adults in and out of the closet: A population-based study. *Journal of Consulting and Clinical Psychology*, 83(5), 890–901. doi:doi:10.1037/ccp0000047

Pachankis, J. E., Hatzenbuehler, M. L., Rendina, H. J., Safren, S. A., & Parsons, J. T. (2015). LGB-affirmative cognitive-behavioral therapy for young adult gay and bisexual men: A randomized controlled trial of a transdiagnostic minority stress approach. *Journal of Consulting and Clinical Psychology*, 83(5), 875–889.

Rock, M., Carlson, T. S., & McGeorge, C. R. (2010). Does affirmative training matter? Assessing CFT students' beliefs about sexual orientation and their level of affirmative training. *Journal of Marital and Family Therapy*, 36(2), 171–184. doi: doi:10.1111/j.1752-0606.2009.00172.x

Rogers, A., Rebbe, R., Gardella, C., Worlein, M., & Chamberlin, M. (2013). Older LGBT adult training panels: An opportunity to educate about issues faced by the older LGBT community. *Journal of Gerontological Social Work*, 56(7), 580–595.

Russett, J. L. (2016). Best practices start with screening: A closer look at screening, brief intervention, and referral to treatment in adolescent, military, and LGBTQ populations. *Journal of Addictions & Offender Counseling*, 37(2), 116–126.

Schrimshaw, E. W., Siegel, K., Downing Jr, M. J., & Parsons, J. T. (2013). Disclosure and concealment of sexual orientation and the mental health of non-gay-identified, behaviorally bisexual men. *Journal of Consulting and Clinical Psychology*, 81(1), 141.

Senreich, E. (2010). Are specialized LGBT program components helpful for gay and bisexual men in substance abuse treatment? *Substance Use Misuse*, 45(7–8),1077–1096. doi:doi:10.3109/10826080903483855

Shelby, R. D., Aronstein, D. M., & Thompson, B. J. (2014). *HIV and social work: A practitioner's guide*. Routledge: New York, NY.

Silvestre, A., Beatty, R. L., & Friedman, M. R. (2013). Substance use disorder in the context of LGBT health: A social work perspective. *Social Work in Public Health*, 28(3–4), 366–376.

Sloan, C. A., Berke, D. S., & Shipherd, J. C. (2017). Utilizing a dialectical framework to inform conceptualization and treatment of clinical distress in transgender individuals. *Professional Psychology: Research and Practice*, 48(5), 301–309. doi:10.1037/pro0000146

Steele, L. S., Daley, A., Curling, D., Gibson, M. F., Green, D. C., Williams, C. C., & Ross, L. E. (2017). LGBT identity, untreated depression, and unmet need for mental health services by sexual minority women and trans-identified people. *Journal of Women's Health*, 26(2), 116–127.

Substance Abuse and Mental Health Services Administration (SAMHSA). (2014). *National survey on drug use and health: Summary of national findings* (HHS Publication No. SMA 15–4927, NSDUH Series H-50). Retrieved from www.samhsa.gov/data/

Sue, D. W., Rasheed, M. N., & Rasheed, J. M. (2015). *Multicultural social work practice: A competency-based approach to diversity and social justice*. John Wiley & Sons.

Taylor, P. (2013). *A survey of LGBT Americans: Attitudes, experiences and values in changing times*. Pew Research Center. Retrieved from www.pewsocialtrends.org/2013/06/13/a-survey-of-lgbt-americans/

Wallace, B. C., & Santacruz, E. (2017). Addictions and substance abuse in the LGBT community: New approaches. *LGBT Psychology and Mental Health: Emerging Research and Advances*, 153–176. Praeger- ABC-CLIO: Santa Barbara, CA.

10 Healthcare Access and Disparities

Lisa E. Cox

PH.D., LCSW, MSW

Kimberly A. Furphy

DHSC, OTR, ATP

CSWE 2015 EPAS Competencies

Competency 1: Demonstrate ethical and professional behavior
Competency 3: Advance human rights and social, economic, and environmental justice
Competency 7: Assess individuals, families, groups, organizations, and communities
Competency 8: Intervene with individuals, families, groups, organizations, and communities

---

Box 10.1 Case: David

David is a 60-year-old gay white male substance use counselor who is contemplating retirement. After 30 years, David's pension and healthcare benefits will provide him fine insurance coverage. Jim, David's long-time African American HIV-infected unmarried partner is ill and less financially stable. Unfortunately, Jim's HIV stage is progressing and requiring David's caregiving assistance. While working, David can escape stress caused by caregiving. The couple experience health disparities as people from the LGBTQIA community who have different types of health coverage. Jim is 70 and now depends on Medicaid assistance. David and Jim both try to keep abreast of the latest healthcare policy changes. They waited a long time before disclosing their sexual orientation and varied health statuses to their health providers because they wanted to avoid stigma.

Introduction

The healthcare system includes multiple professionals including physicians, nurses, hospitalists, occupational and physical therapists, health social workers, and others. Facilities or settings where healthcare professionals (HCPs) render services include outpatient clinics, hospitals, medical centers, rehabilitation facilities, mental health centers, long-term care, and hospice. HCPs also work at educational venues that help people prevent disease, and at institutions and laboratories focused on detection, planning, research, and planning. An assortment of health related activities have been created to prevent, detect, and treat mental health, physical and cognitive disorders and to improve people's well-being. Such services fall under the auspices of 'healthcare.' People's experiences vary insofar as how well they are able to access and experience healthcare activities and services.

This chapter offers definitions of healthcare access and health disparities. Interventions will also be examined, from the controversial and harmful conversion and reparative therapies to the helpful methods of **motivational interviewing**, trauma-informed care, cognitive behavioral therapy, and psychodynamic modalities.

Healthcare Access, Disparities, and Health Disparities

Gaining access involves helping people obtain appropriate healthcare resources in order to preserve or improve their health. Access is a rather complex notion that requires evaluation and exploration. Generally, if services are available and there are enough available services, then there exists an opportunity to get healthcare and have access to services. Yet, how well populations gain access depends on financial, organizational, and socio-cultural barriers that limit service utilization. Stigma exemplifies such a barrier. Access to healthcare is measured in terms of use and such depends on the acceptability, affordability, and physical accessibility of services and not just mere supply. Available services require relevance and effectiveness if a population is to gain access to satisfactory health outcomes. The barriers to access and availability of services require consideration in the context of multiple perspectives, health needs, and cultural settings of diverse societal groups. Equity of access might be measured by availability, utilization, or service outcomes.

Access to healthcare is important for the LGBTQIA population. Essentially, access to health services connotes the timely use of personal health services to achieve the best health outcomes. This includes timely entry into the healthcare system, accessing a place where needed healthcare services are provided, and finding a trustworthy and communicative provider. Healthcare access can help people be knowledgeable about their overall physical, mental and social health status, prevent disease and disability, detect and treat health conditions, prevent death, improve life expectancy, and enhance quality of life.

LGBTQIA people face challenges with access to healthcare. Barriers to access include insurance coverage differences, geographic proximity and caliber of healthcare systems, physicians' and other HCPs' cultural competence levels and more. Figure 10.1 illustrates multiple barriers experienced by LGBTQIA people. For example, environmental factors such as rural vs.

Figure 10.1 Health Care Disparities for LGBTQIA People

urban healthcare system resources matter. People's emotional state, and intellectual strengths for coping with changing physical realities, affect the type of specialized or home healthcare services one can access. What occupation one has held has implications for healthcare benefits and pensions received. And, one's social support networks and spiritual resources—where one gets their meaning in life—are instrumental in helping LGBTQIA people have success or failure in receiving adequate and appropriate healthcare services.

Disparities in healthcare access to services affect both individuals and society. Limited access to healthcare affects people's ability to reach their full potential, and negatively affects their quality of life. Barriers to healthcare services include high cost, lack of insurance coverage, lack of availability, and stigma. These barriers to accessing quality healthcare services potentially lead to delays in getting appropriate care, unmet health needs, the inability to get preventive services, and unwanted hospitalizations.

Healthcare disparities are "differences in the quality of healthcare that are not due to access-related factors or clinical needs, preferences or appropriateness of intervention" (Institute of Medicine; IOM, 2002). This means that healthcare disparities are merely one particular aspect of health disparities. Although the overall effect of these disparities is considered small, relative to other health determinants, it is often thought to have the most relevance to the medical community since it is the most amenable to changes within the healthcare system (HealthyPeople.gov, n.d.).

The term **health disparities** appears to be understood intuitively, yet much of its actual meaning exacts controversy. Generally speaking, not all differences in health status between groups are considered to be disparities. Only differences which systematically and negatively affect less advantaged groups are classified as disparities. In the United States, discussion about disparities has focused mostly on ethnic and racial disparities. In the broader international literature, socioeconomic status (SES) and gender disparities, disparities between disabled and non-disabled people, and disparities by sexual orientation have also been considered.

Perhaps a major point requiring discussion is whether, within these definitions, differences which are not likely to be changed by social or policy interventions should be included? For example, what about those caused by genetic differences between racial and ethnic groups? What about considerations for people making the transition from one gender to the other? Often, difficulty exists in differentiating disparities related to non-genetic vs. genetic influences. Yet, from a social justice standpoint, it is important to focus on differences for which society has a role in creating and ameliorating.

SES presents a complex measurement issue for studies related to health disparities. Intersecting diversity factors prevalent in the LGBTQIA community range, and the theory of intersectionality can apply. Imagine the difference in SES for a person who is gay, African American, HIV-infected, and uninsured to a professional gay white man who is insured, married, and very healthy. Reconsider the characters in Box 10.1 again—sexual orientation and gender identity intersect with SES when we consider how David has insurance, a pension, and options for healthcare that his partner, Jim, does not.

The concept of SES represents a composite of multiple factors, including income, education, childhood income level, wealth, and parental education. Too often, in health disparities research, this complexity is distilled down to the use of one, or no more than two, of these factors. Ideally research concerning the SES link to health disparities should incorporate multiple factors. An additional consideration in measuring gender and SES in the study of health disparities is how to consider the complex ways these constructs can interact with each other. For example, being from a lower SES group affects the health of LGBTQIA people differently than the general heterosexual population and such nuances must be included into the conceptualization and study of health disparities. Both David and Jim will have different healthcare access and disparity issues than will Barak and Michelle Obama or Donald and Melania Trump.

To help clients like David, Jim, and others, social workers must be advocates against stigma, educators about healthcare resources and policies, and counselors regarding the best use of insurance and community resources. Social workers can intervene to combat health disparities across macro, mezzo, and micro levels of practice. Involved social workers can coordinate health fairs, work in AIDS Service Organization clinics, run support groups for LGBTQIA people who have received recent health diagnoses, and counsel partners and family members about health related issues and services.

History of Healthcare for the LGBTQIA Community

For countless generations, LGBTQIA people have experienced discrimination resulting in an inability to access healthcare services as easily as their heterosexual counterparts (Rounds, McGrath, & Walsh, 2013, p. 99). This is due, in part, to a stigma associated with the term 'homosexuality,' which was listed as a mental illness in the *Diagnostic and Statistical Manual of Mental Disorders* until 1973, when the American Psychological Association (APA) replaced the term 'homosexuality' with the diagnosis of 'sexual orientation disturbance.' It was not until 1987 that the APA agreed to remove terms related to 'homosexuality' from the DSM completely (Burton, 2015, p. 87). Anti-LGBTQIA interpretation of religious doctrines has historically increased stigma and discrimination, which has in some cases fueled violence against LGBTQIA persons. In addition, the rise in incidence of HIV and AIDS since the early 1980s resulted in fear and discrimination of not only HIV-infected people, but particularly for gay men, whom were perceived as the primary conduit through which the virus spread. Historically, this LGBTQIA discrimination has negatively affected state and national policy governing the healthcare practice with and the well-being of LGBTQIA people (Bogart, Revenson, Whitfield, & France, 2013, p. 1; Anastas, 2013, p. 302).

Anti- LGBTQIA marriage laws, like the 1996 Defense of Marriage Act (DOMA), prohibited same-sex partners from marrying and thus from receiving the same benefits from individuals in heterosexual relationships, including access to their partner's employer sponsored health plans. In many jurisdictions, there was also a lack of access to family medical leave for the care of same-sex domestic partners (Anastas, 2013, p. 305). Prior to the institution of same-sex marriage in many states, visitation and medical decision-making for a sick same-sex partner was not permitted (Anastas, 2013, p. 305). Often, there was a failure to accept same sex partners as health proxies (Strong & Folse, 2015). In addition, immigrants who were married to same-sex spouses who were United States' citizens were not considered family members, so were ineligible for the visas granted to those in heterosexual marriages (Anastas, 2013, pp. 305–306). With the same-sex marriage laws often under scrutiny and on the agenda for state and national elections, it was important for healthcare workers to monitor these marriage laws to know what rights were afforded to their LGBTQIA clients and to advocate for those rights when the laws were not being upheld by HCPs.

Although laws have changed, social workers cannot become lax. In the future, it will be important for social workers to monitor how the situation progresses or regresses. In particular, in the coming years, now that we are post *Obergefell v. Hodges*—the court case that requires that all states must recognize the relationship and benefits for people who are legally married—social workers must educate others about this case law and its implications for healthcare access.

Discrimination against LGBTQIA individuals by HCPs is often born out of a **heteronormative paradigm**, where HCPs assume that all patients are heterosexual and therefore proceed with care as such (Morrison & Dinkle, 2012, p. 123). Misgendering a client (referring to a client with an incorrect pronoun or assumption about their gender) also occurs. LGBTQIA patients, in turn, have been apprehensive in disclosing their sexual orientation and gender identity to their HCPs for fear of negatively affecting the care they will receive. Their apprehension is not without support, as an early 1994 survey reported that 67% of health professionals surveyed said they had observed inferior care provided to lesbian and gay patients because of their reported sexual orientation (Schatz & O'Hanlan, 1994). Healthy People 2020 reported that there is a clear shortage of culturally aware providers, who are knowledgeable about LGBTQIA health (HealthyPeople.gov, n.d.). Other studies found that healthcare provider training programs lack essential content to train HCPs to be culturally competent with the LGBTQIA community (Lim, Brown, & Kim, 2014, p. 25; Bidell, 2013, p. 300). Health practice trends also perpetuate discrimination. Medical forms do not address LGBTQIA concerns by not including options for identifying sexual orientation, sexual identity, gender identity, or pronouns. There is also an absence of LGBTQIA health literature or signage available in most primary care physician offices and hospitals (Strong & Folse, 2015).

There is, however, hope on the horizon. Recent new anti-discrimination laws for the LGBTQIA community have been enacted, which has led to considerable increases in societal acceptance of this group (Witek, 2014). This has resulted in several federal, state, and local health initiatives that are supportive of the LGBTQIA community.

The United States Department of Health and Human Services, in its Healthy People 2020 program, highlighted the LGBTQIA community as a target group for concern and improvement (HealthyPeople.gov, n.d.). This is in contrast to Healthy People 2010, which emphasized the elimination of health disparities to provide equal access to healthcare to all patients and identified the LGBTQIA population as having health disparities, but without emphasis on the need for improvement (Healthy People 2010, n.d.). In 2010, President Obama, in his Presidential Memorandum on Hospital Visitation, asked for greater compassion and understanding towards all families dealing with medical crises. This memorandum required federally funded hospitals to respect the stated visitation preferences of LGBTQIA patients (Obama, 2010). The 2011 Institute of Medicine (IOM) report outlined current LGBTQIA research, identified gaps in knowledge, and provided recommendations for furthering the knowledge base (IOM, 2011).

The Joint Commission (2011) provided healthcare organizations with information about patient–family engagement, patient assessment, end-of-life care and directives, among others, to better understand and meet the needs of LGBTQIA patients. President Obama signed the Patient Protection and Affordable Care Act (PPACA or ACA) into law in 2010 (Patient Protection and Affordable Care Act, 2010). Since then, legally married same-sex couples are protected under the ACA. In addition, the ACA protects LGBTQIA patients from discrimination based on their health status, including HIV status, and does not place limits on medical coverage, such as monthly or annual limits on HIV medications. And, because of LGBTQIA health disparities like increased use of tobacco and risk of obesity, the ACA provides for wellness and prevention programs with no additional costs above the monthly premium. The 2013 repeal of DOMA gave equal rights to same-sex couples and led the way for an increase in the number of states with same-sex marriage laws, which increased access to health insurance for same-sex partners wanting to enroll in their spouse's employer health insurance plan. It is important that social workers are aware of the laws to ensure that their clients are receiving all benefits afforded to them and to advocate for them when such benefits are withheld.

Healthcare Organizations' Need to Train

In addition to new state and federal initiatives supporting the rights of LGBTQIA individuals, there has been a response by healthcare organizations to provide training to staff to be cognizant of LGBTQIA concerns. Such trainings provide HCPs with the skills and knowledge necessary to provide advocacy for and guidance to their LGBTQIA clients. Fenway Health in Boston developed education modules for HCPs to help improve cultural competency skills when working with LGBTQIA clients (Makadon, Mayer, Potter, & Goldhammer, 2007). Services and Advocacy for Gay, Lesbian, Bisexual and Transgender Elders (SAGE) offers trainings for those working in long-term care (LTC) facilities in meeting the needs of LGBTQIA nursing home residents (Anastas, 2013, p. 305). GLMA: Health Professionals Advancing LGBT Equality (previously known as the Gay & Lesbian Medical Association), an association of lesbian, gay, bisexual, and transgender (LGBT) healthcare professionals, including social workers, functions to ensure quality in healthcare for LGBTQIA individuals and HCPs through public policy advocacy resource dissemination related to LGBTQIA health (GLMA, n.d.). The Human Rights Campaign (HRC) Health Equality Index initiative offers recognition to hospitals and other healthcare organizations that document their ability to meet four foundational criteria for LGBTQIA care in order to offer LGBTQIA-friendly workplace policies and affirmative care to LGBTQIA patients (HRC, n.d.). Social workers should ensure that they consistently participate in trainings and seek out opportunities to advance their knowledge and skills in assessment, intervention, and advocacy for their LGBTQIA clients in order to assist them as they navigate through the system in meeting their unique healthcare needs.

Current Trends in Healthcare for the LGBTQIA Population

At times, health issues affecting LGBTQIA individuals parallel those of the general population, but researchers have also demonstrated that LGBTQIA individuals can have unique health needs and have experienced disparities in care (Makadon, 2011, p. 220). LGBTQIA youth are more likely to attempt suicide and be homeless; have higher rates of tobacco, alcohol, and other drug use; and have a higher prevalence of certain mental health issues (Lim, Brown, & Kim, 2014, p. 27). Many older LGBTQIA individuals have spent a good part of their lives hiding their sexual orientation and gender identity from others, including HCPs, due to past experience with discrimination and victimization (Foglia & Fredriksen-Goldsen, 2014, S41). They are less likely to feel comfortable coming out of the closet so have less family and community supports available to them and often rely on friends or other non-traditional caregivers for their care (Makadon, 2011, p. 223; Lim, Brown, & Kim, 2014, p. 27). Historically, older LGBTQIA individuals also faced additional barriers to optimal health because of self-imposed isolation due to stigma and a lack of culturally appropriate social services and providers. Older LGBTQIA couples have also had to utilize their own resources for wills and advanced directives because they did not have the protections of other married couples until the passage of gay marriage laws (Makadon, 2011, p. 223). Transgender individuals are less likely than lesbians, gay men, bisexuals, and heterosexuals to have health insurance (HealthyPeople.gov, n.d.). They also have a high prevalence of attempted suicide and are more frequently victims of violence. For LGBTQIA veterans, until its repeal and termination in 2011, the 'Don't Ask, Don't Tell' policy had barred openly gay men and lesbians for 18 years from serving in the military. Fortunately, the Veteran's Health Administration (VHA) developed a strategic plan for fiscal years 2013–2018. This outlined a plan for veterans to receive timely, high quality, personalized, safe, effective, and equitable healthcare regardless of gender, race, age, or sexual orientation (VHA, n.d.).

The IOM, in its 2011 report, discussed LGBTQIA people as a **sexual minority**. As such, some LGBTQIA individuals suffer from chronic and sustained high levels of **minority stress** due to the stigmatization of being in a minority group and history of past practices of discrimination, according to the **minority stress model** (Brooks, 1981; Meyer, 1995; Meyer, 2003). Due to this stress, health issues, both physical and mental, are often higher in the LGBTQIA population than in their heterosexual counterparts (Sabin, Riskind, & Nosek, 2015, p. 1831). The incidence of obesity is high for lesbians and bisexual women and, as such, these groups also have higher rates of diabetes and heart disease (Beohmer, Bowen, & Bauer, 2007, p. 1136). Lesbian women are also less likely to seek preventive services for reproductive cancer, yet lesbians and bisexual women are at greater risk to be diagnosed with breast and colon cancer (Beohmer, Bowen, & Bauer, 2007, p. 1139). Gay and bisexual men, especially those who are African

American, are at higher risk for HIV (CDC, 2017a). From 2010–2014, the incidence of HIV diagnoses in Hispanic/Latino gay and bisexual men increased by 13% (CDC, 2017a). Transgender people, especially transgender women, are also at great risk for HIV infection. In 2013, the number of transgender people who received an HIV diagnosis was three times the national average (CDC, 2017b). This is due to many factors including the use of injectable hormones with shared syringes, high levels of drug abuse compared to the general population, homelessness, prostitution, insensitivity to transgender issues by HCPs, and overall stigma and discrimination in healthcare, education, employment, and housing (CDC, 2017b). The prevalence of smoking is reportedly 27% to 71% higher among gay and bisexual men, and 70% to 350% higher among lesbians and bisexual women, than it is the general population (Burkhalter, et al., 2009, p. 1312). There are also higher rates of alcohol and drug abuse among LGBTQIA individuals (HealthyPeople.gov, n.d.). Mental health problems are more prevalent in the LGBTQIA population than in the general population (Makadon, 2011, p. 223). Gay and bisexual men have more depression, panic attacks, suicidal ideation, and psychological distress than do heterosexual men (Cochran, Mays, & Sullivan, 2003, as cited in Makadon). Lesbian and bisexual women are at greater risk of generalized anxiety disorder, depression, antidepressant use, and psychological distress (Cochran, Mays, & Sullivan, 2003, p. 53). Gay and bisexual men have more body image and eating disorders than do heterosexual men. Rates of domestic violence and sexual violence in the LGBTQIA community, particularly for transgender individuals, are as high or are higher than in the general population (Rhodes, McCoy, Wilkin, & Wolfson, 2009, p. 1083; Rothman, Exner, & Baughman, 2011; Stotzer, 2009).

It is important that social workers be vigilant in recognizing the unique healthcare needs of their LGBTQIA clients and in determining the barriers they may face during their healthcare experiences. In doing so, social workers will be better equipped to advocate for their clients and to provide their clients with guidance as they seek out HCPs to meet their needs.

Ways to Decrease Disparities and Improve Current Access to Healthcare

Because there are disparities in health and healthcare access for LGBTQIA individuals and there have been recent policies and programs to address some of these disparities, it is imperative that social workers and other HCPs advocate for further change to help support and expand the initiatives that are in place.

The 2015 *Obergefell v. Hodges* ruling ensured that employers offering a **fully insured healthcare plan** to their employees with an opposite sex spouse must offer that same plan to their employees with a same-sex spouse. Notably, employers offering **self-insured health plans** do not follow state insurance law and may have a loophole to avoid coverage to same-sex spouses (Arendshort, 2015). These employers may, however, be subject to discrimination lawsuits based on **Title VII of the Civil Rights Act of 1964** (Arendshort, 2015). For this reason, it is less likely this situation would occur. Social workers and their LGBTQIA clients should be aware of the implications of both types of employer sponsored healthcare plans as they consider employment options and apply for employer benefits, and should know about options available to them to advocate for benefits they may need.

HCPs and organizations should also improve efforts to collect appropriate demographic information related to sexual orientation and gender identity, so that data from this can be used to further research and offer other health initiatives for the LGBTQIA community (Gates, 2011; Silvestre, 2003). Curriculum standards for all health professionals should require training and education in working with LGBTQIA patients (Wheeler & Dodd, 2011, p. 309). Better yet, greater support for funding of research that examines further the health disparities within the LGBTQIA population and the LGBTQIA cultural competence of health providers would better ensure that the needs of the LGBTQIA population are met by HCPs trained to provide care for their unique needs (Wheeler & Dodd, 2011, p. 309).

Given these current trends in healthcare for the LGBTQIA population, interventions are required to maintain quality of life and good physical, cognitive, and mental health. The next section addresses an array of interventions to help minimize health disparities.

Interventions

An assortment of treatment modalities have documented some effectiveness in helping LGBTQIA people cope better with health concerns and navigate health access and disparities. The utility of motivational interviewing, **trauma informed care**, CBT, and psychodynamic modalities are discussed. Aspects of inter-professional education and practice also are explored. This section will first entertain a brief discussion about historical approaches to interventions and the use of conversion therapy (NASW, 2015).

Conversion and Reparative Therapies/Methods

People seek mental health services for multiple reasons, and ought to have a breadth of knowledge about human sexuality and communicating about human sexual development. When such education does not occur, some LGBTQIA people have been forced or feel pressured to seek conversion therapy. Unfortunately, social workers who practice in schools, hospitals, child welfare, or other contexts still encounter LGBTQIA youth who have parents or guardians who want to change their identity through the use of conversion and reparative approaches.

Conversion and reparative therapies have been a historical and controversial approach used with the LGBTQIA community. Historically, concerns have circled around children and adults being forced into harmful conversion programs. Now there is also the issue of LGBTQIA adults seeking to 'change' on their own, from religion, family, cultural, or other influences. The term sexual orientation change efforts (SOCE) typically includes reparative therapy, conversion therapy, and/or transformational ministries (Venn-Brown, 2015). The use of sexual orientation change efforts might comprise psychotherapy, aversion therapy, medical, religious and spiritual approaches, and sometimes even sexual violence (often referred to as 'corrective rape') (Anastas, 2013). Believers in these therapies claim that scientific data show these methods to be effective; however, many others disagree (APA, 2009; Guevin, 2013; Panozzo, 2013). NASW's Position Statement (NASW, 2015) has discredited and highly criticized SOCE, in conjunction with other major medical, psychiatric, psychological, and professional mental health organizations. The NASW Policy Statement on LGB issues and the NASW Policy Statement on Transgender and Gender Identity issues provide guidelines for social work practice with LGBT clients and communities, and these statements do *not* support SOCE (SAMHSA, 2015). This policy statement suggests that social workers must be aware that there are proponents of conversion and reparative therapies, especially within some cultures and religions. Therefore, social workers must work to educate communities and advocate for greater understanding.

Motivational Interviewing

What motivates people to change or be willing to access healthcare? Miller and Rollnick (1991) reflect on how Prochaska and DiClemente's (1983) six stages of change offer ways to assess people's readiness to change and roll with resistance. Motivation is a key dimension of adherence, so 'motivation' could be defined as the "probability that a person will enter into, continue, and adhere to a specific change strategy" (Miller & Rollnick, 1991, pp. 19–20). Several scholars have identified effective motivational approaches (Hanson & Gutheil, 2004; van Wormer, 2007) listed in Box 10.2.

Box 10.2 Motivational Interviewing Approaches

Giving ADVICE
Removing BARRIERS
Providing CHOICE
Decreasing DESIRABILITY
Practicing EMPATHY
Providing FEEDBACK
Clarifying GOALS
Active HELPING

(Miller & Rollnick, 1991)

A motivational interviewing approach might work very well with LGBTQIA people because they are often ambivalent about coming out and the change this decision may have on their life. In motivational interviewing, the social worker does not assume an authoritarian role; and, strategies are persuasive rather than coercive, and supportive more than argumentative. There are general principles associated with motivational interviewing that many social work and other scholars have employed. For example, social workers can express empathy towards LGBTQIA people. Social workers can also develop discrepancy, avoid argumentation, roll with resistance, and support the self-efficacy of their LGBTQIA clients (Hanson & Gutheil, 2004; Miller & Rollnick, 1991; van Wormer, 2007).

Very often, economic and social conditions affect people's efforts to improve their health and lifestyles. For example, some services or healthcare systems reinforce patient passivity, thereby making a person's best efforts to promote change through individual consultations and engaging in motivational interviewing impossible (Rollnick, Miller, & Butler, 2008, pp. 157–158). Barriers within healthcare systems and beyond influence people's motivations for health change behavior. Redesigning services, being courteous, collaborative and conscientious, and connecting people to community resources facilitates healthcare access for all.

Unfortunately, "communication traps" can hinder communication or increase client resistance (Hohman, 2012, p. 101). When social workers, for example, fall into the traps of questioning/answering, blaming, playing expert, shaming, labeling, or taking sides, clients may shut down (Hohman, 2012). Schumacher and Madson (2015, pp. 100–106) offer tips and strategies for addressing these communication faux pas and for helping clients who are making very slow progress. To address slow progress, social workers may wish to use evocative questions, assess importance and confidence, and revise or change the existing plan. Motivational interviewing provides endless possibilities for use with LGBTQIA clients, such as not blaming people who get angry because of challenges accessing healthcare.

Trauma-Informed Care

Trauma is common and it has societal, economic, and physical health effects. Psychobiology reveals how humans are wired to adapt, manage, and learn from stressful events. General literature on post-traumatic stress disorder (PTSD) shows how it can be diagnosed following just a single traumatic event, while epidemiological research indicates how a person's risk of PTSD or trauma increases with the number of traumatic experiences (Pantalone, Hessler, & Simoni, 2010; Ruben et al., 2017). Many LGBTQIA people experience one or more hate crimes in their life, and they may also have experienced a range of life experiences and microaggressions that contribute to traumatic responses or even PTSD (Ryan, Russell, Huebner, Diaz, & Sanchez, 2010). Some LGBTQIA people may feel there are few 'safe' spaces to feel accepted and open. Social workers need to know about resources for assisting LGBTQIA clients with trauma. There is a list of resources at the end of this chapter to consult for greater clarity.

CBT and Psychodynamic Modalities

The goal of cognitive-behavioral therapy (CBT) is reduced emotional distress, greater self-efficacy, and improved coping skills and activities, rather than intellectual awareness or insight, a goal that is more psychodynamic (Dobson & Dobson, 2009). Cognitive-behavioral therapists do not view psycho-education as a stand-alone treatment. Numerous types of understanding exist in CBT, such as awareness of triggers, emotions, cognitions, behavioral patterns, or understanding of the functional links among these factors. For problem resolution or true change to happen, clients must become aware and behave differently. CBT focuses on *doing* that leads to experiential *insight* and cognitive change (O'Donohue, Fisher, & Hayes, 2003).

Some researchers and clinicians (Craig, Austin, & Allesi, 2013; Ross, Doctor, Dimito, Kuehl, & Armstrong, 2007) question the utility of CBT and query "Does CBT ignore sociological contexts and feminist models of depression?" The feminist model argues that depression in women might be a natural response to our society that undermines and victimizes women more than men such that more women experience poverty, sexual assault and sexual harassment and so on. Hence models that solely focus on 'what is wrong with the self,' rather than including awareness of 'what is wrong with our societal structures' might harm the LGBTQIA population. Social workers should be sensitive, address holistic notions, and entertain person-in-the environment concepts and approaches.

With CBT, therapeutic collaboration between the person seeking healthcare and professional providers, and warmth, genuineness, and empathy are important. Otherwise, clients may become dissatisfied, drop out or terminate treatment, or respond poorly (Pearsons, 2008).

Research on **psychodynamic psychotherapy** has typically been of two principal types: investigations of the process of therapy and studies designed to measure treatment effects or outcomes (Brandell, 2004, p. 373). Often HCPs are asked to assemble their concise clinical assessment after only one meeting with a person. In clinical social work practice, clinical assessment has been geared to evaluating psychopathology, developmental derailments, and dysfunction as well as a person's strengths and assets. While social work has tended to emphasize environment and resources, other therapists include the important psychodynamic concepts of *transference* and *countertransference* in their dynamic assessments. A comprehensive psychodynamic-oriented assessment would consider the following components: diagnostic summary, mental status examination results, assessment of ego/superego functions and object relational capacities, competence, provider's subjective experience of a person, genetics, and a treatment plan (Rubenstein, 2012).

Assessment is central to determining if interventions are effective. Such a formal assessment and treatment plan can tell providers about a person's strengths, weaknesses, and salient aspects about their history. Assessment and intervention results may be informative about complex clinical data and the client's narrative, thereby effectively going beyond simple check-list information. Multi-disciplinary views and assessments are also important; therefore, the following section discusses the benefits of engaging in inter-professional practice when helping to minimize health disparities for LGBTQIA people.

Inter-Professional Practice

Inter-professional education occurs when two or more professions learn about, from, and with each other to enable effective collaboration and improve health outcomes (Nelson, Tassone, & Hodges, 2014, p. 7). In other words, inter-professional education/practice (IPE) is collaboration between professionals across disciplines. This approach was created because of the lack of knowledge between health professionals that caused mis-communication and errors (Nimmagadda & Murphy, 2014; Schaefer & Larkin, 2015). The goal of IPE is to provide improved and more affordable healthcare for populations served and to aid people better on an individual basis (Addy, Browne, Blake, & Bailey, 2015).

Intersections of diversity occur in the lives of LGBTQIA people who social workers and other therapists assist. Intersectionality is a theoretical basis for understanding the diverse identities of clients/patients. In this theory, some clients may experience a compounding of oppression or pri-vilege when society marginalizes their identities. For example, a female lesbian of color may experience more challenges and stigmatization than a gay white male. Even though both share a potentially marginalizing LGBTQIA identity, gender and race may compound oppression for the female lesbian of color in ways that the gay white male will not experience.

Inter-professional education/professional practice (IPE/P) can counter negative consequences of intersectionality. There is an interesting intersec-tion of professions (e.g. social work, occupational therapy, etc.), and an expanded potential for intersecting identities of each of these same profes-sionals' own diverse identities (e.g. gender, race, ethnicity, sexual orienta-tion, etc.). Professionals who have experienced similar marginalization through intersectionality can present as role models for clients/patients. Intersectionality connotes the privileging and marginalization of a person as whole. Diversity intersections between professionals and clients/patients can help a person when they are trying to meet their needs if those intersections work in favor of that person. Adversely, diversity intersections can prohibit someone from meeting their human needs if the levels of diversity they carry do not work cohesively (Cox, Tice, & Long, 2015). Social workers, occupation therapists, and a sundry of HCPs assess people across intersections of diversity. Following are two examples of frameworks offered by social work and occupational therapist professionals.

Box 10.3 Case: Val

Val was stressed after receiving a breast cancer diagnosis six months after her 50th birthday. Val subsequently underwent a double mastectomy two months ago and has recently returned to work after approval to do so by her physician. She does still have chemotherapy treatments to complete and has been attending occupational therapy due to some limitations in the use of her shoulders from the surgery. Val is a long-time softball coach in a university-based athletics program and her wife of two years is her assistant coach. They have been in a committed relationship for 15 years and have a 14-year-old daughter. Each day, as she drives to her beloved job, she worries about her treatment options and care from the myriad of HCPs with whom she is now required to interact. Val dreads both the upcoming medical treatment(s) and therapies, and conversations with HCPs as she has had previous experiences where her doctors did not consider her then partner as a member of her immediate family. She also hates the thought of dealing with insurance companies and follow-up appointments at outpatient imaging centers. She also is concerned about her ability to continue working to support her wife and their daughter.

Let us now examine Val's case using an inter-professional approach between the two disciplines of social work and occupational therapy. We will present an introduction to each discipline's practice frameworks, and a discussion about how professionals in these two disciplines can work interprofessionally to address Val's concerns while being sensitive to her needs.

Social Work Frameworks

The social work profession draws upon an assortment of frameworks, including person-in-environment worldview, systems theory, strengths perspective, and intersectionality. Social work values self-determination and the dignity and worth of all people. Social work professionals who work in health, mental health, substance abuse, children and family services, or gerontology settings all require assessment skills to help LGBTQIA people access healthcare and reduce health disparities. Several theoretical orientations frame social workers' thinking and subsequent practice endeavors. Assessment skills help clients gain healthcare access and strong assessment skills help social workers identify areas where LGBTQIA clients are disenfranchised from healthcare access and experience greater disparities. Scholars (Emlet, 2016; Foglia & Fredriksen-Goldsen, 2014) have established the linkage of economic disparities, social support risks, double stigma, and homophobia to realized health disparities. The person-in-environment and strengths perspective frameworks offer useful approaches and concepts to help HCPs to assist LGBTQIA people who experience health disparities.

Person-in-environment (PIE) was created from scientific views and the evidence-based ecological systems theory. PIE highlights evidence-based and problem-solving approaches and encourages social workers to assess experiences of stigma and trauma (Dybicz, 2015).

The strengths perspective emphasizes how a client system has assets, in the form of resources, support, and knowledge. This perspective focuses on the positive aspects of a client's life to resolve issues for which they are seeking help (Cox, Tice, & Long, 2015). Social workers operating from a strengths perspective would urge other HCPs on their team to consider the transference or countertransference issues at play when caring for a patient/client who identifies as LGBTQIA.

Systems theory explores the many systems that make up a client. The systems used to assist a client are typically comprised of clients, friends, family, religion, and education. Systems theory is used to distinguish goal(s) and to decide what needs must be met in order to reach these goal(s) (Cox, Tice, & Long, 2015). Social workers ascribing to a systems theory approach would help LGBTQIA clients assess their social supports and viable resources in healthcare.

Occupational Therapy Frameworks

Occupational therapists are uniquely poised to work with LGBTQIA individuals and to assist with reducing the health disparities that are apparent within the LGBTQIA population. The profession's core belief is that there is a positive relationship between occupation, various kinds of life activities in which individuals, groups, or populations engage, and health. People are viewed as occupational beings and, as such, must engage in occupations to live productive, satisfying, and healthy lives. Services that occupational therapists provide can have rehabilitative effects for those who have an illness or who have sustained an injury. They can also promote health and wellness for those who may be at risk of illness or injury to ensure optimal occupational functioning.

The American Occupational Therapy Association's (AOTA, 2014) *Occupational Therapy Practice Framework (OTPF)* stated that,

> Occupational therapy practitioners use their knowledge of the transactional relationship among the person, his or her engagement in valuable occupations, and the context in which occupations are performed to design occupation-based intervention plans that facilitate change or growth in client factors (body functions, body structures, values, beliefs,

and spirituality) and skills (motor, process, and social interaction) needed for successful participation.

(AOTA, 2014, S1)

Occupational therapists seek to understand their clients in order to determine what guides their occupational choices. Social workers (SWs) and occupational therapists (OTs) often collaborate inter-professionally. While SWs assess strengths and consider PIE, OTs assess LGBTQIA clients' functional status. SWs and OTs draw upon common professional values that acknowledge the growth and well-being of people. The case of Val (Box 10.3) demonstrates how SWs and OTs collaborate. Occupation is important from a physical, psychological, and spiritual well-being standpoint of both the client and client system. The importance of physical functioning in one's role leads to success in one's life. For economic success, if Val can keep her job, she will retain a sense of meaning in her life, and she will achieve financial security to support her housing and basic needs. Feeling fulfilled may also support Val's spiritual needs and relationships.

Sexual identity is a core component of personal identity. It can influence the occupational choices LGBTQIA clients/patients make. Furthermore, their values and beliefs could be based upon who they are as a member of the LGBTQIA community. Sexuality is an Activity of Daily Living (ADL) and can be addressed with clients who are LGBTQIA as part of a holistic approach to treating the whole person (McRae, 2013, p. 2).

The Model of Human Occupation (MOHO) is based on open systems theory, with intake conceptualized as a person attending to information of interest (Kielhofner, 2008). Processing occurs with the resultant output being occupation. MOHO further states that humans consist of three interrelated components that serve to explain how occupation is motivated, patterned, and performed (Kielhofner, 2008). *Volition* refers to the motivation for occupation or the individual's drive to engage in certain activities. The OT seeks to understand why individuals are motivated to do what they do based on their values, interests, and personal causation. *Habituation* is the process by which occupation is organized into patterns or routines; that is, through doing, behavior forms into patterns and routines emerge. The OT seeks to understand what it is that the individual has done that has influenced their daily life patterns and routines. *Performance capacity* refers to the physical and mental abilities that underlie skilled occupational performance. The OT determines how well this person can do the things they are motivated to do. MOHO also emphasizes that to understand human occupation, the therapist must understand the physical and social environments in which occupation takes place (Kielhofner, 2008). This is a theoretical bridge area with social work. Additionally, through acting in various physical and social contexts, individuals receive feedback from what they do, process that feedback, which is then taken back into the system (intake), creating change over time. In applying this Model, occupational therapists seek to understand the motivations of their clients in the choices they make for occupational performance. Therefore, the OT can utilize this Model with LGBTQIA clients to determine the motivations for their participation in occupations that lead to unhealthy or healthy behaviors, habits, and routines. They can seek to create change through interventions (feedback) within the contexts in which they participate in their favored occupations.

Let us consider these two professional frameworks while revisiting Val's case (Box 10.3). Consider, for example, Val driving to work. As she frequently does during her drive, Val is thinking about an upcoming tournament in which her team is to compete. She plans how she will prepare her team to face a highly ranked team. However, she is also concerned that her need to attend OT therapy sessions will impede her ability to prepare the team fully for the tournament. As she pulls into work, she calls her OT to see if they can rearrange her therapy schedule in order for her to place more time into the team's preparations. The OT considers Val's request and wonders why she cannot have her assistant coach run the practices during Val's absence. She then recalls that Val's wife is the assistant coach and likes to attend the sessions so she can assist Val with exercises as necessary. Although the OT knows that ultimately it would be best for Val to attend her therapy sessions, she also realizes that Val loves her job and has, on several occasions, stated that she knows it was her job that got her to remain positive during the diagnosis, surgery, and now post-surgery treatment. The OT also realizes that Val's partner is an important part of her recovery and is a necessary and valuable support system in Val's life. The OT then works with Val to establish a schedule that would meet Val's work schedule better, while also allowing her to participate in her therapy. The OT considers that Val's work, her occupation, is important to her and motivates her to work towards recovery. It gives her pleasure and it likely has played a valuable role in keeping Val emotionally healthy to endure the physical impact of the cancer diagnosis. In addition, the OT realizes the support of Val's partner as being another valuable part of her recovery. In approaching Val's situation in this way, the OT has approached Val from a client-centered perspective, one in which would likely alleviate Val's apprehension in approaching her and disclosing her needs during future therapy sessions.

While in her therapy session, Val discusses with her OT her feelings of despair and anxiety. She states that she has always been a very positive, strong person, but has recently had a short fuse and has verbally lashed out at her wife and daughter. She states that she is very concerned that she will need to take time off from work to fully recover and is concerned with what the loss of income would mean to her family should she need more time off than she would be allotted through her employer. In addition, she has been thinking more about her own mortality, and how that would affect her family.

The OT asks Val if she would like to speak with a social worker about her concerns, as the social worker would likely have more resources to share with Val on her concerns about her income and benefits. Val agreed, but stated that she would prefer that the social worker attend an OT session to speak with her, as she cannot take more time off from her job. The OT contacts the social worker who, in turn, attends Val's next therapy session. Together, Val, her wife, the OT, and the social worker come up with a plan for Val, including contacting her employer to determine what exact benefits she is entitled to and then developing a subsequent action plan to address potential income gaps should she be out of work for an extended period. After meeting with the social worker to develop this plan, Val also agrees to meet weekly with the social worker for CBT to address the triggers to her anxiety and ways to address her responses to anxiety more appropriately.

Advocacy in Healthcare Contexts

The attitudes towards LGBTQIA people, particularly patients with HIV/ AIDS, have changed over the years. When people with HIV/AIDS experience felt or perceived stigma, their motivation to get healthcare is hindered. They fear seeking help because they feel as though they will be judged and not receive the same degree of care if they disclose their illness. This fear of accessing healthcare can easily be life threatening. For example, in the early 1990s, Americans viewed HIV-infected people as unworthy of care and deserving quarantine. Only gradually has this fear of contagion and indictment on deserving treatment changed (LaVeist, 2005, p. 201).

The LGBTQIA population can at times struggle to gain equal access to healthcare. The reason for this unequal access is due to fear, stigma, and bias of HCPs. When LGBTQIA people do decide to access healthcare, biases and stigma may still be a problem; and, the provider may not be aware of the patient's individual needs. As a result, they may not be receiving the same care as heterosexuals (LaVeist, 2005, p. 291). Living with HIV/AIDS may indeed lead to experiencing stigma.

LGBTQIA populations in the United States can experience significant health disadvantages such as stigma, reduced social supports, and financial disparities (Whitehead, Shaver, & Stephenson, 2016, p. 1). Fears and experiences of stigma and disclosure of sexual orientation and/or gender identity to HCPs are significant barriers to healthcare utilization for LGBTQIA people in both urban and rural samples. In addition, higher scores on stigma scales have been associated with lower utilization of health services.

Conclusion

In summary, health disparities are apparent in the LGBTQIA community. Social work practitioners, occupational therapists, and other HCPs will continue to interact with clients and colleagues who are LGBTQIA. Particular theoretical frameworks and interventions can be more helpful to understand the very different healthcare access experiences LGBTQIA people face. Ethical social work and occupational therapy practice requires a wide-ranging acceptance and understanding of gender and sexual diversity, as well as skills to activate the strengths of their LGBTQIA clients. Working successfully with LGBTQIA people who need healthcare services and resources requires HCPs to reject negative value judgments derived from oppressive cultural norms, and to explore their own biases and tendencies.

Acknowledgment: Thank you to Felicia Mainiero, M.S.W. for her time and work locating selected literature, proofreading references, and assembling thoughts about social work frameworks.

Questions to Consider

1   How has the history of healthcare in the LGBTQIA community affected their ability to access health services?
2   What recent federal, state, and/or local initiatives have helped to reduce the disparity in healthcare access for LGBTQIA individuals?
3   What can healthcare professionals do to decrease healthcare disparities and improve access to healthcare services for the LGBTQIA community?
4   Which interventions might be most useful in helping LGBTQIA people live and cope well?
5   How might health access be maximized and health disparities be minimized for LGBTQIA people requiring healthcare?
6   What healthcare related policies require consideration when helping LGBTQIA people not to experience health disparities?
7   How can inter-professional educators collaborate to help LGBTQIA people prevent health disparities?

Resources

Websites

Gay and Lesbian Medical Association: 1326 18th Street, NW: Washington, DC 20036; 202.600.8037 www.glma.org

National LGBT Health Education Center www.lgbthealtheducation.org/ This site offers health information to LGBTQIA people

National Council for Behavioral Health www.thenationalcouncil.org/ This site provides information about trauma informed care

National Clearinghouse on Family Violence (The National Council) https://ncadv.org/resources offers a Handbook on Sensitive Practice for Health Care Practitioners

The NW (Northwest) Network of Bi, Trans, Lesbian and Gay Survivors of Abuse www.nwnetwork.org/ This site provides LGBTQIA-specific support for survivors of abuse

U.S. Department of Veteran Affairs www.va.gov provides sexual trauma information for women's medical providers and practice guidelines for the delivery of trauma informed care and GBLTQ culturally informed practice

Support Groups

CENTERLINK—The Community of LGBT Centers www.lgbtcen ters.org/localstatenational-groups.aspx
Gay Parent LGBT Magazine www.gayparentmag.com/support-groups

Exercises: Complete the Activity, then Check Your Knowledge

Website with activities https://lgbtrc.usc.edu/education/activities/
Activity https://lgbtrc.usc.edu/files/2015/05/Thats-Gay.pdf
Answers https://lgbtrc.usc.edu/files/2015/05/Answers.pdf

References

Addy, C. C., Browne, T., Blake, E. W., & Bailey, J., (2015, March). Enhancing interprofessional education: Integrating public health and social work perspectives. *American Journal of Public Health*, 105 Suppl. 1, S106–S108. doi: doi:10.2105/AJPH.2014.302502

American Occupational Therapy Association (AOTA) (2014). Occupational therapy practice framework: Domain & process (3rd ed.). *American Journal of Occupational Therapy*, 68, S1–S48. doi:doi:10.5014/ajot.2014.682006

American Psychological Association (APA). (2009). *Publication manual of the American psychological association*. Washington, D.C.: American Psychological Association.

Anastas, J. W. (2013). Policy, practice and people: Current issues affecting clinical practice. *Clinical Social Work Journal*, 41(3), 302–307.

Arendshort, J. (2015). Employee benefits after the Supreme Court's same sex marriage decision. Retrieved from www.jdsupra.com/legalnews/employee-benefits-after-the-supreme-17004/

Beohmer, U., Bowen, D., & Bauer, G., (2007). Overweight and obesity in sexual-minority women: Evidence from population-based data. *American Journal of Public Health*, 97(6), 1134–1140. doi:doi:10.2105/AJPH.2006.088419

Bidell, M., (2013). Addressing disparities: The impact of a lesbian, gay, bisexual, and transgender graduate counseling course. *Counseling and Psychotherapy Research*, 13 (4), 300–307. doi:doi:10.1080/14733145.2012.741139

Bogart, L. M., Revenson, T. A., Whitfield, K. E., & France, C. R. (2013). Introduction to the special section on lesbian, gay, bisexual, and transgender (LGBT) health disparities: Where we are and where we're going. *Annals of Behavioral Medicine*, 47, 1–4. doi:doi:10.1007/s12160-013-9574-7

Brandell, J. R. (2004). *Psychodynamic social work*. New York, NY: Columbia University Press.

Brooks, V.R. (1981). The theory of minority stress. In V. R. Brooks (ed.), *Minority stress and lesbian women* (pp. 71–90). Lexington, MA: Lexington Books.

Burkhalter, J., Warren, B., Shuk, E., Primavera, L., Ostroff, J. E., & Ostroff, J. S. (2009). Intention to quit smoking among lesbian, gay, bisexual, and transgender smokers. *Nicotine & Tabacco Research*, 11(11), 1312–1320. doi:doi:10.1093/ntr/ntp140

Burton, N. (2015). Depression, the curse of the strong. In *The meaning of madness*, 2nd ed. (pp. 78–107). Devon, UK: Acheron Press.

Centers for Disease Control and Prevention (CDC). (2017a). HIV in the United States: At a Glance. Retrieved from www.cdc.gov/hiv/statistics/overview/atagla nce.html

Centers for Disease Control and Prevention (CDC). (2017b). HIV among transgender people. Retrieved from www.cdc.gov/hiv/group/gender/transgender/ index.html

Cochran, S. D., Mays, V. M., & Sullivan, J. G. (2003). Prevalence of mental disorders, psychological distress, and mental health services use among lesbian, gay, and bisexual adults in the United States. *Journal of Consulting and Clinical Psychology*, 71(1), 53–61.

Cox, L. E., Tice, C. J., & Long, D. D. (2015). *An introduction to social work: An advocacy-based profession.* Boston: SAGE Publications, Inc.

Craig, S., Austin, A., & Allesi, F. (2013). Gay affirmative cognitive behavioral therapy for sexual minority youth: A clinical adaptation. *Clinical Social Work Journal*, 41(3), 258–266.

Dobson, D., & Dobson, K. S. (2009). *Evidence-based practice of cognitive-behavioral therapy.* New York, NY: The Guilford Press.

Dybicz, P. (2015). From person-in-environment to strengths: The promise of postmodern practice. *Journal of Social Work Education*, 51(2), 237–249.

Emlet, C. A. (2016). Social, economic, and health disparities among LGBT older adults. *Generations*, 40(2), 16–22.

Foglia, M. B., & Fredriksen-Goldsen, K. I. (2014). Health disparities among LGBT older adults and the role of non-conscious bias. *LGBT Bioethics: Visibility, Disparities, and Dialogue*, special report, Hastings Center Report, 44(5), S40–S44. doi: doi:10.1002/hast.369

Gates, G., (2011). *How many people are lesbian, gay, bisexual, and transgender?*Los Angeles: The Williams Institutes, UCLA School of Law.

GLMA (n.d.). GLMA home page. Retrieved from http://glma.org/

Guevin, V. M. (2013). Homosexuality and reparative therapy. *Ethics & Medics*, 38(9), 1–2.

Hanson, M., & Gutheil, I.A. (2004). Motivational strategies with alcohol-involved older adults: Implications for social work practice. *Social Work*, 49(3), 364–372.

Healthy People 2010 (n.d.). Home page. Retrieved from www.healthypeople.gov/ 2010/

HealthyPeople.gov (n.d.). Healthy People 2020. Retrieved from www.healthypeop le.gov

Hohman, M. (2012). *Motivational interviewing in social work practice.* New York, NY: The Guilford Press.

Human Rights Campaign (HRC) (n.d.). The healthcare equality index. Retrieved from www.hrc.org/hei

Institute of Medicine (IOM). (2002). *Unequal treatment: Confronting racial and ethnic disparities in health care.* Washington, DC: National Academies Press.

Institute of Medicine (IOM). (2011). *The health of lesbians, gay, bisexual, and transgender people: Building a foundation for better understanding.* Washington, DC: National Academies Press. Retrieved from www.nap.edu/read/13128

Joint Commission. (2011). Advancing effective communication, cultural competence, and patient- and family- centered care for the lesbian, gay, bisexual, and transgender (LGBT) community: A field guide. Oakbrook Terrace, IL. Retrieved from www.jointcommission.org/assets/1/18/LGBTFieldGuide.pdf

Kielhofner, G. (2008). *Model of human occupation: Theory and application*, 4th ed. Philadelphia, PA: Lippincott, Williams & Wilkins.

LaVeist, T. A. (2005). *Minority populations and health: An introduction to health disparities in the United States*. San Francisco, CA: Jossey-Bass A Wiley

Lim, F. A., Brown, D. V., & Kim, S. M. J. (2014). Addressing health care disparities in the lesbian, gay, bisexual, and transgender population: A review of best practices. *American Journal of Nursing*, 114(6), 24–34 doi:doi:10.1097/01.NAJ.0000450423.89759.36

Makadon, H. J. (2011). Ending LGBT invisibility in health care: The first step in ensuring equitable care. *Cleveland Clinic Journal of Medicine*, 78(4), 220–224. doi:doi:10.3949/ccjm.78gr.10006

Makadon, H., Mayer, K., Potter, J., & Goldhammer, H. (2007). *Fenway guide to lesbian, gay, bisexual, and transgender health*. Boston, MA: American College of Physicians.

McRae, N. (2013). *Sexuality and the role of occupational therapy*. Bethesda, MD: AOTA. Retrieved from www.aota.org/~/media/Corporate/Files/AboutOT/Professional/WhatIsOT/RDP/Facts/Sexuality.pdf

Meyer, I. H. (1995). Minority stress and mental health in gay men. *Journal of Health & Social Behavior*, 36(1), 38–56.

Meyer, I. H. (2003). Minority stress and mental health in gay men. In L. D. Garnets & D. C. Kimmel (eds.), *Psychological perspectives on lesbian, gay, and bisexual experiences*, 2nd ed. (pp. 699–731). New York: Columbia University Press.

Miller, W. R., & Rollnick, S. (1991). *Motivational interviewing: Preparing to change additive behavior*. New York, NY: The Guilford Press.

Morrison, S., & Dinkle, S. (2012). Heterosexism and healthcare: A concept analysis. *Nursing Forum: An Independent Voice for Nursing*, 47(2), 123–130.

NASW. (2015). *Sexual orientation change efforts (SOCE) and conversion therapy with lesbians, gay men, bisexuals, and transgender persons*. Washington, D.C.: Author.

Nelson, S., Tassone, M., & Hodges, B. D. (2014). *Creating the health care team of the future: The Toronto model for interprofessional education and practice*. Ithaca, NY: The Cornell University Press.

Nimmagadda, J., & Murphy, J. I. (2014). Using simulations to enhance interprofessional competencies for social work and nursing students. *Social Work Education*, 33(4), 539–548.

Obama, B. (2010). Presidential memorandum: Hospital visitation. Retrieved from www.whitehouse.gov/the-press-office/presidential-memorandum-hospital-visitation

O'Donohue, W., Fisher, J. E., & Hayes, S. C. (ed.). (2003). *Cognitive behavioral therapy: Applying empirically supported techniques in your practice*. Hoboken, NJ: John Wiley & Sons, Inc.

Panozzo, D. (2013). Advocating for an end to reparative therapy: Methodological grounding and blueprint for change. *Journal of Gay & Lesbian Social Services*, 25(3), 362–377.

Pantalone, D. W., Hessler, D. M., & Simoni, J. M. (2010). Mental health pathways from interpersonal violence to health-related outcomes in HIV-positive sexual minority men. *Journal of Counseling & Clinical Psychology*, 78(3), 387–397.

Patient Protection and Affordable Care Act (2010) 42 U.S.C. § 18001.

Pearsons, J. B. (2008). *The case formulation approach to cognitive-behavioral therapy.* New York, NY: The Guilford Press.

Prochaska, J., & DiClemente, C. (1983). Stages and processes of self-change in smoking: Toward an integrative model of change. *Journal of Consulting and Clinical Psychology,* 5, 390–395.

Rhodes, S. D., McCoy, T. P., Wilkin, A. M., & Wolfson, M. (2009). Behavioral risk disparities in a random sample of self-identifying gay and non-gay male university students. *Journal of Homosexuality,* 56(8), 1083–1100.

Rollnick, S., Miller, W. R., & Butler, C. C. (2008). *Motivational interviewing in health care: Helping patients change behavior.* New York, NY: The Guilford Press.

Ross, L. E., Doctor, F., Dimito, A., Kuehl, D., & Armstrong, M. S. (2007). Can talking about oppression reduce depression? Modified CBT group treatment for LGBT people with depression. *Journal of Gay & Lesbian Social Services,* 19(1), 1–15.

Rothman, E. F., Exner, D., & Baughman, A. L. (2011). The prevalence of sexual assault against people who identify as gay, lesbian, or bisexual in the United States: A systematic review. *Trauma, Violence & Abuse,* 12(2), 55–66. doi: doi:10.1177/1524838010390707

Rounds, K. E., McGrath, B. B., & Walsh, E. (2013). Perspectives on provider behaviors: A qualitative study of sexual and gender minorities regarding quality of care. *Contemporary Nurse: A Journal for The Australian Nursing Profession,* 44(1), 99–110. doi:doi:10.5172/conu.2013.44.1.99

Ruben, M. S., Shiperd, J. C., Topor, D., AhnAllen, C. G., Sloan, C. A., Walton, H. M., Matza, A. R., & Trezza, G. R. (2017). Advancing LGBT health care policies and clinical care within a large academic health care system: A case study. *Journal of Homosexuality,* 64(10), 1411–1431.

Rubenstein, G. (2012). Internalized homophobia from a psychodynamic perspective: A case of identification with the aggressor? *European Psychiatry, Supplemental,* 27, 1.

Ryan, C., Russell, S. T., Huebner, D., Diaz, R., & Sanchez, J. (2010). Family acceptance in adolescence and health of LGBT young adults. *Journal of Child and Adolescent Psychiatric Nursing,* 23(4), 205–213.

Sabin, J. A., Riskind, R. G., & Nosek, B. A. (2015). Health care providers' implicit and explicit attitudes toward lesbian women and gay men. *American Journal of Public Health,* 105(9), 1831–1841. doi:doi:10.2105/AJPH.2015.302631

Schaefer, J., & Larkin, S. (2015). Interprofessional education in undergraduate social work education. *Journal of Baccalaureate Social Work,* 20(1), 179–188.

Schatz, B., & O'Hanlan, K. (1994). *Anti-gay discrimination in medicine: Results of a national survey of lesbian, gay and bisexual physicians.* American Association of Physicians for Human Rights (AAPHR).

Schumacher, J. A., & Madson, M. B. (2015). *Fundamentals of motivational interviewing: Tips and strategies for addressing common clinical challenges.* New York, NY: Oxford University Press.

Silvestre, A. (2003). Ending health disparities among vulnerable LGBT people. *Clinical Research and Regulatory Affairs,* 20(2), ix–xii.

Stotzer, R. (2009). Violence against transgender people: A review of United States data. *Aggression & Violent Behavior,* 14(3), 170–179.

Strong, K. L., & Folse, V. N. (2015). Assessing undergraduate nursing students' knowledge, attitudes, and cultural competence in caring for lesbian, gay, bisexual, and transgender patients. *Journal of Nursing Education,* 54(1), 45–49. Doi: doi:10.3928/01484834-20141224-07

Substance Abuse and Mental Health Services Administration (SAMHSA). (2015). *Ending conversion therapy: Supporting and affirming LGBTA youth.* (HHS Publication No. (SMA) 15–4928). Retrieved from http://store.samhsa.gov/shin/content/SMA15-4928/SMA15-4928.pdf

van Wormer, K. (2007). Principles of motivational interviewing geared to stages of change: A pedagogical challenge. *Journal of Teaching in Social Work*, 27(2), 21–35. Doi: doi:10.1300/J067v27no1_02

Venn-Brown, A., (2015). Sexual orientation change efforts within religious contexts: A personal account of the battle to heal homosexuals. *Sensoria: A Journal of Mind, Brain & Culture*, 11(1), 81–91.

Veteran's Health Administration (VHA). (n.d). VHA Strategic Plan FY 2013–2018. Retrieved from www.va.gov/health/docs/VHA_STRATEGIC_PLAN_FY2013-2018.pdf

Wheeler, D. P., & Dodd, S. (2011). LGBTQ capacity building in health care systems: A social work imperative. *Health and Social Work*, 36(4), 307–309.

Whitehead, J., Shaver, J., & Stephenson, R. (2016). Outness, stigma, and primary health care utilization among rural LGBT populations. *PLOS ONE*, 11(1), 1–17. doi:doi:10.1371/journal.pone.0146139

Witek, B. (2014). Cultural change in acceptance of LGBT people: Lessons from social marketing. *America Journal of Orthopsychiatry*, 84(1), 19–22. doi:doi:10.1037/h0098945

11 Legal Systems and Violence

Casey Bohrman

PH.D., MSW, LSW

CSWE 2015 EPAS Competencies

Competency 1: Demonstrate ethical and professional behavior
Competency 2: Engage diversity and difference in practice
Competency 3: Advance human rights and social, economic and environmental justice
Competency 5: Engage in policy practice

LGBTQIA individuals are at higher risk of violence and for getting involved in the criminal justice system than cisgender heterosexually identified people. Because of the far-reaching impacts of violence and criminal justice involvement, this chapter will have relevance for social workers in all fields, not just those interested in forensic social work. The chapter will begin with a discussion about the various forms of violence experienced by LGBTQIA individuals and an examination of some of the settings where that violence is most likely to occur. The chapter will then transition to a focus on the criminal justice system: why LGBTQIA individuals are at increased risk for involvement, special challenges faced by LGBTQIA individuals in the system and how that involvement can impact other areas of life.

Frames for Understanding Violence

What comes to mind when you hear the term violence? Most people think of **physical violence**, also called direct or interpersonal violence, where an individual or group of individuals directly cause harm to other individuals (Galtung, 1969). Physical abuse of children, intimate partner violence, bullying and mass shootings would all be examples of physical violence.

While the majority of this chapter will focus on physical violence, it is important to acknowledge that there are other, more insidious forms of violence, perpetrated against LGBTQIA individuals. **Structural violence** is the harm imposed on individuals by social structures that unevenly distribute resources and perpetuate racism, sexism, heterosexism and other forms of oppression (Farmer, Nizeye, Stulac, & Keshavjee, 2006; Galtung,

1969). Individuals in the LGBTQIA community are impacted by structural violence in that they are more likely to be poor, experience housing and job discrimination, experience homelessness and criminal justice involvement, as well as a range of other systematic disadvantages (Albelda, Badgett, Schneebaum, & Gates, 2009; Meyer et al., 2017). LGBTQIA people of color are at even higher risks of all of these problems because of the intersection of racism and heterosexism.

Additionally, LGBTQIA people experience **symbolic violence**. This form of violence occurs when individuals understand the current social structure and social norms to be commonsense and even ideal (Bourdieu, 1977). Symbolic violence against LGBTQIA-identified people often takes the form of heterosexist assumptions and homophobic/transphobic beliefs. From children's books, to popular television and movies, people in the US are taught that families consist of a mother, father and their children. Families with more than one mother or father or with the presence of gender non-conforming adults are seen as aberrations. Receiving the message that something is wrong with you or your family is symbolic violence. In certain institutions such as some religions, people are taught that being gay is a sin. Being bombarded with that message, and perhaps even believing it, is a form of symbolic violence. In many institutions, being gay or transgender is not explicitly condemned, though systems and social spaces are set up exclusively for cisgender heterosexuals. Having to navigate institutions that are not set up for people like you is a form of symbolic violence. Social workers need to be aware of these forms of violence, as they can have implications for an individual's mental health as well as their ability to meet their basic needs. Social workers should pay particular attention to the ways in which their agencies could be enacting symbolic violence.

Box 11.1 Case: Rain

Rain, who was assigned female at birth but currently identifies as gender-queer, is being physically abused by their male partner. They go into a domestic violence agency for services. The social worker doing the intake faces a number of challenges. The intake form asks whether the client is male or female. The intake worker is not sure which to check. The social worker identifies a need for therapy, but the therapy groups are divided by gender so she does not know where to assign Rain. Rain is clearly getting frustrated by the intake and asks to use the bathroom. There are no gender-neutral bathrooms, so Rain uses the women's bathroom. A woman inside the bathroom gets angry at a "man" being in the women's bathroom and tells Rain to leave. Rain does. They do not go back to the intake, but instead go home and do not come back to the agency.

In what ways is symbolic violence being enacted by the agency and what were the consequences? How could the social worker help to ameliorate some of this violence?

Bullying in School

In educational institutions, young LGBTQIA people must navigate the symbolic violence of school programs and buildings being designed for cis-gender heterosexuals, but sometimes they must also cope with harassment, threats and physical violence. People who identify as gay, lesbian, bisexual or transgender from a young age, or even those who exhibit traits not typically associated with their gender, are at increased risk of being bullied. **Bullying** occurs when there is a power imbalance between victim and perpetrator (such as a difference in size) and there are repeated acts over time intended to cause harm to the victim (Olweus, 1993). According to the 2013 Gay, Lesbian and Straight Education Network (GLSEN) *National Student Climate Survey* of LGBTQIA students grades 6–12, 74% were verbally harassed, 36% were physically harassed (such as being shoved) and 17% were physically assaulted (such as being punched or attacked with a weapon) because of their sexual orientation (Kosciw, Greytak, Palmer, & Boesen, 2014). Rates of bullying are highest for LGBTQIA youth of color and for transgender, gender-queer or other non-cisgender students. Students reporting harassment were more likely to have poorer attendance, lower GPAs, lower self-esteem and higher rates of depression. More than half of those students who experienced harassment and physical attacks did not report the incident because they did not believe it would help or believed it would make the situation worse. Of those who did report, more than 60% said that nothing was done about the reports (Kosciw, Greytak, Palmer, & Boesen, 2014).

    Cyberbullying is similar to bullying in person, except that it occurs through electronic communication such as chatrooms, social media, e-mail and text messages. Some of the ways in which cyberbullying may be different from traditional bullying is that the internet offers the opportunity for anonymity and the lack of face to face contact makes bullies even less empathic. Additionally, it is more difficult to police people on the internet than in person (Cassidy, Faucher, & Jackson, 2013). LGBTQIA youth are more than twice as likely to experience cyberbullying as non-LGBTQIA youth (Schneider, O'Donnell, Stueve, & Coulter, 2012). They are at risk of being targeted because of their sexuality and at risk of being outed online. However, it's important to recognize that many LGBTQIA youth use the internet to connect with others and find support networks. The internet also provides a place for youth to be open about their sexuality and to meet potential partners (Varjas, Meyers, Kiperman, & Howard, 2013). While finding supports and meeting people online can be of benefit to LGBTQIA youth, it also creates opportunities for online predators to prey on youth. Regardless of a young person's sexual orientation or gender identity, it can be useful for social workers to talk with youth about how they are using the internet, helping them explore the benefits and drawbacks of certain online activities.

Social workers can also play a key role in supporting students who experience bullying for any reason, including their sexual orientation or gender identity. Social workers should be particularly attuned to LGBTQIA youth who experience bullying, because compared to other youth who are victimized, LGBTQIA youth are more likely to engage in sexually risky behavior, abuse substances and attempt suicide as a result of the bullying (Bontempo & D'Augelli, 2002). Posting signs and stickers that indicate your office is a safe space, a place where people of all sexual orientations and genders are welcomed and respected, can help students to feel more comfortable approaching you about challenges they have faced in school due to heterosexism and homophobia.

While most students in the GLSEN survey reported that their school had some type of anti-bullying policy, only 10% said that this policy specifically addressed bullying related to sexual orientation and gender identity. Social workers can advocate for more inclusive anti-bullying policies as well as examine all school policies for forms of symbolic violence. For example, some schools do not have inclusive dress code policies or do not allow students to form LGBTQIA student clubs. Social workers can support students to form LGBTQIA and ally organizations and to advocate for more inclusive policies.

Box 11.2 Case: Keisha

Keisha, who identifies as a lesbian, was bullied throughout high school ever since her ex-girlfriend outed her. She used to play on the basketball team, but when people found out she was gay, all the other players did not want her in the locker room with them. They would put her clothes in the shower and make homophobic comments towards her. She loved basketball, but could not put up with the bullying. She had several close friends who supported her, but was afraid that her family would not be supportive if they ever found out. She became depressed and thought about suicide. She was frequently absent from school and eventually charged with truancy. On one of the days she was at school, a boy in the hallway started saying that he was going to get a hold of her and "turn her straight." Fed up with the bullying, she pushed him away, a fight ensued, and she was charged with assault. She is facing expulsion from school, but the principal first wants her to meet with the school social worker.

What factors may have contributed to her altercation with the young man? What interventions might you consider at the micro, mezzo and macro levels?

Hate Crimes against LGBTQIA Individuals

While bullying primarily impacts youth, adults can also be targeted because of their sexual orientation or gender identity. After the 1969 Stonewall uprising, when LGBTQIA activists fought back against bullying by police, more individuals were publically identifying as LGBTQIA and were organizing for their rights. As a result of this organizing, there were violent backlashes against individuals and groups of LGBT people. Up until recently, the largest massacres of LGBTQIA individuals was the 1973 arson of a gay church in New Orleans in which 32 people were killed (Downs, 2016). However, in 2016, 49 LGBT individuals were killed in a mass shooting in an Orlando nightclub (Alvarez, Perez-Pena, & Hauser, 2016; Downs, 2016). In addition to the threat of mass violence, LGBTQIA individuals face regular harassment, threats and even physical violence. It is important to note that not all LGBTQIA individuals face the same risk of violent victimization. People who are trans, black or brown, or are undocumented are at the highest risk of victimization (National Coalition of Anti-Violence Programs; NCAVP, 2015).

One of the ways the US has attempted to curb violence against individuals targeted based on their identity is through **hate crime** legislation. While the definitions of hate crimes vary by state, they typically refer to people being victimized by physical violence, harassment or property damage because of their identity (Green, McFalls, & Smith, 2001). Of those who are targeted by bias-motivated violence, LGBTQIA individuals face the highest risk of violence (Potok, 2011). However, not all states have laws that distinguish hate crimes from other violent crimes (Human Rights Campaign, 2014; Potok, 2011). Even among states that do have these laws, sexual orientation and gender identity are not always protected classes (Human Rights Campaign, 2014).

While many LGBTQIA activists have pressed for more inclusive hate crime legislation, others are more cautious about this approach to reducing violence (Silvia Rivera Law Project, 2018). The biggest critique of hate crime legislation is that it does not actually deter people from committing crimes (Franklin, 2002; Moran, 2001). Another concern is that because of institutionalized racism in the criminal justice system, it will be mostly black and brown individuals who will get prosecuted for hate crimes (Spade & Willse, 2000). The notion of a hate crime also connotes an idea that most violence against LGBTQIA individuals is perpetrated by strangers, when in reality, for LGBTQIA individuals, particularly trans individuals, hate crimes are more likely to be committed by someone known to the victim (NCAVP, 2015).

this one

Whether an attack is considered a hate crime or not, LGBTQIA individuals may be afraid to contact law enforcement for assistance. A study on LGBTQIA individual's experiences with the police found that during 1992–2000, negative interactions with police outnumbered positive ones (Wolff & Cokley, 2007). People had problems with operators not sending assistance, officers mocking LGBTQIA victims or even blaming them for the crime. However, the study's authors did find that the trend had reversed from 2000 onward, with more people having positive experiences with police officers than negative ones. While police relations with the LGBTQIA communities are improving, it is important for social workers to recognize potential concerns about contacting police, particularly for LGBTQIA people from black and brown communities where race, sexuality and gender identity all may complicate police interactions.

Bias-motivated crimes result from environments that perpetuate symbolic violence, where the lives of LGBTQIA individuals are devalued and seen as a threat to social norms. While the criminal justice system provides one avenue for dealing with violence once it has occurred, social workers should also be focused on finding ways to prevent bias-motivated violence. Broader efforts to combat symbolic violence through challenging stereotypes and heterosexist policies can ultimately be some of the best ways to prevent hate crimes (Gavrielides, 2012).

Violence in the Family

Fear of contacting the police may also complicate situations in which an LGBTQIA person is experiencing violence perpetrated by a spouse or someone they are dating. With the limited research available, LGBTQIA adults appear to experience similar rates of intimate partner violence to non-LGBTQIA adults (Brown & Herman, 2015). **Intimate partner violence** is defined as a pattern of controlling and coercive behaviors perpetrated by an individual in an intimate relationship and can include physical abuse, emotional abuse and sexual abuse (Yawn, Yawn, & Uden, 1992).

When an LGBTQIA person is thinking about leaving a violent relationship, they face some barriers that are similar to people in non-LGBTQIA relationships. They may fear missing their partner, retaliation from their partner, financial implications or may be embarrassed to reach out for help (Scherzer, 1998; Turell, 2000). Additionally, people in LGBTQIA relationships face unique barriers to leaving. Not all people in LGBTQIA relationships are out to everyone in their social networks. An LGBTQIA person may not want to seek help for fear of disclosing their sexual orientation or for fear that their partner will out them to other people (Ard & Makadon, 2011; Roch, Morton, & Ritchie, 2010). Additionally, some women in relationships with other women may not recognize that they are in an abusive relationship, falsely believing that only men can perpetrate violence (Hassouneh & Glass, 2008).

Not only are there individual barriers to leaving violent relationships, there are also institutional barriers to accessing services unique to LGBTQIA individuals. Some people believe that services are only available to cisgender heterosexual women, and in some communities this may be accurate, particularly when it comes to shelters (Goldberg & Meyer, 2013). There is also a fear that even if people are able to access services, the staff may not be trained to work with LGBTQIA individuals and may even be homophobic (Brown & Herman, 2015). Social workers can take an active role in addressing these institutional barriers by ensuring that agencies who deal with intimate partner violence are inclusive in their services and conduct outreach to the LGBTQIA community to help people feel safe in accessing their services.

LGBTQIA Adults in the Criminal Justice System

LGBTQIA individuals have a long and complicated relationship with the criminal justice system. Historically there were many aspects of being LGBTQIA that were criminalized. During colonial times a man could be put to death for having sex with another man (Crompton, 1976). Up until 1961, **sodomy**, defined as any sexual activity besides vaginal intercourse, was illegal in every state (Kane, 2003). These statutes included sexual behavior by heterosexual couples, but nine states rewrote those statutes so that they would only pertain to gay and lesbian couples. Even though sodomy laws were found unconstitutional in 2003, 12 states continue to have such laws on the books (Kane, 2003). While sodomy laws are virtually impossible to enforce, their presence represents the ongoing belief that there is something wrong with sexual activity outside of the heterosexual norm (Goodman, 2001). Therefore, sodomy laws can be considered another form of symbolic violence.

In addition to the criminalization of sexual activity, LGBTQIA individuals also had their dress regulated by sumptuary laws, which could sometimes require a person to dress according to their gender. People could be arrested for being "disguised" as another gender (Capers, 2008). While most of these laws came off the books in the 1980s, they continue to inform our society's perceptions that people who dress outside their assigned gender norm are more likely to be engaging in other behaviors that violate societal norms and laws (Mogul, Ritchie, & Whitlock, 2011). For example, LGBTQIA individuals are more likely to be targeted by police and arrested for quality of life crimes like loitering and public intoxication (Amnesty International, 2005).

Encounters with police can be particularly scary for transgender individuals. Few trans individuals have identification that matches their gender and while it is illegal for police officers to strip people to identify their gender, the practice is thought to be widespread (Hanssens, Moodie-Mills, Ritchie, Spade, & Vaid, 2014). While police profile trans individuals as sex workers, it is important for social workers to recognize that there are actually a large number of trans women engaging in **sex work** (Herbst et al., 2008). Police officers sometimes use the presence of condoms to be proof that someone is engaging in sex work, putting sex workers at greater risk for HIV and other sexually transmitted infections (Hussey, 2015). Their involvement in sex work may be related to the structural violence they face in other institutions making them at greater risk of poverty. Trans people face employment discrimination, have trouble accessing services because they lack state identification necessary for many services and have few social supports to provide financial assistance than cisgender individuals (Poteat et al., 2015).

LGBTQIA individuals who end up in jail or prison are at higher risk of sexual assault than their non-LGBTQIA peers. The largest national survey of LGBTQIA prisoners to date, *Coming Out of Concrete Closets*, was conducted by Pink and Brown, an organization of LGBTQIA prisoners and their allies (Lydon, Carrington, Low, Miller, & Yazdy, 2015). The authors found that the majority of respondents reported harassment, discrimination, physical assault and unwanted sexual touching by staff. More than 10% reported being sexually assaulted by staff. Rates of harassment and discrimination from other inmates were even higher than that by staff, with more than a third of LGBTQIA people reporting being sexually assaulted by other inmates. In 2003, The Prison Rape Elimination Act (PREA) was enacted to reduce sexual assaults in prison by putting into place standards for assault prevention and reporting; however, most states are not yet in full compliance with the law (Bureau of Justice Assistance, 2014).

LGBT people become even more vulnerable when they are placed in facilities that do not align with their gender, especially when transgender women are being placed in men's jails (Sexton, Jenness, & Sumner, 2010). One way that states attempt to protect LGBTQIA individuals is through the use of **solitary confinement**. Yet, solitary confinement is associated with a wide range of physical and mental health problems such as depression, anxiety, hallucinations, paranoia, stomach pain, headaches and weight loss (Smith, 2006). There has been so much concern about the health impacts of solitary confinement that it has been banned in juvenile facilities. While PREA bans placing a person in solitary confinement just because of their sexual orientation or gender identity, many people report that it is still happening (Center for American Progress & Movement Advancement Project, 2016). The *Coming Out of Concrete Closets* study found that the majority of currently incarcerated LGBTQIA people surveyed reported spending time in solitary confinement (Lydon, Carrington, Low, Miller, & Yazdy, 2015).

Negative experiences in prison can continue to impact people after they are released. People who were victimized while in prison are more likely to violate parole or be re-arrested, both of which contribute to someone's risk of returning to prison (Listwan, Hanley, & Colvin, 2012). Even for those individuals who do not experience victimization in prison, incarceration often has lasting effects. LGBTQIA individuals face further discrimination in the job market when they have a criminal record. With a criminal record, particularly if it involves drug charges, individuals may face barriers to receiving public benefits and educational assistance. Additionally, in some states, people with felony convictions are not allowed to vote, further enacting structural violence on LGBTQIA individuals with a record. The impacts of these consequences of incarceration may be worse for certain subsets of the LGBTQIA population such as people with disabilities or people of color.

Box 11.3 Case: Chanda

You are working in an immigrant services organization with Chanda, a 62-year-old woman from Cambodia, who needs help getting her Medicaid reactivated. Her son, Heng, usually helps her with this process, but he was incarcerated for drug possession with intent to distribute. Chanda tells you that when she and Heng emigrated from Cambodia 28 years ago they moved to a poor section of the city where they had poor quality schools and high levels of violence and drug activity. Her son has been in and out of jail most of his adult life, so she has learned to deal with his absence. However, this time she is particularly distraught. She hasn't been able to eat and is even having trouble getting out of bed. She reports that her son is being harassed in jail both by the guards and by other inmates. Her son is gay and possesses what some considered to be stereotypically female characteristics. The warden has told him that the only thing they can do is place him in solitary confinement where he will be alone in his jail cell 23 hours a day. Some officers have also suggested that if he could try acting a bit more masculine fewer people would bother him. He refuses to go to solitary, but feels like he can't take it anymore. Chanda is feeling helpless and hopeless. What types of violence is Heng experiencing? What types of things would you want to help Chanda with?

If someone like Chanda came to your office, to whom would you refer her in order to obtain help for her son? Research online what types of organizations help with prisoner advocacy in your community.

LGBTQIA Youth in the Juvenile Justice System

LGBTQIA youth are also at increased risk of ending up in the criminal justice system. Youth in the juvenile justice system are almost twice as likely to identify as LGBTQIA as are those in the general population (Majd, Marksamer, & Reyes, 2009). There are a wide range of reasons why LGBTQIA youth are more likely to end up in the juvenile justice system than heterosexual cisgender youth. School bullying and a general school environment that is not supportive of LGBTQIA youth can lead to increased school absences, which puts youth at risk for truancy charges. For those youth who are already on probation, missed days of school can be considered probation violations. For those youth who are charged with a crime, missed days of school can contribute to the perception that they are a flight risk, increasing the likelihood that they will be detained while they await trial (Majd, Marksamer, & Reyes, 2009).

Another reason LGBTQIA youth are more likely to get caught up in the juvenile justice system is that they are more likely to experience homelessness. According to Swift (2012), LGBTQIA adolescents represent nearly 40% in the homeless youth population. Some parents cannot accept their children's sexuality or gender identity, which may lead to children being kicked out or to children running away. Additionally, LGBTQIA youth are more likely to be physically and sexually abused, which may also contribute to them attempting to leave home (Friedman et al., 2011).

Running away, like truancy, is a **status offense** (non-criminal act considered to be illegal because the perpetrator is not an adult) that can result in probation or even incarceration. Additionally, homeless youth may end up in the juvenile system because they may be charged with quality of life crimes such as loitering or they may be caught engaging in survival crimes such as theft or sex work. Trans homeless youth are more likely to engage in sex work, but also get profiled as sex workers and accused of engaging in sex work for merely hanging out in public (Amnesty International, 2005; Hussey, 2015).

One way that advocates have sought to protect youth engaged in sex work is through safe harbor laws. These laws divert youth engaged in sex work from the criminal justice system and provide them with services (Butler, 2015). In essence, these laws view people engaged in sex work as victims. It is important for social workers who want to work with this population to understand that people engaged in sex work, even youth, do not always view themselves as victims. It is not always clear whether sex work is voluntary or coerced (Tyler & Johnson, 2006). When people are engaging in sex work as a means of survival, they may have such limited options that the concept of choice becomes muddled. Some people see other benefits to sex work beyond the money. For example, for some trans sex workers, the sex worker community can provide a sense of community and a source of social support. Additionally, for some trans individuals sex work can provide a validation of their gender identity and a sense that someone finds them sexually attractive (Poteat et al., 2015). By linking youth to resources that reduce the need for survival crimes, social workers can help youth feel empowered to make decisions about what is best for them.

If LGBTQIA youth do end up in the juvenile justice system, they face a number of unique challenges. If they have been rejected by their families, it makes it particularly difficult to navigate the juvenile justice system. If their parents are not involved, they may be detained for their safety. One of the challenges with detaining LGBTQIA youth is that it may be difficult to find a site that will accept them. In their report on LGBTQIA youth in the juvenile justice system, Majd, Marksamer and Reyes (2009) found that facilities would refuse to accept LGBTQIA youth because they thought they might be victimized or might victimize other youth. Some also believed that LGBTQIA youth would somehow interfere with their programming. Because of the lack of options, LGBTQIA youth, even those who have not committed severe crimes, may end up in the highest security detention centers because they are the only facilities which are required to accept everyone.

Findings from Pasko's (2010) study of people who worked in juvenile corrections revealed that the majority of professionals thought that being gay was caused by a history of sexual assault and several staff members felt that gay youth should undergo behavioral modification or even medical treatment because of their sexuality. To minimize discrimination from staff and other youth inside, LGBTQIA youth may feel the need to be strategic in their gender presentation, particularly because LGBTQIA youth are significantly more likely to be sexually assaulted by other youth then their heterosexual cisgender peers (Beck, Cantor, Hartge, & Smith, 2013).

It's important for social workers to recognize and build upon the resilience of young people in the juvenile justice system who identify as LGBTQIA. Data from Mountz's (2016) study of LGBTQIA youth who had been in female juvenile detention centers indicated that youth found healing through activism, collective performance and working with other queer youth. The support from the LGBTQIA community as well as the drive for social change made them feel safer and more empowered. She also found that mentors, including social workers, played a crucial role in the lives of these youth. Mentors challenged the youth not to internalize blame by helping them understand the ways in which oppression, biased policies and stigma against those individuals with a record could make their lives more difficult. The mentors also instilled hope, connected the youth with resources and provided consistent presence. Depending on the social worker's role and function, they may not have the capacity to serve as a long-term mentor for a young person, therefore they may want to consider linking youth to mentors, particularly ones that identify as LGBTQIA.

Conclusion

Like anyone else, LGBTQIA individuals can be victims or perpetrators of physical violence. Social workers must also recognize the barriers LGBTQIA individuals may face when attempting to access services for victims of violence. Trauma theory suggests that "hurt people hurt people," meaning some people experience so much violence that they are no longer able to cope and they may be at risk for hurting other people (Bloom &

Farragher, 2010). LGBTQIA people are at high risk of physical, symbolic and structural violence, all of which can impact their school performance, financial stability, physical and mental health (Albelda, Badgett, Schneebaum, & Gates, 2009; Bontempo & D'Augelli, 2002; Kosciw, Greytak, Palmer, & Boesen, 2014; Lick, Durso, & Johnson, 2013; NCAVP, 2015). Some may internalize the impacts through behaviors such as substance use and self-harming, while others may externalize their emotions by harming others. Therefore, social workers may work with LGBT individuals who have committed physical violence or have otherwise broken the law. In this work, social workers must recognize the challenges facing LGBTQIA individuals in the criminal justice system and advocate to make changes whenever possible.

Symbolic and structural violence intersect with all fields of social work; therefore, all social workers can help to prevent violence through combatting stigma and working towards making policies more inclusive at their agencies as well as the local, state and federal government level. Social workers should also recognize that certain groups within the LGBTQIA population, such as people of color, face higher risks of violence than others. Social workers need to be aware of how these intersecting identities may make people leery of accessing assistance from the government or even certain social services. While the ideal is to reduce or even prevent all violence, for now social workers can help LGBTQIA people to find supports they feel comfortable with in order to begin to heal from the violence they have experienced.

Questions to Consider

1   Describe the differences between physical and interpersonal violence, structural violence and symbolic violence. Why is it important for social workers to know about these forms of violence?

2   How are bullying and cyberbullying forms of violence?

3   What are the rates of hate crimes in your geographical jurisdiction? Are they under- or over- reported? Does your town, city, county or state have hate crimes legislation enacted? How effective are hate crimes laws in changing the climate and safety for LGBTQIA citizens?

4   How does LGBTQIA identity intersect with family life? What issues surround intimate partner violence (IPV) in LGBTQIA families? How might a family's reaction to their LGBTQIA child's identity be the catalyst for experiences of violence and entry into the legal system?

5   In what ways have laws on the books promoted criminalization of LGBTQIA clients? How might laws currently affect LGBTQIA people in ways that bring them into encounters with law enforcement and the criminal justice system?

6   What risks do LGBTQIA people face when incarcerated? Why do LGBTQIA people experience greater rates of sexual assault and solitary confinement?

Resources

Anti-Violence Project http://avp.org/ The Anti-Violence Project provides support and advocacy to LGBTQ people who have been victims of violence. They also coordinate the National Coalition of Anti-Violence Programs and provide links to local service providers.

Audre Lorde Project http://alp.org/ The Audre Lorde project organizes people around issues that impact LGBTQ people of color. They have campaigns related to community violence and to the criminal justice system.

Forge Sexual Violence Project http://forge-forward.org/ Forge Forward provides direct services to trans victims of violence, but also provides training and technical support to other domestic violence agencies. They provide free webinars and publications.

INCITE! http://incite-national.org/ INCITE! was created for radical feminists of color and engaging in activism around violence against women, gender non-conforming and trans people of color. They provide electronic resources and posters that you can download for free.

Lambda Legal www.lambdalegal.org/issues/police-and-criminal-justice Lambda Legal is the oldest and largest LGBTQ legal rights organization. They engage in high impact litigation, education and policy advocacy including advocacy focused on the criminal justice system. They provide legal updates and a place for LGBTQ people to share their stories about experiences in the criminal justice system.

Pink and Black www.blackandpink.org/ Pink and Black is a feminist, anti-racist, anti-capitalist organization of LGBTQ people in prison and their allies dedicated to abolishing the prison industrial complex. They run a pen pal program for LGBTQ prisoners, produce a newspaper for people in prison, provide support to people being victimized in prison and conduct workshops and trainings.

Sex Workers Outreach Project www.swopusa.org/ Sex Workers Outreach Project is a national social justice organization aimed at decreasing violence and stigma directed towards sex workers. The website offers information about local chapters, obtaining services for sex workers, and information about sex work.

Sylvia Rivera Law Project www.srlp.org/ Named after LGBTQ rights pioneer, Silvia Rivera, this group has a legal clinic and engage in policy advocacy across a number of realms including hate crime laws, juvenile detention center policy, prison policy and policing policy. The website provides free publications and training guides.

References

Albelda, R., Badgett, M. V. L., Schneebaum, A., & Gates, G. J. (2009). *Poverty in the lesbian, gay and bisexual community*. Los Angeles: The Williams Institute, University of California, Los Angeles School of Law.

Alvarez, L., Perez-Pena, R., & Hauser, C. (2016, June 13). Orlando gunman was 'cool and calm' after massacre, police say. *New York Times*. Retrieved from www. nytimes.com/2016/06/14/us/orlando-shooting.html?_r=0

Amnesty International (2005). *Stonewalled: Police abuse and misconduct against lesbian, gay, bisexual and transgender people in the U.S.* Retrieved from: www.amnesty.org/en/documents/AMR51/122/2005/en/

Ard, K. L., & Makadon, H. J. (2011). Addressing intimate partner violence in lesbian, gay, bisexual, and transgender patients. *Journal of General Internal Medicine*, 26(8), 930–933. doi: doi:10.1007/s11606–11011–1697–1696

Beck, A., Cantor, D.Hartge, J., & Smith, T. (2013). *Sexual victimization in juvenile facilities report by youth, 2012.* Washington, D.C.: U.S. Department of Justice, Office of Justice Programs, Bureau of Justice Statistics. Retrieved from www.bjs.gov/content/pub/pdf/svjfry12.pdf

Bloom, S. L., & Farragher, B. (2010). *Destroying sanctuary: The crisis in human service delivery systems.* New York: Oxford University Press.

Bontempo, D. E., & D'Augelli, A. R. (2002). Effects of at-school victimization and sexual orientation on lesbian, gay, or bisexual youths' health risk behavior. *Journal of Adolescent Health*, 30(5), 364–374.

BourdieuP. 1977. *Outline of a theory of practice.* Cambridge: Cambridge University Press.

Brown, T. N. T. & Herman, J. L. (2015). *Intimate partner violence and sexual abuse among LGBTQ people.* The Williams Institute at UCLA Law School. Retrieved from http://williamsinstitute.law.ucla.edu/wp-content/uploads/Intimate-Partner-Violence-and-Sexual-Abuse-among-LGBTQ-People.pdf

Bureau of Justice Assistance (2014). *States and territories responses to the May 15, 2014 Prison Rape Elimination deadline.* Retrieved from www.bja.gov/Programs/PRE Acompliance.pdf

Butler, C. N. (2015). Bridge over troubled water: Safe harbor laws for sexually exploited minors. *North Caroline Law Review*, 93(5), 1281–1338.

Capers, I. B. (2008). Cross dressing and the criminal. *Yale Journal of Law and the Humanities*, 20, 7–33.

Cassidy, W., Faucher, C., & Jackson, M. (2013). Cyberbullying among youth: A comprehensive review of current international research and its implications and application to policy and practice. *School Psychology International*, 34(6), 575–612. doi: doi:0143034313479697

Center for American Progress & Movement Advancement Project (2016). *Unjust: How the broken criminal justice system fails LGBT people.* Retrieved from www.lgbtmap.org/file/lgbt-criminal-justice.pdf.

Crompton, L. (1976). Homosexuals and the death penalty in colonial America. *Journal of Homosexuality*, 1(3), 277–293.

Downs, J. (2016). *Stand by me: The forgotten history of Gay Liberation.* New York: Basic Books.

Farmer, P. E., Nizeye, B., Stulac, S., & Keshavjee, S. (2006). Structural violence and clinical medicine. *Pubic Library of Science Medicine*, 3(10), e449. doi:doi:10.1371/journal.pmed.0030449

Franklin, K. (2002). Good intentions: The enforcement of hate crime penalty-enhancement statutes. *American Behavioral Scientist*, 46(1), 154–172.

Friedman, M. S., Marshal, M. P., Guadamuz, T. E., Wei, C., Wong, C. F., Saewyc, E. M., & Stall, R. (2011). A meta-analysis of disparities in childhood sexual abuse, parental physical abuse, and peer victimization among sexual minority and sexual nonminority individuals. *American Journal of Public Health*, 101(8), 1481–1494. doi: doi:10.2105/AJPH.2009.190009

Galtung, J. (1969). Violence, peace, and peace research. *Journal of Peace Research*, 6(3), 167–191.

Gavrielides, T. (2012). Contextualizing restorative justice for hate crime. *Journal of Interpersonal Violence*, 27(18), 3624–3643. doi: doi:10.1177/0886260512447575

Goldberg, N. & Meyer, I. (2013). Sexual orientation disparities in history of intimate partner violence: Results from the California Health Interview Survey. *Journal of Interpersonal Violence*, 28(5), 1109–1118. doi: doi:10.1177/0886260512459384

Goodman, R. (2001). Beyond the enforcement principle: Sodomy laws, social norms, and social panoptics. *California Law Review*, 89(3), 643–740. doi: doi:10.2307/3481180

Green, D. P., McFalls, L. H., & Smith, J. K. (2001). Hate crime: An emergent research agenda. *Annual Review of Sociology*, 27, 479–504.

Hanssens, C., Moodie-Mills, A. C., Ritchie, A. J., Spade, D., & Vaid, U. (2014). *A roadmap for change: Federal policy recommendations for addressing the criminalization of LGBTQ people and people living with HIV*. New York: Center for Gender & Sexuality Law at Columbia Law School. Retrieved from: https://web.law.colum bia.edu/sites/default/files/microsites/gender-sexuality/files/roadmap_for_change_ full_report.pdf

Hassouneh, D. & Glass, N. (2008). The influence of gender role stereotyping on women's experiences of female same-sex intimate partner violence. *Violence against Women*, 14(3), 310–325. doi: doi:325.10.1177/1077801207313734

Herbst, J. H., Jacobs, E. D., Finlayson, T. J., McKleroy, V. S., Neumann, M. S., Crepaz, N., & HIV/AIDS Prevention Research Synthesis Team. (2008). Estimating HIV prevalence and risk behaviors of transgender persons in the United States: A systematic review. *AIDS and Behavior*, 12(1), 1–17. doi: doi:10.1007/ s10461-10007-9299-9293

Human Rights Campaign (2014). *A guide to state-level advocacy following enactment of the Mathew Shepard and James Byrd, Jr. Hate Crimes Prevention Act*. Retrieved from http://hrc-assets.s3-website-us-east-1.amazonaws.com//files/assets/resources/HRC-Hate-Crimes-Guide-2014.pdf

Hussey, H. (2015, February). *Beyond 4 walls and a roof: Addressing homelessness among transgendered youth*. Center for American Progress. Retrieved from https://cdn.am ericanprogress.org/wp-content/uploads/2015/02/TransgenderHomeless-report2. pdf

Kane, M. (2003). Social movement policy success: Decriminalizing state sodomy laws, 1969–1998. *Mobilization: An International Quarterly*, 8(3), 313–334.

Kosciw, J. G., Greytak, E. A., Palmer, N. A., & Boesen, M. J. (2014). *The 2013 national school climate survey: The experiences of lesbian, gay, bisexual and transgender youth in our nation's schools*. Retrieved from the Gay, Lesbian and Straight Education Network website: www.glsen.org/article/2013-national-school-climate-survey

Lick, D. J., Durso, L. E., & Johnson, K. L. (2013). Minority stress and physical health among sexual minorities. *Perspectives on Psychological Science*, 8(5), 521–548.

Listwan, S. J., Hanley, D., & Colvin, M. (2012). *The prison experience and reentry: Examining the impact of victimization on coming home, final report*. U.S. Department of Justice. Retrieved from www.ncjrs.gov/pdffiles1/nij/grants/238083.pdf

Lydon, J., Carrington, K., Low, H., Miller, R., & Yazdy, M. (2015). *Coming out of concrete closets: A report on Black and Pink's national LGBTQ prisoner survey.* Retrieved from www.blackandpink.org/wp-content/upLoads/Coming-Out-of-Concrete-Closets.-Black-and-Pink.-October-21-2015..pdf

Majd, K., Marksamer, J., & Reyes, C. (2009). *Hidden injustice: Lesbian, gay, bisexual, and transgender youth in juvenile courts.* Equity Project. Retrieved from www.nclrights.org/wp-content/uploads/2014/06/hidden_injustice.pdf

Meyer, I. H., Flores, A. R., Stemple, L., Romero, A. P., Wilson, B. D., & Herman, J. L. (2017). Incarceration rates and traits of sexual minorities in the United States: National Inmate Survey, 2011–2012. *American Journal of Public Health*, 107(1), 267–273. doi:doi:10.2105/AJPH.2016.303576

Mogul, J. L., Ritchie, A. J., & Whitlock, K. (2011). *Queer (in) justice: The criminalization of LGBTQ people in the United States* (Vol. 5). Boston: Beacon Press.

Moran, L. (2001). Affairs of the heart: Hate crime and the politics of crime control. *Law and Critique*, 12(3), 331–344.

Mountz, S. E. (2016). That's the sound of the police state-sanctioned violence and resistance among LGBTQ young people previously incarcerated in girls' juvenile justice facilities. *Affilia*, 31(3), 287–302. doi: doi:10.1177/0886109916641161

National Coalition of Anti-Violence Programs (NCAVP) (2015). *Lesbian, gay, bisexual, transgender, queer and HIV-affected intimate partner violence in 2014.* New York, NY: Author. Retrieved from www.avp.org/storage/documents/2014_IPV_Report_Final_w-Bookmarks_10_28.pdf

Olweus, D. (1993). *Bullying: What we know and what we can do.* Oxford: Blackwell Publishing.

Pasko, L. (2010). Setting the record "straight": Girls, sexuality, and the juvenile correctional system. *Social Justice*, 37(1), 7–26.

Poteat, T., Wirtz, A. L., Radix, A., Borquez, A., Silva-Santisteban, A., Deutsch, M. B., ... & Operario, D. (2015). HIV risk and preventive interventions in transgender women sex workers. *The Lancet*, 385(9964), 274–286.

Potok, M. (2011, February 12). *Anti-gay hate crimes: Doing the math.* Southern Poverty Law Center. Retrieved from www.splcenter.org/fighting-hate/intelligence-report/2011/anti-gay-hate-crimes-doing-math

Roch, A., Morton, J., & Ritchie, G. (2010). *Out of sight, out of mind: Transgender people's experiences of domestic abuse, Scotland.* Retrieved from LGBT Youth Scotland Website: www.lgbtyouth.org.uk/files/documents/DomesticAbuseResources/transgender_DA.pdf

Scherzer, T. (1998). Domestic violence in lesbian relationships: Findings of the lesbian relationships research project. *Journal of Lesbian Studies*, 2, 29–47. doi: doi:10.1300/J155v02n01_03

Schneider, S. K., O'Donnell, L., Stueve, A., & Coulter, R. W. (2012). Cyberbullying, school bullying, and psychological distress: A regional census of high school students. *American Journal of Public Health*, 102(1), 171–177. doi: doi:10.2105/AJPH.2011.300308

Sexton, L., Jenness, V., & Sumner, J. M. (2010). Where the margins meet: A demographic assessment of transgender inmates in men's prisons. *Justice Quarterly*, 27(6), 835–866. doi:doi:10.1080/07418820903419010

Sylvia Rivera Law Project (2018). *SRLP on hate crime laws.* Retrieved from https://srlp.org/action/hate-crimes/

Smith, P. S. (2006). The effects of solitary confinement on prison inmates: A brief history and review of the literature. *Crime and Justice*, 34(1), 441–528. doi: doi:10.1086/500626

Spade, J. & Willse, C. (2000). Confronting the limits of gay hate crimes activism: A radical critique. *Chicano/a Latino/a Law Review*, 21(1), 38–52.

Swift, J. (2012, July 17). *LGBTQ youth over represented in juvenile justice system.* Retrieved from www.jjie.org/LGBTQ-youth-overrepresented-juvenile-justice-system

Turell, S. C. (2000). Seeking help for same-sex relationship abuses. *Journal of Gay & Lesbian Social Services*, 10(2), 35–49. doi:doi:10.1300/J041v10n02_02

Tyler, K. A. & Johnson, K. A. (2006). Trading sex: Voluntary or coerced? The experiences of homeless youth. *Journal of Sex Research*, 43(3), 208–216.

Varjas, K., Meyers, J., Kiperman, S., & Howard, A. (2013). Technology hurts? Lesbian, gay, and bisexual youth perspectives of technology and cyberbullying. *Journal of School Violence*, 12(1), 27–44. doi: doi:10.1080/15388220.2012.731665

Wolff, K. B. & Cokely, C. L. (2007). To protect and to serve? An exploration of police conduct in relation to the gay, lesbian, bisexual, and transgender community. *Sexuality and Culture*, 11, 1–23. doi: doi:10.1007/s12119–12007–9000-z

Yawn, B. P., Yawn, R. A., & Uden, D. L. (1992). American Medical Association diagnostic and treatment guidelines on domestic violence. *Archives of Family Medicine*, 1, 39.

12 Economics and the Workplace

Joseph Nicholas DeFilippis

PH.D., MSW

CSWE 2015 Educational Policy and Accreditation Standards

Competency 2: Engage diversity and difference in practice
Competency 3: Advance human rights and social, economic, and environmental justice
Competency 4: Engage in practice-informed research and research-informed practice
Competency 5: Engage in policy practice
Competency 8: Intervene with individuals, families, groups, organizations, and communities

Introduction

Popular culture has helped to create a dominant narrative in the United States about LGBT people that suggests that they are all affluent. For decades on television, from *Will and Grace* to *Modern Family*, LGBT characters have been limited largely to that of well-off, cosmopolitan White gay men (GLAAD, 2015; Ulaby, 2013). The landscape is fairly similar at the movies where, for example, in 2015 the overwhelming majority of LGBT characters in Hollywood films were also White males (GLAAD, 2016). Yet the LGBT community is not limited to affluent White gay men. This limited range of characters does not depict an accurate representation of LGBT communities and has contributed to a tremendously misleading image of the economic lives of LGBT people. In reality, queer women, transgender people, and LGBT people of color, senior citizens, and immigrants face a range of structural obstacles that put them at great risk of economic insecurity or poverty.

This chapter will explore the economic lives of U.S. LGBT communities, providing information to help social workers to develop an intersectional understanding of LGBT people. It will also identify recommendations for change, and highlight information and skills that social work students need in order to strengthen their competency in working with LGBT populations.

Why is the pay gap of women there only one we talk about a pay gap

Income and Poverty Rates of LGBT People

LGBT people have lower income levels and higher poverty rates than their *gap for LGBT* heterosexual and cisgender peers in the general population (Badgett et al., 2013; DeFilippis, 2016; Pew Research Center, 2013). The unemployment rates for lesbian, gay, and bisexual people are more than 40% higher than they are for heterosexual Americans, and the unemployment rate for transgender people is double the national rate (Movement Advancement Project (MAP) et al., 2013); however, even when LGBT people have jobs, they earn less. Although 28% of the general population of U.S. adults earned less than $30,000 a year, 39% of LGB people earned less than that amount, and for bisexuals the rate was even higher at 48% (Pew Research Center, 2013). A 2014 report found that almost one-third of LGBT adults (approximately 2.4 million people) did not have enough money to feed themselves or their family (Gates, 2014). The following sections briefly examine what existing research tells us about income and poverty among different LGBT populations, and demonstrate how, despite media depictions to the contrary, economic inequality and poverty are a crisis in all LGBT communities.

Gay and Bisexual Men

Gay White men are generally in better financial standing than other segments of the LGBT community, yet are still not as economically privileged as the media indicates. Gay and bisexual men of all races earn less than heterosexual men (Badgett et al., 2013; Gates, 2014). Gay men earn up to one-third less income than similarly qualified heterosexual males (Krehely & Hunt, 2011). In addition, gay and bisexual men have poverty rates higher than those of heterosexual men, with 20% of gay men and 25% of bisexual men living in poverty (Badgett et al., 2013; MAP et al., 2014).

Lesbian and Bisexual Women

Twenty-three percent of lesbians and 30% of bisexual women live in poverty, compared with 21% of heterosexual women (MAP et al., 2014). Lesbian couples have higher poverty rates than both gay male couples and different-sex couples (Badgett et al., 2013). Lesbians and bisexual women are 50% more likely to receive food stamps and public assistance than are heterosexual women (Badgett et al., 2013). Race compounds poverty for lesbian and bisexual women. Bisexual and lesbian women of color have lower incomes than White women, and disproportionately higher rates of homelessness and poverty (DeFilippis, 2016).

Transgender People

Transgender communities face much higher rates of unemployment, poverty, and homelessness than the general public. Research shows that 60–65% of transgender people live below the poverty line (DeFilippis, 2016). Compared to the typical person in the United States, transgender people are 400% more likely to have a household income under $10,000, and are 200% more likely to be unemployed (Center for American Progress & MAP, 2015; Grant et al., 2011). Almost 20% reported being homeless at some point in their lives (Sears & Badgett, 2012).

Even when employed, transgender people earn lower wages than their cisgendered peers (Center for American Progress & MAP, 2015). The earnings of female transgender workers fell by nearly one-third following their gender transitions (Schilt & Wiswall, 2008). Ninety percent of transgender people surveyed have reported experiencing harassment and discrimination at their jobs (Sears & Badgett, 2012).

LGBT People of Color

LGBT people of color must contend with racism, in addition to homophobia and transphobia, and earn less than do White LGBT people or heterosexual people of color (Bond et al., 2009; Dunn & Moodie-Mills, 2012; Human Rights Campaign, 2009). African American LGBT people have higher poverty rates than their White or heterosexual counterparts (Albelda et al., 2009; Badgett et al., 2013; MAP et al., 2013). Similarly, Latino LGBT people have higher poverty rates than heterosexual, cisgendered Latinos or White LGBT people (Albelda et al., 2009), and Two-Spirit or LGBT Native Americans face greater economic insecurity than their heterosexual, cisgendered peers or White LGBT people (Albelda et al., 2009; Badgett et al., 2013).

Asian/Pacific Islander or Latino LGBT people are disproportionately immigrants (MAP et al., 2012), and there are an estimated 904,000 LGBT adult immigrants in the United States (MAP et al., 2013). Consequently, they grapple with other obstacles that all non-citizens face, including lower wages, lack of access to services, and xenophobic discrimination and violence. Undocumented LGBT immigrants are particularly vulnerable to poverty (DasGupta, 2012).

Transgender people of color face poverty at particularly high rates. Black transgender people have unemployment rates that are double those of other transgender people and four times the rate of the general population (National Black Justice Coalition et al., 2011). One third of Black transgender people live in extreme poverty, with 34% earning an annual income of less than $10,000 per household. In addition, Latino transgender people are five times as likely to live in extreme poverty compared to the general Latino population (MAP et al., 2013), and American Indian and Alaskan Native transgender and gender non-conforming people have rates of extreme poverty that are nearly six times that of the general U.S. population (Grant et al., 2011).

Rural LGBT People

Poverty rates for same-sex couples living in rural areas are twice as high as they are for same-sex couples who live in large cities (Badgett et al., 2013). Lesbian couples who live in rural areas are more than three times as likely to be poor than lesbian couples in large, urban areas. This is not true for all rural people; there is not this level of discrepancy between heterosexuals living in urban areas compared to those in rural areas. In fact, rural LGB people are also poorer than their heterosexual rural peers (Badgett et al., 2013).

LGBT Older Adults

LGBT older adults also struggle with economic instability (Fredriksen-Goldsen et al., 2011). One-fifth of older LGBT people live on less than $20,000 a year, and 65% have incomes of less than $45,000 a year (DeFilippis, 2016; Smith et al., 2010). Older lesbian couples are twice as likely to live in poverty as their heterosexual married peers (DeFilippis, 2016). The majority of older LGBT people do not have children or family members to support them financially as they age, or to provide other forms of support, such as taking them shopping or to doctors' appointments (Hollibaugh, 2012).

The Causes of LGBT Poverty

There are many reasons why LGBT people have lower income levels and higher rates of poverty. This section will explore some of the primary causes of these disparities.

Over-Criminalization

One reason for LGBT poverty is because LGBT communities are disproportionately criminalized by the police and other institutions. Queer immigrant activist Veronica Bayetti Flores argues,

> When we're talking about queer bodies, immigrant bodies, black and brown bodies, disabled bodies, those disrupt white supremacy and heteropatriarchy – that's the context in which we see criminalization of communities that disrupt the social order by surviving, existing and thriving.
>
> (Taterka, 2015, para 4)

Severe disciplines and punishments disproportionately criminalize LGBT youth in schools. Lesbian, gay, and bisexual youth are more likely than their heterosexual peers to be expelled from school (MAP et al., 2013). Gender non-conforming girls are three times more likely to experience severe disciplinary actions at school than other students (Hollibaugh & Weiss, 2015).

Because they are frequently targeted for homophobic and/or racial harassment and violence at school, LGBT youth of color are at particularly high risk for being subject to disciplinary action by school officials or law enforcement (MAP et al., 2013). In addition, they are monitored more closely than other students. The overwhelming majority (79–87%) of LGBT youth of color have been approached by security or law enforcement in their middle or high school years (Lambda Legal, 2015; Taterka, 2015). Among African American LGBT youth, 69% have been sent to detention and 31% have been suspended (MAP et al., 2013). These interactions put LGBT youth (especially LGBT youth of color) into the school-to-prison pipeline.

The criminalization of LGBT youth is not limited to the schools. LGBT youth represent up to 40% of the homeless youth population, and these young people are often arrested for committing crimes related to homelessness, such as sleeping in public spaces or violating youth curfew laws (Hunt & Moodie-Mills, 2012). Approximately 300,000 LGBT youth (of which more than 60% are Black or Latino) are arrested or detained each year (Hunt & Moodie-Mills, 2012). Although LGBT youth comprise only 5–7% of the youth in our country, they represent 13–15% of those in the juvenile justice system. Once arrested, an LGBT youth is more likely than other youth to be convicted as an adult (MAP et al., 2013).

This dynamic continues into adulthood. There is a consistent pattern of homophobic and transphobic harassment by police, immigration officials, and federal surveillance agencies that includes profiling, searches and detention, selective law enforcement, and sexual and physical abuse (Taterka, 2015; Whitlock, 2012). Racism compounds the police's homophobic and transphobic treatment of LGBT people, resulting in the often-abusive monitoring of youth, homeless people, street vendors, and sex workers, who are disproportionately queer and people of color (Queers for Economic Justice, 2010; Taterka, 2015; Whitlock, 2012). This includes being stopped, strip-searched, and/or assaulted by police. After a lifetime of being over-criminalized, many LGBT people have police records, making it more difficult to obtain jobs.

Survival Economies

Because of experiences of discrimination and criminalization, many LGBT people end up with no choice but to work in low-wage jobs with no benefits. People who are already vulnerable and marginalized within the dominant culture because of their sexual orientation, gender identity, race, class, education level, or citizenship status are more likely to be forced into exploitative, non-unionized jobs, or jobs in underground economies. These jobs often involve menial, physical, and/or dangerous labor, leading to increased risk for disability and illness (Taterka, 2015). Due to discriminatory and exploitative working conditions, low-income LGBT people disproportionately live with high levels of physical and psychological fatigue, disabilities, injuries, and illness, making it even harder to achieve economic stability (Taterka, 2015).

Some LGBT people seek out work in "gay establishments" (such as bars, restaurants, clubs, or stores) because "gender expression and sexuality will not be disciplined in the same ways as in professional jobs" (Hollibaugh & Weiss, 2015, p. 22). This approach also presents challenges, as work in these settings often includes unpredictable schedules and unregulated salaries, yielding little economic security (Hollibaugh & Weiss, 2015). In addition, if workers lose their jobs or age out of work and need to retire, these "off the books" jobs leave the workers ineligible for crucial benefits such as unemployment insurance or social security (Taterka, 2015).

Many LGBT people turn to illegal activities in order to survive, often exchanging sex or drugs for food, cash, or a place to sleep, sometimes while they were also working in legal low-wage jobs (Hollibaugh & Weiss, 2015; Shah, 2012). Transgender and homeless LGBT people, including youth, are particularly likely to engage in sex work for survival; however, sex work is precarious and labor laws offer no protections. Sex workers do not have the right to organize, are subject to exploitation, criminalization, incarceration and health risks, and may experience violence at the hands of customers, police, and others. Despite these realities, many LGBT sex workers believe that taking low-wage, temporary work (often in homophobic or transphobic workplaces) is not necessarily a better option (Hollibaugh & Weiss, 2015; Shah, 2012).

Employment Discrimination

Those LGBT people who are able to obtain legal work receive lower salaries than their heterosexual, cisgender peers. The reason for this wage gap is because of the discrimination that LGBT workers experience in hiring, promotion, and retention at their jobs.

Workers (both LGBT people and their non-LGBT coworkers) consistently report witnessing workplace discrimination based on sexual orientation or gender identity (Sears & Mallory, 2011). Twenty-seven percent of lesbian, gay, and bisexual people have experienced workplace harassment and 7% have lost a job because of their sexual orientation (Gates, 2011a). Almost 60% of bisexual people report hearing anti-bisexual jokes and comments on the job (Tweedy & Yescavage, 2015). The rates of workplace discrimination are even higher (38%) for those LGB people who are open to their coworkers about their sexual orientation on the job (Gates, 2011a).

Transgender people report even higher rates of transphobic employment discrimination than LGB people (DeFilippis, 2016). A large majority (78%) of transgender people have experienced at least one form of anti-trans harassment or mistreatment at work, and 47% have been discriminated against in hiring, promotion, or job retention. (Sears & Mallory, 2011).

Older LGBT adults also experience workplace discrimination and have reported discrimination in the forms of not being hired for a job (22%), not being given a job promotion (21%), and being fired (14%) on the basis of their sexual orientation or gender identity (Fredriksen-Goldsen et al., 2011).

In addition to discrimination based upon their sexual orientation and/or gender identity, LGBT workers of color experience high rates of discrimination and additional challenges in the workplace due to racial discrimination. The combination of homophobia/transphobia and racism results in almost 50% of Black LGBT people and over 75% of Asian and Pacific Islander LGBT people reporting experiences of discrimination at work (MAP et al., 2013).

There are approximately 267,000 LGBT immigrants in the U.S. without legal authorization, 92% of whom are people of color (MAP et al., 2013). Their lack of legal documentation means that most of them have no choice but to work in minimum-wage jobs and jobs without benefits. In addition, fear of deportation makes it harder for them to speak up about legal violations, such as the withholding of wages (DasGupta, 2012; MAP et al., 2013).

Neoliberal Policies

In addition to the issues of discrimination documented earlier, many LGBT people are poor because of the same economic trends that leave other people poor. It is not possible to understand LGBT income and poverty without examining the impact of 40 years of neoliberal economic policies that give more power to corporations and less power to government. The neoliberal belief in small government has resulted in a shredded social safety net, stagnating minimum wages, and weaker labor unions, contributing to American poverty among all groups, including LGBT people.

Unionized workers are paid up to 30% more than non-unionized workers, and are more likely to have job-related health coverage, paid leave, and guaranteed pensions than non-unionized employees (Peralta, 2015; Walters & Mishel, 2003). Yet after 40 years of **neoliberal policies**, union membership has fallen to its lowest level since the Great Depression (Peralta, 2015). In the 1950s, 30% of American workers were union members, but today, less than 12% of American workers are in unions (Meyerson, 2012). Workers' bargaining power has declined in these years, resulting in economic growth going to the top of the income distribution (Peralta, 2015). Employers have replaced union workers with long-term temporary workers who work side by side with permanent employees but receive less pay and no benefits (Peralta, 2015). During this same period, income inequality has widened tremendously to the highest level the country has ever recorded (Guo, 2016).

In 2017, the federal minimum wage was $7.25 an hour. After taxes and deductions, most full-time minimum wage earners take home $225 a week or $12,000 a year, putting them at just a few dollars over the official poverty line (Komlos, 2015). About 2.6 million people earn the federal minimum wage or less (Bureau of Labor Statistics, 2016). In addition, despite popular belief, these minimum wage workers are not all high school students earning extra money. In fact, 89% are over the age of 20, 56–61% are women, and 40% are Black or Latino (U.S. Department of Labor, 2016; Weissmann, 2013). Additionally, low-wage workers are worse off than they were 40 years ago. People are working longer hours for less pay. From 1973 to 2013, hourly compensation of a typical worker only increased 9% even though productivity increased 74% (Mischel et al., 2015). In fact, the real minimum wage (adjusting the minimum wage for inflation) has seen a drastic decline in the past four decades. When adjusted for inflation, the 1968 minimum wage should be $10.90 today, rather than our current rate of $7.25 per hour (Komlos, 2015). This means that the minimum wage has actually been reduced by one-third in recent decades. This has real consequences for LGBT people. LGBT people of color are disproportionately included in this group, frequently working minimum wage jobs without health insurance, paid sick days, or retirement savings (MAP et al., 2013).

In addition, because of four decades of neoliberal policies designed to shrink the social safety net, the poor get less aid from the government than they once did (Stanley et al., 2016). In 1996, President Bill Clinton signed the Personal Responsibility and Work Opportunity Reconciliation Act (PRWORA) of 1996, a law that overhauled our welfare system. As a result of this law, fewer poor people qualify for government aid. Before welfare reform, over 13 million poor people received cash assistance from the government, whereas today only 3 million of the poor do. When LGBT individuals and families are actually able to access benefits, those benefits are not sufficient. After adjusting for inflation, cash assistance benefits for poor families decrease in value every year. For 99% of recipients nationally, these benefits are now at least 20% below their 1996 levels (Stanley et al., 2016). Because of new time limitations, between 500,000–1,000,000 people lost access to food stamps in 2016, despite otherwise having incomes low enough to continue to qualify. The government scheduled cuts of $8.7 billion from the SNAP program over the next ten years. This particularly affects LGBT people because same-sex couples are almost twice as likely than different-sex couples to receive food stamps (Gates, 2014).

Special Dilemmas

LGBT Families

Research indicates that 6 million American people (children and adults) have a parent who is LGBT (Gates, 2013). Approximately 2 million children are currently being raised in LGBT families, and that number will grow in the next decade (MAP et al., 2012). An estimated 3 million LGBT American adults (37% of all LGBT adults) have had a child at some time in their lives (Gates, 2013). Thousands of these children are biological or step-children, and tens of thousands more are grandchildren, siblings, nieces, or nephews. In addition, same-sex couples raising children are four times more likely than their different-sex counterparts to be raising an adopted child, and six times more likely to be raising foster children (Gates, 2013).

Same-sex couples who are parents and their children are more likely to be racial minorities than are other families (Gates, 2013). Same-sex couples with children are more racially and ethnically diverse than are heterosexual married parents (MAP et al., 2012). In addition, same-sex couples of color are more likely to be parenting than are White same-sex couples (MAP et al., 2012). LGBT parents are also more likely to be binational than heterosexual-headed households, with nearly half of binational, same-sex couples raising children (MAP et al., 2011).

Children raised in same-sex households are much more likely to be poor than those raised by heterosexual married families, largely because the families of lesbian couples and couples of color are much more likely to be poor (Albelda et al., 2009). The average household income for same-sex couples raising children is 20% less ($15,500) than it is for heterosexual couples (Burns, 2012). Single LGBT adults raising children are three times more likely than comparable heterosexual, cisgender individuals to be living near the official poverty line, and married or partnered LGBT couples with children are twice as likely (Gates, 2013). LGBT families of color are more likely to be living in poverty than other families. In fact, African American children in gay male households have the highest poverty rate (52.3%) of children in any household type in America (Badgett et al., 2013).

Many LGBT families do not have access to the benefits of marriage. Approximately 9 million American adults identify as LGBT (Gates, 2011b). Of them, 982,000 people (491,000 couples) have entered same-sex marriages (Associated Press, 2016). This means almost 90% of LGBT people (approximately 8 million people) are not in same-sex marriages. Many are bisexuals in opposite-sex marriages, and many others are cohabitating same-sex couples. Millions of LGBT people are not living in households structured around romantic coupling. These families are unable to access the benefits that are limited only to married couples.

This reflects larger trends among heterosexual America. Only one-fifth of U.S. households are now comprised of mother, father, and their biological children under the age of 18. The majority of American households take different forms. They are comprised of single people, single parents, couples who are cohabitating with or without children, grandparents raising children, friends, multi-generation homes, extended families, and blended families with children being raised alongside their half- and step-siblings.

For LGBT communities, families are built in all of those ways, as well as in a range of additional structures. LGBT people have historically built families in a wide variety of formations, many of which are not built around romantic relationships (DeFilippis, 2015; DeFilippis et al., 2015). Lesbian couples may often inseminate with sperm donated by a friend or family member. Sometimes the donor (often a single or partnered gay male) remains active in the child's life and works to co-parent the child with the lesbian mother or mothers. Other times, gay men may have children with the help of a hired surrogate or with a friend who volunteers to be a surrogate. Many of these options for family creation bring with them considerable expenses (Boggis, 2001).

Other families are not structured around child-rearing. LGBT people are more likely than the population as a whole to be a caregiver for someone who is not legally related (MAP et al., 2013). For instance, increasingly, older LGBT adults come together as housemates to create "Golden Girls"-like homes, living together and/or making legal contracts to care for each other (DeFilippis, 2015). In addition, since the 1980s, LGBT people have built on-going, long-term care-giving relationships that provide support to those living with extended illness such as HIV/AIDS. For a century, queer communities of color have participated in ballroom and house communities, which are homes organized around drag culture and which provide housing, social, and economic supports. LGBT people are also more likely than their heterosexual siblings to take in an aging parent in order to care for them (Hu, 2005); LGBT families of color are more likely to be multi-generational and include extended family and kin.

Eligibility for many work-related benefits are designed around marriage and traditional family structure, and do not reflect the reality of LGBT families. To access most job-related benefits, couples must be married, and employees must have a legal parental relationship with the people for whom they are caring. These narrow eligibility requirements do not recognize the myriad of family configurations listed earlier, leaving LGBT families without access to crucial resources.

Access to the Social Safety Net

Many social welfare programs presume that children are being raised by legally married parents, using this narrow definition of family to determine aid eligibility. The result is that cash assistance, health insurance, food and nutrition support, child care assistance, housing subsidies, educational loans, and other aid may not be available to LGBT families (MAP et al., 2012). In addition, some immigrant families are ineligible for safety net programs. Without access to these benefits, low-income LGBT families lack crucial support. Because of a larger culture of stigma telling LGBT families that they are not "real families," they may not even realize that they qualify for aid even when they are actually eligible (MAP et al., 2012).

Additionally, when low-income LGBT families and individuals do seek assistance, high numbers experience obstacles and discrimination applying for and receiving public assistance and Social Security (Arkles et al., 2010; Audre Lorde Project, 2010; Legal Services NYC, 2016; Queers for Economic Justice, 2010). Many count on support such as Medicaid, HIV/AIDS benefits, SNAP (food stamps), Supplemental Security Income, Social Security Disability (SSD), and TANF (welfare), yet they experience discrimination and harassment. When applying for assistance, 30–50% report being denied benefits (Legal Services NYC, 2016; Queers for Economic Justice, 2010).

Because of workplace discrimination, transgender people must often seek public assistance. Yet, they are particularly vulnerable to harassment when applying, and are consistently denied access to benefits. In the years following the 1996 welfare reform, unemployed transgender people who applied for public assistance reported being so severely harassed at mandatory welfare work sites that they chose to give up benefits and turn to sex work on the streets, where they felt safer (Blum et al., 2000). Activists report that this harassment has continued at welfare offices in the years since (Arkles et al., 2010; Legal Services NYC, 2016; Queers for Economic Justice, 2010).

Homelessness

LGBT youth are often kicked out by homophobic parents or run away because of homophobic abuse, and face high rates of homelessness. In an 11-city study of homeless youth aged 14 to 21, 20% identified as bisexual, 9.9% identified as gay or lesbian, 6.8% identified as transgender, and 4.1% identified their sexual orientation as "something else" (Administration for Children and Families, 2016). The average homeless youth spends almost two years living on the streets, and the majority lack a safe place to stay, a phone, help with school, and access to places to study, rest, or do laundry. Over 60% have been assaulted (raped, beaten up, and/or robbed). Among homeless youth who identify as gay or lesbian, 44% are Black and 26% are Latino (Quintana et al., 2010). Native American young people are also over-represented among LGBT homeless youth (Aratani, 2009).

Many of these homeless youth grow up to be homeless adults. In addition, LGBT adults may also become homeless because of the income disparities and obstacles to benefits faced by LGBT people. More research is needed about homelessness among LGBT adults, but anecdotal evidence suggests that it may be at crisis levels. For instance, a study of 722 men who have sex with men in Los Angeles found that 50% were homeless (Shoptaw et al., 2009). Another study found that 29% of San Francisco's homeless adults identified as LGBT (Green, 2015). In a survey of 171 low-income LGBT New Yorkers, 70% of them had been or were currently homeless (Queers for Economic Justice, 2010).

Many homeless shelters are run by faith-based organizations and religious groups that discriminate against LGBT people. At both these and at publicly run shelters, homeless LGBT people have reported facing discriminatory and dangerous treatment. This treatment includes having been denied services, stopped and searched by police, falsely arrested, and/or physically and sexually assaulted (Queers for Economic Justice, 2010). Residents attempting to file grievances are retaliated against, kicked out, transferred arbitrarily to another shelter, or subject to inspections in the middle of the night.

Transgender people are at particularly high risk of homelessness. Between 20–40% of transgender and gender-non-conforming people have experienced homelessness (DeFilippis, 2016; Grant et al., 2011). These rates are disproportionate with other populations and clearly constitute a crisis.

When transgender people seek shelter, they encounter apathy, hostility, and/or violence at the hands of shelter staff (Duggan, 2012; Motta, 2011; Queers for Economic Justice, 2010). In most cities, homeless transgender people cannot choose whether they are placed in the men's or women's system, and they are forced to reside where they are assigned (Duggan, 2012; Motta, 2011). Transgender women are frequently placed in male shelters, where they face the risk of violence, rape, and murder. Transgender shelter residents face so much violence in the shelters that they often feel safer returning to the streets (Duggan, 2012; Motta, 2011; Mottet & Ohle, 2003). Transgender or gender-non-conforming people who do stay in the shelters face discrimination and harassment at every stage of their residence, including in the intake processes, use of restrooms and showers, sleeping arrangements, and accessing services (Duggan, 2012; Queers for Economic Justice, 2010). They report having their confidentiality violated, being harassed by staff and other residents, and being subject to violence.

Social Work Practice Considerations

Macro-level Recommendations

On the macro level, advocates and activists have worked for years at the state and federal levels to pass laws preventing discrimination in the workplace. As of 2018, only 19 states and Washington, D.C., have made it illegal for employers to discriminate against LGBT people. Three other states protect workers on the basis of sexual orientation but not gender identity. Advocacy efforts exist in the remaining states to add legal protections, but a federal law would make that local work unnecessary. The Equality Act, a bill introduced in the United States Senate and House of Representatives in 2017, sought to amend the Civil Rights Act of 1964 to prohibit discrimination based on sexual orientation and gender identity in employment, education, housing, public accommodations, credit, jury service, and federally funded programs.

While anti-discrimination laws are important, there are significant limitations to them. Not all jobs are covered by anti-discrimination laws. Most laws only cover companies with at least 15 employees, and not all jobs done by low-income people are legally recognized as work. Childcare, welfare work sites, and underground economies such as sex work are often not subject to regulation or protections. Moreover, most anti-discrimination laws have a short statute of limitations and require that a charge of discrimination be filed within a year of the discrimination. This has limited the number of people who can file discrimination claims. Finally, it is often very difficult to prove discrimination. Providing evidence demonstrating why you were not hired is very difficult (if not impossible) to do, and it is not much easier to prove why you were denied a promotion or terminated.

Employment non-discrimination laws will also be of little help to those who will still be unable to get jobs. If the only remedy for poverty is non-discrimination laws, then poverty rates will not improve for non-workers, such as people with disabilities, retired seniors, undocumented immigrants who cannot work, and those with other complicating legal issues.

An exclusive focus solely on ending discrimination fails to address other structural issues that cause poverty. Too often, social workers end up focusing only on the issue of discrimination, without addressing the larger economic context in which that discrimination is embedded. While it is crucial to address identity-based discriminations such as homophobia, transphobia, sexism, and racism, it is equally important to examine the role of capitalism and neoliberal policies if we are actually to combat inequity and poverty in any meaningful way. Otherwise, we are saying that LGBT poverty is acceptable, as long as it is comparable to heterosexual poverty, whereas social workers must challenge poverty in all of its iterations and contexts. Although it is important for social workers to support laws such as the Equality Act, it cannot be mistaken as the only policy solution that is needed. Social workers must target their interventions to include policies and broader economic issues, such as raising the minimum wage, supporting labor unions, and strengthening the social safety net programs. Winning marriage equality so that LGBT people can access their partners' benefits is not enough when those benefits are being diluted and discontinued more broadly across the nation.

In addition to devoting more resources to the social safety net, social workers must also advocate for more LGBT families to have access to the safety net of government programs and protections. As a result of marriage equality and the assumption that all LGBT people can now get benefits through marriage, many states and corporations are now doing away with protections for non-married families. Social workers must consider the needs and recognition of diverse family structures and advocate on behalf of all families. We must accommodate the reality of how LGBT and other 21st century families actually engage in parenting and other forms of care-giving, such as kinship care, multi-generational parenting, and caring for elderly or sick relatives.

Mezzo-level Recommendations

Social workers must address homophobia and transphobia that exists at agencies serving low-income people (Arkles et al., 2010; Audre Lorde Project, 2010; Duggan, 2012; Legal Services NYC, 2016; Motta, 2011; Mottet & Ohle, 2003; Queers for Economic Justice, 2010). In particular, homeless shelters and welfare offices are sites where many LGBT people experience so much discrimination that they cannot access the crucial programs and benefits they need. Social workers can partner with LGBT activists to conduct staff trainings in developing culturally sensitive policies, services, and interactions with LGBT clients, so that these clients have access to the services and benefits that can help alleviate poverty.

In addition, social workers can work with their local schools to reduce punishments that send students on to the streets, such as expulsions and suspensions, where they are more likely to be stopped by the police. In addition, we can work to eliminate police presence in the schools, and reduce the over-reliance on criminalization as a disciplinary strategy. A lifetime of police surveillance of LGBT people (particularly people of color and transgender people) begins in schools, and this school-to-prison pipeline contributes to LGBT poverty.

Micro-level Recommendations

Social workers engaged in micro-level work with LGBT people will enhance their effectiveness by utilizing intersectional approaches to assessment of clients. Too often, social workers presume that LGBT people's biggest obstacles are homophobia or transphobia. While that is possible, it is equally likely that poverty or racism are even greater issues in their lives. An intersectional lens helps social workers to understand the complexity of the lives of people who are simultaneously LGBT and also people of color, immigrants, older adults, and/or low-income. Social workers must consider poverty and material needs when doing assessment and referrals with LGBT clients, so that they can help them access resources such as social services, benefits, or jobs that can alleviate their poverty.

Social workers must also engage in casework or clinical work that recognizes the diverse forms of care-giving and family creation in which many LGBT people are engaged. Focusing only on marriage and legally recognized children fails to recognize the myriad of other relationships that may be central to the lives of LGBT clients.

Final Considerations: Social Work Knowledge, Values, and Skills

In order to work with LGBT people, social workers need to answer certain questions, while committing to specific social work values and developing particular social work skills. This section identifies some of them.

What a Social Worker Needs to Know

- Does your community have LGBT non-discrimination laws? Do they cover employment? Do they cover gender identity, or just sexual orientation?
- At what amount is your state's minimum wage set? Is this a livable wage?
- Does your client have a job? Does this job pay a living wage and provide benefits? Do they feel safe and respected at their job?
- For what individual benefits might your client qualify? Are these benefits sufficient?
- What benefits would be available for the type of family your client has created? Is marriage mandatory to access them, or are they available to a wide range of family types?
- Do the homeless shelters in your community allow transgender people to self-determine whether they want to reside in a male shelter or female shelter? Are LGBT couples or families allowed to live together in the family shelters? Do your community's welfare offices serve LGBT people in non-discriminatory ways?

Social Work Values and Ethical Considerations

Working with LGBT people on issues of employment discrimination and poverty is clearly in keeping with the National Association of Social Worker's (NASW) Code of Ethics. A central value in social work is the pursuit of *social justice*, about which the Code of Ethics explicitly states, "Social workers' social change efforts are focused primarily on issues of poverty, unemployment, discrimination, and other forms of social injustice". Social workers must work to end the crisis of LGBT poverty that has been caused by these forms of social injustice. The Code of Ethics also stresses *the importance of human relationships*. It states, "social workers seek to strengthen relationships among people in a purposeful effort to promote, restore, maintain, and enhance the well-being of individuals, families, social groups…" and consequently social workers must partner with LGBT clients to combat their poverty and find ways of supporting the different caregiving relationships and families that they have built. In addition, the Code of Ethics requires that social workers actively work to increase their *competence*. There is no way for social workers to competently serve LGBT clients without an understanding of the epidemic of poverty facing these communities.

Social Work Skills to Strengthen Competency

In order for social workers to work effectively with LGBT populations, they must develop their knowledge about economic policies that affect workers and the local and national laws that protect against discrimination. They must also learn about the concrete impact of criminalization and the long-term legal and economic repercussions of having a criminal record. Social workers should develop skills to intervene with clients disenfranchised by having such a record. They must also increase their understandings of family diversity and the different family compositions of their LGBT clients. Finally, they must become aware of local and federal programs and develop their skills at connecting clients to public assistance and other benefit programs.

Questions to Consider

1   How do income and poverty rates vary across LGBT populations? What factors should social workers consider about income and poverty for LGBT clients when framed within the theoretical perspective of intersectionality?
2   What structural issues of injustice affect poverty levels for LGBT people?
3   Why might employment be challenging for LGBT people, especially for those who identify as transgender?
4   What are "neoliberal policies" in the United States? How have they affected Americans and specifically, the financial well-being of LGBT people?
5   How has the Personal Responsibility and Work Opportunity Reconciliation Act of 1996 impacted poverty rates for LGBT individuals and families? What is important to consider when examining this and other policies, such as the Equality Act?
6   What are the pros and cons of legal marriage for LGBT couples and families? What presumptions should social workers avoid making about LGBT clients based on marital status?
7   How does criminalization affect poverty rates? Why are some LGBT people at higher risk? How can you, as a social worker, intervene in the "school-to-prison" pipeline?
8   In what ways can social workers advocate for a stronger social safety net for LGBT people and all who face poverty?
9   What factors place LGBT people at higher risk of homelessness? What issues should social workers address at shelters and other agencies to prepare them to be more welcoming and supportive of LGBT people?

10 What resources exist in your local area to support LGBT people in addressing poverty, employment, and workplace discrimination?

Resources

Further Reading

The Movement Advancement Project (MAP) www.lgbtmap.org is an independent think tank that provides research and analysis about LGBT people. Its website has various reports focused on various relevant policies and issues.

National LGBTQ Task Force www.thetaskforce.org/category/reports-studies/ This national advocacy organization regularly produces reports about LGBT issues, including some focused on LGBT people who are low-income or people of color.

A New Queer Agenda http://sfonline.barnard.edu/a-new-queer-agenda/ A New Queer Agenda is a special issue of The Scholar & the Feminist Online, with articles focusing on issues impacting LGBT people who are low-income and/or people of color.

Queers for Economic Justice (archive) http://q4ej.blogspot.com closed in 2014, but this site has many of their publications and positions statements about issues impacting low-income LGBT communities:

The Williams Institute http://williamsinstitute.law.ucla.edu The Williams Institute at UCLA Law, dedicated to conducting independent research on sexual orientation and gender identity law and public policy, has many reports about LGBT people's income and poverty rates.

In addition, these authors regularly write about low-income LGBT people: Joseph Nicholas DeFilippis, Kenyon Farrow, Amber Hollibaugh, Yasmin Nair, and Dean Spade.

Organizations

The following is a list of 30 community-based organizations located across the country. These organizations address issues facing LGBT people who are low-income, people of color, immigrants, and/or incarcerated:

1 **Affinity Community Services** (Chicago, IL) www.affinity95.org
2 **allgo** (Austin, TX) www.allgo.org
3 **Audre Lorde Project** (New York, NY) www.alp.org
4 **Arizona Queer Undocumented Immigrant Project** (Phoenix, AZ) http://azquip.tumblr.com/
5 **Black and Pink** (Boston, MA) www.blackandpink.org
6 **BreakOUT!** (New Orleans, LA) www.youthbreakout.org
7 **BSeedz** (Denver, CO) http://coavp.org/bseedz

8 **Center for Artistic Revolution** (Little Rock, AR) www.artisticrevo
   lution.org
9 **Community United Against Violence** (San Francisco, CA) www.
   cuav.org
10 **Esperanza Peace and** Justice Center (San Antonio, TX) www.espera
   nzacenter.org
11 **Familia: Trans Queer Liberation Movement** (Los Angeles, CA)
   http://familiatqlm.org
12 **FIERCE** (New York, NY) www.fiercenyc.org
13 **First Nations Two-Spirit Collective** (national) www.facebook.
   com/First-Nations-Two-Spirit-Collective-228560843858693/
14 **Gender** Justice L.A. (Los Angeles, CA) www.facebook.com/
   GenderJusticeLA
15 **Hearts on a Wire Collective** (Philadelphia, PA) www.scribd.com/
   user/78046739/Hearts-on-a-Wire
16 **Immigrant Youth Coalition** (Los Angeles, CA) http://theiyc.org/
17 **The National Black Justice Coalition** (Washington, DC) http://
   nbjc.org
18 **National Queer Asian Pacific Islander Alliance** (Washington, DC)
   www.nqapia.org
19 **El/La Para Translatinas** (San Francisco, CA) http://ellaparatransla
   tinas.yolasite.com
20 **Providence Youth Student Movement** (Providence, RI) www.
   prysm.us
21 **Queer Undocumented Immigrant Project of the United We
   Dream Network** (national) http://unitedwedream.org/
22 **Queer Women of Color Media Arts Project** (San Francisco, CA)
   www.qwocmap.org
23 **SONG: Southerners on New Ground** (Durham, NC) www.south
   ernersonnewground.org
24 **SPARK (**Atlanta, GA) www.sparkrj.org
25 **Streetwise and Safe** (New York, NY) http://streetwiseandsafe.org
26 **Sylvia Rivera Law Project** (New York, NY) www.srlp.org
27 Transgender, Gender Variant **and** Intersex Justice **Project** (Oakland,
   CA) www.tgijp.org
28 **The Transgender Law Center** (Oakland, CA) http://transgenderla
   wcenter.org
29 **TransLatin@ Coalition** (national) http://translatinacoalition.org/
30 **Women With A Vision** (New Orleans, LA) http://wwav-no.org

References

Administration for Children and Families (2016). *Final report – street outreach program data collection study*. Administration for Children and Families, Family and Youth

Services Bureau, Street Outreach Program. Retrieved from www.acf.hhs.gov/fysb/resource/street-outreach-program-data-collection-study

Albelda, R., Badgett, M.V.L., Schneebaum, A., & Gates, G. (2009). *Poverty in the lesbian, gay and bisexual community*. The Williams Institute, UCLA School of Law, UC Los Angeles. Retrieved from www.law.ucla.edu/williamsinstitute/pdf/LGBPovertyReport.pdf

Aratani, Y. (2009). *Homeless children and youth, causes and consequences*. National Center for Children in Poverty. Retrieved from http://nccp.org/publications/pdf/text_888.pdf

Arkles, G., Gehi, P., & Redfield, E. (2010). The role of lawyers in trans liberation: Building a transformative movement for social change. *Seattle Journal for Social Justice*, 8(2), 579–641.

Associated Press (June 22, 2016). Same-sex marriages in U.S. since Supreme Court ruling estimated to be 123,000. *CBS News*. Retrieved from www.cbsnews.com/news/same-sex-marriages-us-supreme-court-ruling-estimate/

Audre Lorde Project (2010). *The winning team: The Welfare Justice Campaign trains Human Resource Administration on policy to address discrimination against trans and gender non-conforming people*. Retrieved from http://alp.org/winning-team-welfare-justice-campaign-trains-human-resource-administration-policy-address-discrimina

Badgett, M.V.L., Durso, L.E., & Schneebaum, A. (2013). *New patterns of poverty in the lesbian, gay, and bisexual community*. The Williams Institute, UCLA School of Law, UC Los Angeles. Retrieved from http://williamsinstitute.law.ucla.edu/wp-content/uploads/LGB-Poverty-Update-Jun-2013.pdf

Blum, R., DeFilippis, J., & Perrina, B.A. (2000). Why welfare is a queer issue. *New York University Review of Law and Social Change*, 26(1&2), 137–219.

Boggis, T. (2001). Affording our families: Class issues in family formation. In M. Bernstein & R. Reimann (Eds.), *Queer families, queer politics: Challenging culture and the state* (pp. 175–181). New York: Columbia University Press.

Bond, L., Wheeler, D.P., Millett, G.A., LaPollo, A.B., Carson, L.F. & Liau, A. (2009). Black men who have sex with men and the association of down-low identity with HIV risk behavior. *American Journal of Public Health*, 99(S1), 92–95.

Bureau of Labor Statistics (2016). *Characteristics of minimum wage workers, 2015*. Retrieved from www.bls.gov/opub/reports/minimum-wage/2015/home.htm

Burns, C. (2012). The gay and transgender wage gap. Center for American Progress. Retrieved from www.americanprogress.org/issues/lgbt/news/2012/04/16/11494/the-gay-and-transgender-wage-gap/

Center for American Progress & Movement Advancement Project (MAP) (2015). Paying an unfair price: The financial penalty for being transgender in America. Retrieved from www.lgbtmap.org/file/paying-an-unfair-price-transgender.pdf

DasGupta, D. (2012). Queering immigration: Perspectives on cross-movement organizing. *A New Queer Agenda: The Scholar and the Feminist Online*, 10(1–2).

DeFilippis, J.N. (2015). Wedding bells are breaking up that old gang of mine. In C. Sickels (Ed.), *Untangling the knot: Queer voices on marriage, relationships & identity* (pp. 123–140). Portland, OR: Ooligan Press.

DeFilippis, J.N. (2016). "What about the rest of us?" An overview of LGBT poverty issues and a call to action. *Journal of Progressive Human Services*, 27(3), 143–174.

DeFilippis, J.N., Anderson-Nathe, B., & Panichelli, M. (2015). Notes on same-sex marriage concerns for feminist social workers. *Affilia*, 30(4), 461–475.

Duggan, A. (2012). 'Nobody should ever feel the way that I felt': A portrait of Jay Toole and queer homelessness. *A New Queer Agenda: The Scholar and the Feminist Online,* 10(1–2). The Barnard Center for Research on Women. Retrieved from http://sfonline.barnard.edu/a-new-queer-agenda/nobody-should-ever-feel-the-way-that-i-felt-a-portrait-of-jay-toole-and-queer-homelessness/0/

Dunn, M. & Moodie-Mills, A. (2012). *The state of gay and transgender communities of color in 2012: The economic, educational, and health insecurities these communities are struggling with and how we can help them.* Center for American Progress. Retrieved from www.americanprogress.org/issues/2012/04/lgbt_comm_of_color.html

Fredriksen-Goldsen, K.I., Kim, H.-J., Emlet, C.A., Muraco, A., Erosheva, E.A., Hoy-Ellis, C.P., Goldsen, J., & Petry, H. (2011). *The aging and health report: Disparities and resilience among lesbian, gay, bisexual, and transgender older adults.* Seattle: Institute for Multigenerational Health. Retrieved from http://caringandaging.org/wordpress/wp-content/uploads/2011/05/Full-Report-FINAL-11-16-11.pdf

Gates, G.J. (2011a). Special analyses using data from the general social survey 2008. The William Institute. Retrieved from http://williamsinstitute.law.ucla.edu/wp-content/uploads/Sears-Mallory-Discrimination-July-20111.pdf

Gates, G.J. (2011b). How many people are lesbian, gay, bisexual and transgender? The William Institute. University of California, Los Angeles. Retrieved from http://williamsinstitute.law.ucla.edu/wp-content/uploads/Gates-How-Many-People-LGBT-Apr-2011.pdf

Gates, G.J. (2013). LGBT parenting in the United States. The Williams Institute. University of California, Los Angeles. Retrieved from http://williamsinstitute.law.ucla.edu/wp-content/uploads/LGBT-Parenting.pdf

Gates, G.J. (2014). Food insecurity and SNAP (food stamps) participation in LGBT communities. The Williams Institute, University of California, Los Angeles. Retrieved from http://williamsinstitute.law.ucla.edu/wp-content/uploads/Food-Insecurity-in-LGBT-Communities.pdf

GLAAD (2015). GLAAD – Where we are on TV report – 2015. GLAAD. Retrieved from www.glaad.org/whereweareontv15

GLAAD (2016). 2016 GLAAD studio responsibility index. GLAAD. Retrieved from www.glaad.org/sri/2016

Grant, J.M., Mottet, L., Tanis, J.E., Harrison, J., Herman, J., & Keisling, M. (2011). *Injustice at every turn: A report of the national transgender discrimination survey.* National Center for Transgender Equality and National Gay and Lesbian Task Force. Retrieved from www.thetaskforce.org/static_html/downloads/reports/reports/ntds_full.pdf

Green, E. (2015). Groundbreaking shelter for LGBT homeless opening in the Mission. *San Francisco Chronicle.* Retrieved from www.sfchronicle.com/bayarea/article/Groundbreaking-shelter-for-LGBT-homeless-opening-6331449.php?t=0769a42b95f294ee0d&cmpid=twitter-premium#photo-8131480

Guo, J. (2016). Income inequality today may be higher today than in any other era. *The Washington Post.* Retrieved from www.washingtonpost.com/news/wonk/wp/2016/07/01/income-inequality-today-may-be-the-highest-since-the-nations-founding/

Hollibaugh, A. (2012). 2, 4, 6, 8: Who says that your grandmother's straight. *A New Queer Agenda: The Scholar and the Feminist Online,* 10(1–2). The Barnard Center for Research on Women. Retrieved from http://sfonline.barnard.edu/a-new-queer-agenda/2-4-6-8-who-says-that-your-grandmothers-straight/

Hollibaugh, A. & Weiss, M. (2015). Queer precarity and the myth of gay affluence. *New Labor Forum*, 24(3), 18–27. doi: doi:10.1177/1095796015599414

Hu, M. (2005). *Selling us short: How social security privatization will affect lesbian, gay, bisexual, and transgender Americans*. National Gay and Lesbian Task Force. Retrieved from www.thetaskforce.org/static_html/downloads/reports/reports/SellingUsShort.pdf

Human Rights Campaign (2009). *At the intersection: Race, sexual orientation and gender*. Retrieved from www.hrc.org/files/documents/HRC_Equality_Forward_2009.pdf pp. 11–13.

Hunt, J. & Moodie-Mills, A. (2012). The unfair criminalization of gay and transgender youth. Center for American Progress. Retrieved from www.americanprogress.org/wp-content/uploads/issues/2012/06/pdf/juvenile_justice.pdf

Komlos, J. (2015). Why raising the minimum wage is good economics. *PBS Newshour*. Retrieved from www.pbs.org/newshour/making-sense/why-raising-the-minimum-wage-is-good-economics/

Krehely, J. & Hunt, J. (2011). *Helping all of our homeless: Developing a gay- and transgender-inclusive federal plan to end homelessness*. Center for American Progress. Retrieved from www.americanprogress.org/issues/2011/01/pdf/lgbt_homelessness.pdf

Lambda Legal (2015). *Protected and Served?* Retrieved from www.lambdalegal.org/sites/default/files/publications/downloads/ps_executive-summary.pdf

Legal Services NYC (2016). Poverty is an LGBT issue: An assessment of the legal needs of low-income LGBT people. Retrieved from www.legalservicesnyc.org/storage/PDFs/lgbt%20report.pdf

Meyerson, H. (2012). If labor dies, what's next?American Prospect. Retrieved from http://prospect.org/article/if-labor-dies-whats-next

Mischel, L., Gould, E., & Bivens, J. (2015). Wage stagnation in nine charts. Economic Policy Institute. Retrieved from www.epi.org/publication/charting-wage-stagnation/

Motta, C. (2011). An interview with Kenyon Farrow. Retrieved from http://wewhofeeldifferently.info/interview.php?interview=105

Mottet, L. & Ohle, J. M. (2003*). Transitioning our shelters: A guide to making homeless shelters safe for transgender people*. National Gay and Lesbian Task Force Policy Institute. National Center for Transgender Equality. Retrieved from http://srlp.org/wp-content/uploads/2012/08/TransitioningOurShelters.pdf

Movement Advancement Project (MAP), BiNet USA, & Bisexual Resource Center (2014). *Understanding issues facing bisexual Americans*. Retrieved from www.lgbtmap.org/file/understanding-issues-facing-bisexual-americans.pdf

Movement Advancement Project (MAP), Center for American Progress, Freedom to Work, Human Rights Campaign, & National Black Justice Coalition (2013). *A broken bargain for LGBT workers of color*. Retrieved from www.lgbtmap.org/file/a-broken-bargain-for-lgbt-workers-of-color.pdf

Movement Advancement Project (MAP), Family Equality Council, & Center for American Progress (2011). *All children matter: How legal and social inequalities hurt LGBT families*. Retrieved from www.lgbtmap.org/file/all-children-matter-full-report.pdf

Movement Advancement Project (MAP), Family Equality Council, Center for American Progress, National Black Justice Coalition, Unid@s, the National Queer Asian Pacific Islander Alliance, & the FIRE Initiative (2012). *LGBT families of color: Facts at a glance.* Retrieved from www.nbjc.org/sites/default/files/lgbt-families- of-color-facts-at-a-glance.pdf

National Black Justice Coalition, the National Gay and Lesbian Task Force, & the National Center for Transgender Equality (2011). *Injustice at every turn: A look at black respondents in the National Transgender Discrimination Survey.* Retrieved from www.thetaskforce.org/downloads/reports/reports/ntds_full.pdf

Peralta, K. (2015). The fall of unions from power. *US News and World Report.* Retrieved from www.usnews.com/news/articles/2015/01/02/workers-weakened-bargaining-power-fuels-income-inequality

Personal Responsibility and Work Opportunity Reconciliation Act of 1996, Pub. L. No. 104-193, 110 Stat. 2105 (1996) (codified in scattered sections of 42 U.S.C.).

Pew Research Center (2013). A survey of LGBT Americans: The LGBT population and its sub-groups. Retrieved from www.pewsocialtrends.org/2013/06/13/a-survey-of-lgbt-americans/#the-lgbt-population-and-its-sub-groups

Queers for Economic Justice (2010). "A fabulous attitude": Low-income LGBTGNC people surviving & thriving on love, shelter & knowledge". *Queers for Economic Justice, Welfare Warriors Research Collaborative.* Retrieved from www.issuelab.org/resources/14891/14891.pdf

Quintana, N.S., Rosenthal, J., & Krehely, J. (2010). *On the streets: The federal response to gay and transgender homeless youth.* Washington, DC: Center for American Progress. Retrieved from www.americanprogress.org/wp-content/uploads/issues/2010/06/pdf/lgbtyouthhomelessness.pdf

Schilt, K. & Wiswall, M. (2008). Before and after: Gender transitions, human capital, and workplace experiences. *The BE Journal of Economic Analysis & Policy,* 8(1). DOI: doi:10.2202/1935-1682.1862

Sears, B. & Mallory, C. (2011). Documented evidence of employment discrimination & its effects on LGBT people. The Williams Institute. University of California, Los Angeles. Retrieved from http://williamsinstitute.law.ucla.edu/wp-content/uploads/Sears-Mallory-Discrimination-July-20111.pdf

Sears, B. & Badgett, L. (2012). Beyond stereotypes: Poverty in the LGBT community. The Williams Institute. University of California, Los Angeles. Retrieved from http://williamsinstitute.law.ucla.edu/headlines/beyond-stereotypes-poverty-in-the-lgbt-community/

Shah, S.P. (2012). Sex work and queer politics in three acts. *A New Queer Agenda: The Scholar and the Feminist Online,* 10(1–2). Retrieved from http://sfonline.barnard.edu/a-new-queer-agenda/sex-work-and-queer-politics-in-three-acts/0/

Shoptaw, S., Weiss, R., Munjas, B., Hucks-Ortiz, C., Young, S., Larkins, S., Victorianne, G., & Gorbach, P. (2009). Homonegativity, substance use, sexual risk behaviors, and HIV status in poor and ethnic men who have sex with men in Los Angeles. *Journal of Urban Health,* 86, 77–92.

Smith, L.A., McCaslin, R., Chang, J., Martinez, P., & McGrew, P. (2010). Assessing the needs of older gay, lesbian, bisexual and transgender people: A service-learning and agency partnership approach. *Journal of Gerontological Social Work,* 53(5), 387–401.

Stanley, M., Floyd, I., & Hill, M. (2016). *TANF Cash benefits have fallen by more than 20 percent in most states and continue to erode.* Center on Budget and Policy Priorities. Retrieved from www.cbpp.org/research/family-income-support/tanf-cash-benefits-have-fallen-by-more-than-20-percent-in-most-states

Taterka, M. (2015). Surviving or thriving: How economic (in)justice matters for LGBT People. *Autostraddle*. Retrieved from www.autostraddle.com/surviving-or-thriving-how-economic-injustice-matters-for-lgbt-people-275453/

Tweedy, A.E. & Yescavage, K. (2015). Employment discrimination against bisexuals: An empirical study. *William and Mary Journal of Women and the Law*, 21(3/5), 699–741.

Ulaby, N. (2013). Who's gay on tv? Dads, journalists, investigators and footmen. National Public Radio. Retrieved at www.npr.org/2013/01/02/168215115/whos-gay-on-tv-dads-journalists-investigators-and-footmen

U.S. Department of Labor (2016). Minimum wage mythbusters. Retrieved from www.dol.gov/featured/minimum-wage/mythbuster

Walters, M. & Mishel, L. (2003) How unions help all workers. Economic Policy Institute. Retrieved from www.epi.org/publication/briefingpapers_bp143/

Weissmann, J. (2013). Who might get a raise if Obama boosts the minimum wage? *The Atlantic*. Retrieved from www.theatlantic.com/business/archive/2013/02/who-might-get-a-raise-if-obama-boosts-the-minimum-wage/273123/

Whitlock, K. (2012). We need to dream a bolder dream: The politics of fear and queer struggles for safe communities. *A New Queer Agenda: The Scholar and the Feminist Online*, 10(1–2) The Barnard Center for Research on Women. Retrieved from http://sfonline.barnard.edu/a-new-queer-agenda/we-need-to-dream-a-bolder-dream-the-politics-of-fear-and-queer-struggles-for-safe-communities/0/

13 Religion and Spirituality

Claire L. Dente

PH.D., MSW, LCSW

CSWE 2015 EPAS Competencies

Competency 1: Demonstrate ethical and professional behavior
Competency 2: Engage diversity and difference in practice
Competency 3: Advance human rights and social, economic and environmental justice
Competency 4: Engage in practice-informed research and research-informed practice
Competency 5: Engage in policy practice
Competency 6: Engage with individuals, families, groups, organizations and communities
Competency 7: Assess individuals, families, groups, organizations and communities
Competency 8: Intervene with individuals, families, groups, organizations and communities
Competency 9: Evaluate practice with individuals, families, groups, organizations and communities

Most social work students state that they are pursuing social work because they want to help people. It is not uncommon for students to share how involved they are in outreach through their church, synagogue or mosque, often providing numerous hours of service to people in need. Some even engage in mission trips to areas of the United States and other countries to render service through organized programs sponsored by faith-based organizations. The profession itself includes religious roots in the history of the emersion of social work (Popple & Leighninger, 2011).

Other students indicate that while they grew up in religious families of various denominations, they have chosen not to participate in their family of origin's faith system anymore. These students often reference disillusionment with their faith system over disagreement on an issue or a negative experience with a religious leader or congregation.

A third group of students will share that they did not grow up with any formal religious orientation. Some say they feel connected to the world and the universe on a spiritual level. It is likely that as a social work student you find yourself in one of these groups or somewhere in between (see Chaves, 2011, for a discussion of recent trends in religion).

This chapter invites you to consider who you are and what you believe about **religion, spirituality** and faith. It challenges you to consider working with LGBTQIA clients who may also embrace or reject religion, spirituality or faith. You can expect to learn about social work knowledge, values and skills related to the intersectionality of religion, spirituality and faith with LGBTQIA identities. As shown at the end of this chapter in the Questions to Consider section, social work knowledge derived from practice and research, social work values articulated in the National Association of Social Work Code of Ethics (NASW, 2008) and social work skills highlighted in the Council on Social Work Education 2015 EPAS Competencies (CSWE, 2015) will provide a foundation for our discussion in this chapter.

Historical Considerations and Personal Values

The intersectionality of religion, spirituality and faith with LGBTQIA identities has had a rocky relationship within many mainstream religions. For the most part, the majority of faith systems have not welcomed people with LGBTQIA identities. There is no shortage of documentation on the challenges LGBTQIA people have faced (Wood & Conley, 2014). Many religious traditions have approached human sexuality from perspectives that elevate heterosexual cisgender relationships within the context of hetero-sexual marriage, with a primary purpose of procreation. This has led to prohibitions regarding sexual contact outside of marriage, the use of birth control and abortion, as well as non-acceptance of 'non-traditional' sexual orientation and gender identity.

While many religious and cultural traditions would support interventions to assist individuals born with a cleft palate or other physical issues, uncertainty and fear can arise when considering transgender identities and the needs of transgender individuals for established medical interventions, including hormone regimens or surgery. Some traditions have emphasized the concept of 'natural law,' which historically has been defined within a heteronormative context. Nonetheless, LGBTQIA people exist in every culture and tradition, and there are LGBTQIA people from all faith traditions.

While history reveals tensions, discussions about LGBTQIA identities among communities of faith have expanded. Advocacy on behalf of civil rights for LGBTQIA people and the passage of gay marriage placed LGBTQIA issues at the forefront of many contexts, including religious and faith systems. Some traditions have recommitted to long-held beliefs of LGBTQIA identities as sinful; others are examining their beliefs within the context of evolving scientific knowledge and informing their understanding through the lived experiences of LGBTQIA people both in and out of their specific faith tradition. Some denominations are even addressing ways to welcome and support LGBTQIA clergy. Moon (2014) observed that there is now a continuum of perspectives from acceptance to rejection of LGBTQIA identities within Judeo-Christian traditions. Social work students and their clients may also identify as LGBTQIA and/or come from faith traditions anywhere along this spectrum of acceptance and rejection. Self-awareness on these identities and beliefs is crucial for social workers to provide competent practice for clients. Consider your own religious, spiritual and faith identities, and then consider your own sexual orientation and gender identity. Are there conflicts between these identities? How have you personally reconciled any differences? How might you support a client in this space, which can sometimes include tension?

Religion and spirituality differ. Researchers embrace nuanced definitions, but most tend to agree that religion involves formal practices of a specific faith system, while spirituality involves the ways people live out their beliefs and make meaning in their life (Altmeyer, Klein, Keller, Silver, Hood & Streib, 2015; Land, 2014; Sheldrake, 2013). Religiosity would involve attending services at one's house of worship and engaging in practices and activities such as formal prayer, reading religious texts and participating in rituals. Spirituality can emerge from the beliefs and practices of a formal religion. The formal prayers learned through one's religion might take on spiritual meaning; however, spirituality does not have to link to a formal religion. Some people feel connected to others and the universe while walking alone in nature; others might live according to their prior religious training to 'love one another,' yet might never go to church. Both of these are examples of spirituality. Spirituality can be broad and expansive in its definition; the manner in which individuals and communities make meaning in life is varied and diverse.

Integrating Faith and LGBTQIA Identities: Micro and Mezzo Considerations

Integrating one's faith and LGBTQIA identity poses challenges, but can also present opportunities for integration of self and spiritual growth. Individuals raised in a faith system that does not welcome LGBTQIA identities face challenges which can include *how, when* or even *if* they should come out to family, friends and faith community. They may find themselves critically examining their own LGBTQIA identity, and attempting to reconcile that identity within the context of the belief system they have cherished. Yet, at a time of great questioning, their formal faith system may not be affirming. Their spiritual home, which could have served as a resource during the coming out process, may no longer be accessible. These individuals come face-to-face with all they believe about their faith, family and even God or another higher power. Many grow to make the distinction between their faith, i.e., what they believe and how it guides their lives, and their faith system, which is the religious institution and its practices, dogma and theology. Negotiating this spiritual crisis can spur spiritual and emotional maturity. Challenging core beliefs from childhood and reexamining them as an adult calls forth mature questioning that can result in a reaffirmation of what one believes and a discarding of that which lacks integrity in forming spiritual and LGBTQIA identities. 'Wrestling with God' or 'testing one's faith in fire,' as some belief systems might frame it, can deepen one's relationship to the transcendent aspects of life and in turn, the daily living of what one truly believes. This can lead to greater integrity and a more authentic experience of living.

It is at this point that many beginning social work students might propose that these clients walk away from an unwelcoming denomination to find a new, more accepting one. While this may seem like a logical approach, it leaps over two very important steps of generalist social work practice that social workers must consider: the skills of engagement and assessment (Kirst-Ashman & Hull, 2015). It is in these two steps that social workers can foster a professional social work relationship with LGBTQIA clients of faith and explore the strengths and challenges of their converging identities. Can you as a social worker connect with this client in this struggle, even if faith is not important to you? Why are these identities both so important to this client? How can you learn more about this particular client's situation and assess the strengths and challenges present? Numerous movies and testimonies depict struggles people of faith experience as they integrate their sexual orientation and gender identity with their faith (Dente, 2015).

Social work students should be aware that there are **'within' and 'between' group differences** in understanding the approaches of religious and spiritual traditions which impact clients. As in research methods and understanding diversity, 'between group' comparisons acknowledge that there are differences between groups of religious traditions, such as how Jewish, Christian, Muslim or Buddhist traditions approach the issue of LGBTQIA identities. 'Within group' comparisons recognize that there are differences within each religious tradition. In Judaism, Orthodox traditions approach LGBTQIA identities more strictly than Reform traditions, which are usually more accepting. Within Christianity, the Episcopal Church will permit gay marriage while the Roman Catholic Church will not. Nuances rise further within groups, e.g., when considering that some strains of the Episcopal Church support gay marriage while others do not; and, while the official stance of the Roman Catholic Church denies gay marriage, there are local LGBTQIA-supportive congregations that welcome LGBTQIA members even if the church cannot witness marriages for them. Social work students should familiarize themselves with resources about faith traditions to help clarify the official positions each takes on LGBTQIA identities. It is also important for social workers to avoid broad generalizations about any specific religious group. Rather, it is important to develop the skills of engagement and assessment to become skillful at talking with clients about their tradition and the context of their specific congregation. If you are unfamiliar with mainstream religious and spiritual traditions, the British Broadcasting Corporation (BBC) website (see Resources later in this chapter) provides a helpful overview of religious traditions (BBC, 2014). The Human Rights Campaign (HRC) website also provides an overview of the relationship of different religious traditions with LGBTQIA issues and people (HRC, 2016a).

Why would a client with an LGBTQIA identity want to maintain their faith identity, even if it means remaining connected to a faith tradition that does not offer full inclusion or celebrate LGBTQIA members? This question tugs at the heart of understanding diversity. Many LGBTQIA people raised with a faith system do not wish to leave that system. For many, their religious traditions weave throughout their culture of origin. Religious practices embed with life milestones, such as one's Bar Mitzvah, Baptism, family weddings and funerals. Many live out the cycle of each year in the observances of Ramadan and Eid al-Fitr, Holy Week and Easter, or Rosh Hashana and Yom Kippur. In fact, many clients find aspects of their faith to provide a source of strength as they negotiate the coming out process, even when the faith system itself might not fully welcome LGBTQIA members. At all life stages, LGBTQIA people of faith might seek their religious system as a source of celebration in joyful times, and strength in times of need, just as any other person might. From a baptism or bris at birth to anointing and pastoral care at death, LGBTQIA identities will interact with spirituality across the lifespan.

There is rising interest in the relationship of spirituality to the coming out process in youth (Bayne, 2016; Gold & Stewart, 2011), and how growing into one's LGBTQIA identity can link with one's faith development (Kocet, Sanabria & Smith, 2011). While LGBTQIA people often left rejecting faith systems in past decades, many LGBTQIA people do not want to discard their faith and now stay, advocating and educating congregations for greater understanding and acceptance of sexual orientation and gender identity. In fact, the integration of one's LGBTQIA identity with one's faith and spirituality has drawn new investigation (Beagan & Hattie, 2015; Levy, 2011). Some scholars have examined the experience of LGBTQIA individuals in the Church of Jesus Christ of Latter Day Saints (Mormons) in integrating faith with LGBTQIA identity (Bradshaw, Dehlin, Heaton, Galliher, Decoo & Crowell, 2015; Dehlin, Galliher, Bradshaw & Crowell, 2015); others have reflected on gay marriage from the Mennonite perspective (Braun, 2014). Numerous studies have explored the Jewish experience, especially among Orthodox Jewish individuals where LGBTQIA identities may be less accepted (Itzhaky & Kissil, 2015; Slomowitz & Feit, 2015). Others have examined the experiences of LGBTQIA people in Roman Catholicism (Figueroa & Tasker, 2014; Greene, Brennan & Britton, 2015; Hall, 2015) and Christian denominations, including the Black Church and conservative evangelical traditions (Dessel & Bolen, 2014; Foster, Bowland & Vosler, 2015; Lassiter, 2015; McGlasson & Rubel, 2015; Toft, 2014). Researchers have also noted the challenges facing LGBTQIA Muslims (Yip,

2015), including Muslim refugees resettling in western locations (Kahn, 2015). Hence, LGBTQIA people of all faiths are seeking to integrate these identities. As social workers, we must be knowledgeable and skillful in ways to support clients in this pursuit.

Family often intrinsically links to one's faith, as many children grow up in a religious tradition espoused by their family of origin. In some cases, families have rejected a member who identifies as LGBTQIA because of the dogma of their faith system, while others have negotiated these differences. The group, Parents, Families & Friends of Lesbians & Gays (PFLAG), provides resources that specifically address support, education and advocacy within multiple traditions and faith communities (PFLAG, 2016). It is important for social workers to ask clients about family support and acceptance, as well as how their community of faith will receive them as LGBTQIA people. It may not be an LGBTQIA person who engages a social worker, but rather, a family member who is struggling with the coming out of their family member. Social workers must be supportive and non-judgmental in assisting these family members through their own process. Some parents may fear that their child is going to hell, or that their religious community will reject the child or family. Others wonder about whether or not they should invite their child to Thanksgiving dinner. Social workers are uniquely poised to listen, to link clients to resources, to provide information and to assist clients through this process. No matter how great or small the concerns, social workers can provide a context of openness and willingness to hear them.

Assessment

Most social workers are not pastoral counselors or clergy, and so we must remember to engage clients within our scope of practice. Nonetheless, we can still include religion and spirituality in our assessment with a client. Social workers engaging with LGBTQIA clients of faith will find it helpful to inquire about the religious and spiritual components of clients' lives. Assessing micro, mezzo and macro dimensions of clients' lives is equally important.

A comprehensive assessment includes gathering information about biological, psychological, social, spiritual and cultural components. A thorough intake or clinical interview can help clients to articulate the importance of religion and spirituality in their lives. Social workers can strengthen engagement with clients who value their religious and spiritual identities by asking about them, as many often overlook these areas. As social workers, we must understand these identities before we can assess them in the lives of our clients. Social workers who may feel uncomfortable inquiring about religion and spirituality should ask themselves why this is so. Is it lack of familiarity and knowledge? If you feel hesitant to ask, spend some time delving into your discomfort. Think about your own experiences, practice asking friends about the religious and spiritual components of their childhood and current life, talk to religious leaders from various traditions, and discuss your hesitation in clinical supervision sessions.

There are assessment approaches social workers can use with clients. Roberts-Lewis (2011) proposed that even beginning social workers can utilize a basic Spiritual Assessment and Ethnographic Interviewing Technique. A basic Spiritual Assessment can provide an overview of a client's positive and negative experience with religion and spirituality, as well as the strengths, challenges, resources and roles these play in their life (Roberts-Lewis, 2011, p. 140). The Goals, Renewal, Action, Connection and Empowerment (GRACE) model also provides a structured approach to help professionals in working with LGBTQIA clients (Bozard & Sanders, 2011). These and other spiritual and religious assessments are available for use with LGBTQIA clients. Social workers should speak with their clinical supervisors and agencies about the best approach to use with clients in their specific agency context.

Community Life and Policy: Mezzo and Macro Considerations

Some formal religious traditions have embraced new scientific knowledge about sexual orientation and gender identity. This informs their stance to approach LGBTQIA people with open arms. Yet, earlier we stated that there has been a history of non-acceptance of LGBTQIA identities within mainstream religious traditions. As you explore different religious traditions, you can see why each one has its particular theological stance on LGBTQIA identities. In some traditions, the belief in a natural law that affirms heterosexuality or a fundamentalist interpretation of Judeo-Christian Biblical scriptures that prohibit homosexuality lays the groundwork for less inclusive approaches (see Vines, 2014, for a discussion of Biblical passages frequently cited as evidence against homosexuality). The legal passage of civil gay marriage intensified the dialogue among religious groups opposed to this issue.

Because some faith systems outright reject diverse LGBTQIA identities, some have espoused **sexual orientation change efforts (SOCE)**. Other terms that encompass this approach include **conversion therapy** or **reparative therapy; transformational therapy** or **transformational ministry**. SOCE approaches specifically aim to 'change' one's sexual orientation or gender identity. The American Psychological Association (APA, 2009) and National Association of Social Workers (NASW, 2015) have issued statements opposing these approaches. Thirteen professional organizations also united as the Just the Facts Coalition (2008) to publish information about the harmful effect of these therapies. Their report targeted educators who work with LGBTQIA youth. It highlighted the lack of empirical evidence supporting change efforts and educated readers about the harmful effects of change efforts. In essence, given the current medical and behavioral science knowledge available, it would be unethical, and in some cases illegal, for social workers to engage in SOCE approaches. Ongoing research demonstrates the lack of evidence for these approaches (Flentje, Heck & Cochran, 2014). Despite statements from professional organizations that SOCE approaches are harmful, some faith systems have persisted in their use. This prompted advocacy by LGBTQIA groups against the use of SOCE, especially in minors whose parents make legal decisions for their physical and mental health care (HRC, 2016b). Testimonies before the legislature (Levovitz, 2015) have contributed to several states outlawing the use of SOCE approaches. According to the HRC (2016b), "California, Illinois, New Jersey, Oregon, Vermont and the District of Columbia have passed laws to prevent licensed mental health providers from offering conversion therapy to minors, and more than 20 states have introduced similar legislation" (HRC, 2016b). Social workers should be aware that SOCE efforts are harmful to clients and may be illegal in jurisdictions.

With the passage of gay marriage, some religious groups and individuals feared they might be forced to engage LGBTQIA people in their houses of worship. Because the United States values separation of church and state, this is not likely. Freedom of religion is protected under the First Amendment of the United States Constitution. Yet, freedom of religion and anti-discrimination laws that protect LGBTQIA people are being positioned as mutually exclusive, in some cases as political tactics to exempt any group with a religious affiliation from the requirements of non-discrimination against LGBTQIA people. The federal **Religious Freedom Restoration Acts (RFRAs)** of 1993 limited the right of government to interfere with the practice of religion. In recent years, many states have enacted state RFRAs (see Bombay, 2014, and McClam, 2015, for a discussion of the history of federal and state RFRAs). Many attribute the recent rise in these acts as a response to the legalization of gay marriage and as a way to seek exemptions from providing professional or business services to LGBTQIA people on the basis of religious beliefs (Sepinwall, 2015). In essence, this could lead to discrimination against LGBTQIA people under the guise of freedom of religion. Scholars have explored whether ministers would now be required to marry LGBTQIA people (Stevens, 2014) or if businesses could refuse services to gay couples seeking to hire them (Oleske, 2015). Of great concern to professional groups like NASW, Tennessee passed a law in 2016 permitting mental health counselors and therapists to exempt themselves from providing services based on religious exemptions, even though each Code of Ethics for psychologists, professional counselors, social workers and marriage and family therapists would suggest otherwise (Wagner, 2016). In 2016, 'bathroom bills' aimed at forcing transgender individuals to use the bathroom of their gender at birth, even when those individuals identify otherwise or may even be in the process of transitioning, invoked U.S. Justice Department and even the Obama White House to act to overturn these laws (Berlinger, 2016; Davis & Apuzzo, 2016).

Thus, in considering religious and spiritual issues that impact LGBTQIA clients, social workers must also consider the climate for LGBTQIA people in the local community. Policies and laws at the state and federal level may seek to both strengthen and challenge lives of LGBTQIA people. Social workers will need to engage both LGBTQIA and religious communities to build bridges. Opportunities are ripe for social work interventions at mezzo and macro levels to work towards educating and reconciling these two groups (Liboro, 2015).

Conclusion

Many LGBTQIA people of faith seek to live according to their belief system and look for inclusion and acceptance in the religious and spiritual communities in which they grew up. At the end of this chapter, you will find a summary of important questions you should consider as you work with LGBTQIA clients of faith. When people are not accepted, some leave their formal religious system, while others stay and work towards greater inclusion. Social workers need to be aware that these are complex interactions for individuals at the intersection of faith and LGBTQIA identities. It is important not to judge clients on their stance and to consider ways that one's religion or spiritualty can also be a great source of strength for those clients who desire this. This chapter has focused primarily on sexual orientation and gender identity and their relationship with religion and spirituality. We must also consider other identities such as age, ethnicity, race, ability and socio-economic status. Social workers must be competent at conducting a comprehensive assessment with clients that includes all of these factors. The family's relationship to their faith and spirituality is also important.

At the mezzo and macro levels, social workers must also be proactive in attending to current laws and policies that examine **religious freedom** and non-discrimination. Social workers can advocate for ways that permit the free exercise of religion while also protecting vulnerable groups such as LGBTQIA people. The Resources section at the end of this chapter provides a listing of web resources that can assist you with finding more information about the issues presented in this chapter. As you continue on your journey through a career in social work, it will be important to update your knowledge and skills on the challenges and strengths of religion, faith and spirituality in the lives of LGBTQIA clients.

Questions to Consider

1   Historically, religious institutions have not welcomed LGBTQIA people. How is that changing today?
2   Religion and spirituality are not always the same construct. How do they differ? Why is it important to understand this distinction for LGBTQIA people?

3   Each social worker brings personal values from their own family, education and life experiences to the practice of social work. The NASW Code of Ethics calls social workers to foster self-determination in clients. How do I increase my awareness of my own personal values and beliefs, especially where they may differ from those of my client?

4   How do LGBTQIA clients integrate their LGBTQIA identity with their religion, spirituality and/or faith?

5   What are ways that one's LGBTQIA and religious/spiritual identities intersect with family, career and life?

6   Social workers assess clients on both LGBTQIA and on religious and spiritual identities. What are ways social workers can do this?

7   There are several strengths and challenges for LGBTQIA clients of faith. What are they?

8   What resources exist for LGBTQIA clients who are seeking a welcoming faith community?

9   What evidence-based research exists in scholarly literature regarding the effect of reparative and conversion therapies?

10 What current or proposed policies and laws exist at the federal, state and local levels regarding religious freedom and sexual orientation, gender and gender identity? How do these laws and policies affect LGBTQIA people?

Resources

General Information

British Broadcasting Company (BBC) www.bbc.co.uk/religion/reli gions provides an archived overview of major world religions.

Human Rights Campaign (HRC) www.hrc.org/explore/topic/religion-fa ith is an LGBTQIA civil rights organization which contains information on religion and faith and the stance of groups to LGBTQIA people.

Institute for Welcoming Resources, a program of the National LGBTQ Task Force www.welcomingresources.org/index.htm is an ecumenical group working for full inclusion of LGBTQIA members in religious groups. Contains extensive resource lists for multiple denominations.

Just the Facts about Sexual Orientation and Youth: A Primer for Principals, Educators and School Personnel www.apa.org/pi/lgbc/p ublications/justthefacts.html is a publication sponsored by many professions in the educational, medical, social and behavioral sciences. It was published to address reparative and conversion therapies.

Lambda Legal www.lambdalegal.org/cgi-bin/iowa/index.html works for civil rights for LGBTQIA individuals. Clients facing discrimination involving religion and sexual orientation or gender identity can find resources here.

NASW Practice: Lesbian, Gay, Bisexual & Transgender www.socia lworkers.org/Practice/LGBT contains links to positions statements on conversion and reparative therapies, as well as other resources for practice.

Parents, Families & Friends of Lesbians & Gays (PFLAG) http://comm unity.pflag.org/page.aspx?pid=655 is a non-denominational group for families and friends whose mission includes support, education and advocacy.

A Sampling of Faith-Specific Resources

There are numerous denominations providing support and welcome to LGBTQIA people. These are some examples and starting points; there are many faiths not listed here.

Christian Traditions

BAPTIST

Association of Welcoming and Affirming Baptists www.awab.org

BRETHREN MENNONITE

Brethren Mennonite Council for Lesbian, Gay, Bisexual and Transgender Interests www.bmclgbt.org

CHRISTIAN/EVANGELICAL CHRISTIAN

Q Christian Fellowship www.qchristian.org
The Reformation Project www.reformationproject.org/about

CHURCH OF JESUS CHRIST OF LATTER DAY SAINTS (LDS/MORMON)

Affirmation: LGBT Mormons, Families and Friends https://affirma tion.org/

EPISCOPAL CHURCH

Official Church Page www.episcopalchurch.org/page/lgbt-church
Integrity USA www.integrityusa.org Episcopalians working for inclusion

LUTHERAN

Reconciling Works: Lutherans for Full Participation www.reconci lingworks.org/resources/sogi/lgbtq

PRESBYTERIAN

More Light Presbyterians https://mlp.org
United Church of Christ (UCC) www.ucc.org/lgbt_resources

Islam

The Muslim Alliance for Sexual & Gender Diversity (MASGD) www. muslimalliance.org

Muslims for Progressive Values www.mpvusa.org/lgbtqi-resources

Judaism

JQ International www.jqinternational.org
Keshet www.keshetonline.org

Roman Catholic

Dignity USA www.dignityusa.org
Fortunate Families www.fortunatefamilies.com
New Ways Ministry www.newwaysministry.org

Supplemental Resources

Activities/Assignments

1   Compare two or more specific faith traditions on their stance on LGBTQIA identities. In what ways does the tradition embrace and/or reject LGBTQIA identities? How has the religious tradition evolved in its stance on LGBTQIA identities? What is the tradition's theology and dogma on LGBTQIA issues? What is the approach religious leaders take in their pastoral care of LGBTQIA members and their families?

2   If you were working with a client who struggled with integrating their faith and LGBTQIA identity, to whom would you refer them from their faith? Are there religious leaders, clergy and congregations who would be resources for the client? How might you build a network of local clergy who could assist clients struggling with their faith and LGBTQIA identity? Create a resource guide of local LGBTQIA-affirming clergy and congregations from various traditions. Be sure to include a wide array of denominations from the community.

3   Conduct your own spiritual history of yourself and your family. What religious tradition(s) have you experienced? How has this tradition's belief system affected your own approach to self and others on LGBTQIA issues? What has changed for you as you grew from childhood into adulthood? Have you continued to embrace this tradition? If you have no formal faith system, what do you believe about life, death, hope, suffering and challenges that philosophers have addressed throughout the centuries? Where do you find meaning?

4   Contact an LGBTQIA group within a specific faith tradition. Interview one of the group's leaders about the issues that are important to LGBTQIA people within that faith tradition. What are some of the unique challenges and strengths for LGBTQIA people within that faith tradition? What is the denomination's official stance? How do individuals come out and integrate their sexual orientation, gender and/or gender identity within that specific faith tradition?

References

Altmeyer, S., Klein, C., Keller, B., Silver, C.F., Hood, R.W. & Streib, H. (2015). Subjective definitions of spirituality and religion: An exploratory study in Germany and the US. *International Journal of Corpus Linguistics*, 20(4), 526–552. doi doi:10.1075/ijcl.20.4.05alt

American Psychological Association (APA). (2009). *Report of the APA task force on appropriate therapeutic responses to sexual orientation*. Retrieved from www.apa.org/pi/lgbt/resources/sexual-orientation.aspx

Bayne, H.B. (2016). Helping gay and lesbian students integrate sexual and religious identities. *Journal of College Counseling*, 19(1), 61–75. doi: doi:10.1002/jocc.12031

Beagan, B.L. & Hattie, B. (2015). Religion, spirituality, and LGBTQ identity integration. *Journal of LGBT Issues in Counseling*, 9(2), 92–117.

Berlinger, J. (2016, May 10). North Carolina's bathroom law: Six points from both sides of the issue. *CNN Politics*. Retrieved from www.cnn.com/2016/05/10/politics/hb-2-point-counterpoint/

Bombay, S. (2014, June 30). What is RFRA and why do we care? *Constitution Daily: Smart Conversation from the National Constitution Center*. Retrieved from http://blog.constitutioncenter.org/2014/06/what-is-rfra-and-why-do-we-care/

Bozard, R.L. & Sanders, C.J. (2011). Helping Christian lesbian, gay, and bisexual clients recover religion as a source of strength: Developing a model for assessment and integration of religious identity in counseling. *Journal of LGBT Issues in Counseling*, 5(1), 47–74. doi: doi:10.1080/15538605.2011.554791

Bradshaw, W.S., Dehlin, J.P., Heaton, T.B., Galliher, R.V., Decoo, E. & Crowell, K.A. (2015). Religious experiences of GBTQ Mormon males. *Journal for the Scientific Study of Religion*, 54(2), 311–329.

Braun, J.G. (2014). Whose Law? Queer Mennonites and same-sex marriage. *Journal of Mennonite Studies*, 32, 97–113.

British Broadcasting Corporation (BBC). (2014). *Featured religions and beliefs (archived)*. Retrieved from www.bbc.co.uk/religion/religions/

Chaves, M. (2011). Religious trends in America. *Social Work & Christianity*, 38(2), 119–132.

Council on Social Work Education (CSWE). (2015). *Educational policy and accreditation standards*. Alexandria, VA: Author.

Davis, J.H. & Apuzzo, M. (2016, May 12). U.S. directs public schools to allow transgender access to restrooms. *The New York Times*. Retrieved from www.nytimes.com/2016/05/13/us/politics/obama-administration-to-issue-decree-on-transgender-access-to-school-restrooms.html?_r=0

Dehlin, J.P., Galliher, R.V., Bradshaw, W.S. & Crowell, K. A. (2015). Navigating sexual and religious identity conflict: A Mormon perspective. *Identity*, 15(1), 1–22. doi: doi:10.1080/15283488.2014.989440

Dente, C.L. (2015). The intersection of religion and sexual orientation: Pedagogy and challenges. *The Journal of Baccalaureate Social Work*, 20, 157–178.

Dessel, A.B. & Bolen, R.M. (Eds.). (2014). *Conservative Christian beliefs and sexual orientation in social work: Privilege, oppression, and the pursuit of human rights*. Alexandria, VA: CSWE Press.

Figueroa, V. & Tasker, F. (2014). "I always have the idea of sin in my mind. …": Family of origin, religion, and Chilean young gay men. *Journal of GLBT Family Studies*, 10(3), 269–297. doi: doi:10.1080/1550428X.2013.834424

Flentje, A., Heck, N.C. & Cochran, B.N. (2014). Experiences of ex-ex-gay individuals in sexual reorientation therapy: Reasons for seeking treatment, perceived helpfulness and harmfulness of treatment, and post-treatment identification. *Journal of Homosexuality*, 61(9), 1242–1268. doi: doi:10.1080/00918369.2014.926763

Foster, K.A., Bowland, S.E. & Vosler, A.N. (2015). All the pain along with all the joy: Spiritual resilience in lesbian and gay Christians. *American Journal of Community Psychology*, 55(1–2), 191–201.

Gold, S.P. & Stewart, D.L. (2011). Lesbian, gay, and bisexual students coming out at the intersection of spirituality and sexual identity. *Journal of LGBT Issues in Counseling*, 5(3/4), 237–258. doi: doi:10.1080/15538605.2011.633052

Greene, D.C., Brennan, C. & Britton, P.J. (2015, August 24). Exploration of psychological distress in gay, bisexual, and heterosexual Roman Catholic priests. *Psychology of Religion and Spirituality*. Advance online publication. doi: doi:10.1037/rel0000047

Hall, D. (2015). Individual choices revisited: Non-heterosexual Christians in Poland. *Social Compass*, 62(2), 212–224. doi: doi:10.1177/0037768615571691

Human Rights Campaign (HRC). (2016a). *Explore: Religion & faith*. Retrieved from www.hrc.org/explore/topic/religion-faith

Human Rights Campaign (HRC). (2016b). *The lies and dangers of efforts to change sexual orientation or gender identity*. Retrieved from www.hrc.org/resources/the-lies-and-dangers-of-reparative-therapy

Itzhaky, H. & Kissil, K. (2015). 'It's a horrible sin. If they find out, I will not be able to stay': Orthodox Jewish gay men's experiences living in secrecy. *Journal of Homosexuality*, 62(5), 621–643.

Just the Facts Coalition. (2008). *Just the facts about sexual orientation and youth: A primer for principals, educators, and school personnel*. Washington, DC: American Psychological Association. Retrieved fromwww.apa.org/pi/lgbc/publications/justthefacts.html

Kahn, S. (2015). Experiences of faith for gender role non-conforming Muslims in resettlement: Preliminary considerations for social work practitioners. *British Journal of Social Work*, 45(7), 2038–2055. doi: doi:10.1093/bjsw/bcu060

Kirst-Ashman, K.K. & Hull, G.H. (2015). *Understanding generalist practice* (7th ed). Stamford, CT: Cengage Brooks/Cole.

Kocet, M.M., Sanabria, S. & Smith, M.R. (2011). Finding the spirit within: Religion, spirituality, and faith development in lesbian, gay, and bisexual individuals. *Journal of LGBT Issues in Counseling*, 5(3/4), 163–179. doi: doi:10.1080/15538605.2011.633060

Land, H. (2014). *Spirituality, religion, and faith in psychotherapy: Evidence-based expressive methods for mind, brain, and body*. Chicago, IL: Lyceum.

Lassiter, J.M. (2015). Reconciling sexual orientation and Christianity: Black same-gender loving men's experiences. *Mental Health, Religion & Culture*, 18(5), 342–353. doi: doi:10.1080/13674676.2015.1056121

Levovitz, M. (2015). Testimony on sexual orientation change efforts. *Journal of Gay & Lesbian Mental Health*, 19(1), 96–99. doi: doi:10.1080/19359705.2014.960758

Levy, D.L. (2011). Christian social workers serving gay and lesbian clients. *Social Work & Christianity*, 38(2), 218–227.

Liboro, R.M. (2015). Community-level interventions for reconciling conflicting religious and sexual domains in identity incongruity. *Journal of Religion and Health*, 54(4), 1206–1220.

McClam, E. (2015, March 30). Religious Freedom Restoration Act: What you need to know. *NBC News*. Retrieved from www.nbcnews.com/news/us-news/india na-religious-freedom-law-what-you-need-know-n332491

McGlasson, T.D. & Rubel, D.J. (2015). My soul to take: A phenomenology of the struggle for an authentic gay spirituality. *Counseling and Values*, 60(1), 14–31.

Moon, D. (2014). Beyond the dichotomy: Six religious views of homosexuality. *Journal of Homosexuality*, 61(9), 1215–1241.

National Association of Social Workers (NASW). (2008). *Code of ethics*. Washington, DC: Author.

National Association of Social Workers (NASW). (2015). *Sexual orientation change efforts (SOCE) and conversion therapy with lesbians, gay men, bisexuals and transgender persons: NASW position statement*. Washington, DC: Author.

Oleske, J.M. (2015). Doric columns are not falling: Wedding cakes, the ministerial exception, & the public-private distinction. *Maryland Law Review*, 75(1),142–162.

Parents, Families & Friends of Lesbians & Gays (PFLAG). (2016). *Welcoming faith communities*. Retrieved from http://community.pflag.org/page.aspx?pid=652

Popple, P.R. & Leighninger, L. (2011). *Social work, social welfare and American society (8th ed.)*. Boston: Pearson/Allyn & Bacon.

Roberts-Lewis, A.C. (2011). Response to Mark Chaves: Practical interventions to assist social work students in addressing religious and spiritual diversity. *Social Work & Christianity*, 38(2), 139–145.

Sepinwall, A.J. (2015). Conscience and complicity: Assessing please for religious exemptions in Hobby Lobby's wake. *University of Chicago Law Review*, 82(4), 1897–1980.

Sheldrake, P. (2013). *Spirituality: A brief history* (2nd ed). West Sussex, UK: Wiley-Blackwell.

Slomowitz, A. & Feit, A. (2015). Does God make referrrals? Orthodox Judaism and homosexuality. *Journal of Gay & Lesbian Mental Health*, 19(1), 100–111.

Stevens, A. (2014). By the power vested in me? Licensing religious officials to solemnize marriage in the age of same-sex marriage. *Emory Law Journal*, 63(4), 979–1020.

Toft, A. (2014). Re-imagining bisexuality and Christianity: The negotiation of Christianity in the lives of bisexual women and men. *Sexualities*, 17(5/6), 546–564. doi: doi:10.1177/1363460714526128

Vines, M. (2014). *God and the gay Christian: The Biblical case in support of same-sex relationships*. New York: Convergent Books/Random House.

Wagner, L. (2016, April 27). Tennessee enacts law letting therapists refuse patients on religious grounds. *The Two-Way: Breaking News from NPR*. Retrieved from www.npr.org/sections/thetwo-way/2016/04/27/475939114/tennessee-enacts-law-letting-therapists-refuse-patients-on-religious-grounds

Wood, A.W. & Conley, A.H. (2014). Loss of religious or spiritual identities among the LGBT population. *Counseling and Values*, 59(1), 95–111.

Yip, A.K-T. (2015). Living out Islam: Voices of gay, lesbian, and transgender Muslims. *Sociology of Religion*, 76(3), 360–361. doi: doi:10.1093/socrel/srv037

14 Aging

Noell L. Rowan

PH.D., LCSW, LCAS, FNAP

Sandra S. Butler

PH.D., MSW

CSWE 2015 EPAS Competencies

Competency 1: Demonstrate ethical and professional behavior
Competency 2: Engage diversity and difference in practice
Competency 3: Advance human rights and social, economic and environmental justice
Competency 4: Engage in practice-informed research and research-informed practice
Competency 5: Engage in policy practice
Competency 7: Assess individuals, families, groups, organizations and communities
Competency 8: Intervene with individuals, families, groups, organizations and communities

Social Work Knowledge

LGBTQIA Older Adults and Historical Context
Health and Caregiving
Mental Health and Substance Use Issues
Obstacles to Accessing Health Care and Long Term Services and Supports
LGBTQIA-Sensitive Social Work Practice with Older Adults

Social Work Values and NASW Code of Ethics

1.01: Commitment to Clients
1.02: Self-Determination
1.04: Competence
1.05: Cultural Competence and Social Diversity
2.06: Referral for Service
4.01: Competence
4.02: Discrimination

Social Work Skills

Understand oppression and discrimination

Recognize and **interpret** social, personal, environmental and health information pertinent to historical context

Recognize health risk and protective factors specific to LGBTQIA aging populations

Articulate stressors and strengths specific to LGBTQIA aging populations and mental health and substance use issues

Identify challenges to health care access for LGBTQIA older adults

Articulate specific aging in place and housing options for LGBTQIA older adults

Understand and **utilize** theories of intersectionality in working with LGBTQIA older adults to identify marginalization and oppression

Implement strengths approach to working with LGBTQIA older adult clients

Identify steps to take to increase cultural sensitivity and competency in working with older LGBTQIA adults

Introduction

In the last five to ten years, topics about LGBTQIA aging have received more attention in the scholarly literature. Publications such as the Institute of Medicine (IOM, 2011) report of LGBT health, funded study by National Institutes of Health and an expansion of publications with special issues in prominent journals have certainly illuminated the focus of this field of research (de Vries & Croghan, 2014; Fredriksen-Goldsen et al., 2011; Fredriksen-Goldsen et al., 2014; Rowan & Giunta, 2014). Also, the burgeoning expansion of the National Resource Center of LGBT Aging (Meyer & Johnston, 2014), originally funded by the United States Administration on Aging, and the incredible work of SAGE (Services and Advocacy of GLBT Elders), with affiliates across the United States, are more pieces of evidence of the increased attention to the LGBTQIA aging populations (www.sageusa. org). Despite this recent emphasis, many questions remain unanswered and services and issues need to be addressed (de Vries & Croghan, 2014). This is a time to expand the knowledge and focus on the particular needs and issues of the aging population of LGBTQIA persons.

LGBTQIA Older Adults and their Historical Context

Estimating the number of LGBTQIA older adults in the U.S. is not an exact science. As stated by Grant (2009), there are both definitional challenges to the categories of **lesbian, gay, bisexual** and **transgender**, and the fact that few national surveys ask about sexual orientation, much less gender identity. Grant (2009) draws on established estimates that LGBTQIA individuals make up from 5 to 10 percent of the U.S. population, leading to an approximation of two to seven million LGBTQIA adults 65 and older. Fredriksen-Goldsen et al. (2011), using the more conservative estimate of 2 percent of adults 50 and older identifying as lesbian, gay or bisexual, estimate the number of LGB adults 50 and older to be two million. Until questions about sexual orientation and identity are asked routinely on national surveys and census polling, these numbers will remain estimates. Nonetheless, as our nation ages with rapidly increasing numbers of people 65 and older, and even more rapidly increasing numbers of people 85 and older, the number of older adults is simultaneously growing.

Older adults today have lived through a historical period that distinguishes them from younger generations and this must be considered by social workers and others in the health and service professions. The current cohort of LGBTQIA adults, age 65 and older, lived their younger, formative years before the gay liberation movement of the 1970s. While **homophobia, heterosexism** and **transphobia** still exist today, they were much more pervasive and accepted 45 years ago, when older LGBTQIA persons were coming of age. Some authors have labeled this cohort of LGBTQIA individuals as the 'prelibation' cohort (e.g., Brotman, Ryan, & Cormier, 2003), as they lived their early years prior to the Stonewall rebellion of 1969, often considered the watershed event that initiated gay civil rights (Kochman, 1997; Morrow, 2001). The Stonewall Inn was a gay bar in New York City, frequently raided by police in the 1960s when being gay was considered a crime. During one such raid, on June 27, 1969, the patrons fought back, resulting in three days of rioting, and marking the start of active resistance to anti-gay violence (Morrow, 2001).

Many older lesbian and gay individuals became aware of their orientation when gay sex was considered illegal. For many years, sodomy laws existed throughout the country until some states repealed them in the 1960s and 1970s. But just three decades ago, in 1986, when the current cohort of older LGBTQIA were young adults or in their middle-age, the Supreme Court upheld Georgia's sodomy law in Bowers v. Hardwick (1986), reminding LGBTQIA individuals that society considered them to be criminals, and underscoring the need to conceal much of who they were (ACLU, 2003). It would be 2003 before the United States Supreme Court overturned that decision in Lawrence v. Texas (2003), which finally struck down the sodomy laws that still existed in 14 states at that time.

Not only were LGBTQIA people considered criminals, they were also labeled as deviants by health care experts. The first two editions of the *Diagnostic and Statistic Manual of Mental Disorders* (DSM-I, 1952 and DSM-II, 1968), published by the American Psychiatric Association, classified 'homosexuals' as child molesters, voyeurs, exhibitionists and people who committed antisocial and destructive crimes (Hidalgo, Peterson, & Woodman, 1985); 'homosexuality' was not removed from the list of DSM disorders until 1973. In the years that being gay was considered a disease, social and health care practitioners—including social workers—subjected gay clients to conversion (to heterosexuality) treatments (Kochman, 1997).

Given this historical context, it is not surprising that many older LGBTQIA individuals might continue to conceal their identities and be distrustful of health care providers. Many have spent their lives 'passing' as heterosexuals out of fear for their safety, their jobs and their loving relationships. At the same time, older LGBTQIA people are facing the same challenges that all people confront as they age that are unrelated to LGBTQIA status, such as loss of physical ability, death of friends and partners and facing new roles in retirement. As Van Wagenen, Driskell, and Bradford (2013) note, the LGBTQIA identity may be extremely salient in some contexts, but not all contexts, and it will intersect with other identities that shape individual experiences as LGBTQIA elders age.

Health and Caregiving

In 2011, the Institute of Medicine (IOM) published an ambitious volume assessing the health of LGBTQIA individuals. In the chapter on older adults, the authors note a paucity of research on this population, but offered a few tentative findings. For example, older lesbian and bisexual women may have higher rates of breast cancer than heterosexual women as they are more likely to have some risk factors for the disease, including never having had children, excessive drinking and obesity (Funders for Lesbian and Gay Issues, 2004; IOM, 2011). Moreover, older lesbians, compared to older heterosexual women, may have a higher rate of risk factors for cardiovascular disease, such as smoking, drinking and obesity, though evidence is conflicting (IOM, 2011). The IOM (2011) notes that the rate of HIV infection is higher among men who have sex with men than for other groups, and the proportion of individuals living with HIV who are age 50 and older is twice that of people younger than age 24. Though some older gay men may view HIV infection as a problem of the young, between 11 and 15 percent of HIV cases diagnosed each year are in people over 50 (Funders for Lesbian and Gay Issues, 2004). *The Aging and Health Report: Disparities and Resilience among Lesbian, Gay, Bisexual, and Transgender Older Adults* (Fredriksen-Goldsen et al., 2011) was another significant report on this topic to be published in 2011. Drawing on the first national federally funded study, *Caring and Aging with Pride* (for more information about this project, see http://age-pride.org/wordpress/caring-and-aging-with-pride-about/), to examine LGBTQIA aging and health, Fredriksen-Goldsen and colleagues outlined health disparities in the population, along with risk and protective factors. The authors reported higher levels of smoking and excessive drinking among lesbian, gay and bisexual adults age 50 and older, as compared to their heterosexual counterparts. Also uncovered was a higher level of obesity and cardiovascular disease among older lesbian and bisexual women, as compared to heterosexual women. Older gay and bisexual men in their study were more likely to report poor physical health as compared to older heterosexual men. Furthermore, older gay and bisexual men were found to be more likely to live alone as they age than are heterosexual men, putting them at greater risk of social isolation, which is linked to poor health, premature chronic disease and death (Fredriksen-Goldsen et al., 2011).

The literature on older LGBTQIA adults identifies a number of risk factors to poorer health, including victimization and discrimination (Fredriksen-Goldsen, Emlet, et al., 2013; Fredriksen-Goldsen, Kim, et al., 2013; Fredriksen-Goldsen et al., 2011; IOM, 2011). Such victimization and discrimination may be particularly severe for transgender adults (Cook-Daniels, 2013). Internalized stigma is also related to poor physical and mental health (Fredriksen-Goldsen, Emlet, et al., 2013). On the other hand, LGBTQIA older adults may approach their elder years with unique resiliency and particular strengths. Such strengths include:

- Coping skills developed through accepting sexual orientation and/or gender identity, which may help individuals adjust to aging and **ageism** in a youth-oriented society; the stigma of being old may seem less profound than the stigma of being queer;
- Creation of strong 'families of choice,' sometimes as a consequence of rejection by families of origin; this social network is then available in times of need;
- Greater flexibility in gender roles than is true among heterosexual and **cisgender** individuals, which can be helpful in the aging process (Butler, 2004).

These risk and protective factors also affect the context of **caregiving** for LGBTQIA older adults. Because, in general, LGBTQIA older adults are more likely to live alone and not to have children than their heterosexual counterparts, they are more likely to turn to **'formal' caregivers** (i.e., paid professional support) when they need assistance (Funders for Lesbian and Gay Issues, 2004). But many have partners, friends or children who become **'informal'** or **'family' caregivers** when illness or disability causes older LGBTQIA individuals to need assistance with **activities of daily living (ADL)**, such as bathing, toileting and eating, or **instrumental activities of daily living (IADL)**, such as shopping, cleaning and driving. In general, LGBTQIA older adults are more likely to receive caregiving from friends and partners, while heterosexual older adults are more likely to receive such care from family members (Grant, 2009; Grossman, D'Augelli, & Dragowski, 2007). A 2006 national survey of lesbian and gay baby boomers found that while three in four respondents expected to be caregivers to someone else, one in five wondered who would take care of them should they need assistance (Metlife Mature Market Institute, 2006). A second national survey of LGBTQIA baby boomers four years later found

LGBTQIA older adults more likely to be providing care than their hetero-sexual counterparts (21 percent vs. 17 percent) and that gay men were providing the most hours of weekly care on average (40.7 hours; Metlife Mature Market Institute, 2010). Caregivers of LGB older adults face some of the same issues encountered by 'all caregivers: emotional, physical and financial strains, along with conflicts with employment responsibilities (Hash, 2006). But, they also often deal with additional concerns related to historical and current discrimination, both felt and anticipated (Brotman et al., 2007; Fredriksen-Goldsen, Kim, Muraco, & Mincer, 2009). We know less about the experiences of caregiving for and by transgender elders. Given that transgender individuals face even greater rejection from families and communities than LGB individuals, accessing appropriate caregivers is of particular concern for older transgender adults (IOM, 2011).

Mental Health and Substance Use Issues

Older LGBTQIA persons have inevitably faced many challenges with self-esteem and overall mental health due to many factors. For lesbian and gay populations, one key factor is the history of the Diagnostic Statistical Manual (DSM) used by mental health providers noting mental illness simply for being 'homosexual' until 1973 (American Psychiatric Association, 2013). Also, the history of Stonewall riots, hate crimes and other legal concerns, as well as ongoing political and religious debates, reinforce a stigma and vul-nerability for LGBTQIA people for risk factors specific to mental health and substance use issues (Austin & Irwin, 2010; Cochran & Cauce, 2006; Hatzenbuehler et al., 2014; IOM, 2011; Putney, 2014; Rowan & Butler, 2014; Wilsnack et al., 2008). Additional stressors such as isolation, financial stress and social inequities create difficulties for older LGBTQIA people when dealing with mental health and substance use disorders (Cahill & South, 2002; Erdley, Anklam, & Reardon, 2014). It is a challenge to understand with certainty the risk for mental illness and substance use disorders of LGBTQIA older adults. Dealing with a plethora of issues including stigma, several threats for marginalization (age, gender, gender expression, gender identity and sexual orientation), inadequate screening by health providers and comorbid health issues pose complexity and concerns (He, Sengupta, Velkoff, & DeBarros, 2005; Hooyman & Kiyak, 2008; Rowan, 2012; Rowan & Butler, 2014). Research indicates that in comparison to heterosexual adults, LGB older adults have significantly higher levels of psychological stress (Fredriksen-Goldsen, Emlet, et al., 2013; Hoy-Ellis, Ator, Kerr, & Milford, 2016).

Studies have shown that many LGBTQIA people have co-occurring mental illness along with substance use disorders, tend to be heavy service utilizers (Cochran & Cauce, 2006; Harley & Hancock, 2016) and that there is a need for more research to better understand the unique challenges faced by these populations (Fredriksen-Goldsen et al., 2011). Other studies show hesitancy for LGBTQIA older adults in disclosing their sexual orientation or gender identity due to a lack of LGBTQIA culturally sensitive assessment and treatment options (Butler, 2004; Erdley et al., 2014; Fredriksen-Goldsen et al., 2014; Mercer et al., 2007). Moreover, one study indicated a high risk of suicidal ideation with a variance by population group: 35 percent for lesbians, 37 percent for gay men, 40 percent for bisexual women, 39 percent for bisexual men and 71 percent for transgender older adults (Fredriksen-Goldsen et al., 2011). The risk of suicide for LGBTQIA older adults has been estimated to be two to four times higher than that of heterosexual individuals (Erdley, et al., 2014; Morrow, 2008). In a comparison of important health factors by sexual orientation, lesbian, gay and bisexual older adults demonstrated increased mental health and disability factors when compared with heterosexual older adults (Fredriksen-Goldsen, Emlet, et al., 2013).

In spite of these risk factors and challenges, many LGBTQIA older adults have demonstrated resilience and a commitment to wellness. For example, Witten (2015) noted that out of 276 older transgender lesbians, the majority indicated that they had been aging successfully and were better prepared for events of later life than the general aging transgender identified population and yet still expressed many fears about later life. Putney, Leafmeeker, and Hebert (2016) contributed a model for change to support older lesbian adults in coping with later life. Their model demonstrates how spirituality, social support and resistance to cultural norms assist in dealing with loss, illness and discrimination. Rowan and Butler (2014) reported that their entire sample of older lesbians recovering from alcoholism indicated that they were at least somewhat good at bouncing back from adversity. Fredriksen-Goldsen et al. (2011) reported that 91 percent of their older LGBTQIA adult sample participated in wellness activities while 82 percent remained at least moderately physically active. Ramirez-Valles, Dirkes, and Barrett (2014) discussed the importance of trustworthy and reliable emotional and social support for older gay men, in particular, having assistance with activities of daily life may make a notable difference in mental health. Key factors in mental health and addictions treatment provisions include having educated and skilled health care providers who can ease the discomfort and the access to culturally sensitive care for LGBTQIA older adults (Doherty, Johnston, Meyer, & Giunta, 2016; Ramirez-Valles et al., 2014; Rowan & Faul, 2011; Rowan, 2012; Rowan & Butler, 2014).

Obstacles to Accessing Health Care and Long-Term Services and Supports

In their national study of older LGBTQIA adults, Fredriksen-Goldsen and colleagues (2011) found that 13 percent of their participants had been denied or received inferior health care because of their sexual orientation or gender identity. For some (4 percent), this had happened three or more times, and for transgender older adults, an alarming 40 percent had this experience. Perhaps not surprisingly, given the history of oppression this older cohort has faced, nearly a quarter of LGBTQIA older adults have not revealed their sexual orientation or gender identity to their primary physician, with bisexual men and women being the least likely to disclose (Fredriksen-Goldsen et al., 2011). The 2006 Metlife national survey of lesbian and gay baby boomers found less than half their sample had strong confidence that their health care providers would treat them with dignity and respect (Metlife Mature Market Institute, 2006). Fears about accessing health care and experiences of discrimination have been documented in smaller studies of LGBTQIA older adults as well (e.g., Brotman et al., 2003; Brotman et al., 2007; Stein, Beckerman, & Sherman, 2010). On the other hand, the 2010 Metlife national survey of LGBTQIA baby boomers found that over half their respondents had great confidence in being treated with dignity and respect by health care professionals at the end of life (Metlife Mature Market Institute, 2010). Perhaps these more recent findings of late middle-age LGBTQIA adults indicate a positive shift for the next cohort of older LGBTQIA individuals.

Notwithstanding the optimistic findings from the 2010 Metlife survey, most studies of services within the **aging network** find that the needs of LGBTQIA older adults are not well met. In 2003, the largest organization representing and serving LGBTQIA older adults, SAGE (Services and Advocacy for Gay, Lesbian, Bisexual and Transgender Elders), conducted a national needs assessment regarding the state of health and social services for this population. The assessment found few LGBTQIA-specific services for older adults and a widespread belief among LGBTQIA elders that they would not be welcome or well understood in mainstream senior service programs (Plumb & Associates, 2003). More recent surveys of aging service providers have underscored the general lack of sensitivity and readiness to meet the needs of this population (Hughes, Harold, & Boyer, 2011; Knochel, Quam, & Croghan, 2011). A national study of Area Agencies on Aging found few provided LGBTQIA services or outreach, though most were willing to receive training, particularly those situated in urban areas (Knochel, Croghan, Moone, & Quam, 2012).

One specific aspect of accessing health care that is of particular concern to older LGBTQIA individuals is that of **long-term care (LTC)**, sometimes referred to as **long-term services and supports (LTSS)**. As mentioned earlier, LGBTQIA older adults are more likely to live alone and less likely to have children than their heterosexual counterparts. This means that should they have chronic health conditions that require long-term assistance, something that becomes increasingly likely in the 'oldest, old,' there is a good possibility that they will need to interact with the LTC system. As is common in aging literature, the term 'oldest, old' refers to people in the 85 and older age group (Nolen et al., 2017). A recent survey conducted by a group of both mainstream and LGBTQIA aging organizations and investigating how LGBTQIA older adults fare in long-term facilities uncovered pervasive discrimination and abuse (Cook-Daniels, 2011). Over two-fifths of the 769 survey respondents, including LGBTQIA older adults, their friends and family, advocates, LTC staff, and health care providers, reported mistreatment. This included: harassment from other residents and staff members; refusal of admission, or if admitted, refusal of basic care; restriction of visitors; lack of acceptance of medical power of attorney from resident's spouse; denial of medical treatment; and refusal to refer to transgender residents by their appropriate name and pronoun. Even more pervasive was the fear of mistreatment; nearly nine in ten of the respondents said they feared LTC staff would discriminate against an 'out' LGBTQIA resident (Cook-Daniels, 2011). This fear of needing to 'go back in the closet' when interfacing with the LTC system was also uncovered by Stein and colleagues (2010) in focus groups held with lesbian and gay elders in both a community setting and a long-term residential setting. Participants reported fear of being rejected or neglected by staff and not being accepted by other residents. They also voiced a preference for gay-friendly care (Stein et al., 2010). Adelman (2016) also underscored both the fears and actual experiences of stigma and mistreatment in both home care and residential settings for LGBTQIA elders dealing with Alzheimer's disease and other forms of dementia.

In a recent special issue on LGBTQIA aging in *Generations (Journal of the American Society on Aging)*, several articles highlighted specific aging-in-place and housing options in response to repeated concerns about social isolation and discrimination against LGBTQIA older adults being common in older adult residences (Kilbourn, 2016; Larson, 2016; Thurston, 2016; Woody, 2016). These articles emphasized housing in large metropolitan areas, such as Chicago, New York, San Francisco and Washington, D.C. that are rising in response to the emerging need for more attention to older LGBTQIA culturally sensitive residential and health care needs. It is likely that in the years to come there will be more LGBTQIA specific housing efforts to address these concerns about stigma and discrimination and social isolation amongst these populations.

LGBTQIA-Sensitive Social Work Practice with Older Adults

As noted earlier, few mainstream aging organizations are well prepared to serve the needs of LGBTQIA clients. While there are a few organizations in cities, such as New York and San Francisco, catering particularly to LGBTQIA older adults, in general, resources are not available to sustain LGBTQIA-specific programs within the aging network. Similarly, ageism in LGBTQIA communities and the fact that funding tends to be directed to younger LGBTQIA individuals, result in a paucity of services specifically for LGBTQIA elders (Hoy-Ellis et al., 2016). Currently, most social and health service organizations report that 'they treat everyone the same;' but, as Moone, Croghan and Olson (2016) so aptly point out, "ignoring differences is not necessarily respecting differences" (p. 74). Individual practitioners and organizations serving older adults must be proactive in order to serve this population better; a heterogeneous population by class, race and other social conditions. Adams (2016) correctly pointed out that practitioners interested in addressing the needs of the most vulnerable population elders should take an intersectional approach to their work by moving beyond a uni-dimensional lens and weaving in race, gender, ability/disability, socioeconomic status, religion and other social positions that impact people's lives.

Drawing on a literature spanning 30 years, Zodikoff and Butler (2015, pp. 560–561) outlined strategies for individual practitioners to increase their sensitivity and competency in working with older LGBTQIA adults. These include:

- Engaging in self-reflection regarding one's own heterosexism, homophobia, transphobia and ageism;
- Recognizing that not all presenting issues are related to being old or being LGBTQIA;
- Honoring relationships and treating identified family as family;
- Finding respectful service providers for referrals;
- Assisting one's clients to broaden their social networks, including making connections to the LGBTQIA community;
- Respecting one's right to privacy and confidentiality and accepting his or her level of disclosure;
- Working to develop more LGBTQIA-friendly resources; and
- Advocating for change in discriminatory policies at all levels: organizational, local, state and federal.

Witten (2016) adds to that list the need to help clients access needed legal assistance, something that may be particularly important for transgender older adults.

Health and social service providers can also take a number of steps to create welcoming and culturally sensitive environments. Moone and colleagues (2016, p. 76) provide a list of ten steps, including actions such as:

- Including LGBTQIA topics or clients in newsletters and marketing materials;
- Updating assessment forms to include LGBTQIA welcoming language;
- Posting non-discrimination policies and using LGBTQIA-recognized visual cues (e.g., the rainbow flag);
- Providing training on LGBTQIA aging to staff and volunteers; and
- Participating in LGBTQIA community events through both sponsorship and attendance.

We are in a time of great transformation for LGBTQIA individuals of all ages: sodomy laws are no longer legal and same-sex marriage is. These are dramatic changes for the current cohort of LGBTQIA elders, of whom many lived through an era in which they were considered both sick and criminal. There is still much work to do. While some states have inclusive civil rights laws, it is still legal to discriminate against LGBTQIA individuals in housing, employment and public accommodations in more than half the states (Fredriksen-Goldsen, 2016). Social workers and other advocates need to continue to fight for federal laws prohibiting such discrimination (Espinoza, 2016).

While our work is not complete in terms of fighting for civil rights, we must remember that we have made much progress. For example, in 2011, the National Resource Center for LGBT Aging was established through a federal grant from the Department of Health and Human Services; this was a historic and significant development. Since that time, it has trained thousands of aging and LGBTQIA service providers and offers resources to all practitioners interested in better serving LGBTQIA older adults (Doherty et al., 2016). Social workers now have the tools they need to become sensitive and inclusive practitioners and strong advocates for LGBTQIA older adults. It is imperative that we do.

Questions for Discussion

1   Discuss the historical period that LGBTQIA older adults have lived through and how this history plays a role in marginalization and oppression.
2   In what year did the Diagnostic Statistical Manual change to take out homosexuality as an illness? Why is this important for cultural sensitivity and competence among social workers?
3   Name some risk and protective health factors specific to older LGBTQIA adults. Why are these factors important in providing culturally sensitive social work practice with LGBTQIA older adults?
4   Name some key factors in mental health and addictions treatment provisions to improve culturally sensitive care for older LGBTQIA adults.
5   Explain the fear of needing to 'go back in the closet' for LGBTQIA older adults. Discuss specific housing options for LGBTQIA older adults and why these are important resources for social workers.
6   Discuss specific strategies that social work practitioners can take to increase sensitivity and competence in working with LGBTQIA older adults.

Resources

Organizations with a Particular Focus on LGBTQIA Aging

Aging with Pride (Research center) www.Age-Pride.org
American Society on Aging, LGBT Aging Issues Network www.aga ging.org/LAIN/
FORGE (Transgender network) www.forge-forward.org
Frank Harr Foundation (LGBTQ education and advocacy in Wilmington, North Carolina) www.frankharrfoundation.com

Girot Circle (LGBT elders of color) www.girotcircle.org
Lavender Seniors of the East Bay www.lavenderseniors.org
LGBT Aging Project www.lgbtagingproject.org
National Resource Center on LGBT Aging www.lgbtagingcenter.org
Old Lesbians Organizing for Change (OLOC) www.oloc.org
Primetimers Worldwide (for gay men) www.primetimersww.org
Services and Advocacy for GLBT Elders (SAGE) www.sageusa.org—
See this website for a list of SAGE affiliates around the country.

References

Adams, M. (2016). An intersectional approach to services and care for LGBT elders. *Generations*, 40 (2), 94–100.

Adelman, M. (2016). Overcoming barriers to care for LGBT elders with Alzheimer's. *Generations*, 40 (2), 38–40.

American Civil Liberties Union (ACLU). (2003, June 16). *History of sodomy laws and the strategy that led to today's decision.* Retrieved from www.aclu.org

American Psychiatric Association. (2013). *Diagnostic and statistical manual of mental disorders* (5th ed.). Washington, DC: Author.

Austin, E. L., & Irwin, J. A. (2010). Age differences in the correlates of problematic alcohol use among southern lesbians. *Journal of Studies on Alcohol & Drugs*, 71, 295–298.

Bowers v. Hardwick, 478 U.S. 186 (1986).

Brotman, S., Ryan, B., Collins, S., Chamberland, L., Cormier, R., Julien, D., Meyer, E., Peterkin, A., & Richard, B. (2007). Coming out to care: Caregivers of gay and lesbian seniors in Canada. *Gerontologist*, 47, 490–503. doi:10.1093/geront/47.4.490

Brotman, S., Ryan, B., & Cormier, R. (2003). The health and social service needs of gay and lesbian elders and their families in Canada. *Gerontologist*, 43, 192–202. doi:10.1093/geront/43.2.192

Butler, S. S. (2004). Gay, lesbian, bisexual and transgender (GLBT) elders: The challenges and resilience of this marginalized group. *Journal of Human Behavior in the Social Environment*, 9 (4), 25–44.

Cahill, S. R., & South, K. (2002). Policy issues affecting lesbian, gay, bisexual, and transgender people in retirement. *Generations*, 26, 49–54.

Cochran, B. N., & Cauce, A. M. (2006). Characteristics of lesbian, gay, bisexual, and Transgender individuals entering substance abuse treatment. *Journal of Substance Abuse Treatment*, 30, 135–146.

Cook-Daniels, L. (2013). Identifying and assisting abuse among LGBT elder clients. *Victimization of the Elderly and Disabled*, 15 (6), 81–96.

Cook-Daniels, L. (2011). Institutional abuse and LGBT long-term care facility residents. *Victimization of the Elderly and Disabled*, 14 (3), 37–38, 47.

de Vries, B., & Croghan, C. F. (2014). LGBT aging: The contributions of community-based research. *Journal of Homosexuality*, 61 (1), 1–20. doi: doi:10.1080/00918369.2013.834794

Doherty, M., Johnston, T. R., Meyer, H., & Giunta, N. (2016). SAGE's National Resource Center on LGBT Aging is training a culturally competent aging network. *Generations*, 40 (2), 78–79.

Erdley, S. D., Anklam, D. D., & Reardon, C. C. (2014). Breaking barriers and building bridges: Understanding the pervasive needs of older LGBT adults and the value of social work in health care. *Journal of Gerontological Social Work*, 57 (2–4), 362–385. doi:doi:10.1080/01634372.2013.871381

Espinoza, R. (2016). Protecting and ensuring the well-being of LGBT older adults: A policy roadmap. *Generations*, 40 (2), 87–93.

Fredriksen-Goldsen, K. I. (2016). The future of LGBT+ aging: A blueprint for action in services, policies, and research. *Generations*, 40 (2), 6–15.

Fredriksen-Goldsen, K. I., Emlet, C. A., Kim, H-J., Muraco, A., Erosheva, E., Goldsen, J., & Hoy-Ellis, C. (2013). The physical and mental health of lesbian, gay male, and bisexual (LGB) older adults: The role of key health indicators and risk and protective factors. *Gerontologist*, 53, 664–675. doi:doi:10.1093/geront/gns123

Fredriksen-Goldsen, K. I., Hoy-Ellis, C. P., Goldsen, J., Emlet, C. A., & Hooyman, N. R. (2014). Creating a vision for the future; Key competencies and strategies for culturally competent practice with lesbian, gay, bisexual and transgender (LGBT) older adults in the health and human services. *Journal of Gerontological Social Work*, 57 (2–4), 80–107.

Fredriksen-Goldsen, K. I., Kim, H. J., Barkan, S. E., Muraco, A., & Hoy-Ellis, C. P. (2013). Health disparities among lesbian, gay male and bisexual older adults: Results from a population-based study. *American Journal of Public Health*, 103, 1802–1809.

Fredriksen-Goldsen, K. I., Kim, H., Emlet, C., Muraco, A., Erosheva, E. A., Hoy-Ellis, C., Goldsen, J., & Petry, H. (2011). *The aging and health report: Disparities and resilience among lesbian, gay, bisexual, and transgender older adults*. Seattle, WA: Institute of Multigenerational Health.

Fredriksen-Goldsen, K. I., Kim, H-J., Muraco, A., & Mincer, S. (2009). Chronically ill midlife and older lesbians, gay men, and bisexuals and their informal caregivers: The impact of the social context. *Sexuality Research & Social Policy*, 6, 52–64. doi:10.1525/srsp.2009.6.4.52

Funders for Lesbian and Gay Issues. (2004). *Aging in equity: LGBT elders in America*. New York: Author.

Grant, J. M. (2009). *Outing Age 2010: Public policy issues affecting gay, lesbian, bisexual and transgender elders*. Washington, DC: Policy Institute, National Gay and Lesbian Task Force.

Grossman, A. H., D'Augelli, A. R., & Dragowski, E.A. (2007). Caregiving and care receiving among older lesbian, gay, and bisexual adults. *Journal of Gay & Lesbian Social Services*, 18, 15–38. doi:doi:10.1300/J041v18n03_02

Harley, D. A., & Hancock, M. T. (2016). Substance use disorders intervention with LGBT elders. In D. A. Harley & P. B. Teaster (Eds.), *Handbook of LGBT elders: An interdisciplinary approach to principles, practices, and policies*. (pp. 473–490). Switzerland: Springer International Publishing.

Hash, K. (2006). Caregiving and post-caregiving experiences of midlife and older gay men and lesbians. *Journal of Gerontological Social Work*, 47, 121–138. doi: doi:10.1300/J083v47n03_08

Hatzenbuehler, M. L., Bellatorre, A., Lee, Y., Finch, B. K., Muennig, P., & Fiscella, K. (2014). Structural stigma and all-cause mortality in sexual minority populations. *Social Science & Medicine*, 103, 33–41. doi: doi:10.1016/j.socscimed.2013.06.005

He, W., Sengupta, M., Velkoff, V. A., & DeBarros, K. A. (2005). *States* (pp. 23–209). Washington, DC: US Government Printing Office.

Hidalgo, H., Peterson, T. L., & Woodman, N. J. (1985). Introduction. In H. Hidalgo, T. L. Peterson, & N. J. Woodman (Eds.), *Lesbian, and gay issues: A resource manual for social workers* (pp. 1–6). Silver Spring, MD: NASW, Inc.

Hooyman, N. R., & Kiyak, H. A. (2008). *Social gerontology: A multidisciplinary perspective*. Boston, MA: Pearson.

Hoy-Ellis, C. P., Ator, M., Kerr, C., & Milford, J. (2016). Innovative approaches address aging and mental health needs in LGBTQ communities. *Generations*, 40 (2), 56–62.

Hughes, A. K., Harold, R. D., & Boyer, J. M. (2011). Awareness of LGBT aging issues among aging services network providers. *Journal of Gerontological Social Work*, 54, 659–677. doi:doi:10.1080/01634372.2011.585392

Institute of Medicine (IOM). (2011). *The health of lesbian, gay, bisexual, and transgender people: Building a foundation for better understanding*. Washington, DC: The National Academies Press.

Kilbourn, S. (2016). Perseverance, patience, and partnerships build elder LGBT housing in San Francisco. *Generations*, 40 (2), 103–105.

Knochel, K. A., Croghan, C. F., Moone, R. P., & Quam, J. K. (2012). Training, geography, and provision of aging services to lesbian, gay, bisexual, and transgender older adults. *Journal of Gerontological Social Work*, 55, 426–443. doi:doi:10.1080/01634372.2012.665158

Knochel, K. A., Quam, J. K., & Croghan, C. F. (2011). Are old lesbian and gay people well served? Understanding the perceptions, preparation, and experiences of aging services providers. *Journal of Applied Gerontology*, 30, 370–389. doi:doi:10.1177/0733464810369809

Kochman, A. (1997). Gay and lesbian elderly: Historical overview and implications for social work practice. In J. K. Quam (Ed.) *Social services for senior gay and lesbians* (pp. 1–10). New York: Harrington Park Press.

Larson, B. (2016). Intentionally designed for success: Chicago's first LGBT-friendly senior housing. *Generations*, 40 (2), 106–107.

Lawrence v. Texas, 539 U.S. 558 (2003).

Mercer, C. H., Bailey, J. V., Johnson, A. M., Erens, B., Wellings, K., Fenton, K. A., & Copas, A. (2007). Women who report having sex with women: British national probability data on prevalence, sexual behaviors, and health outcomes. *American Journal of Public Health*, 97, 1126–1133.

Metlife Mature Market Institute. (2010). *Still out, still aging: The Metlife study of lesbian, gay, bisexual and transgender baby boomers*. New York: Author.

Metlife Mature Market Institute. (2006). *Out and aging: The Metlife study of lesbian and gay baby boomers*. New York: Author.

Meyer, H., & Johnston, T. R. (2014). The National Resource Center on LGBT Aging provides critical training to aging service providers. *Journal of Gerontological Social Work*, 57 (2–4), 407–412.

Moone, R. P., Croghan, C. F., & Olson, A. M. (2016). Why and how providers must build culturally competent, welcoming practices to serve LGBT elders. *Generations*, 40 (2), 73–77.

Morrow, D. F. (2001). Older gays and lesbians: Surviving a generation of hate and violence. *Journal of Gay & Lesbian Social Services*, 13, 151–169.

Morrow, D. (2008). Older gays and lesbians. *Journal of Gay and Lesbian Social Services*, 13 (1–2), 151–169.

Nolen, S. C., Evans, M. A., Fischer, A., Corrada, M. M., Kawas, C. H., & Bota, D. A. (2017). Cancer-Incidence, prevalence, and mortality in the oldest-old. A comprehensive review. *Mechanisms of Ageing and Development*, 164, 113–126.

Plumb, M. & Associates. (2003). *National needs assessment and technical assistance audit.* New York: Senior Action in a Gay Environment.

Putney, J. (2014). Older lesbian adults psychological well-being: The significance of pets. *Journal of Gay and Lesbian Social Services*, 1–17.

Putney, J., Leafmeeker, R. R., & Hebert, N. (2016). "The wisdom of age": Perspectives on aging and growth among lesbian older adults. *Journal of Gerontological Social Work*, 1–18.

Ramirez-Valles, J., Dirkes, J., & Barrett, H. A. (2014). GayBy boomers' social support: Exploring the connection between health and emotional and instrumental support in older gay men. *Journal of Gerontological Social Work*, 57 (2–4), 218–234.

Rowan, N. L. (2012). Older lesbian adults with alcoholism: A case study for practitioners. *Journal of Geriatric Care Management*, 22 (1), 19–24.

Rowan, N. L., & Butler, S. S. (2014). Resilience in attaining and sustaining sobriety among older lesbians with alcoholism. *Journal of Gerontological Social Work*, 57 (2–4), 176–197.

Rowan, N. L., & Faul, A. C. (2011). Gay, lesbian, bisexual, and transgender people and chemical dependency: Exploring successful treatment. *Journal of Gay and Lesbian Social Services*, 23(1), 107–130.

Rowan, N. L. & Giunta, N. (2014). Introduction: Building capacity in gerontological social work for lesbian, gay, bisexual, and transgender older adults and their loved ones. *Journal of Gerontological Social Work*, 57 (2–4), 75–79.

Stein, G. L., Beckerman, N. L., & Sherman, P. A. (2010). Lesbian and gay elders and long-term care: Identifying the unique psychosocial perspectives and challenges. *Journal of Gerontological Social Work*, 53, 421–435. doi:doi:10.1080/01634372.2010.496478.

Thurston, C. (2016). The intersectional approach in action: SAGE Center Bronx. *Generations*, 40 (2), 101–102.

Van Wagenen, A. V., Driskell, J., & Bradford, J. (2013). "I'm still raring to go": Successful aging among lesbian, gay, bisexual and transgender older adults. *Journal of Aging Studies*, 27, 1–14.

Wilsnack, S. C., Hughes, T. L., Johnson, T., Bostwick, W. B., Szalacha, L. A., Benson, P., & Kinnison, K. E. (2008). Drinking and drinking-related problems among heterosexual and sexual minority women. *Journal of Studies on Alcohol & Drugs*, 69, 129–139.

Witten, T. (2015). Elder transgender lesbians: Exploring the intersection of age, lesbian sexual identity, and transgender identity. *Journal of Lesbian Studies*, 19 (1), 73–89.

Witten, T. M. (2016). The intersectional challenges of aging and being a gender non-conforming adults . *Generations*, 40 (2), 63–70.

Woody, I. (2016). Mary's House: An LGBTQ/SGL-friendly, alternative environment for older adults. *Generations*, 40 (2), 108–109.

Zodikoff, B., & Butler, S. S. (2015). Lesbian, gay, bisexual, and transgender (LGBT) older adults. In D. Kaplan & B. Berkman (Eds.) *Handbook of social work in health and aging* (2nd ed., pp. 555–564), New York: Oxford University Press.

15 Global Issues

Christina M. Chiarelli-Helminiak

PH.D., MSW

Michele Eggers Barison

PH.D., MSW[1]

2015 CSWE Educational Policy

Competency 2: Engage diversity and difference in practice
Competency 3: Advance human rights and social, economic, and environmental justice
Competency 5: Engage in policy practice

Global Issues

The profession of social work has a history steeped with advocating for the rights of vulnerable and oppressed populations. As a whole, advocacy on behalf of lesbian, gay, bisexual, trans, and intersex (LGBTI) populations deserves more attention, as explicit and underlying discrimination and violence against LGBTI individuals is far too common domestically and abroad. Cultural norms and laws worldwide openly allow the **human rights** of LGBTI individuals to be violated on a daily basis. As a social worker, one must practice in a way that promotes the realization of human rights for all individuals including those in the global LGBTI community.

This chapter provides an overview of LGBTI issues at the international level from a human rights-based frame. The chapter begins with an overview of international discrimination, including some of the countries with laws against homosexuality and the consequences. The chapter summarizes the history of LGBTI rights within the United Nations system and how **international laws** have been applied to the rights of LGBTI individuals. The chapter then moves into issues affecting LGBTI immigrants and refugees. Finally, the chapter provides information for social workers who work with international LGBTI clients or who plan to work on LGBTI rights abroad.

Global Violence and Discrimination

Across the globe there is a wide spectrum of anti-gay laws. Approximately 76 out of 193 member states of the **United Nations** have laws in place that criminalize LGBTI individuals on the basis of sexual orientation or gender identity (**United Nations Human Rights Council**, 2015). These range from propaganda or morality laws, limiting LGBTI expression, to **buggery** or **sodomy laws**. The scope of penalties for committing an act deemed illegal consists of receiving a fine or limited jail time to life in prison or the death penalty (International Lesbian, Gay, Bisexual, Trans and Intersex Association (ILGA) 2016). For example, in Malawi in 2010 a trans woman and straight man were sentenced up to 14 years in prison after being found guilty of sodomy (Cheney, 2012). In 2012, four men in Iran were sentenced to death for sodomy (Han & O'Mahoney, 2014, p. 269). Further, not all laws punish male and female identified individuals equally. According to ILGA (2016), 73 countries criminalize relationships between males as opposed to 45 countries that criminalize relationships between females. Thus, laws are an inherent part of a culture in which they are constructed, interpreted, and enforced differently worldwide.

In every region of the world, LGBTI individuals are persecuted for their sexual orientation or gender identity and expression (Han & O'Mahoney, 2014). Anti-gay laws often promote a permissive environment of violence. For example, Ireland (2013) stated, "Sodomy laws legitimize antigay actions and sentiments in institutions and society and constrict the political space available for those who struggle to reduce them" (p. 52). Further, since the passing of anti-gay propaganda legislation in Russia in 2013, there has been an increase in violence by vigilante groups toward LGBTI individuals (Nichols, 2014). Thus, when anti-gay laws construct LGBTI individuals as criminals, a cultural environment of permissive harm is fostered, rendering subjugation and maltreatment invisible as an accepted cultural norm (Mullen, 2015).

According to the United Nations High Commissioner for Human Rights (2011), LGBTI communities are targets for brutal violence, often with no state protection. For example, in Jamaica police allegedly participated and encouraged the stabbing and stoning of a gay man that resulted in his death. In Indonesia, a gay couple was allegedly beaten and sexually assaulted by police officers the day after they reported to have been assaulted by multiple community members. In El Salvador, a transgender woman was held in a male prison where she was gang-raped multiple times with the involvement of prison officials. In Bangladesh, a woman was arrested for being a lesbian and while in custody was beaten and raped by police (United Nations Human Rights Council, 2015). In immigration detention centers in the United States, gay and transgender individuals are reportedly placed in solitary confinement, in addition to being tortured and sexually assaulted. In Ecuador, 200 to 300 clinics focused on sexual orientation change efforts (SOCE) exist with the purpose of curing young lesbians of their sexual orientation (Astraea Lesbian Foundation for Justice, 2015). Reports indicated that women have suffered mental/emotional, physical, and sexual abuse, including rape, within these clinics. Regardless of the Ecuadorian government assurance to abolish anti-gay laws, they continue to exist.

Laws that criminalize sexual orientation or gender expression and identity as outside of specific cultural norms, whether intentionally or unintentionally, repress LGBTI populations. Criminalization produces and sustains stigma, limits access to essential resources and services, denies state protection from abuse and often sanctions state violence. Consequently, criminalization dehumanizes and relegates LGBTI individuals and communities to a category of *other*, which sustains a permissive environment of discrimination and violence.

Layers of established social norms, such as attitudes and behaviors, manifest as lack of political will at various levels of government; subsequently, these restrict the social, economic, and political agency of LGBTI individuals and communities. Thus, anti-gay laws and subsequent harmful cultural attitudes, beliefs, and practices toward LGBTI communities are a violation of international human rights laws (United Nations Human Rights Council, 2015).

History of LGBTI Rights within the United Nations

The **Universal Declaration of Human Rights** (UDHR) is based on the notion that all individuals have inherent rights. According to Article 1 of the UDHR, "All human beings are born free and equal in dignity and rights" (United Nations, 1948). The foundation of these rights is based on each individual's right to equality and non-discrimination. This ideal that everyone has equal rights has been supported by 193 countries across the globe, yet the realization of rights for LGBTI persons has still not been achieved 70 years after the UDHR was adopted.

LGBTI rights are cause for much debate due to the range of cultural acceptance within societies. While the development of the United Nations and UDHR were reactions to the atrocities of World War II, including the detainment and execution of men convicted of homosexuality and other forms of sexual deviance in Nazi Germany, the inclusion of rights based on sexual orientation were notably excluded from the UDHR (Encarnación, 2014; Plant, 1986; United Nations, 2016). Customary cultural norms and traditions are often touted as reasons for the lack of recognition of LGBTI rights at the United Nations.

Although the United Nations historically remained silent on rights specific to LGBTI individuals, the **Yogyakarta Principles** (Yogyakarta, 2007) (see Box 15.1) were developed in response to the widespread discrimination and violence faced by LGBTI populations. These principles, such as the right to non-discrimination and the right to human and personal security, apply international human rights law concerning sexual orientation and gender identity. Since being developed, some nation-states have affirmed their commitment to applying the Yogyakarta Principles in future policies, even though the principles are not legally binding (United Nations High Commissioner for Human Rights, 2011). For example, Ettelbrick and

Zerán (2010) found Bolivia's Constitution to include the prohibition of discrimination based on sexual orientation or gender identity. Ettelbrick and Zerán also highlighted how across the globe countries have been slow to incorporate the Yogykarta Principles in national policies.

Box 15.1 Yogyakarta Principles

The Yogyakarta Principles include 29 principles specific to the human rights of LGBTI individuals. In 2006, a group of academics, judges, human rights defenders, and former and current members of human rights treaty bodies developed the document in Yogyakarta, Indonesia. The Principles and related recommendations are still the most comprehensive document detailing the rights of LGBTI individuals in line with international law. The Yogyakarta Principles provide guidance on the states' obligations to promote and protect human rights in relation to sexual orientation and gender identity.

Two important landmark actions instigated subsequent positive movement toward the recognition of LGBTI rights. In 2010, the United Nations finally acknowledged and actively advocated for LGBTI rights after Secretary General Ban Ki-moon called on all member states to end the criminalization of homosexuality. The Secretary General recognized the severe impact of anti-gay laws on LGBTI individuals in more than 70 countries. He declared that the realization of universal human rights are designed to be inclusive of everyone, thus should overcome cultural norms, societal traditions, and personal biases that interfere with the attainment of rights specific to LGBTI persons (United Nations, 2010). The next year, in 2011, the UN Human Rights Council adopted the first resolution on human rights, sexual orientation, and gender identity (United Nations Human Rights Council, 2011). This resolution reinforced the rights of LGBTI individuals inherently guaranteed by the UDHR and other key human rights documents. Further, the resolution called for research on the impact of discriminatory laws and practices and requested recommendations on how international law could be used effectively to end violence against LGBTI individuals and communities. Secretary General Ban Ki-moon's call for action and the Human Rights Council's resolution resulted in the first United Nations Human Rights Council report in 2011 on LGBTI rights.

The historic 2011 United Nations report provided the context through which international law is structured to protect the human rights of LGBTI persons. Despite the existence of such protection of rights, the report documented incidents of violence, including rape, torture, and murder; discriminatory laws, which resulted in incidents of arbitrary arrests and detention and the death penalty; and discriminatory practices related to employment, health care, education, benefits, gender recognition, and restriction of freedom of expression, association, and assembly. The report also provided examples of how nation states are moving toward meeting their obligations to uphold the rights of LGBTI individuals, including training programs for law enforcement, public education campaigns in schools and communities, and policy changes at the state level. While not exhaustive, the report provided eight recommendations, including prompt investigation of all murders and incidents of violence related or perceived to be related to sexual orientation or gender identity; prevention of violence targeting LGBTI persons; protection for LGBTI persons seeking asylum; repeal of laws targeting homosexuality; policies focused on anti-discrimination; protection of freedom to expression, association, and assembly; law enforcement training and school-based education; and legal protection and recognition of transgendered persons (United Nations High Commissioner for Human Rights, 2011). Subsequent to the release of the report, the Human Rights Council held its first panel discussion and debate on LGBTI issues (United Nations High Commissioner for Human Rights, 2012).

Analyses of documented LGBTI human rights violations across the globe led to the development of recommendations for nation states, advocates, and individuals on how to utilize international law as a means of upholding human rights. Thus, in 2012, the United Nations High Commissioner for Human Rights produced and disseminated a booklet, *Born Free and Equal.* This booklet highlighted core obligations related to the rights of LGBTI persons. The five core legal obligations include: (1) "protect individuals from homophobic and transphobic violence"; (2) "prevent torture and cruel, inhumane, and degrading treatment of LGBTI persons"; (3) "decriminalize homosexuality"; (4) "prohibit discrimination based on sexual orientation and gender identity"; and (5) "respect freedom of expression, association, and peaceful assembly" (United Nations High Commissioner for Human Rights, 2012, p. 5).

In 2013, the United Nations launched a global public education campaign, *UN Free & Equal,* "to raise awareness of sexual, gender and bodily diversity, and promote equal rights and fair treatment of lesbian, gay, bi, trans and intersex people everywhere" (United Nations High Commissioner for Human Rights, 2015, p. 2). The campaign included an active online presence and featured citizens and celebrities from around the globe working to secure equal rights for LGBTI individuals. Viewers can access an impressive number of relevant videos and other materials on the website, translated into many of the diverse languages of **United Nations member states** (see Resources section at the end of this chapter for web addresses).

In 2015, the United Nations Human Rights Council produced a second report on LGBTI rights. This report highlighted steps taken across the globe to eliminate discrimination and violence directed toward LGBTI individuals, including implementation of laws and legal protections, such as marriage or civil unions and legal gender recognition of transgendered individuals, and the elimination of laws that criminalized homosexuality.

While the report acknowledged progress made in all regions of the world since 2011, it also recognized ongoing violence and discrimination based on sexual orientation and gender identity. The report included nine recommendations to address violence, ranging from the implementation of hate crime laws to the elimination of SOCE, such as **conversion therapy**, and other involuntary medical and mental health interventions. Recommendations related to the inclusion of sexual orientation and gender identity in anti-discrimination laws, and youth-targeted education to include anti-bullying and sexuality education (United Nations, 2016).

Most recently, in 2016 the United Nations Human Rights Council established an **Independent Expert**, known as a **Special Rapporteur**, to generate reports and provide advice to the Human Rights Council pertaining to LGBTI issues globally (United Nations High Commissioner for Human Rights, 2016b). According to the United Nations High Commissioner for Human Rights (2016a), the directive of the Independent Expert is:

> ... to assess the implementation of existing international human rights instruments with regard to ways to overcome violence and discrimination against persons on the basis of their sexual orientation or gender identity, and to identify and address the root causes of violence and discrimination.
>
> (para. 16)

The focus on the inclusion of LGBTI rights within the United Nations human rights frame has been instrumental in the movement toward achieving LGBTI rights globally (Encarnación, 2014); however, little evidence has been reported on how protective policies have changed harmful societal and cultural attitudes, beliefs, and practices. Despite the efforts of the United Nations and specific member states, equality has not been achieved as evidenced by continuing discriminatory practices and acts of violence perpetrated against LGBTI individuals across the globe.

Although the United Nations lacks authority to mandate countries to enact legal protection, international laws highlight the importance to protect LGBTI persons from violence and discrimination. These laws frequently influence policy changes at national levels. However, despite well-intentioned international law regarding the prohibition of human rights violations based on sexual orientation or gender identity, limited processes are in place to denounce abuse that still occurs. A critical concern is that nation-states both guarantee and violate human rights simultaneously (Dominelli, 2007). Dominelli highlights a key limitation of the United Nations Declaration of Human Rights. She states,

> ... the social, political, economic, and civil rights it encompasses are located in the framework of a nation-state responsible for enforcing provisions and punishing violations. Without independent compliance

mechanisms, a country's failure to adhere to the UDHR requirements is a serious drawback to realizing its ideals.

(p. 22)

Right to Asylum

The violence against LGBTI persons coupled with the lack of state protection and infrastructure to report human rights violations forces those targeted to leave their communities and flee abroad (Ireland, 2013; Schutzer, 2012). Article 14 of the UDHR and subsequent 1951 Convention Relating to the Status of Refugees recognized the right to asylum from persecution in other countries (United Nations High Commissioner for Refugees, n.d.). Anker and Ardalan (2012) state that refugee claims of actual or fear of persecution must be based on one of the five legal grounds, "race, religion, nationality, membership to a particular social group, or political opinion" (p. 542). Although sexual orientation is not specifically stated, it is generally understood that sexual orientation meets the requirement under membership to a particular social group.

The Convention related to the Status of Refugees provides a mechanism to protect LGBTI individuals from persecution when states fail to offer protection; however, the convention differs from other human rights treaties in that there is no human rights committee to monitor state implementation (Anker & Ardalan, 2012; Schutzer, 2012). Thus, every United Nations member state determines its own process for deciding who qualifies for refugee status and what the definition of persecution is. This can be problematic as it invites global discrepancies toward the realization of the right to asylum depending on individual state interpretation of the convention. Further, processes for determining refugee status and asylum are often in contradiction to each other.

Anker and Ardalan (2012) discuss the use of a **social visibility test** in some nation-states whereby the person who is seeking asylum has to prove their sexual orientation or gender identity in order to make the case that they are at risk of or currently experiencing persecution. For example, in the 2009 U.S. case of Razkane v. Holder (2009), Razkane was not seen as possessing effeminate mannerisms and therefore not identified as a homosexual. Thus, court decisions based on social visibility are subjective and depend on stereotypes, which lead to incorrect conclusions further harming those who are seeking protection (McKinnon, 2016).

Contrary to decisions for asylum based on social visibility is the reasoning of discretion. For example, in the United Kingdom,

> [D]iscretion reasoning entail[s] a reasonable expectation that persons should, to the extent that is possible, co-operate in their own protection, by exercising self-restraint such as avoiding any behavior that would identify them as gay; never telling anyone they were gay; only expressing their sexuality by having anonymous sex in public places;

pretending that their partner is a 'flatmate'; or indeed remaining celibate.

(Millbank, 2009, p. 393).

According to Schutzer (2012), courts in the United Kingdom and Australia have a history of denying protection for asylum due to the rationale that an applicant is able to hide their sexual orientation or gender identity as a means to avoid persecution. This assumes that hiding one's identity is by choice and not forced because of extreme repression faced by the LGBTI community. The focus of interpretation then is shifted to the behavior of the individual seeking asylum, rather than the harms committed against the asylum seeker (Heller, 2009). The fact that LGBTI individuals have to hide who they are should be proof enough that their countries of origin are not safe and they are at risk of persecution. Schutzer (2012) adds, "when the conditions in a country as insti-gated or condoned by the State compel LGB[TI] individuals to conceal their sexual identity, those individuals are being persecuted" (p. 678).

Multiple issues present themselves when states are free to determine refugee status and asylum outside of international standards or monitoring. Asylum decisions are embedded within an already repressive state environ-ment toward LGBTI individuals and communities, resulting in the mis-application or misunderstanding of the law and subsequent denial of protection for LGBTI refugees seeking asylum (Schutzer, 2012). Thus, the actual process of seeking asylum can be oppressive toward a group already experiencing marginalization (Heller, 2009). Social work, therefore, is well positioned to support LGBTI individuals and communities abroad and refugees seeking asylum locally based on our professional commitment to advocate for marginalized populations.

International Social Work

Social work is a profession that knows no geographic boundaries and more social workers are choosing international social work as a career path. Healy (2012) conceptualized the purposes of international social work as "promot[ing] global social justice and human well-being and ensur[ing] the ongoing relevance of locally based practice by calling attention to global realities that affect local conditions" (p. 12). International social work occurs both domestically, when working with individuals and communities who have migrated to the United States and abroad when social workers from the United States practice social work internationally.

Values and Ethics

Social workers base their work on the ethical obligation to promote social justice for vulnerable and oppressed populations (National Association of Social Workers (NASW) 2008). While the NASW (2008) does not specifically address human rights in its *Code of Ethics*, it does provide some guidance in its *International Policy of Human Rights* affirming that our focus on social justice necessitates approaching our work from a human rights frame. The international policy specifically states that social workers must advocate for the realization of human rights for vulnerable populations and denounce rights violations, including those based on sexual orientation (Wheeler & McClain, 2015).

The **International Federation of Social Workers** (IFSW, 2016), of which the NASW is a member, provides a global presence and perspective for the profession. The IFSW works closely with the United Nations to promote social work values and holds Special Consultative Status with the United Nations Economic and Social Council (ECOSOC) and the United Nations Children's Fund (UNICEF). The IFSW (2012) specifically incorporates tenets of human rights and social justice throughout its Statement of Ethical Principles (see Box 15.2). The IFSW (2014) explicitly states, "people whose sexual identity, sexual orientation or gender expression differs from the norm are vulnerable to oppression and marginalization" (p. 1). In its policy on *Sexual Orientation and Gender Expression*, the IFSW specifies that social workers have an ethical obligation to promote the rights of LGBTI persons based on their limited access to the full enjoyment of equality. The IFSW specifies issues affecting LGBTI individuals to include: criminalization, pathology, sin, cultural, and **intersectionality** and calls on social workers to work on LGBTI advocacy related to: the right to life, liberty, and security; interpersonal violence; economic inequality; health disparities; HIV/AIDS; and youth and education.

Box 15.2 International Federation of Social Workers' Statement of Ethical Principles

Similar to the NASW (2008) *Code of Ethics*, the IFSW (2012) provides guidance to social workers through its *Statement of Ethical Principles*.
  The principle on human rights and human dignity is based on:

- Respecting the right to self-determination;
- Respecting the right to participation;
- Treating each person as a whole; and
- Identifying and developing strengths.

The principle on social justice is based on:

- Challenging negative discrimination;
- Recognizing diversity;
- Distributing resources equitably;
- Challenging unjust policies and practices; and
- Working in solidarity.

(IFSW, 2012)

Social Work with Immigrant and Refugee Populations

According to Heller (2009), social work rarely acknowledges the needs and experiences of LGBTI immigrants and asylum seekers. Immigration and LGBTI concerns are both critical contemporary issues; however, these are seldom addressed in the literature as overlapping or interrelated (Chávez, 2011). Thus, there is limited research in this area and consequently a lack of social work response in practice and policy advocacy. Yet, multiple issues impact LGBTI immigrant and refugee experience in the United States. Many LGBTI refugees are victims of repeated government, community, or family violence in their countries of origin and may experience symptoms of trauma, isolation, internalized homophobia, depression, and discrimination based on race, class, or gender identity and expression (Morales, 2013). In addition, LGBTI refugees and immigrants of color experience distinctive issues around discrimination related to racism, being a sexual minority and an immigrant (Gray, Mendelsohn, & Omoto, 2015). LGBTI asylum seekers have to navigate multiple stressors in connection to their identity within various interlocking systems of oppression (Reading & Rubin, 2011). Thus, LGBTI asylum seekers experience multiple traumas, which are intensified due to limited access to community support and social and economic resources.

Social workers advocating for the rights of LGBTI immigrants and refugees need to recognize that people who identify as LGBTI are diverse in culture, ethnicity, class, and gender identity and expression (Heller, 2009). Not all LGBTI refugees are treated equal under laws and those who are already marginalized in society are the most impacted by discriminatory policies and processes. Thus, intersectionality is an essential lens to reveal the vulnerability of LGBTI refugee realities because the range of experience and identity are distinct and interact with race, class, gender, and sexuality among other systems of oppression, which render these individuals and groups at risk of extreme human suffering (Farmer, 2005). Social workers practicing with diverse populations need to be aware of their own social location of race, class, gender, and nation and how these influence their perception of others (Healy & Kamya, 2014; Heller, 2009). In maintaining social work's professional values and ethics in promoting human rights and social justice, we need to ensure that we are not creating more harm to an already vulnerable population.

Harmful cultural attitudes and beliefs are built into societal structures and subsequently manifest as discriminatory attitudes and practices within multiple institutions (Maiorana, Kassie, & Myers, 2013). For example, LGBTI individuals experience health disparities due to ignorance and discrimination embedded within health institutions. Thus, the unique health needs of LGBTI migrants are often underserved (Chávez, 2011). In addition, the Convention relating to the Status of Refugees explicitly states that, "refugees should not be penalized for their illegal entry or stay... [and] that the seeking of asylum can require refugees to breach immigration rules" (United Nations High Commissioner for Refugees, n.d., p. 3). However, fear of deportation limits access to needed resources and services for undocumented LGBTI individuals.

Lastly, LGBTI immigrants and refugees who migrate to the United States may not be aware of local discriminatory laws, such as North Carolina's Public Facilities Privacy & Security Act, which discriminates against transgendered individuals by mandating a person uses the public bathroom that corresponds with their biological sex (General Assembly of North Carolina, 2016). Thus, social workers can be attentive to providing LGBTI immigrants and refugees with information regarding U.S. legislation that protects or discriminates against them and advocate for asylum criteria that realizes the complexity of sexual identity and expression (Heller, 2009).

International Social Work with LGBTI Populations

Social workers advocating for LGBTI rights abroad must not only be aware of the laws in the country in which they are working, but the cultural and societal norms as well. Just as domestic violence and sexual assault against women often go unreported, so does violence targeted at LGBTI individuals for fear of retribution by the perpetrator, criminal justice system, and/or the public. Discriminatory laws can also be used to justify derogatory treatment of LGBTI individuals. Social workers must be attentive to how laws and institutional homophobia or heterosexism affect the population they are working with when considering how to approach treatment and advocacy when practicing abroad.

Social workers practicing internationally must also be aware of what they bring from their own cultural background and should practice in a culturally responsive manner reflective of their social location of race, class, gender, sexuality, and nationality among others. Wetzel (2001) put Amnesty International's recommendations for advocating for LGBTI rights into context for social work suggesting that:

- all approaches must be LGBTI-sensitive;
- one must be particularly sensitive to cultural differences in the use of language because self-definitions and perceptions of sexuality vary between and within cultures;
- a gender-specific perspective must be maintained in all research and action strategies;
- respect for the wishes and needs of victims of human rights abuse is paramount when deciding on action techniques; and
- one must be strategic... within the context of long-term objectives.

(p. 29)

Prior to practicing abroad, social workers would benefit not only from foundational education in social work, but expanding their knowledge in other disciplines as well. Consider obtaining some education in interdisciplinary fields such as human rights and feminist, gender, and/or sexuality studies. Such background in interdisciplinary studies pairs social work knowledge, skills, and values with an understanding from an often critical perspective that challenges hetero-normative standards. Additionally, international studies or a concentration in the region of the world where the social worker anticipates being employed will heighten understanding of the culture. Having fluency in the written and spoken language of the host country is also ideal when planning to work abroad.

Risks for Social Workers

Social workers are equally vulnerable to the laws and policies constructed within a specific political climate. Social workers who focus on LGBTI rights in regions where discriminatory laws are still present and violence toward LGBTI individuals is commonplace should reasonably be prepared for risk of physical harm or personal security. Reports of LGBTI rights activists being attacked are numerous. For example, in 2009, a bill was introduced in Uganda to criminalize a person who has knowledge of and fails to report homosexual activity or who supports gay rights (Ireland, 2013). Further, Human Rights Watch (2014) found an increase of violent incidents in Russia directed at LGBTI individuals and activists following the passage of a 2013 anti-LGBTI propaganda law.

While safety in any job setting cannot be guaranteed, social workers should take steps to protect themselves. Research local and international laws to have an understanding of what your rights are if you experience discrimination or violence based on your work. Develop relationships with the local criminal justice system so they are familiar with the importance of your work in protecting the rights of vulnerable populations. Keep family and friends abreast of the work you are doing and where you are travelling. Develop relationships with other local LGBTI organizations and have knowledge of their resources and services. Memorize the phone number of a local legal organization that can assist you. For example, *Universitarios por la Diversidad* (Universities for Diversity) in Santo Domingo, Dominican Republic, has lawyers on call 24 hours a day, seven days a week to provide legal assistance. Social workers can be aware of their surroundings and be familiar with whom they are working and travelling. Finally, safely documenting any incidences of discrimination and violence experienced while working is essential. Witness, an international organization, provides training on how to use video to document human rights violations. As with any work environment, being aware of the associated risks is the first step in maintaining safety.

Conclusion

Multiple interlocking systems of oppression such as race, class, gender, and sexuality create and sustain violence toward LGBTI individuals and communities worldwide. Various countries lack anti-discrimination laws, an infrastructure to report repression and violence, and often sanction violence toward LGBTI individuals and communities, leaving no state protection. When social norms are in conflict with international human rights standards the act of criminalizing LGBTI individuals, especially with the death penalty, is persecutory and a gross violation of human rights (Schutzer, 2012). According to Cheney (2012),

> If the LGBTI community… is not at least allowed to live free of fear of death at the hands of the state, such discrimination paves the way for further human rights abuses against any number of others categorized as minorities.
>
> (p. 90)

Thus, criminalization promotes discrimination and violence toward LGBTI individuals and communities exemplifying a multidimensional issue that elicits a multidimensional response. Social work is well positioned to advocate for the human rights of LGBTI individuals through our professional values and ethics. Social workers need to understand the depth and breadth of human rights violations that are at stake when LGBTI individuals and communities are continually persecuted. The role of social work locally and abroad should be nothing short of working toward the decriminalization of homosexuality and gender identity and expression outside of the cultural and societal norms of any given country.

Questions for Consideration

1   Socially constructed laws are laws that are manifest within a particular political climate. In what ways are laws impacting LGBTI individuals and communities worldwide socially constructed?
2   What is intersectionality?
3   How does intersectionality provide a framework for understanding the experiences of LGBTI immigrants and refugees?
4   Why is it important to understand intersectionality in relation to the criminalization of sexual orientation or gender identity?
5   What are the barriers to achieving the right to asylum for LGBTI individuals and communities?
6   How do the values and ethics of the social work profession offer a framework to advocate for the rights of LGBTI individuals and communities locally and abroad?

Resources

Amnesty International   www.amnestyusa.org/our-work/issues/LGBTI-rights is a grassroots organization working toward the realization of human rights in the United States and abroad.

European Union Agency for Fundamental Rights (FRA) http://fra. europa.eu/en/theme/LGBTI is an organization dedicated to ensuring that the fundamental human rights of all people within the European Union are protected.

Freedom House https://freedomhouse.org/our-work is an independent organization dedicated to the promotion of political and civil rights, supporting activists defending human rights, and to ensure democratic government processes.

Human Rights First www.humanrightsfirst.org/campaigns/support-huma n-rights-LGBTI-people-caribbean is a U.S.-based organization working toward creating a political climate toward the realization of human rights.

Human Rights Watch www.hrw.org/topic/LGBTI-rights is a non-governmental organization that gathers information regarding human rights abuses in order to advocate for human rights globally.

International Commission of Jurists (ICJ) www.icj.org/themes/sexua l-orientation-and-gender-identity/ is made up of judges and lawyers from around the world to protect human rights through legal systems.

International Day Against Homophobia, Transphobia, and Biphobia http://dayagainsthomophobia.org/ is a global campaign to help raise awareness about discrimination and violence experienced by LGBTI individuals and communities worldwide.

International Federation of Social Workers (IFSW) http://ifsw.org/ is an international social work organization, working toward social justice and human rights globally.

International Lesbian, Gay, Bisexual, Trans and Intersex Association (ILGA) http://ilga.org/ is a non-governmental organization advocating for LGBTI rights. ILGA produces maps that tracks worldwide protection, recognition, and criminalization of sexual orientation.

International Lesbian, Gay, Bisexual, Transgender, Queer, and Intersex Youth & Student Organization (IGLYO) www.iglyo.com/ is a youth membership organization funded by European governmental entities. IGLYO seeks to engage youth and student participation in LGBTQI issues.

Outright Action International (formerly known as the International Gay and Lesbian Human Rights Commission) www.outrightinterna tional.org/ is a non-governmental organization advocating for LGBTI rights from the local to global level. Outright increases the capacity of LGBTI individuals and activists by offering a variety of trainings.

Trans Murder Monitoring Project (TMM) http://tgeu.org/tmm/ is a collaboration of Transgender Europe and Liminalis, an online magazine. TMM collects and provides global data on the homicides of trans and/or gender diverse people.

United Nations Free and Equal Campaign www.unfe.org/ is the United Nations' global public education campaign focused on promoting LGBTI rights worldwide.

Witness https://witness.org/ is a non-governmental organization that educates individuals on documenting human rights violations globally to influence change.

Worldwide Movement for Human Rights www.fidh.org/en/issues/ LGBTI-rights/ is a campaign of the International Federation for Human Rights, a non-governmental organization. The federation advocates for LGBTI rights through intervention at the European Court of Human Rights.

Yogyakarta Principles in Action www.ypinaction.org/ is a website hosted by ARC International, a non-governmental organization focused on raising the recognition of LGBTI rights through the United Nations' systems. The Yogyakarta Principles in Action website provides guidance on implementing the principles for activists and tracks how the principles are utilized globally.

Note

1 In congruence with feminist theories, the authors are listed alphabetically. All authors contributed equally.

References

Anker, D. E., & Ardalan, S. (2012). Escalating persecution of gays and refugee protection: Comment on queer cases make bad law. *International Law & Politics*, 44(2), 529–557.

Astraea Lesbian Foundation for Justice. (2015). Ecuador LGBTI: Landscape analysis of political, economic, and social conditions. Retrieved from www.astraeafounda tion.org/uploads/files/Reports/Astraea%20Ecuador%20Landscape%202015.pdf

Chávez, K. R. (2011). Identifying the needs of LGBTQ immigrants and refugees in Southern Arizona. *Journal of Homosexuality*, 58, 189–218.

Cheney, K. (2012). Locating neocolonialism: Tradition and human rights in Uganda's gay death penalty. *African Studies Review*, 55(2), 77–95.

Dominelli, L. (2007). Human rights in social work practice: An invisible part of the social work curriculum. In E. Reichert (Ed.), *Challenges in human rights: A social work perspective* (pp. 16–43). New York: Columbia University Press.

Encarnación, O. G. (2014). Human rights and gay rights. *Current History*, 113(759), 36–39.

Ettelbrick, P. L., & Zerán, A. T. (2010). *The impact of the Yogyakarta principles on international human rights law development: A study of November 2007 – June 2010.* Retrieved from www.ypinaction.org/files/02/57/Yogyakarta_Principles_Impact_ Tracking_Report.pdf

Farmer, P. (2005). *Pathologies of power: Health, human rights, and the new war on the poor.* Berkeley, CA: University of California Press.

General Assembly of North Carolina. (2016). *House bill 2: Public facilities privacy & security act.* Retrieved from www.ncleg.net/Sessions/2015E2/Bills/House/PDF/H2v4.pdf

Gray, N. N., Mendelsohn, D. M., & Omoto, A. M. (2015). Community connectedness, challenges, and resilience among gay Latino immigrants. *American Journal of Community Psychology*, 55, 202–214.

Han, E. & O'Mahoney, J. (2014). British colonialism and the criminalization of homosexuality. *Cambridge Review of International Affairs*, 27(2), 268–288.

Healy, L. M. (2012). Defining international social work. In L. M. Healy & R. J. Link (Eds.), *Handbook of international social work: Human rights, development, and the global profession* (pp. 9–15). New York: Oxford.

Healy, L. & Kamya, H. (2014). Ethics and international discourse in social work: The case of Uganda's anti-homosexual legislation. *Ethics and Social Welfare*, 8(2), 151–169.

Heller, P. (2009). Challenges facing LGBT asylum-seekers: The role of social work in correcting oppressive immigration processes. *Journal of Gay & Lesbian Social Sciences*, 21, 294–308.

Human Rights Watch. (2014). *License to harm: Violence and harassment against LGBTI people and activists in Russia.* Retrieved from www.hrw.org/report/2014/12/15/license- harm/violence-and-harassment-against-LGBTI-people-and-activists-russia

International Federation of Social Workers (IFSW). (2012). *Statement of ethical principles.* Retrieved from http://ifsw.org/policies/statement-of-ethical-principles/

International Federation of Social Workers (IFSW). (2014). *Sexual orientation and gender expression.* Retrieved from http://cdn.ifsw.org/assets/ifsw_102638-5.pdf

International Federation of Social Workers (IFSW). (2016). *What we do.* Retrieved from http://ifsw.org/what-we-do/

International Lesbian, Gay, Bisexual, Trans and Intersex Association (ILGA). (2016, June). *Sexual orientation laws in the world: Criminalisation.* Retrieved from http://ilga.org/downloads/04_ILGA_WorldMap_ENGLISH_Crime_May2016.pdf

Ireland, P. R. (2013). A macro-level analysis of the scope, causes, and consequences of homophobia in Africa. *African Studies Review*, 56(2), 47–66.

Maiorana, A., Kassie, N., & Myers, J. J. (2013). On being gay in Barbados: Bullers and battyboys and their HIV risk in a societal context of stigma. *Journal of Homosexuality*, 60, 984–1010.

McKinnon, S. L. (2016). *Gendered asylum: Race and Violence in U.S. law and politics.* Chicago, IL: University of Illinois Press.

Millbank, J. (2009). From discretion to disbelief: Recent trends in refugee determinations on the basis of sexual orientation in Australia and the United Kingdom. *International Journal of Human Rights*, 13(2–3), 391–414.

Morales, E. (2013). Latino lesbian, gay, bisexual, and transgender immigrants in the United States. *Journal of LGBT Issues in Counseling*, 7, 172–184.

Mullen, M. (2015). Reassessing the focus of transnational justice: The need to move structural and cultural violence to the centre. *Cambridge Review of International Affairs*, 28(3), 462–479.

National Association of Social Workers (NASW). (2008). *Code of ethics.* Retrieved from www.naswdc.org/pubs/code/code.asp

Nichols, J. (2014, January). Young and gay in Putin's Russia. *The Huffington Post.* Retrieved from www.huffingtonpost.com/2014/01/14/vice-young-gay-russia_n_4595791.html

Plant, R. (1986). *The pink triangle: The Nazi war against homosexuals.* New York: New Republic Books.

Razkane v. Holder, Jr., No. 08-9519 (10th Cir. 2009)

Reading, R., & Rubin, L. R. (2011). Advocacy and empowerment: Group therapy for LGBT asylum seekers. *Traumatology*, 17(2), 86–98.

Schutzer, M. (2012). Bringing the asylum process out of the closet: Promoting the acknowledgment of LGB refugees. *The Georgetown Journal of Gender and the Law*, 13, 669–707.

United Nations. (1948). *Universal declaration of human rights*. Retrieved from www.un.org/en/universal-declaration-human-rights/

United Nations. (2010). *Universal decriminalization of homosexuality a human rights imperative – Ban*. Retrieved from www.un.org/apps/news/story.asp?NewsID=37026#.V36kOvkrL4a

United Nations. (2016). *History of the United Nations*. Retrieved from www.un.org/en/sections/history/history-united-nations/

United Nations High Commissioner for Human Rights. (2011). *Discriminatory laws and practices and acts of violence against individuals based on their sexual orientation and gender identity*. Retrieved from www2.ohchr.org/english/bodies/hrcouncil/docs/19session/A.HRC.19.41_English.pdf

United Nations High Commissioner for Human Rights. (2012). *Born free and equal: Sexual orientation and gender identity in international human rights law*. Retrieved from www.ohchr.org/Documents/Publications/BornFreeAndEqualLowRes.pdf

United Nations High Commissioner for Human Rights. (2015). *UN free and equal campaign progress report 2015*. Retrieved from www.unfe.org/wp-content/uploads/2017/05/2015-UNFE-Report.pdf

United Nations High Commissioner for Human Rights. (2016a). *Council establishes mandate on protection against violence and discrimination based on sexual orientation and gender identity*. Retrieved from www.ohchr.org/en/NewsEvents/Pages/DisplayNews.aspx?NewsID=20220&LangI D=E

United Nations High Commissioner for Human Rights. (2016b). *Special procedures of the Human Rights Council*. Retrieved from www.ohchr.org/EN/HRBodies/SP/Pages/Welcomepage.aspx

United Nations High Commissioner for Refugees. (n.d.). *Convention and protocol relating to the status of refugees*. Retrieved from www.unhcr.org/en-us/3b66c2aa10

United Nations Human Rights Council. (2011). *Human rights, sexual orientation and gender identity*. Retrieved from http://arc-international.net/wp-content/uploads/2011/09/HRC-Res-17-19.pdf

United Nations Human Rights Council. (2015). *Discrimination and violence against individuals based on their sexual orientation and gender identity*. Retrieved from http s://documents-dds-ny.un.org/doc/UNDOC/GEN/G15/088/42/PDF/G1508842.pdf?OpenElement

Wetzel, J. W. (2001). Human rights in the 20th century: Weren't gays and lesbians human? In M. E. Swigonski, R. Mama, & K. Ward (Eds.), *From hate crimes to human rights: A tribute to Matthew Shepard* (pp. 15–31). New York: Harrington Park Press.

Wheeler, D. P., & McClain, A. (2015). *Social work speaks* (10th ed.). Washington, DC: ASW Press.

Yogyakarta. (2007). *Principles on the application of international human rights law in relation to sexual orientation and gender identity*. Retrieved from www.yogyakartaprinciples.org/principles_en.pdf

Glossary of Key Terms

Key chapter(s) indicated in parenthesis.

Activities of daily living (ADL)   This phrase refers to basic personal tasks of everyday life including bathing, dressing, using the toilet, transferring (to and from bed or chair), caring for incontinence, and eating (Paying for Senior Care, 2016). (14)

Adoption   A process whereby a person assumes the parenting of a child from that person's biological or legal parent or parents, and in doing so, permanently transfers all rights and responsibilities, along with filiation, form the biological parent or parents. (4)

Aging out   Individuals who have reached the legal age of independent status and the foster care system is no longer required to provide assistance. (5)

Ageism   This term refers to the inequitable, discriminatory, unfair, and/or biased treatment of older adults, including prejudice or discrimination against a particular age group. (14)

Agender   A person who does not identify as having a gender identity that can be categorized as male/masculine or female/feminine. (8)

Aging network   This phrase refers to a network headed by the U.S. Administration on Aging and includes 56 State Agencies on Aging, 629 Area Agencies on Aging, 246 Native American aging programs, over 29,000 service providers, and thousands of volunteers. (14)

Ally   This term refers to someone who stands by and supports a community other than their own; for LGBTQIA populations, this usually refers to a heterosexual and/or cisgender person. (1, 6)

Asexual   This term identifies someone who does not feel sexually attracted to a person of any gender. (1, 6)

Bigender   A person who experiences gender identity as two genders at the same time or whose gender identity may vary between genders (including non-binary genders). (8)

Biological sex   This refers to the body with which a person was born, including chromosomes, genitalia, and hormones. (1)

Bisexual or Bi   This term refers to someone who is attracted to both sexes. (1, 6, 14)

Bi-phobia   Fear, prejudice, and marginalizing behaviors directed towards bisexual individuals (Human Rights Campaign, 2018). (7)

Bullying   Repeated acts over time intended to cause harm to the victim, particularly when there is a power imbalance between victim and perpetrator. (11)

Buggery laws   Originating in England, buggery laws vary across nations; these laws made sodomy, bestiality, and/or anal intercourse a crime, especially when occurring between two men. (15)

Caregiving/caregiver   (see also 'Formal' caregivers) This term refers to a person who provides assistance, care, and aid to someone in need on a regular basis. Caregiving can occur between family members or through professional services. (14)

Cisgender   A term used to refer to a person whose gender identity aligns with the sex they were assigned at birth. (1, 8, 12, 14)

Civil union   This was a legal agreement offered by a few states before the legalization of gay marriage. Rights varied by state, although all provided greater rights than a domestic partnership, but far less than marriage. Civil unions did not include federal recognition of the relationship. (2)

Closed adoption   A process by which a family adopts an infant, and records of the biological parent(s) are not disclosed. (4)

Closeted/In the closet   This refers to someone who does not disclose their LGBTQIA identity(ies), keeping the identity(ies) 'secret.' Some remain closeted out of fear, and at times for self-protection or preservation. (6)

Cognitive Behavioral Therapy (CBT)   CBT is a short-term goal-oriented psychotherapy treatment that takes a hands on practical approach to problem-solving. The goal of CBT is to change people's thinking or behavior patterns that are causing them difficulty. (10)

Coming out (of the closet)   The process of identifying oneself as LGBTQIA to self, family, friends, co-workers, society, and within the LBGTQIA community. Coming out is an ongoing process in each new setting; it can be a normative process but also may involve risks in some settings. (6)

Conversion therapy   (see also Sexual Orientation Change Efforts (SOCE): Reparative therapy and Transformational therapy/ministry) A controversial practice under the sexual orientation change effort (SOCE) umbrella that aims to change ('convert') a person's sexual orientation or gender identity to a heterosexual and/or cisgender identity. Such practices are not sanctioned by the medical, social, or behavioral sciences. In some states, it is illegal to conduct these practices with minors; and, the National Association of Social Workers does not support these approaches. (13, 15)

Cultural humility   This refers to practicing with awareness and sensitivity to what a social worker does/does not know about another culture, population, or society. Cultural humility espouses respectful openness for life-long learning at micro, mezzo, and macro levels. (2)

Culturally sensitive practice The skill by which individuals and systems work respectfully and effectively with individuals, families, and communities in a manner that acknowledges, supports, and values their culture. (5)

Cyberbullying Similar to bullying in person, cyberbullying occurs through electronic communication such as chatrooms, social media, e-mail, and text messages. (11)

DOMA DOMA refers to the Defense of Marriage Act, the law that defined marriage as the union between one man and one woman. The Supreme Court overturned DOMA in 2013. (2)

Domestic adoption This refers to the adoption of a child born in the United States. (4)

Domestic partnership Prior to gay marriage, this provided some legal recognition of a couple's relationship, with varying benefits across states. It was considered the lowest form of relationship recognition in terms of legal rights, with some states not providing much, if any, benefit at all. California was the first state to offer them in 1999. (2)

Facilitated/unlicensed adoption An adoption process facilitated by a person for a fee. It has the least amount of supervision and oversight, and is illegal in many jurisdictions. (4)

Family of choice A person's chosen family, which has great significance within the LGBTQIA community for many people who are rejected by their family of origin. (2)

Family of origin A person's biological family or legally adoptive family. (2)

'Formal' caregivers This phrase refers to individuals who are paid to give care, e.g., personal care aides and certified nursing assistants (Lai, 2003). (14)

Foster adoption A child placement in which parents' rights have not yet been severed by the court, or, in which birth parents are appealing the court's decision; however, the foster parents agree to adopt the child if/ when parental rights are terminated. (4)

Foster care A temporary arrangement provided by a public or private social agency that removes children from their homes because of a serious or dangerous situation and moves them to a setting that provides them full-time care. (5)

Fully insured healthcare plan This model is the traditional way most employers offer health insurance benefits to their employees. The company pays a monthly fixed premium to the insurance carrier based on the number of enrolled employees in that month. The insurance carrier collects the premiums and pays for employee healthcare claims based on the outlined policy coverage. The employee (and their dependents) pay deductibles and co-payments, as indicated in the plan. (10)

Gay   This term typically refers to men attracted to men, but used also as an umbrella term to refer to the LGBTQIA community as a whole. (1, 6, 14)

Gay marriage   (see Marriage equality and Same-sex marriage) Gay marriage involves two people of the same sex getting married; it became the law of the land in the United States on June 26, 2015, through the U.S. Supreme Court ruling in the case, Obergefell v. Hodges. (2)

Gender   Socially and culturally constructed behavioral and role expectations for male, female, and transgender individuals. Gender can be understood as a multidimensional system of expectations with micro, mezzo, and macro level influence (Marsiglia & Kulis, 2008). (6, 7)

Genderqueer   A non-binary identity, e.g., a person whose gender identity is neither male nor female, is between or beyond genders, or is some combination of genders, sometimes feeling as though neither captures their gender identity (6, 8)

Gender nonbinary   Gender binary refers to limiting the understanding of gender solely as two forms, male or female, and sex as two distinct genitalia for men or for women, with no variation inclusive of transgender or intersex identities (Gender Spectrum, 2017). Gender nonbinary expands the notion of gender and sex beyond these two (binary) options. It includes variations often described as transgender and intersex (8)

Gender dysphoria   This term categorizes the feelings of discomfort or disconnect a transgender person may have with his/her/their body. Gender Dysphoria replaced Gender Identity Disorder in the American Psychiatric Association's *Diagnostic and Statistical Manual 5 (DSM-5)* in an effort to reduce stigma. It refers to the difference between a person's gender identity and the gender others would assign him/her/them. To meet diagnostic criteria, the difference must be verbally expressed and present for at least six months (American Psychiatric Association, 2013). (6, 8)

Gender expression   This refers to how we present our gender identity (feminine, masculine, other) in society and may be subject to cultural variations. This may occur through dress, mannerisms, speech, behavior, interests, and activities. (1, 6)

Gender fluid/Genderfluid   A person whose gender identity is not confined to one specific gender. Gender may shift fluidly along the spectrum of gender, and may shift toward the masculine or the feminine across time. (6, 8)

Gender identity   This refers to my internal sense of my gender, which could be male, female, transgender, genderqueer, or other. This may or may not match the assigned gender based on sex characteristics at birth (female, male, intersex, other). Gender identity differs from biological sex and sexual orientation. (1, 6, 8)

Gender identity disorder   (see Gender dysphoria.)

Gender non-binary Terminology that reflects those who do not identify gender as consisting solely of two traditional options of male or
female. (1)

Gender non-conforming Someone who resists societal expectations of
gender expression based on the gender binary and often does not conform to expectations of masculinity and femininity (1, 6)

Gender role (see also Gender expression) Similar to gender expression,
this refers to "The set of functions, activities, and behaviors commonly
expected of boys/men and girls/women by society" (Gender Spectrum,
2017). (1)

Hague Convention adoption Hague Convention on the Protection
of Children and Co-Operation in Respect of Intercountry Adoption
(Hague Convention) refers to the international agreement signed by
many (but not all) countries including the United States. The Hague
Convention established standards of practice for international adoptions. (4)

Hate crime Physical violence, harassment, or property damage motivated
by animosity towards an individual or group because of their identity. (11)

Health disparities These refer to differences in health status between
groups, which systematically and negatively affect less advantaged
groups. (10)

Healthcare disparities These are "differences in the quality of health
care that are not due to access-related factors or clinical needs, preferences or appropriateness of intervention" (Institute of Medicine
(IOM), 2002). (10)

Heteronormative paradigm A perspective that assumes heterosexuality
is the only sexual orientation and that sexual relations and marriage are
only fitting between man and woman. (10)

Heteronormativity The belief that 'normal' people fall along a distinct
gender binary (male or female), which prescribes certain roles and
marginalizes all who defy this binary as abnormal/atypical/unnatural; it
typically supports marriage inequality and/or tries to define LGBTQIA
relationships along the gender binary. (2, 6)

Heterosexism A socio-cultural value system that reifies heterosexuality as
the standard of normal and healthy sexuality and expressions of intimate
love. In this value system, non-heterosexual love and intimate partner
relationships are devalued (Murphy & Dillon, 2011). It may lead to
discrimination that conceals, stigmatizes, and/or marginalizes the
LGBTQIA community, as this paradigm presumes heterosexuality in
people and may also conclude that a heterosexual identity is superior or
preferred to an LGBTQIA identity. (2, 7, 14)

Heterosexual A sexual orientation with opposite sex attraction, often
referred to as 'straight,' where men are attracted to women, and women
are attracted to men. (1, 6)

Homelessness The condition of not having permanent housing. (5)

Homophobia/homophobic   Originally directed at gay and lesbian people, homophobia involved negative attitudes and feelings, particularly anger, irrational fear, hatred, or prejudice directed towards members of the LGBTQIA community. (4, 6, 7, 14)

Human rights   Inherent rights that all humans have by virtue of being human. (15)

Independent adoption   An adoption process where an attorney assists prospective adoptive and birth parents through the adoption process; neither party seeks services through an agency. (4)

Independent Expert or Special Rapporteur   A Special Rapporteur is an honorary position appointed by the Human Rights Council to advise and report on human rights related to a specific country or theme. Mr. Vitit Muntarbhorn, an international law professor from Thailand, was the first UN Independent Expert on violence and discrimination based on sexual orientation and gender identity, appointed in 2016. In 2017, there were 12 country and 44 thematic mandates, including Mr. Muntarbhorn as Independent Expert on protection against violence and discrimination based on sexual orientation and gender identity. (15)

'Informal' or 'family' caregivers   These include individuals not paid to give care and generally include family members and friends; they are sometimes called 'family caregivers' (Lai, 2003). (14)

Instrumental activities of daily living (IADL)   Everyday tasks including housework, managing money, taking medication, preparing meals, shopping, and caring for pets (Paying for Senior Care, 2016). (14)

Intercountry adoption   A type of adoption in which an individual or couple become the legal and permanent parent(s) of a child who is a national of a different country. In general, prospective parents must meet the legal adoption requirements of their country of residence and those of the country whose nationality the child holds. (4)

Internalized homophobia   Feelings of shame, discomfort, or embarrassment about one's identity which may result from consistent negativity expressed towards the LGBTQIA community. (9)

International Federation of Social Workers (IFSW)   IFSW is an international social work organization, working towards social justice and human rights globally. (15)

International law   Legal standards recognized by nation states to hold each other accountable. (15)

Intersectionality   Individuals may have identities that overlap or intersect in ways that compound oppression and discrimination. Intersectionality involves an analytic strategy and source of knowledge production that critically deconstructs social structures that justify privileged identities and the subjugation of non-white, non-male, and non-heterosexual individuals. Intersectionality challenges society to construct multidimensional understandings of the lived experiences of all human beings, the complex systems of power and oppression, and effective paths for liberation (Dill & Zambrana, 2013). (1, 2, 6, 7, 15)

Intersex A person born with atypical sexual or reproductive anatomy, chromosomes, and/or hormones that do not fit within the categories of binary male or female identities. (1, 6, 15)

Intimate partner violence A pattern of controlling and coercive behaviors perpetrated by an individual in an intimate relationship and can include physical abuse, emotional abuse, and sexual abuse. (11)

Joint adoption This involves two unmarried people desiring to adopt a child together at the same time; few states permit this option (Family Equality Council, 2018). (4)

Lesbian This term identifies a woman whose primary romantic, emotional, and sexual attraction is to other women. (1, 6, 14)

LGBTQIA adoption Adoption by lesbian, gay, bi-sexual, transgender, or queer-identified people. (4)

LGBTQIA An acronym for the Lesbian, Gay, Bisexual, Transgender, Queer/Questioning, Intersex, Asexual/Ally communities. (7)

Licensed private agency adoption An adoption process where birth parents relinquish their parental rights to an agency, and prospective adoptive parents work with an agency to adopt. (4)

Long-term care (LTC)/Long-term services and supports (LTSS) These phrases refer to a range of services and supports a person may need to meet personal care needs. They generally do not refer to medical care, but rather assistance with Activities of Daily Living (ADLs) and Instrumental Activities of Daily Living (IADLs). (14)

Marriage equality This term is descriptive of the movement towards equal rights for same-sex couples; in some circles it became favored over the terms 'gay marriage' or 'same-sex marriage' because it focused on equality over a special right being conferred. (2)

Minority stress High levels of chronic stress faced by members of stigmatized minority groups. (10)

Minority stress model A model that states that sexual 'minorities' (LGBTQIA people) experience chronic stress due to stigmatization, which can arise from actual experiences of discrimination and violence, perceived stigma, internalized homophobia, or concealment of one's own sexual orientation or identity. (7, 10)

Minority Stress Theory (MST) A theory focused on social stigmas and their impacts on the identity development process and bio-psychosocial functioning of stigmatized individuals. (7)

Misgendering The act of using an incorrect or inaccurate name or pronoun for an individual, thus identifying them by a gender that is not theirs. This occurs both intentionally and unintentionally, and can be upsetting to transgender and non-binary people. (8)

Mixed marriage This term has a broad scope and can refer to spouses of different sexual orientation, races, nationalities, and/or religions. (2)

Motivational interviewing   This refers to a therapeutic approach that is goal oriented and client-centered, designed to elicit behavioral change by helping people to explore and resolve ambivalence. (10)

Neoliberal policies   Economic policies that allocate more power to corporations and less power to government, thus promoting 'smaller government.' These approaches endorse "free trade, capital and labor mobility, privatization, and fiscally solvent social welfare systems" (Kirchick, 2017). Concerns raised suggest that neoliberal beliefs unsteady the social safety net, stagnate minimum wages, and weaken labor unions, which can increase poverty rates in the U.S. among all groups, including LGBTQIA people. (12)

Nonbinary   This term encompasses gender identities that do not fall exclusively in man/male or woman/female categories of gender (Webb et al., 2015). A nonbinary person may identify as being both a man and a woman at the same time, somewhere between those two genders, or off of the gender spectrum entirely. Nonbinary may describe a myriad of individuals in this subset of gender identity; however, nonbinary people may also use other terms to describe themselves. (8)

Non–Hague Convention adoption   (see also Hague Convention adoption) These adoptions do not adhere to the Hague Convention guidelines. (4)

Open adoption   A form of adoption in which the biological and adoptive families have access to varying degrees of each other's personal information and have an option of contact or use of an intermediary to facilitate communications. (4)

Pangender   A person who does not limit their identity to one gender, and may identify as many genders, mixed gender, or a third gender. (6, 8)

Pansexual   Someone who is attracted to a person of any sex or gender, including those who identify as transgender, gender-fluid, agender, intersex, and others. (1, 6)

Physical violence   An individual or group of individuals directly causing harm to other individuals (also called interpersonal violence or direct violence). (11)

Public agency adoption   An adoption process where public agencies, and private agencies contracted by public agencies, locate and prepare adoptive families to adopt children from foster care. (4)

Psychodynamic psychotherapy   Is a form of depth psychology where the primary focus is to reveal the unconscious content of a person's psyche, in order to alleviate psychic tension(s). (10)

Queer   Queer is an umbrella term, formerly a derogatory slur against LGBTQIA people, reclaimed by some to reframe its original meaning and to provide an inclusive space. It can include anyone identified as LGBTQIA, or someone who does not feel like other possible identities capture who they are. (1, 6)

Questioning   Refers to individuals who are exploring or unsure of their sexual orientation and/or gender identity. (1, 6)

Racism   A complex socio-political and economic form of discrimination and oppression based on the racial identity of an individual, family, and/or community. Some scholars have identified four types of racism: ideological, institutionalized, personally mediated, and internalized racism. (Jones, 2000; Miller & Garran, 2008). (7)

Religion   This includes formal faith systems, traditions, and denominations. Religious practices include reading sacred books, observing specific practices such as prayer and attending services, and adhering to the theology, teachings, practices, and dogma of a specific faith tradition. (13)

Religious freedom   Religious freedom is the right to practice one's religion, as protected by the First Amendment of the Constitution of the United States. This protection consists of the Establishment Clause, which guards against government promotion of any religion; and, the Free Exercise Clause, that grants protection to practice any religion a person may choose, or, not to practice a religion at all (see ACLU Department of Public Education, 2018). (13)

Religious Freedom Restoration Act (RFRA)   The federal law, the Religious Freedom Restoration Act of 1993, Pub. L. No. 103–141, 107 Stat. 1488 (November 16, 1993) was enacted to protect religious freedom from government intervention. A Supreme Court case ruling in 1997 determined that this law applied at the federal level, but not at the state level. Some state legislatures enacted their own RFRA's since that time, and these statutes have been used to protect individuals from being required to serve LGBTQIA individuals on religious grounds. RFRAs may be viewed as controversial when they appear to pit freedom of religion against LGBTQIA civil liberties (for more information, see Robinson, 2003). (13)

Reparative therapy   (see also Sexual Orientation Change Efforts (SOCE), Conversion therapy and Transformational therapy/ministry) A controversial practice under the sexual orientation change effort (SOCE) umbrella that aims to change ('repair') a person's sexual orientation or gender identity to a heterosexual and/or cisgender identity. Such practices are not sanctioned by the medical, social, or behavioral sciences. In some states, it is illegal to conduct these practices with minors, and the National Association of Social Workers does not support these approaches. (13)

Same-sex marriage   (see also Marriage equality and Gay marriage) Same-sex marriage involves two people of the same sex getting married; it became the law of the land in the United States on June 26, 2015, through the U.S. Supreme Court ruling in the case, Obergefell v. Hodges. (2)

SCOTUS   Supreme Court of the United States. (2)

Second-parent adoption or co-parent adoption   This type of adoption allows a second parent to adopt a child in the home even if the parents do not have a legally recognized relationship. In this way, the 'first parent' does not lose their legal rights and the child can have two 'legal' parents. (Family Equality Council, 2018; National Center for Lesbian Rights (NCLR), 2018). (4)

Self-insured health plan   A plan where employers operate their own health plan with fixed costs (administrative fees, other fees, stop-loss premiums) and variable costs (monthly healthcare claims). (10)

Sex   A medical term designating a certain combination of gonads, chromosomes, external gender organs, secondary sex characteristics, and hormonal balances; sex is commonly thought of as simply male or female, but also includes intersex. (6)

Sex work   The exchange of sexual services for money or material goods. (11)

Sexism   A complex socio-political and economic form of discrimination and oppression based on gender identity (Morrow & Messinger, 2006). (7)

Sexual behaviour   The sexual activity in which and with whom a person chooses to engage. (1)

Sexual identity   The way a person identifies their sexual orientation, e.g., as gay, lesbian, bisexual, heterosexual, etc. (1)

Sexual minority   Refers to groups whose sexual identity, sexual orientation, and/or sexual practices differ from the majority of society, and usually refers to LGBTQIA people. (10)

Sexual orientation   A person's sexual orientation indicates to whom they are attracted physically, emotionally, sexually, and romantically. Sexual orientation is often subjected to a binary designation of straight or gay, but it exists on a continuum rather than a system of specific categories. (1, 6)

Sexual orientation change efforts (SOCE)   These are non-sanctioned efforts to change a person's sexual orientation (or transgender identity) to a heterosexual and cisgender identity. SOCE approaches include conversion therapies, reparative therapies, and/or transformational therapies/ministries that may include talk therapy, use of medications, behavior modification, and aversion therapies. Scientific evidence does not support these approaches; instead, evidence has indicated that these approaches may cause harm to the individual instead. For this reason, several states have legally banned their use with youth. When SOCEs have been used, it has often been for religious reasons within faith systems that do not support LGBTQIA identities or view them as sinful. (13)

Social services   Services provided by public, private, or non-profit agencies to individuals, families, and communities. (5)

Social visibility test   Related to international cases of people seeking asylum, a person must visually represent as belonging to a particular social group. (15)

Sodomy   Any sexual activity other than vaginal intercourse. (11)

Sodomy laws   The crime of consensual or forced anal or oral sex between persons or person and animal. (15)

Solitary confinement   Isolation of an individual in a single prison cell so that person has minimal contact with others. (11)

Special Rapporteur or Independent Expert   A Special Rapporteur is an honorary position appointed by the Human Rights Council to advise and report on human rights related to a specific country or theme. Mr. Vitit Muntarbhorn, an international law professor from Thailand, was the first UN Independent Expert on violence and discrimination based on sexual orientation and gender identity, appointed in 2016. In 2017, there were 12 country and 44 thematic mandates, including Mr. Muntarbhorn as Independent Expert on protection against violence and discrimination based on sexual orientation and gender identity. (15)

Spirituality   Spirituality refers to the ways people make connection and meaning in their lives, and how they live out their beliefs. It involves a deepened approach to understanding the integral components of a person's life, and may or may not include formal religious practices. (13)

Status offense   A non-criminal act considered illegal because the person engaging in the act is not an adult. (11)

Stigmatization theory   A theory that explores the socio-cultural origins, processes, and bio-psychosocial impacts of the stigmatization on individuals, families, and groups (Goffman, 1963). (7)

Strengths perspective   This theoretical approach views individuals and communities with awareness of the potential that exists, rather than focusing on the problems. It highlights ability over deficits and pathology. (1)

Structural violence   Harm imposed on individuals by social structures that unevenly distribute resources and perpetuate racism, sexism, heterosexism, and other forms of oppression. (11)

Symbolic violence   Harm imposed on individuals when the current social structure and social norms, which privilege certain groups, are understood to be commonsense and even ideal. (11)

Title VII of the Civil Rights Act of 1964   This statute prohibits discrimination by covered employers (those employers with 15 or more employees working daily for 20 or more calendar weeks) on the basis of race, color, religion, sex, or national origin. (10)

Transformational therapy/ministry   A practice under the sexual orientation change effort (SOCE) umbrella that is not sanctioned by medical, social, or behavioral professions. Transformational therapy aims to change ('transform') a person's sexual orientation or gender identity to a heterosexual and/or cisgender identity. (13)

Transgender   A term used to refer to individuals whose current gender identity does not align with the sex they were assigned at birth. The prefix trans- is Latin for 'other side.' (1, 6, 7, 8, 14)

Transphobia/transphobic   Negative attitudes and feelings, particularly anger, irrational fear, hatred or prejudice, and discrimination directed towards transgender people. (4, 6, 7, 14)

Trauma informed care Is an organizational structure and treatment framework that involves understanding, recognizing, and responding to the effects of all types of trauma. (10)

United Nations (UN) Created after World War II, the United Nations is an international intergovernmental organization charged with maintaining global order and cooperation. (15)

United Nations Human Rights Council (HRC) The HRC is an intergovernmental body made up of 47 elected member state representatives charged with strengthening human rights. The HRC assesses human rights in each member state through the Universal Periodic Review and reports directly to the United Nations General Assembly. (15)

United Nations member states or nation states Member states are countries that have successfully sought membership in the United Nations and accepted the related obligations as outlined in the UN Charter. The UN formed in 1945 with 51 original members and has grown to 193 member states currently. (15)

Universal Declaration of Human Rights (UDHR) The Universal Declaration of Human Rights adopted in 1948 by the UN General Assembly defines universal human rights for all individuals through 30 articles. (15)

'Within' and 'between' group differences This concept from research and diversity language highlights that differences exist between groups within a category, as well as within each group. A category of religion consists of different groups, such as Judaism, Christianity and Islam. There are differences between each group—they believe different truths, read different holy texts and may say different prayers. Although members of each one of these groups may share some similarities with the other members within their group, they also have differences. For examples, some Christian, Muslim and Jewish people are very religiously conservative, and others are more religiously progressive. Social workers cannot assume that all Jewish, Muslim or Christian people are alike because there are within group differences. (13)

Yogyakarta Principles 29 principles and related recommendations developed to address the promotion and protection of human rights specific to sexual orientation and gender identity. (15)

References

ACLU Department of Public Education. (2018). *Your right to religious freedom*. New York, NY: Author. Retrieved from www.aclu.org/other/your-right-religious-freedom

American Psychiatric Association. (2013). *DSM-5: Diagnostic and statistical manual of mental disorders* (5th ed.). Washington, DC: Author.

Dill, B. T. & Zambrana, R. E. (2013). Critical thinking about inequality: An emerging lens. In S. J. Ferguson (Ed). *Race, gender, sexuality, social class: Dimensions of inequality*. Los Angeles: Sage.

Family Equality Council. (2018). *50 states of adoption*. Retrieved from www.familye quality.org/get_informed/families_for_all/50_states_of_adoption/

Gender Spectrum. (2017). *Understanding gender*. Retrieved from www.gendersp ectrum.org/quick-links/understanding-gender/

Goffman, E. (1963). *Stigma: Notes on the management of spoiled identity*. New York, N.Y.: Simon & Schuster.

Human Rights Campaign. (2018). *Bisexual FAQ*. Retrieved from www.hrc.org/ resources/bisexual-faq

Institute of Medicine (IOM). (2002). *Unequal treatment: Confronting racial and ethnic disparities in health care*. Washington, DC: National Academies Press.

Jones, C. P. (2000). Levels of racism: A theoretic framework and a gardener's tale. *American Journal of Public Health*, 90(8), 1212–1215.

Kirchick, J. (2017, June 4). I'm a neoliberal and I'm proud. *Los Angeles Times*. Retrieved from www.latimes.com/opinion/op-ed/la-oe-kirchick-neoliberalism -defense-20170604-story.html

Lai, C. K. I. (2003). *Formal caregivers, informal caregivers, and carers*. Retrieved from Reflections on Nursing Leadership website at www.reflectionsonnursingleader sihp.org

Marsiglia, F.F. & Kulis, S. (2008). *Diversity, oppression, and change*. Chicago, IL: Lyceum Books.

Miller, J. & Garran, A.M. (2008). *Racism in the Unites States: Implications for the helping professions*. Belmont, CA: Brooks/Cole.

Morrow, D. F. & Messinger, L. (Eds). (2006). *Sexual orientation and gender expression in social work practice: Working with gay, lesbian, bisexual, and transgender people*. New York: Columbia University Press.

Murphy, B. C. & Dillon, C. (2011). *Interviewing in action in a multicultural world*. Belmont, CA: Brooks/Cole.

National Center for Lesbian Rights (NCLR). (2018). *Adoption by LGBT parents*. Retrieved from www.nclrights.org/wp-content/uploads/2013/07/2PA_state_list. pdf

Paying for Senior Care. (2016). *Activities & instrumental activities of daily living-Defini- tions, importance and assessments*. Retrieved from www.payingforseniorcare.com

Robinson, B. A. (2003, December 24). *Religious freedom restoration acts: Federal legis- lation*. Ontario Consultants on Religious Tolerance. Retrieved from www.reli gioustolerance.org/rfra1.htm

Webb, A., Matsuno, E., Budge, S., Krishnan, M., & Balsam, K. (2015). Non-binary gender identities fact sheet. APA Division 44: *The Society for the Psychological Study of Lesbian, Gay, Bisexual, and Transgender Issues*. Washington, DC: APA. Retrieved from www.apadivisions.org/division-44/resources/advocacy/non-binary-facts.pdf

Index

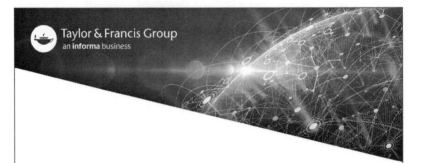